This volume contains the X/1999 installments from Animerica Extra, the Anime Fans's Comic Magazine, Vol. 1, No. 1 through Vol. 2, No. 5 in their entirety.

STORY & ART BY CLAMP

ENGLISH ADAPTATION BY FRED BURKE

Translation/Lillian Olsen
Touch-Up Art & Lettering/Wayne Truman
Cover Design/Viz Graphics
Editor/Julie Davis

Senior Maketing Manager/Dallas Middaugh
Senior Sales Manager/Ann Ivan
Editor-in-Chief/Hyoe Narita
Publisher/Seiji Horibuchi

Printed in Canada

Published by Viz Communications, Inc.
P.O. Box 77010 • San Francisco, CA 94107

10 9 8 7 6 5 4 3
First printing, August 1999
Third printing , October 2000

X/1999 GRAPHIC NOVELS TO DATE

VOLUME 1: PRELUDE
VOLUME 2: OVERTURE
VOLUME 3: SONATA
VOLUME 4: INTERMEZZO
VOLUME 5: SERENADE
VOLUME 6: DUET

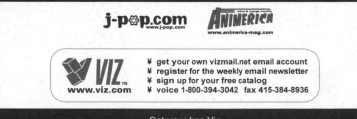

ANIMERICA EXTRA GRAPHIC NOVEL

X/1999™
SERENADE

BY CLAMP

X/1999
THE STORY THUS FAR

The End of the World has been prophesied…and time is running out. Kamui Shiro is a young man who was born with a special power—the power to decide the fate of the Earth itself.

The story opens with Kamui's reappearance in Tokyo after a six-year absence. Almost immediately upon his arrival, he's challenged to a psychic duel by a number of "men in black." These men turn out to be "curse zombies"—psychic constructs sent by a powerful being to spy on Kamui. Kamui defeats the curse zombies handily, but their presence is an uneasy reminder that others recognize something special about Kamui.

At school, one of Kamui's childhood friends, Kotori Monou, recognizes him almost immediately, but Kamui turns her away with a somber warning: "Don't get involved with me. Never talk to me again. Things are different from six years ago."

Heartbroken, Kotori stumbles away crying. Falling unconscious, she sinks into a vision of the End of the World, featuing the world shattering like a glass ball, and Kamui as its destroyer. She awakens in the school infirmary to the news that a young man matching Kamui's description had carried her in. Since Kotori has a heart condition, her brother Fuma is worried by her collapse, and takes her home.

Kamui himself is then injured in a duel—his opponent, Saiki, is rescued by the sword-wielding Arashi, while Kamui is tended to by Fuma and another mysterious young man, the young priest Sorata, who explains much of Kamui's destiny to the confused young man.

Meanwhile, Fuma and Kotori's father, priest of the Togakushi shrine, is confronted by a young man, Nataku, intent on obtaining the sacred sword kept by the shrine. Mr. Monou fights bravely, but in vain—the sword is carried off by Nataku, and Mr. Monou dies in Fuma's arms, whispering a warning about the end of the world. Soon after this, Kamui discovers his mother's sister, Tokiko Magami, working as the school nurse. Tokiko tells Kamui of the strange circumstances surrounding his birth, but mysteriously disappears before she can explain more. Finally, Sora decides that Kamui must meet the seeress Hinoto, whose visions may finally provide Kamui with the answers he had been searching for. Within Hinoto's secret hideaway, Kamui comes face to face with his ultimate destiny, and the choice he must face.…

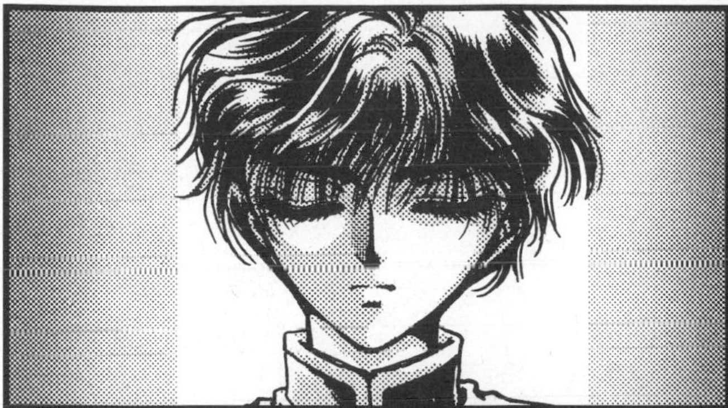

Kamui
A moody, distant young man, Kamui was taken from Tokyo at a young age by his mother, who wished to protect those closest to them from the fate surrounding Kamui and herself. After six years, Kamui returns to Tokyo in obedience of his mother's cryptic instructions to him, even as she was dying in a mysterious fire that consumed their apartment. Kamui has little understanding of the true nature of his destiny, and despite his powerful psychic abilities, he wants only to live a normal life.

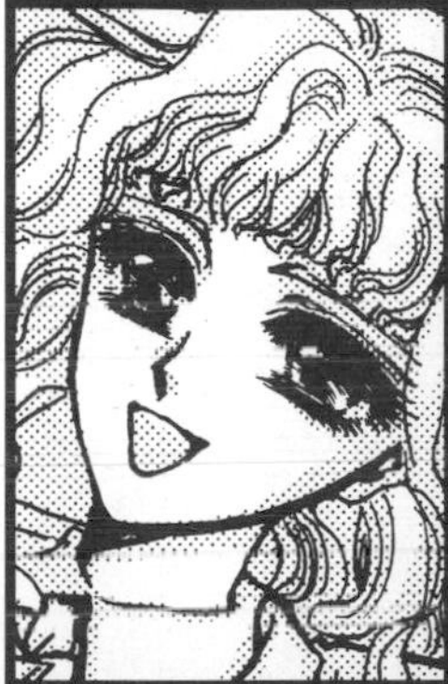

Kotori
Beautiful, and fragile due to a heart condition, Kotori was one of Kamui's best Kamui when they were children. In fact, Kamui promised to marry Kotori when they grew up. On occasion, Kotori has had startling visions of the future, and the fate of the Earth.

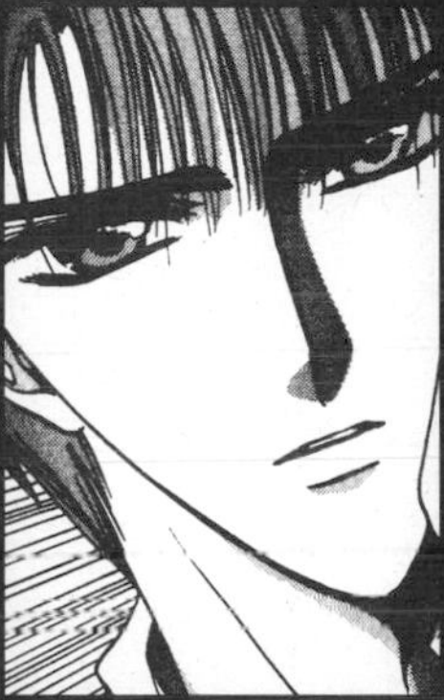

Fuma
Kotori's brother, Fuma was also great friends with Kamui when they were both children. Fuma and Kotori's mother died in a gruesome incident, and since then, Fuma has been very protective of his fragile sister. Now that Kamui has returned, Fuma feels somewhat ambivalent about Kamui, and his affect on Kotori.

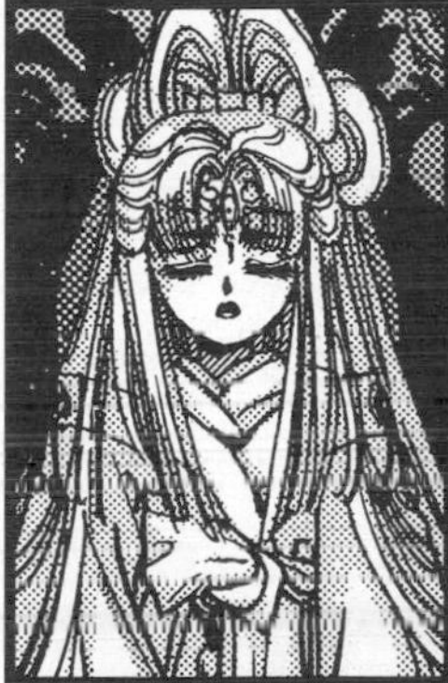

Hinoto
A blind prophetess who lives in a secret chamber underneath Tokyo's Diet building, Hinoto is a powerful psychic whose dreams of the future have never failed to come true. Lately, her dream has been of the world's destruction, and her vision places Kamui at the heart of the cataclysm to come—a great battle between the "Dragons of Heaven" and the "Dragons of Earth" for the Earth itself.

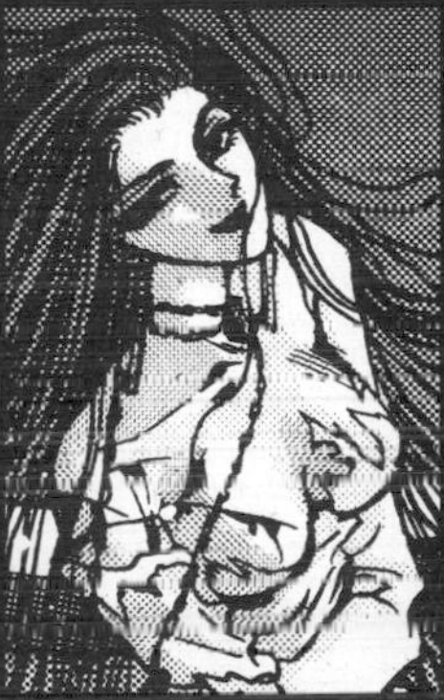

Kanoe
Hinoto's younger sister, Kanoe is also a seeress, but she has her own vision of the future which, with the help of her own group of powerful followers, the "Seven Harbingers," she plans to bring about.

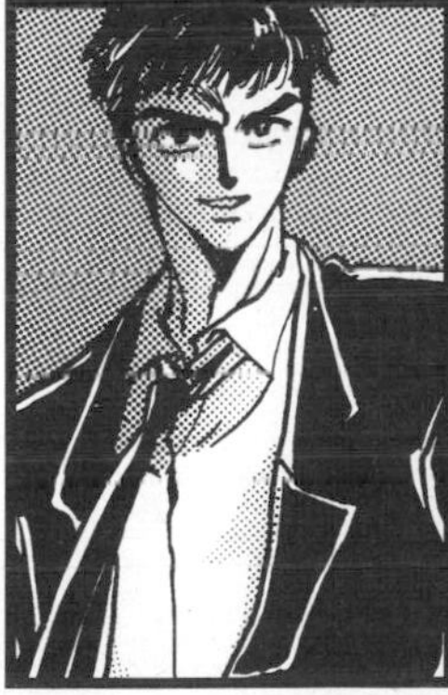

Sorata
A young priest from the shrine at Mt. Koya in Japan, Sorata was raised by priests who recognized his great power from a young age. Sent to Tokyo by his mentor, "Stargazer," Sora has sworn to protect Kamui with his life.

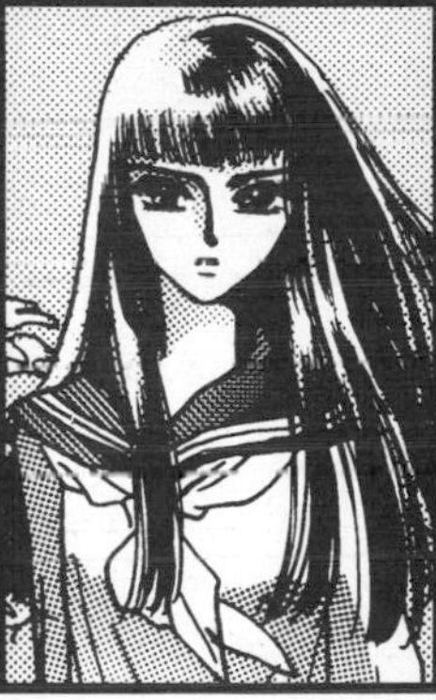

Arashi
A somber young woman who can summon a mystical sword that grows from the very palm of her hand, Arashi is one of the "Seven Seals" surrounding the priestess, Hinoto. Sora takes an immediate liking to the beautiful young woman.

"**X/1999** demands your attention... This title is a self-contained, intellectual series that, while begrudgingly gives the reader plenty of gratuitous action and violence manages to stand apart from that and entice readers with the beauty of its art and the seriousness of the story."

EX.: The Online World of Anime & Manga

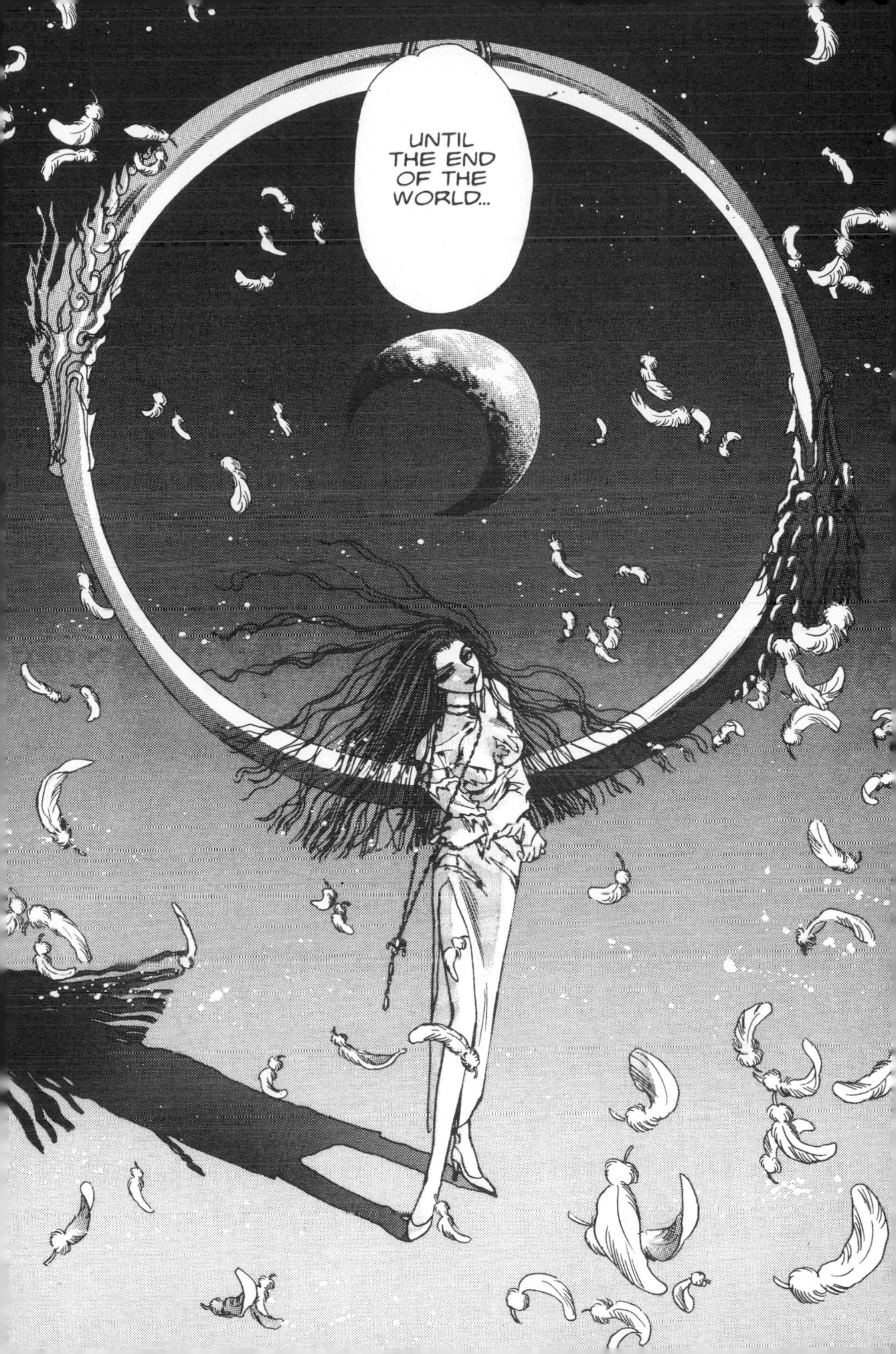
UNTIL THE END OF THE WORLD...

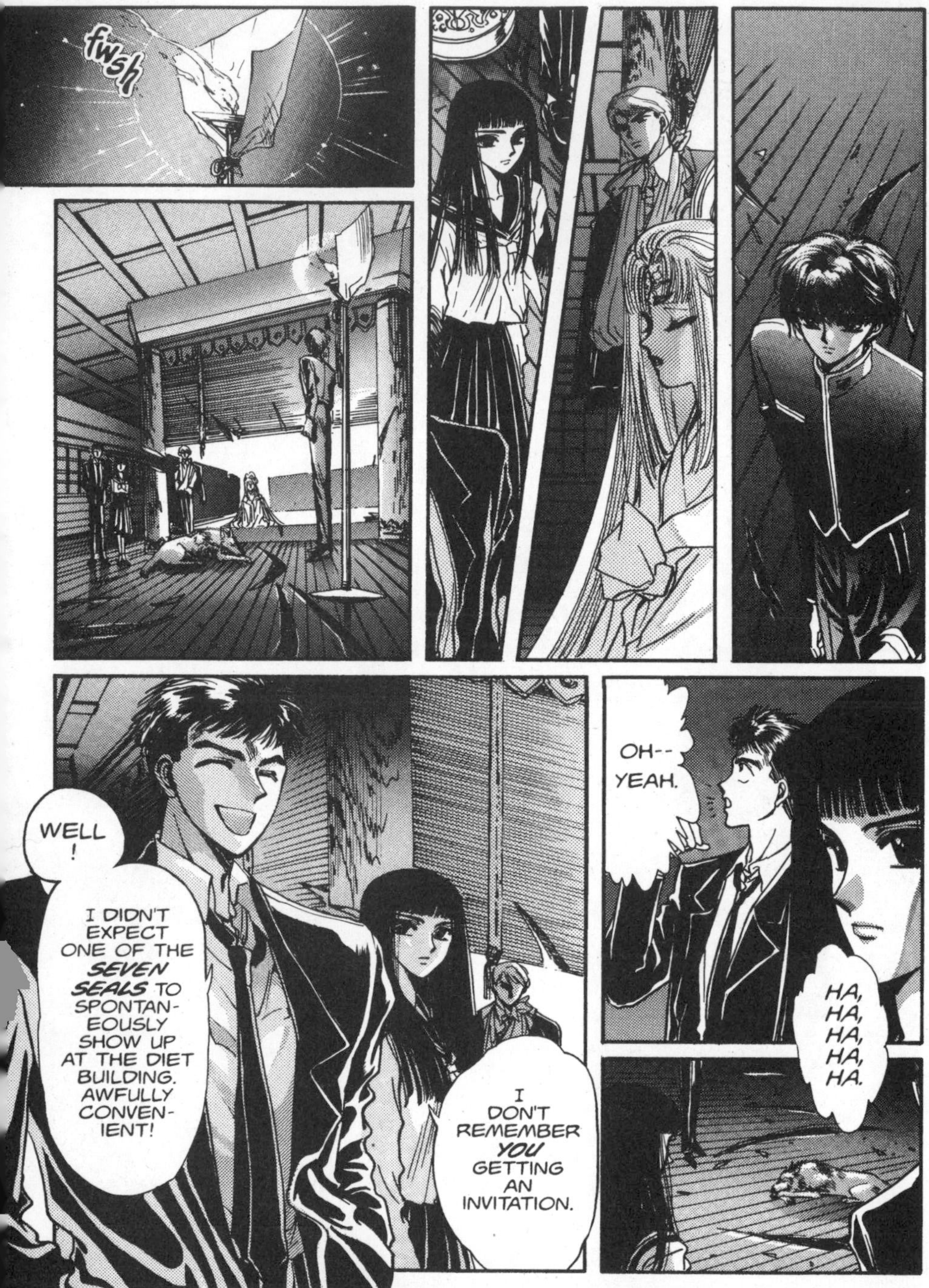
fwsh
WELL!
I DIDN'T EXPECT ONE OF THE SEVEN SEALS TO SPONTANEOUSLY SHOW UP AT THE DIET BUILDING. AWFULLY CONVENIENT!
I DON'T REMEMBER YOU GETTING AN INVITATION.
OH-- YEAH.
HA, HA, HA, HA, HA.

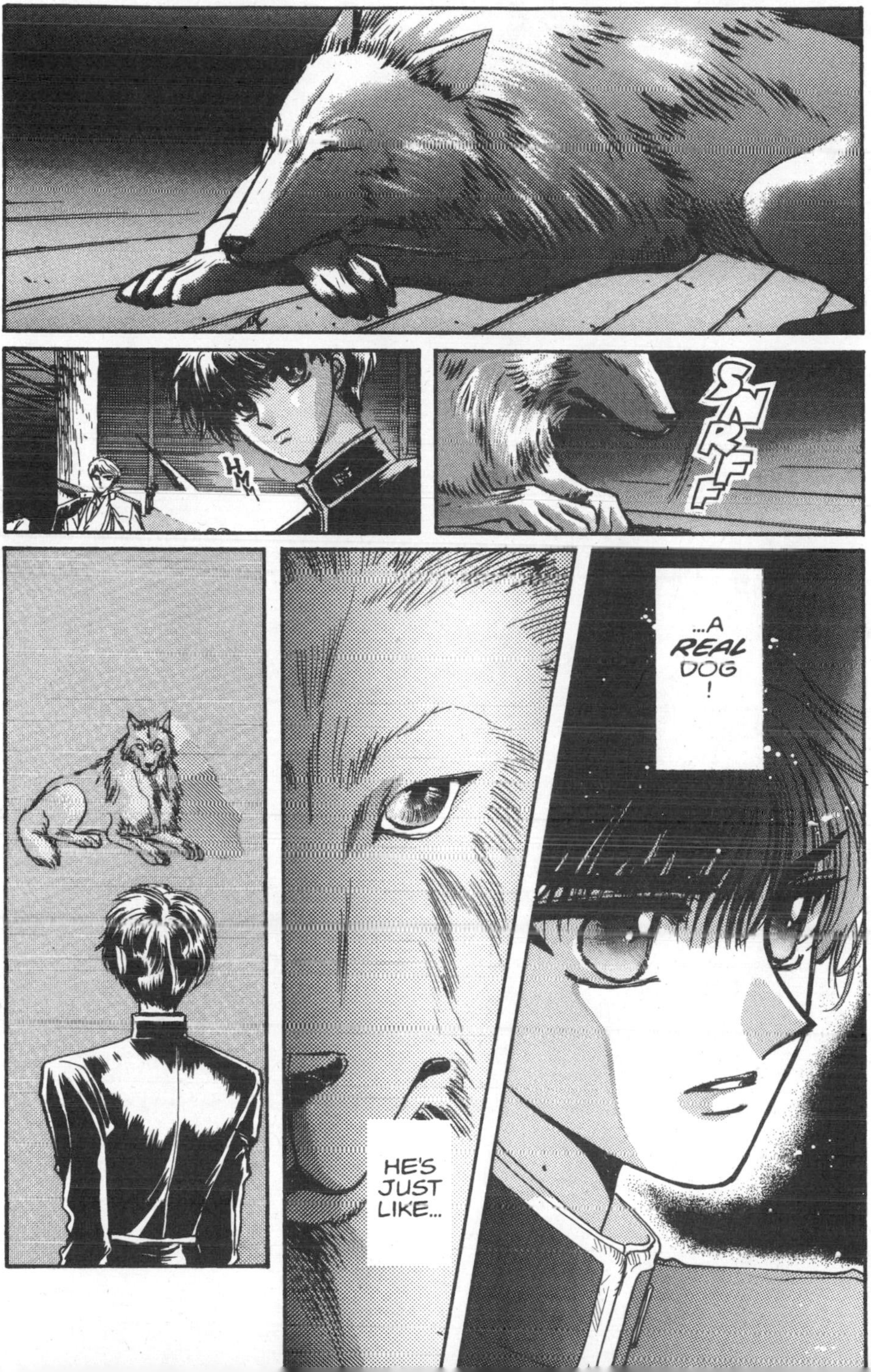
HMM
SNARFF
...A REAL DOG !
HE'S JUST LIKE...

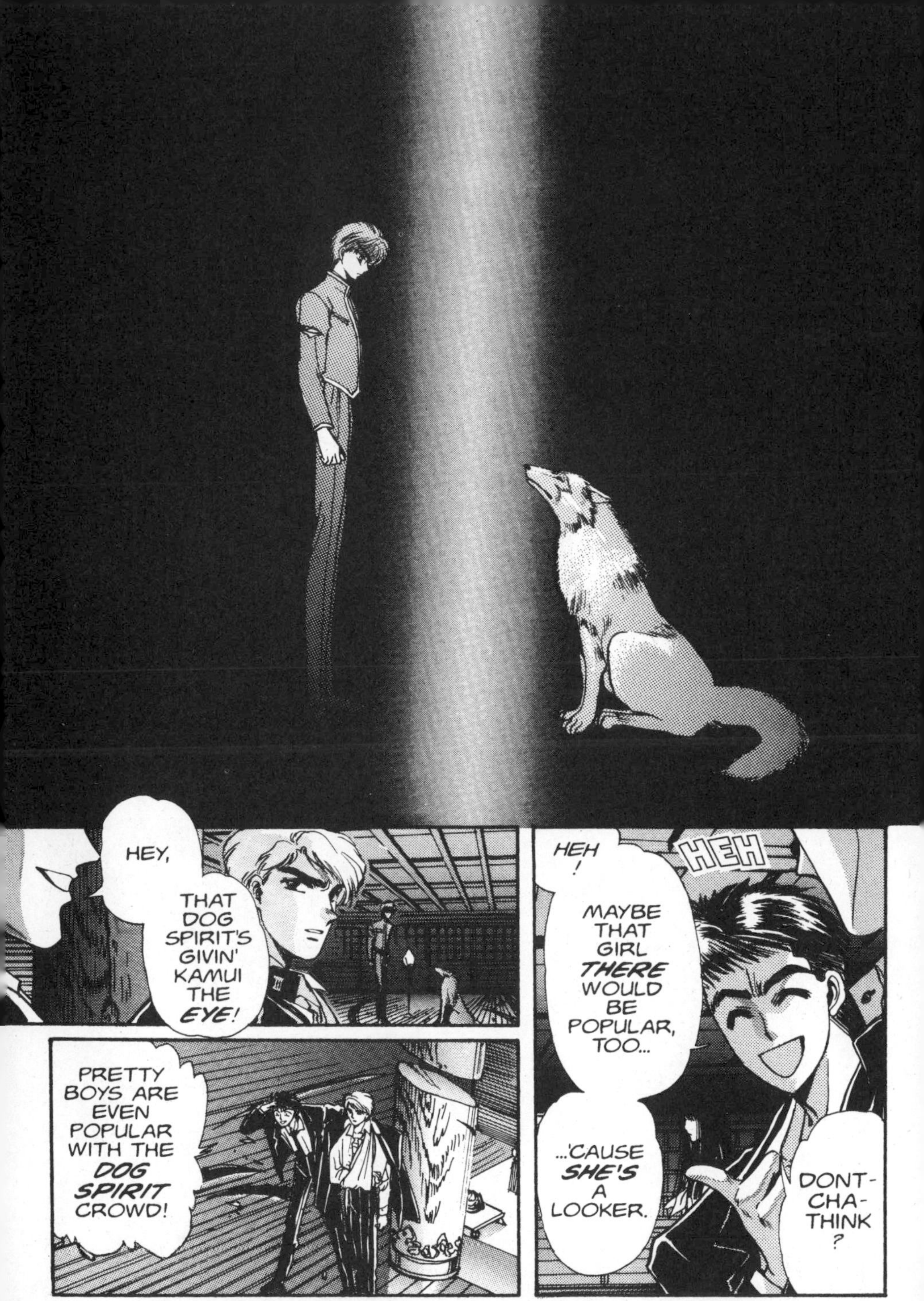

HEY,
THAT DOG SPIRIT'S GIVIN' KAMUI THE *EYE*!
PRETTY BOYS ARE EVEN POPULAR WITH THE *DOG SPIRIT* CROWD!
HEH!
HEH
MAYBE THAT GIRL *THERE* WOULD BE POPULAR, TOO...
...'CAUSE *SHE'S* A LOOKER.
DONT-CHA-THINK?

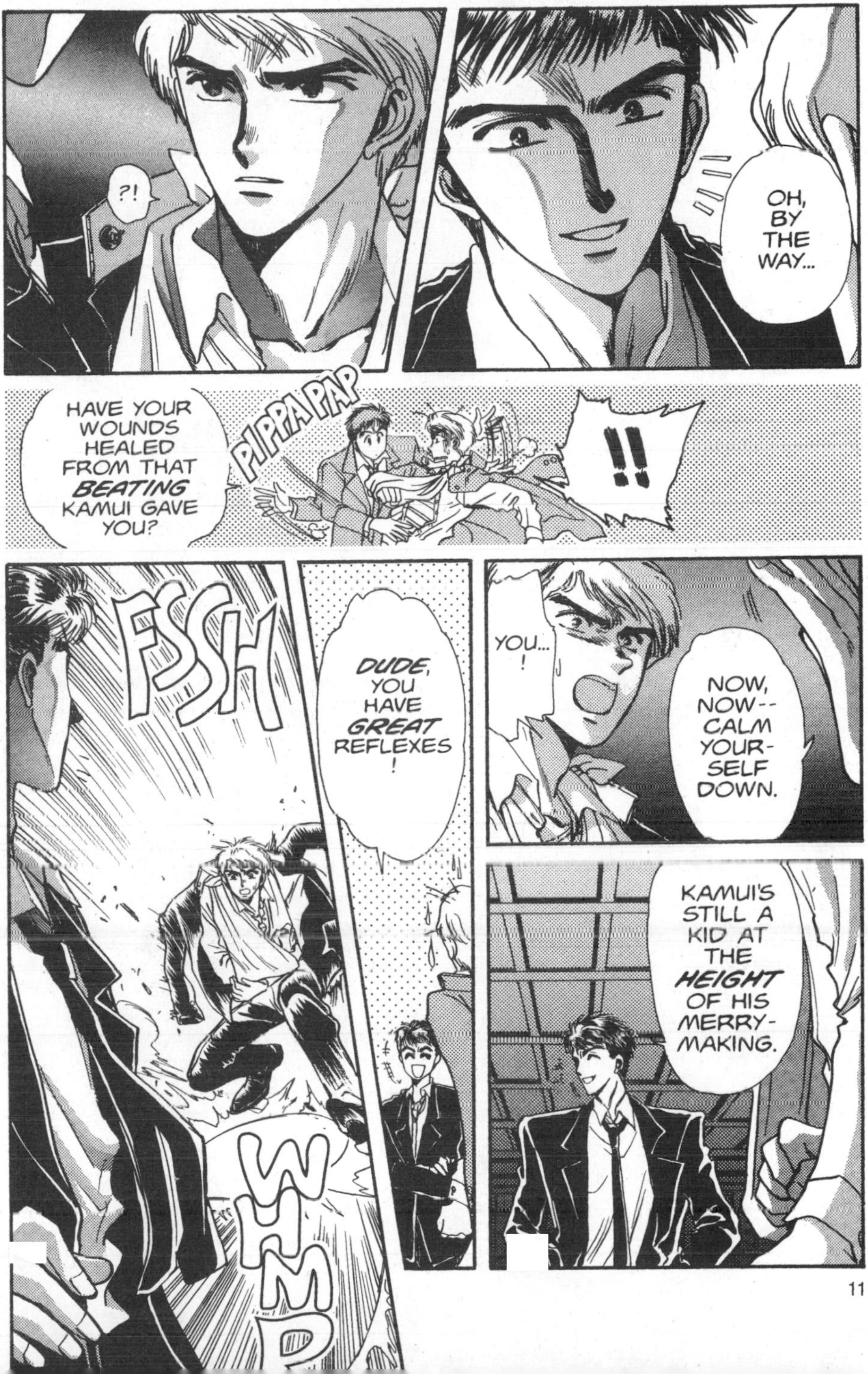
?!
OH, BY THE WAY...
HAVE YOUR WOUNDS HEALED FROM THAT *BEATING* KAMUI GAVE YOU?
PIPPA PAP
!!
FSSH
WHMP
DUDE, YOU HAVE *GREAT* REFLEXES!
YOU...!
NOW, NOW-- CALM YOURSELF DOWN.
KAMUI'S STILL A KID AT THE *HEIGHT* OF HIS MERRY-MAKING.

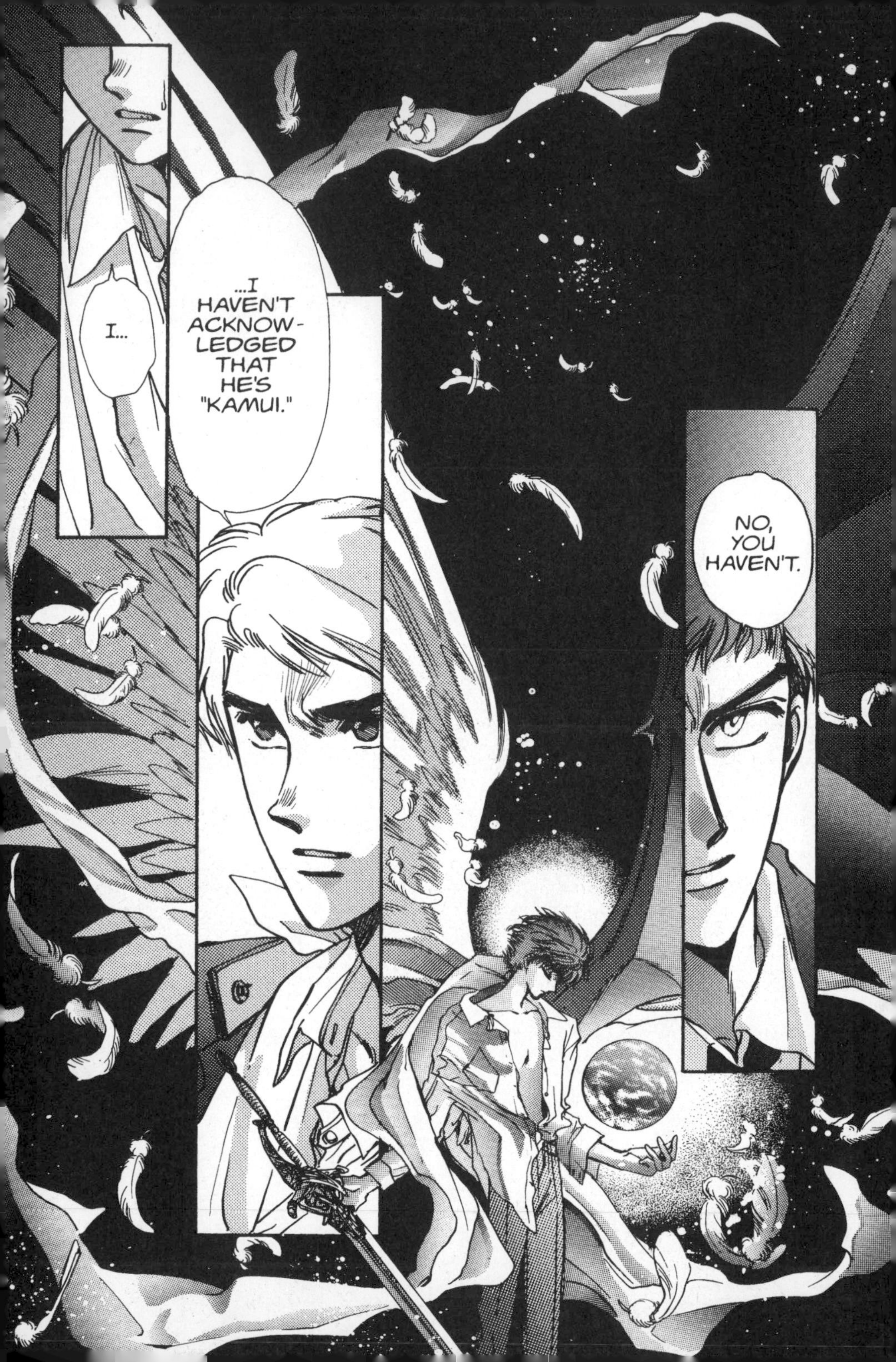
I...
...I HAVEN'T ACKNOW-LEDGED THAT HE'S "KAMUI."
NO, YOU HAVEN'T.

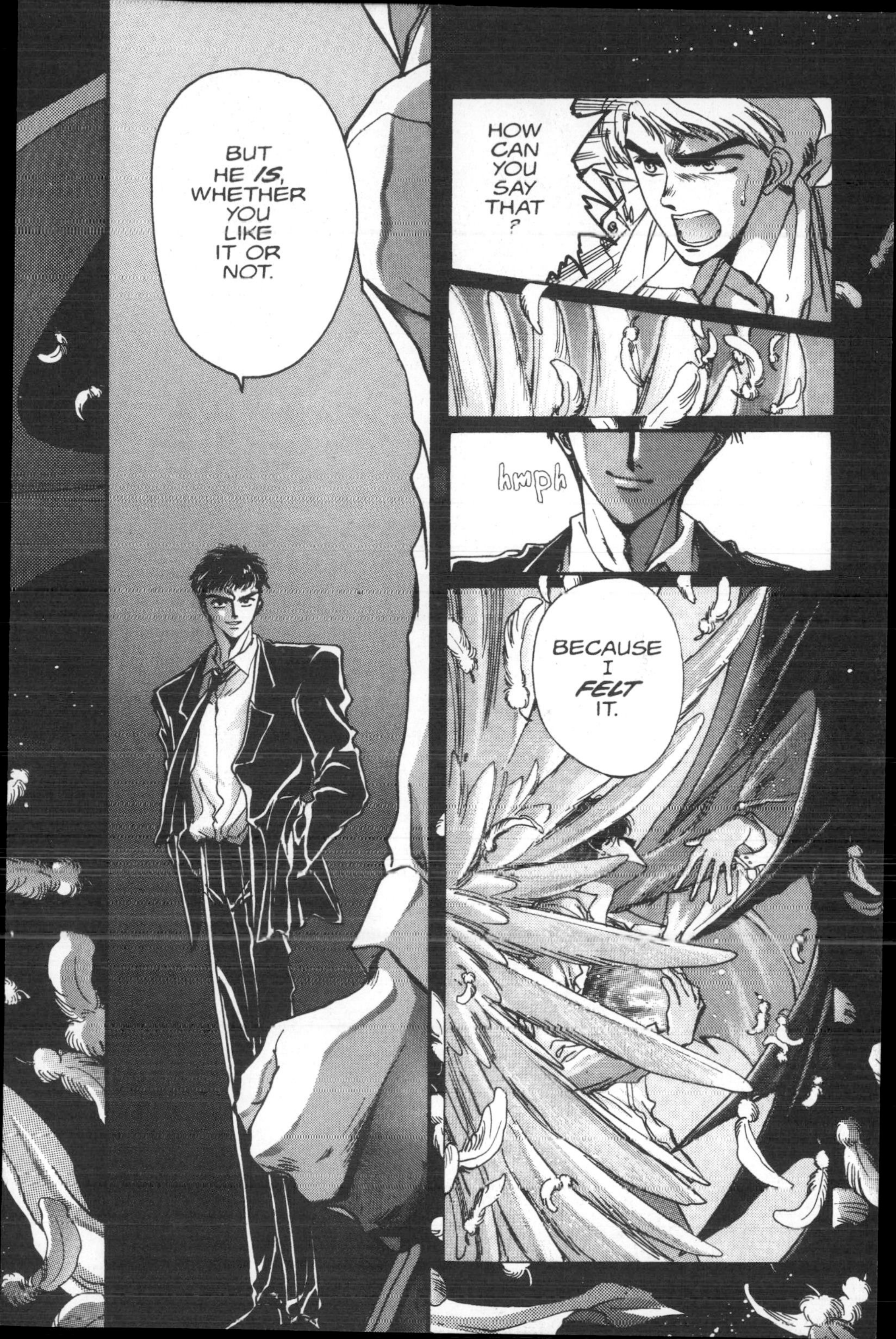
BUT HE IS, WHETHER YOU LIKE IT OR NOT.
HOW CAN YOU SAY THAT?
hmph
BECAUSE I FELT IT.

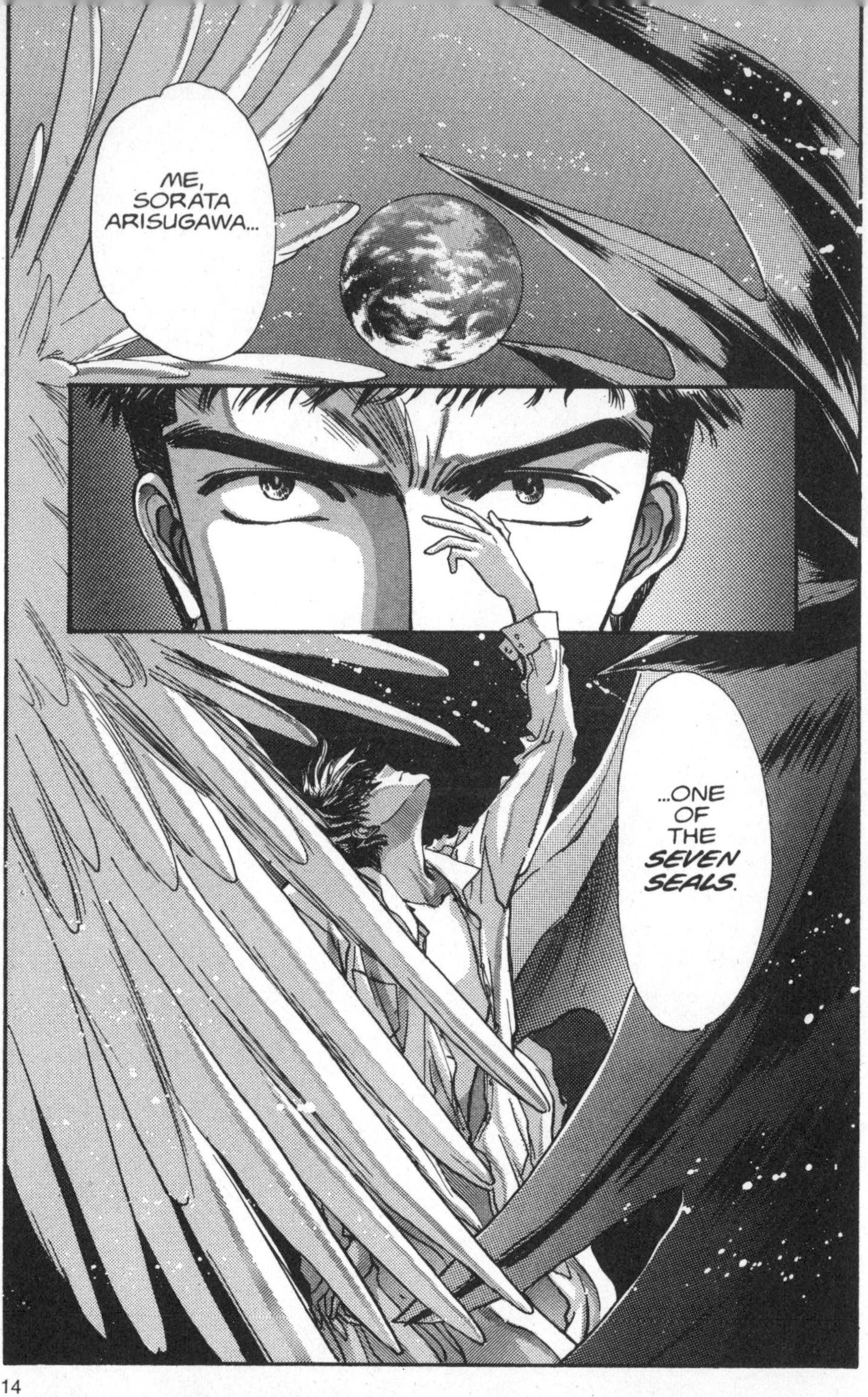
ME, SORATA ARISUGAWA...
...ONE OF THE SEVEN SEALS.

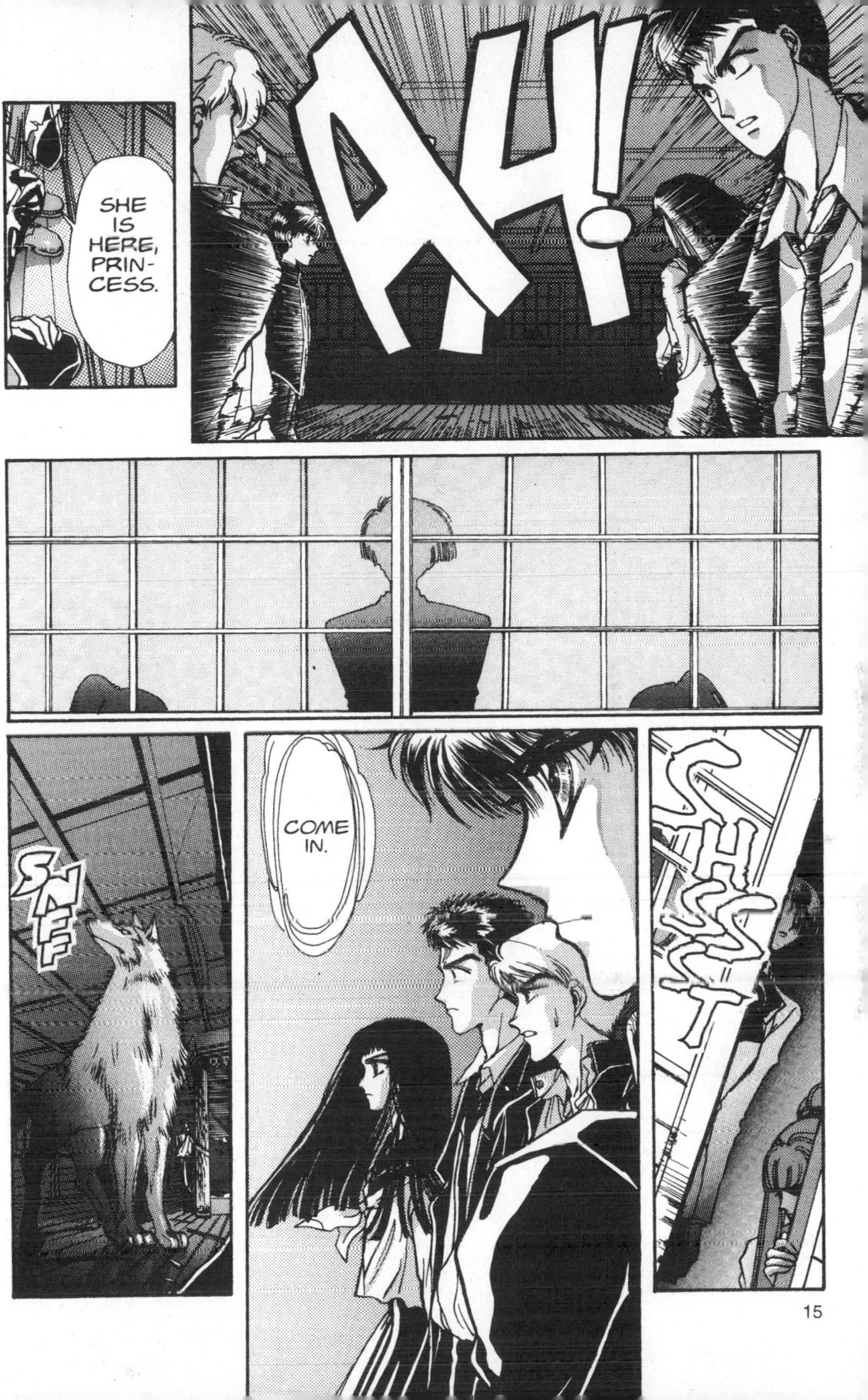
SHE IS HERE, PRINCESS.
AH!
SNIFF
COME IN.
SHSSST

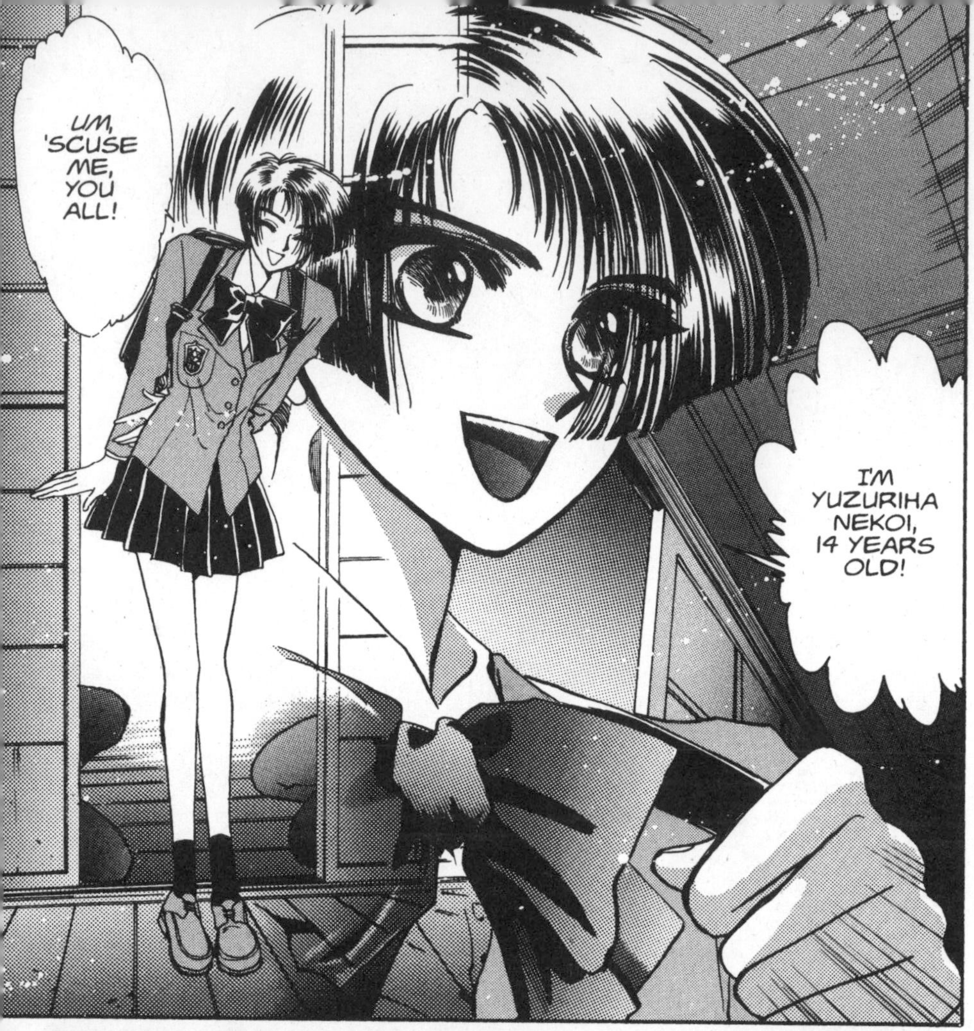
UM, 'SCUSE ME, YOU ALL!
I'M YUZURIHA NEKOI, 14 YEARS OLD!
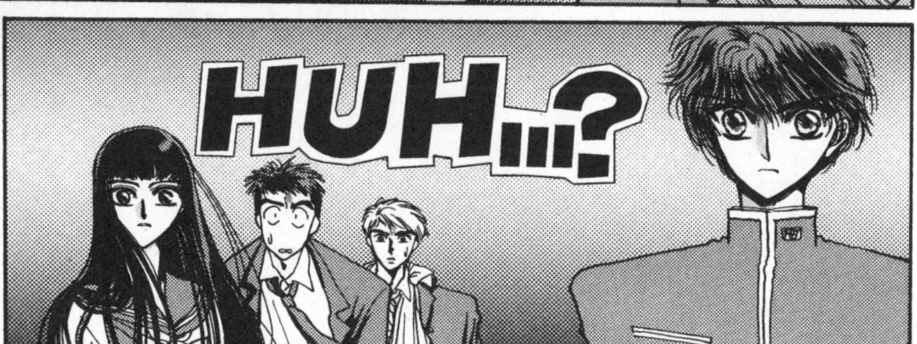
HUH...?

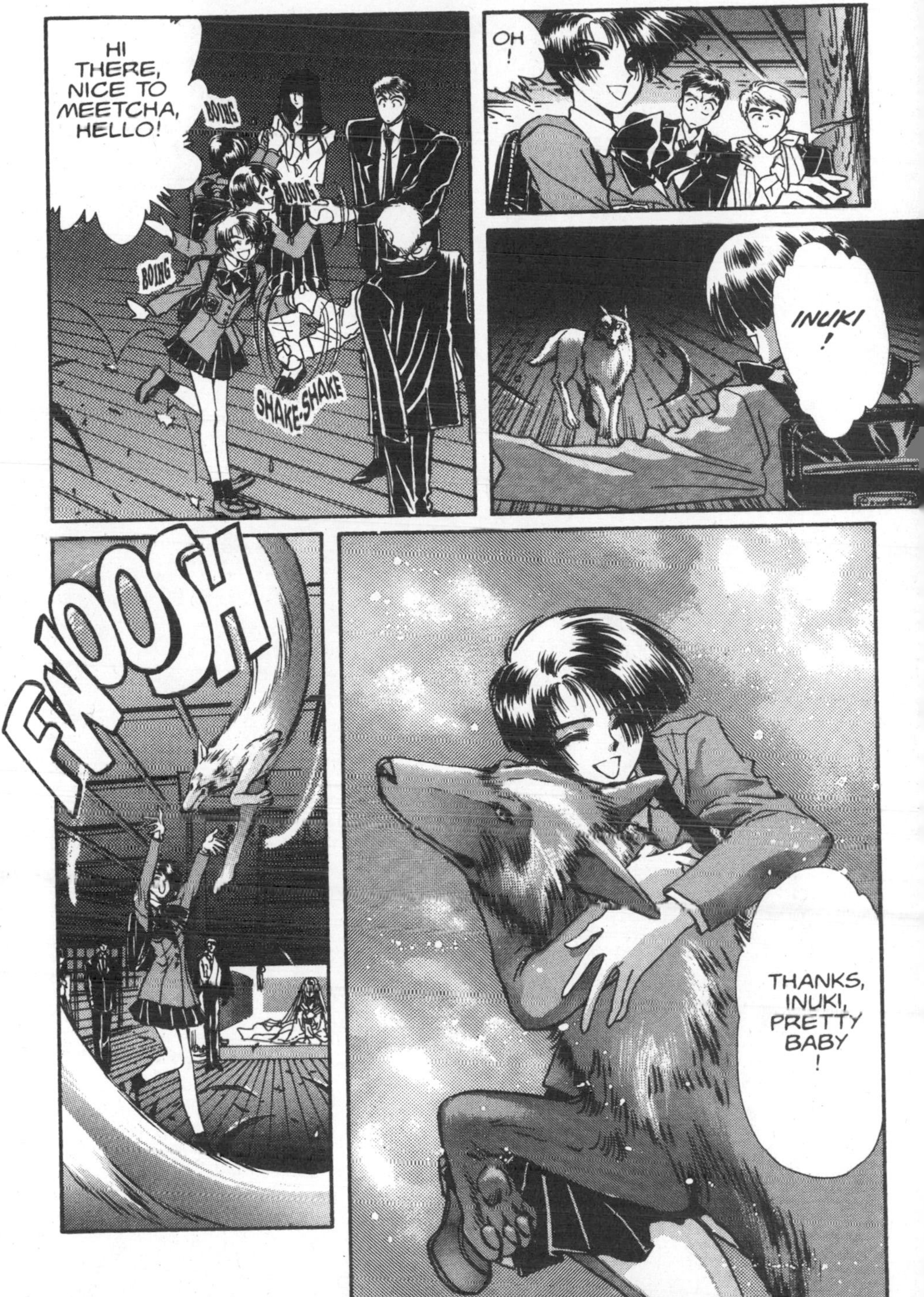
HI THERE, NICE TO MEETCHA, HELLO!
BOING
BOING
BOING
SHAKE-SHAKE
OH!
INUKI!
FWOOSH
THANKS, INUKI, PRETTY BABY!

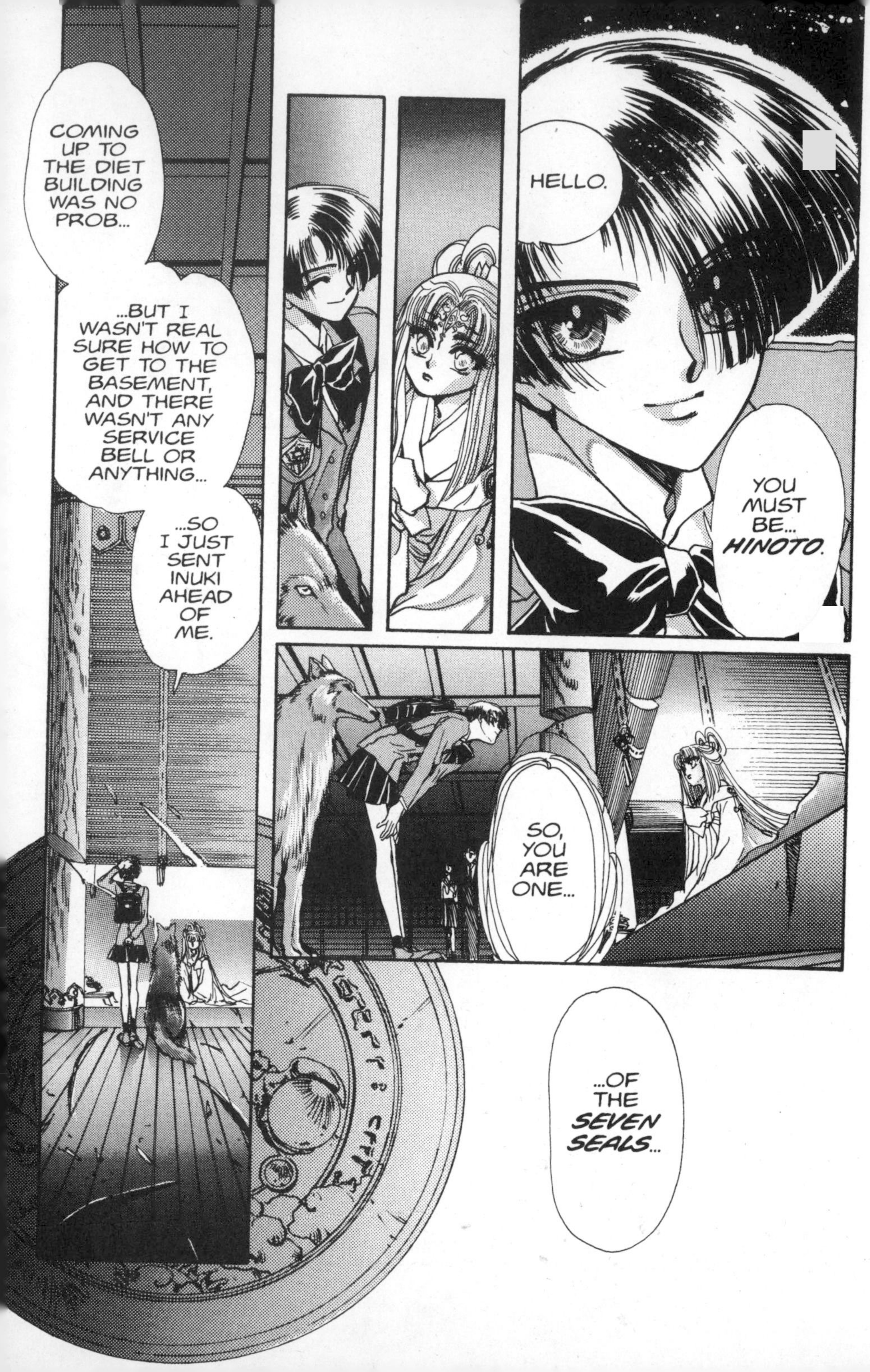
COMING UP TO THE DIET BUILDING WAS NO PROB...
...BUT I WASN'T REAL SURE HOW TO GET TO THE BASEMENT, AND THERE WASN'T ANY SERVICE BELL OR ANYTHING...
...SO I JUST SENT INUKI AHEAD OF ME.
HELLO.
YOU MUST BE... *HINOTO*.
SO, YOU ARE ONE...
...OF THE *SEVEN SEALS*...

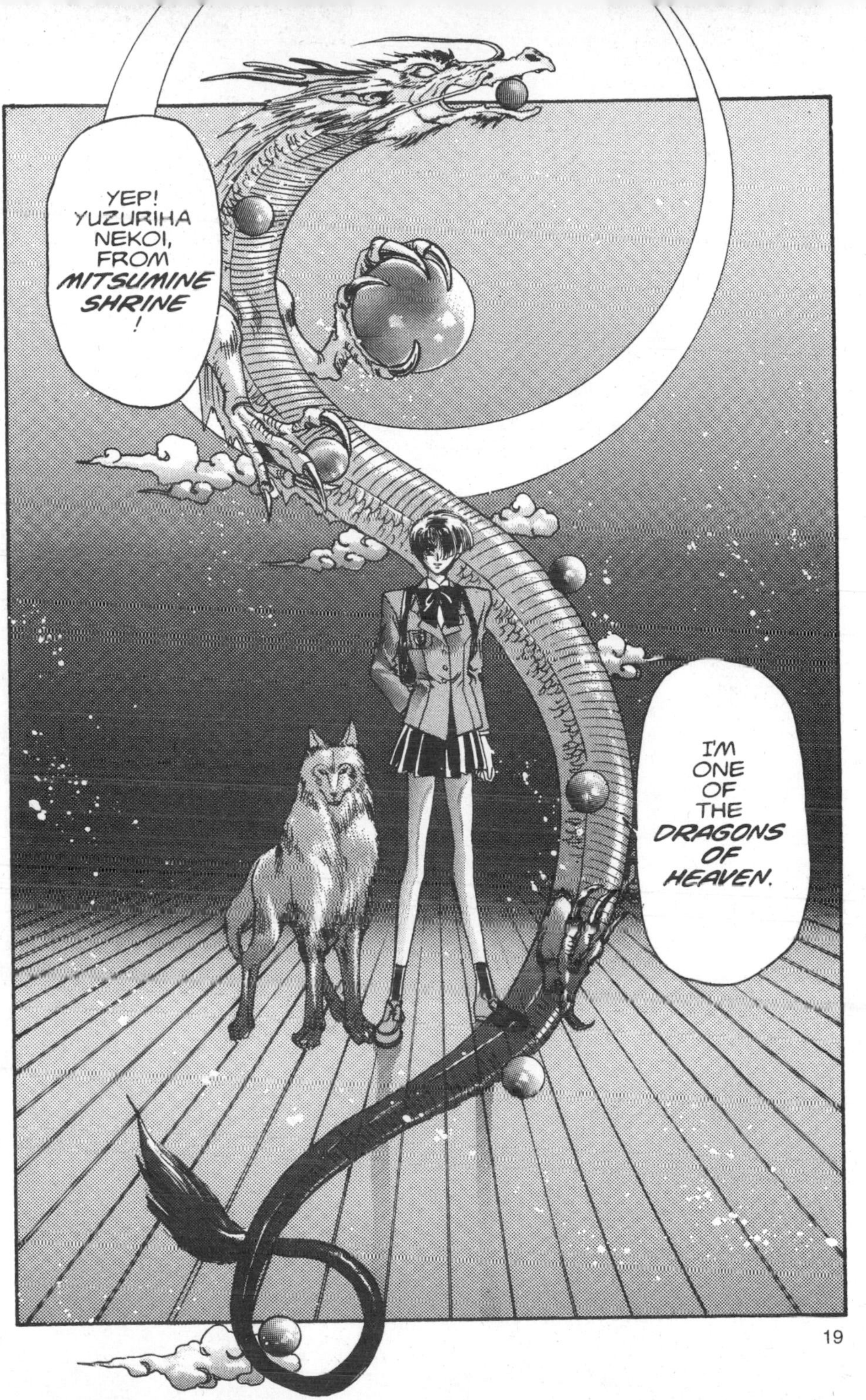
YEP! YUZURIHA NEKOI, FROM MITSUMINE SHRINE!
I'M ONE OF THE DRAGONS OF HEAVEN.

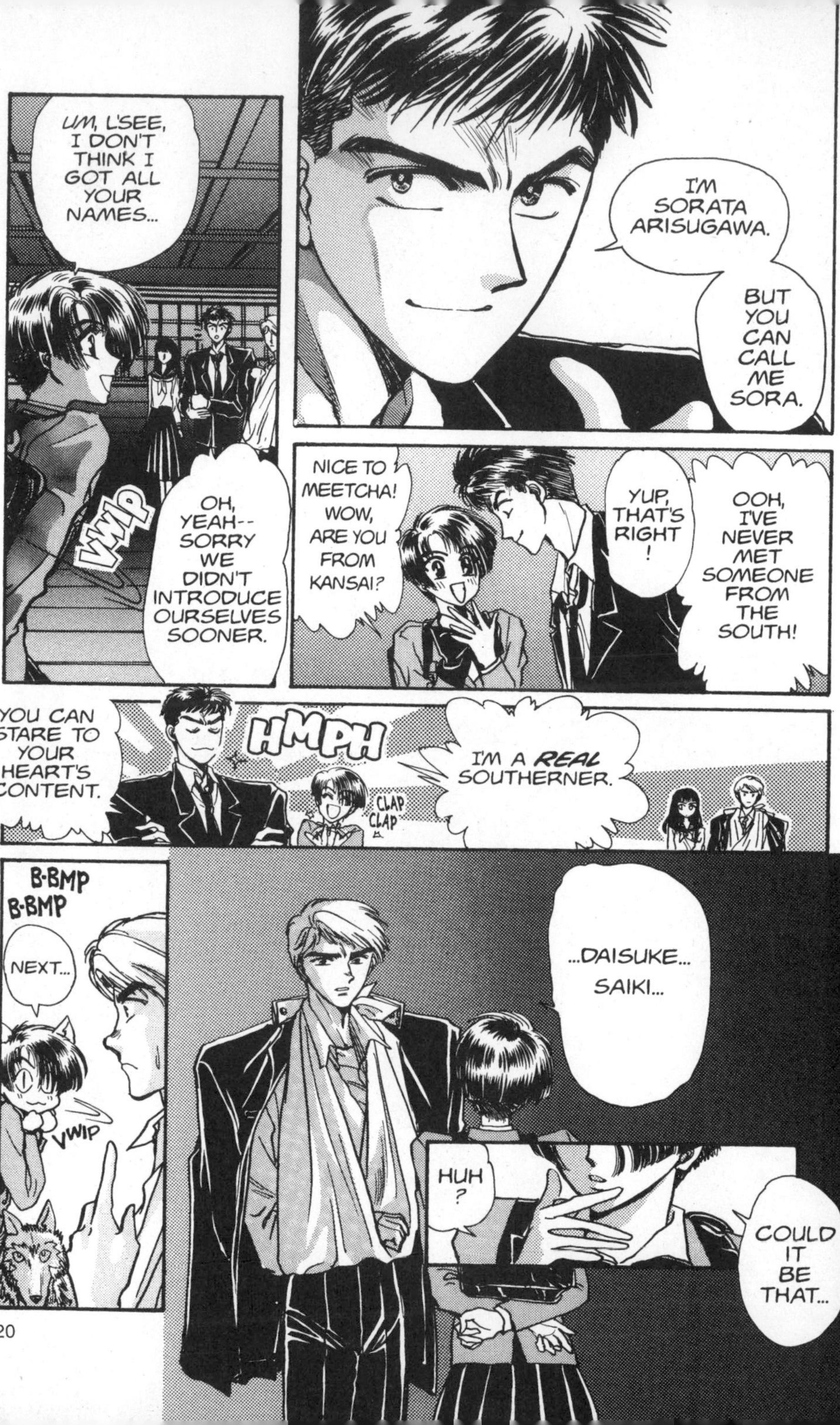
UM, L'SEE, I DON'T THINK I GOT ALL YOUR NAMES...
VWIP
OH, YEAH-- SORRY WE DIDN'T INTRODUCE OURSELVES SOONER.
I'M SORATA ARISUGAWA.
BUT YOU CAN CALL ME SORA.
NICE TO MEETCHA! WOW, ARE YOU FROM KANSAI?
YUP, THAT'S RIGHT!
OOH, I'VE NEVER MET SOMEONE FROM THE SOUTH!
YOU CAN STARE TO YOUR HEART'S CONTENT.
HMPH
I'M A *REAL* SOUTHERNER.
CLAP CLAP
B-BMP
B-BMP
NEXT...
VWIP
...DAISUKE... SAIKI...
HUH?
COULD IT BE THAT...

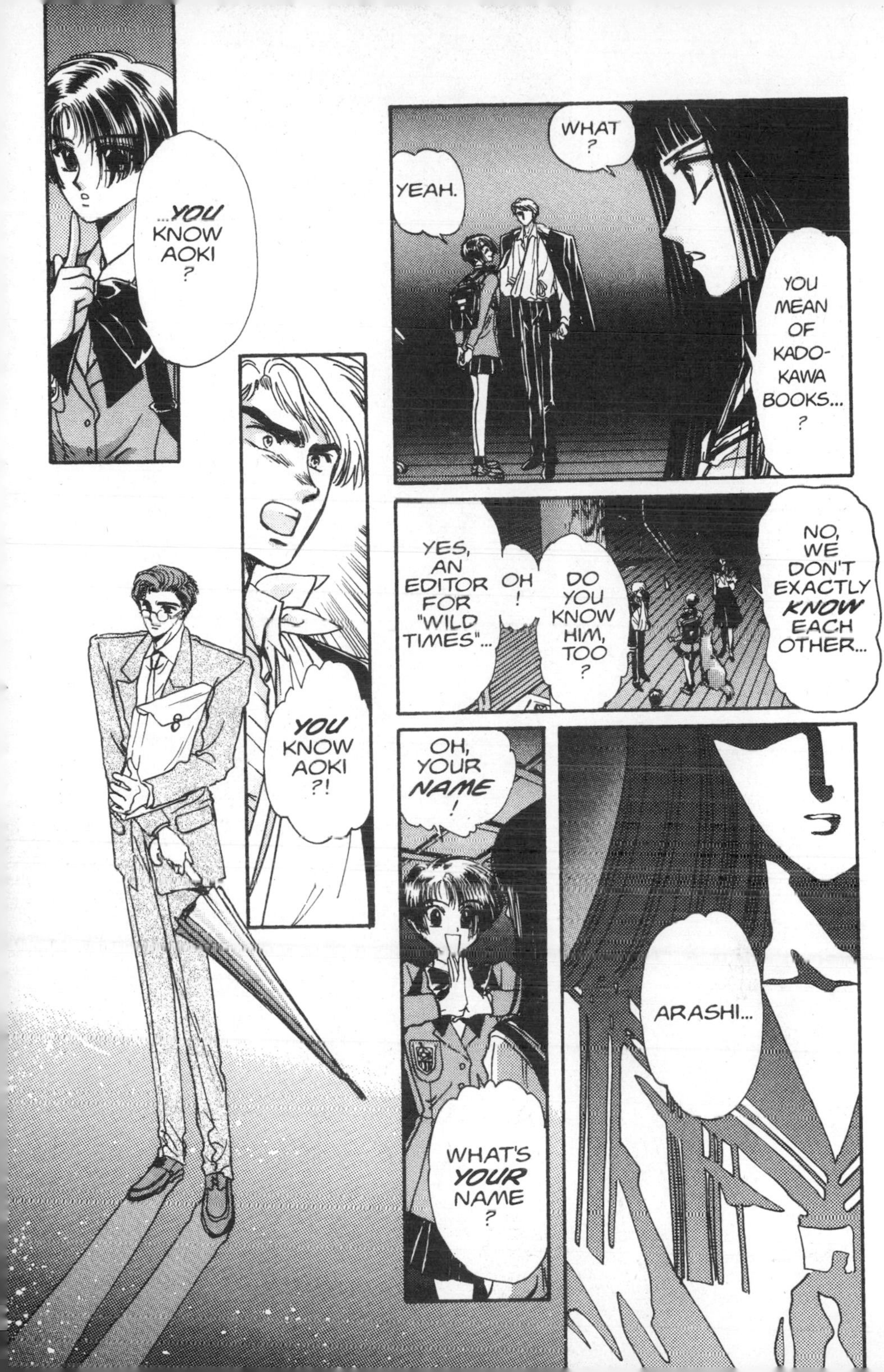
...YOU KNOW AOKI?
YEAH.
WHAT?
YOU MEAN OF KADO-KAWA BOOKS...?
YOU KNOW AOKI?!
YES, AN EDITOR FOR "WILD TIMES"...
OH!
DO YOU KNOW HIM, TOO?
NO, WE DON'T EXACTLY KNOW EACH OTHER...
OH, YOUR NAME!
WHAT'S YOUR NAME?
ARASHI...

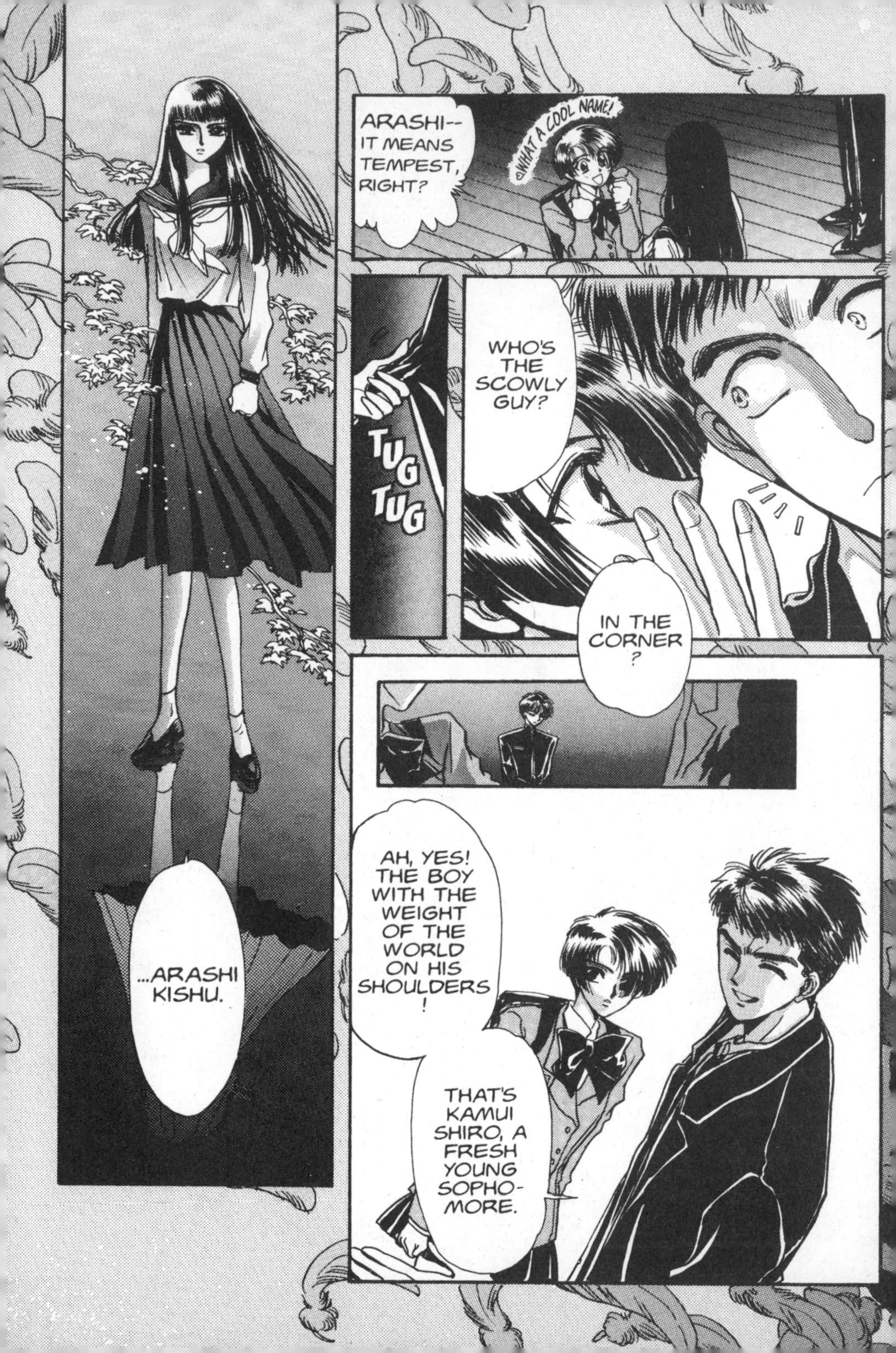
...ARASHI KISHU.
ARASHI-- IT MEANS TEMPEST, RIGHT?
WHAT A COOL NAME!
TUG TUG
WHO'S THE SCOWLY GUY?
IN THE CORNER?
AH, YES! THE BOY WITH THE WEIGHT OF THE WORLD ON HIS SHOULDERS!
THAT'S KAMUI SHIRO, A FRESH YOUNG SOPHO-MORE.

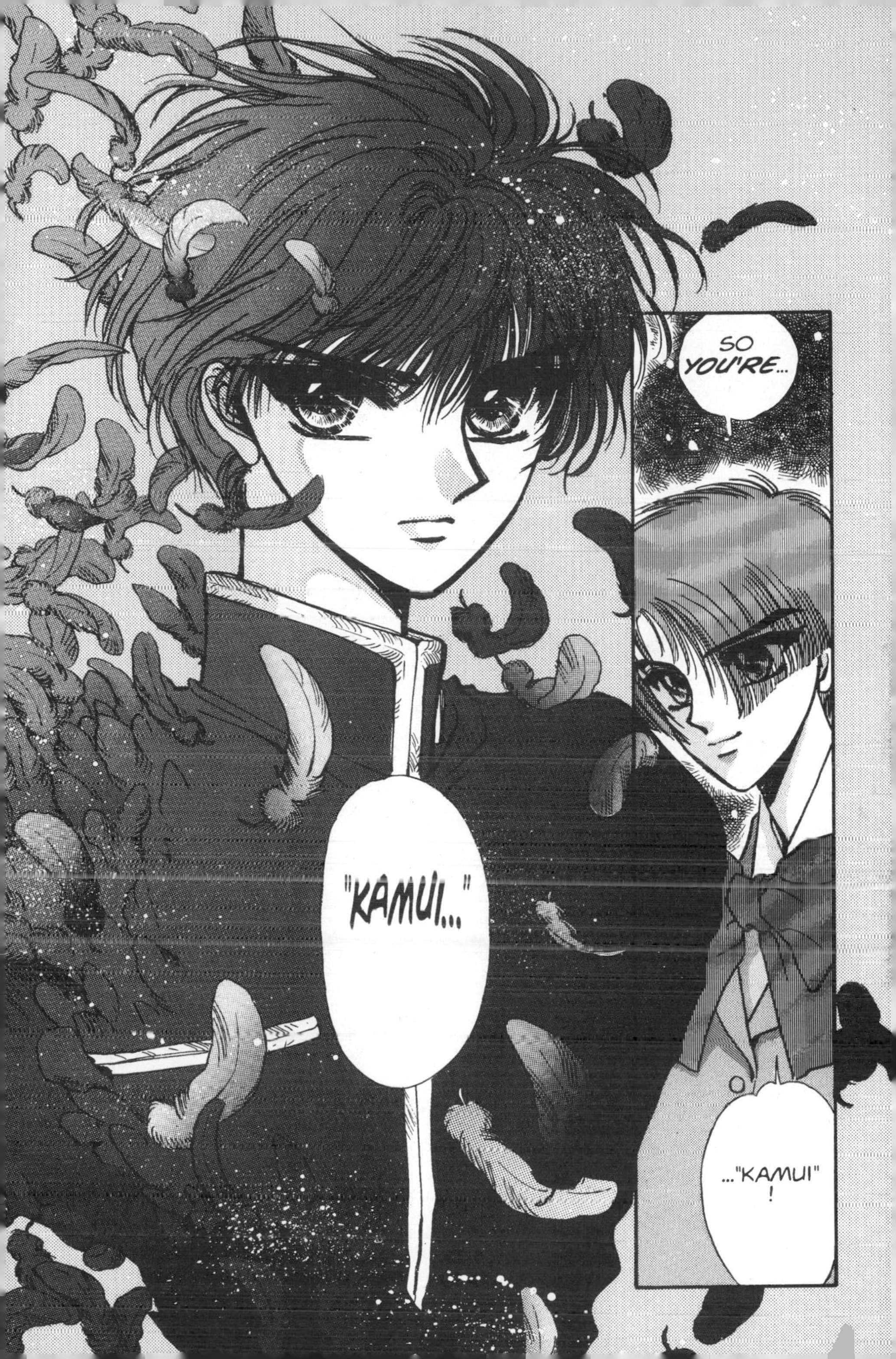
"KAMUI..."
SO YOU'RE...
..."KAMUI"
!

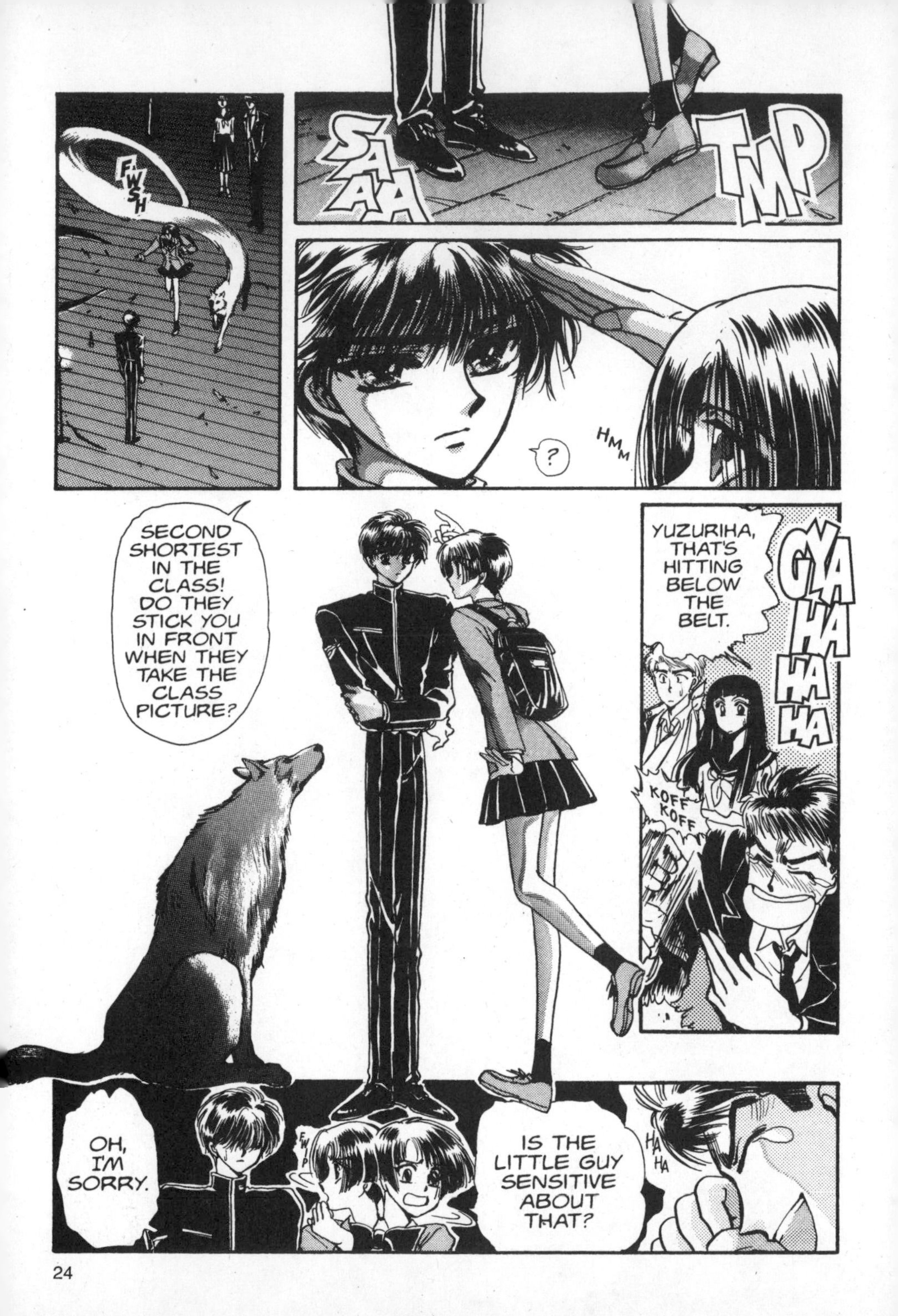
FWSH
SAAA
TMP
?
HMM
SECOND SHORTEST IN THE CLASS! DO THEY STICK YOU IN FRONT WHEN THEY TAKE THE CLASS PICTURE?
YUZURIHA, THAT'S HITTING BELOW THE BELT.
GYAHAHAHAHA
KOFF KOFF
OH, I'M SORRY.
FWIP
IS THE LITTLE GUY SENSITIVE ABOUT THAT?
HA HA

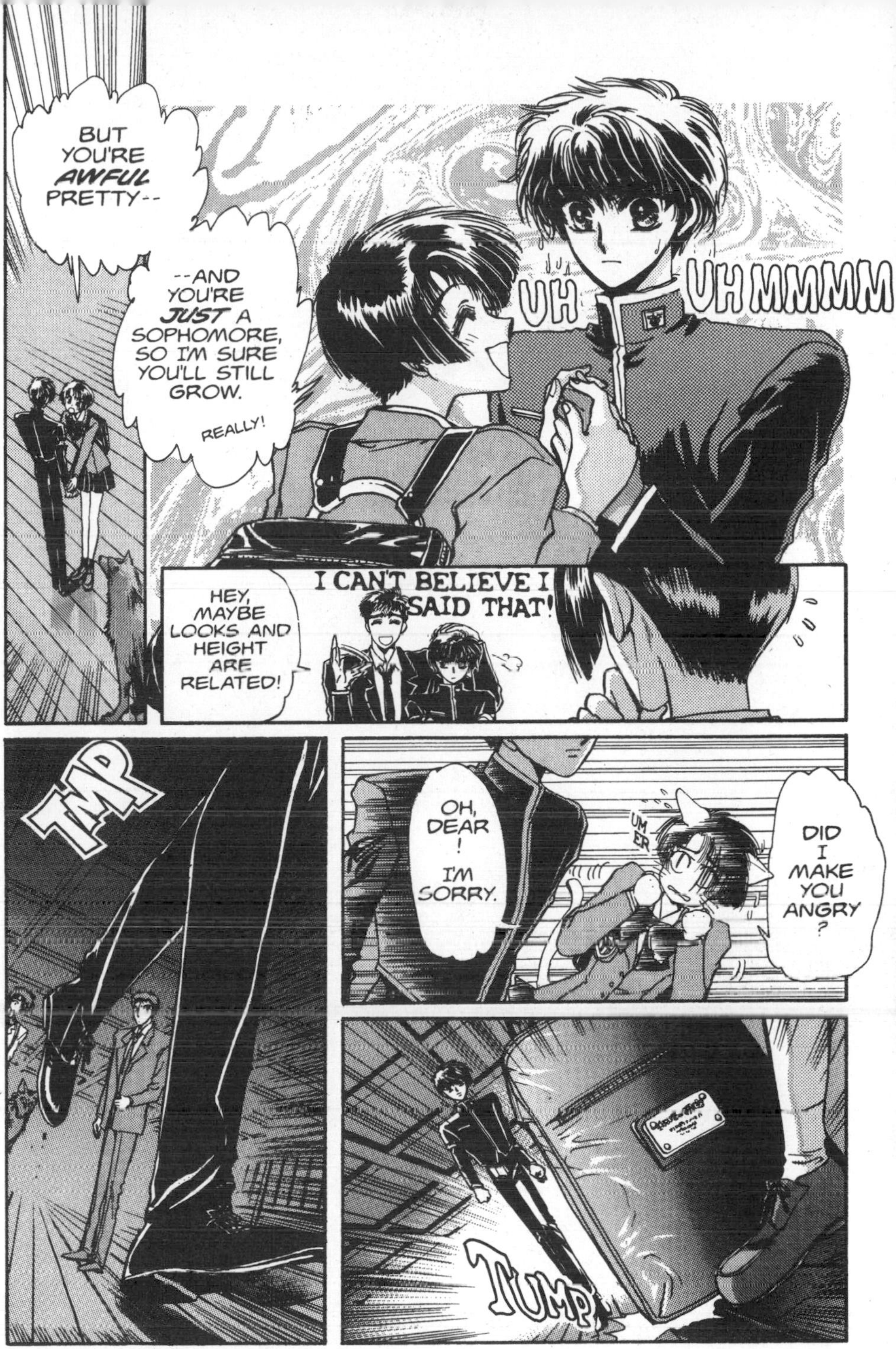
BUT YOU'RE AWFUL PRETTY--
--AND YOU'RE JUST A SOPHOMORE, SO I'M SURE YOU'LL STILL GROW.
REALLY!
UH
UH MMMMM
HEY, MAYBE LOOKS AND HEIGHT ARE RELATED!
I CAN'T BELIEVE I SAID THAT!
TMP
OH, DEAR! I'M SORRY.
UM ER
DID I MAKE YOU ANGRY?
TUMP

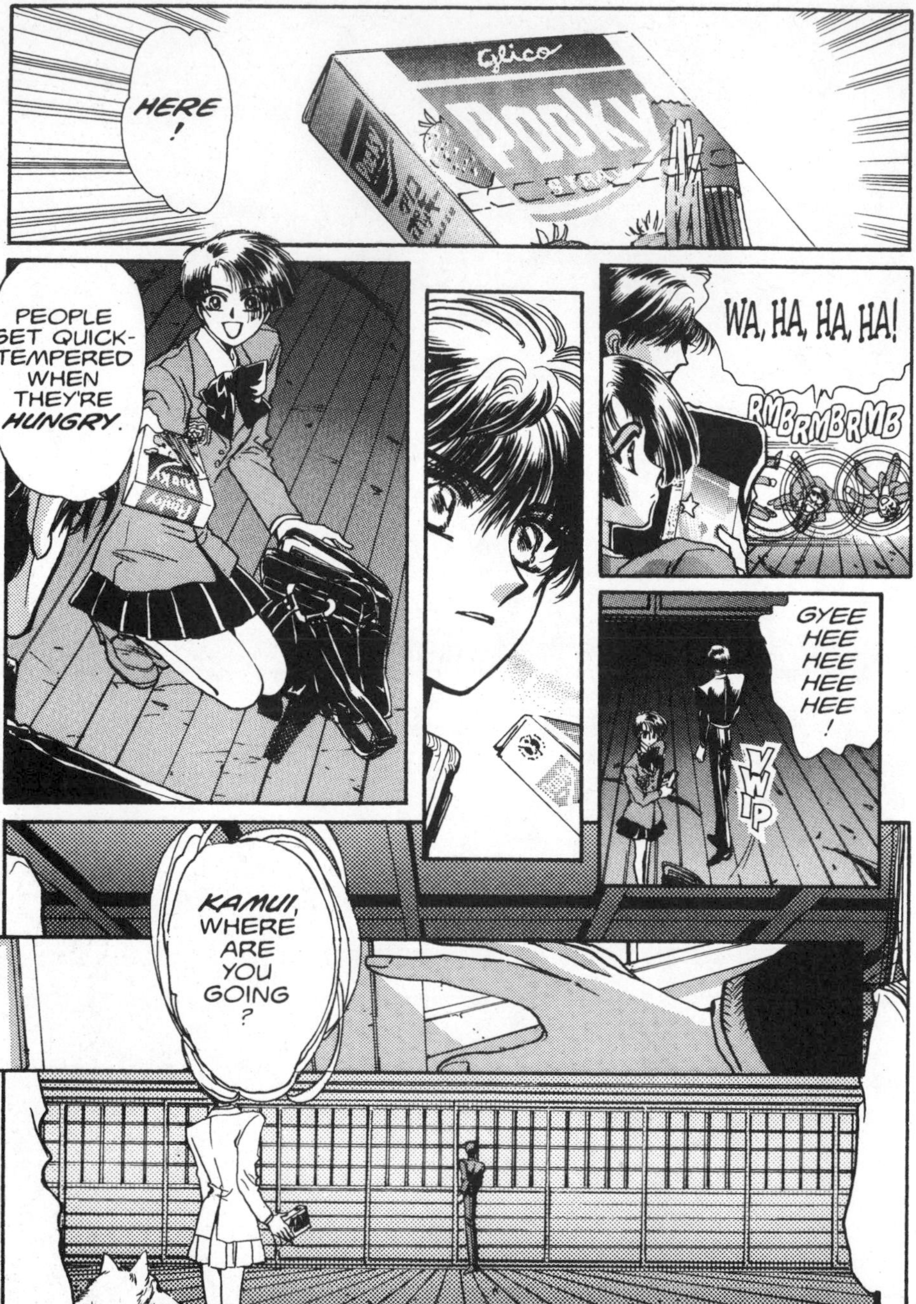
HERE!
glico
POCKY
PEOPLE GET QUICK-TEMPERED WHEN THEY'RE *HUNGRY*.
WA, HA, HA, HA!
RMBRMBRMB
GYEE HEE HEE HEE HEE!
VWIP
KAMUI, WHERE ARE YOU GOING?

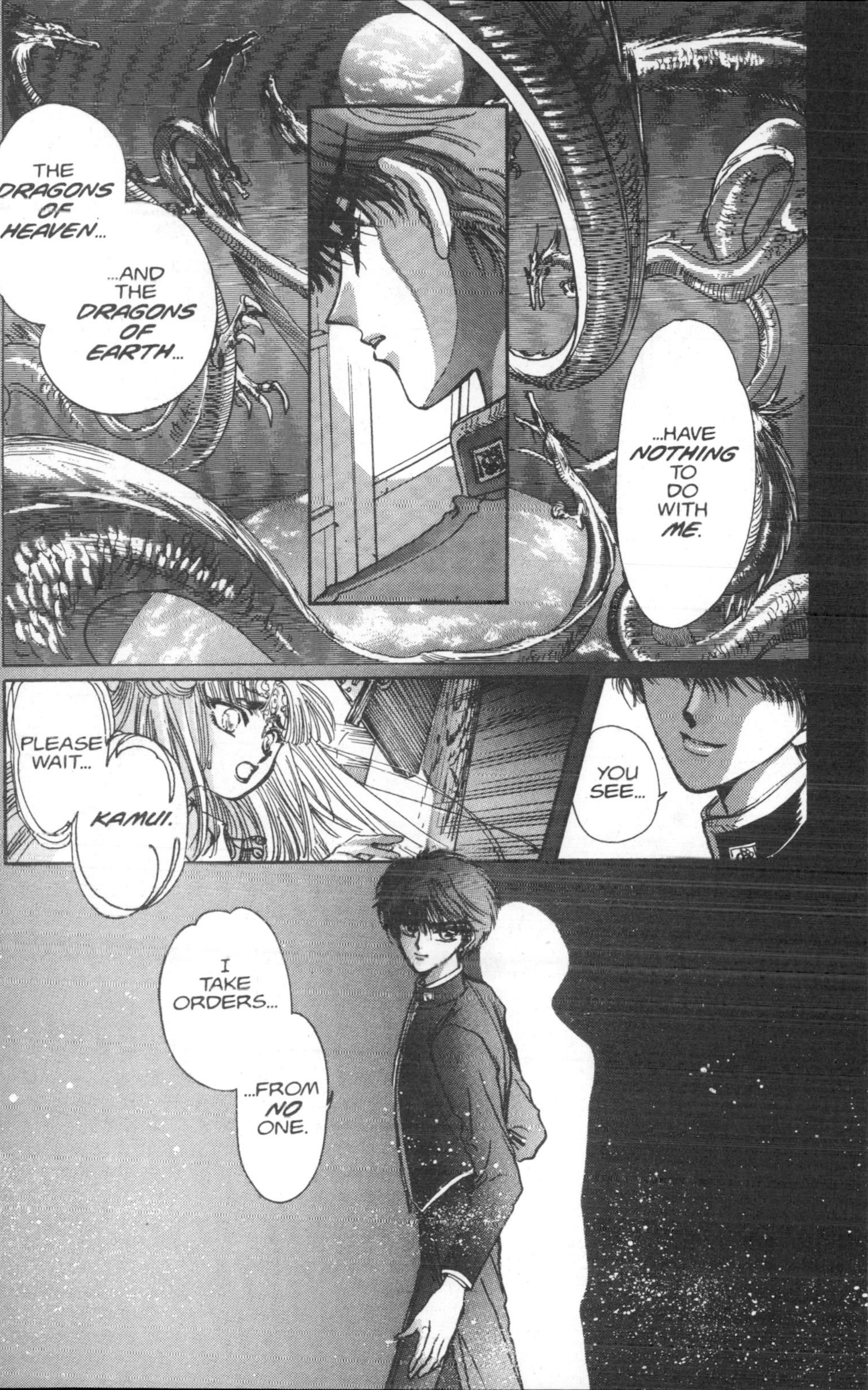
THE *DRAGONS OF HEAVEN*...
...AND THE *DRAGONS OF EARTH*...
...HAVE *NOTHING* TO DO WITH *ME*.
PLEASE WAIT...
KAMUI.
YOU SEE...
I TAKE ORDERS...
...FROM *NO* ONE.

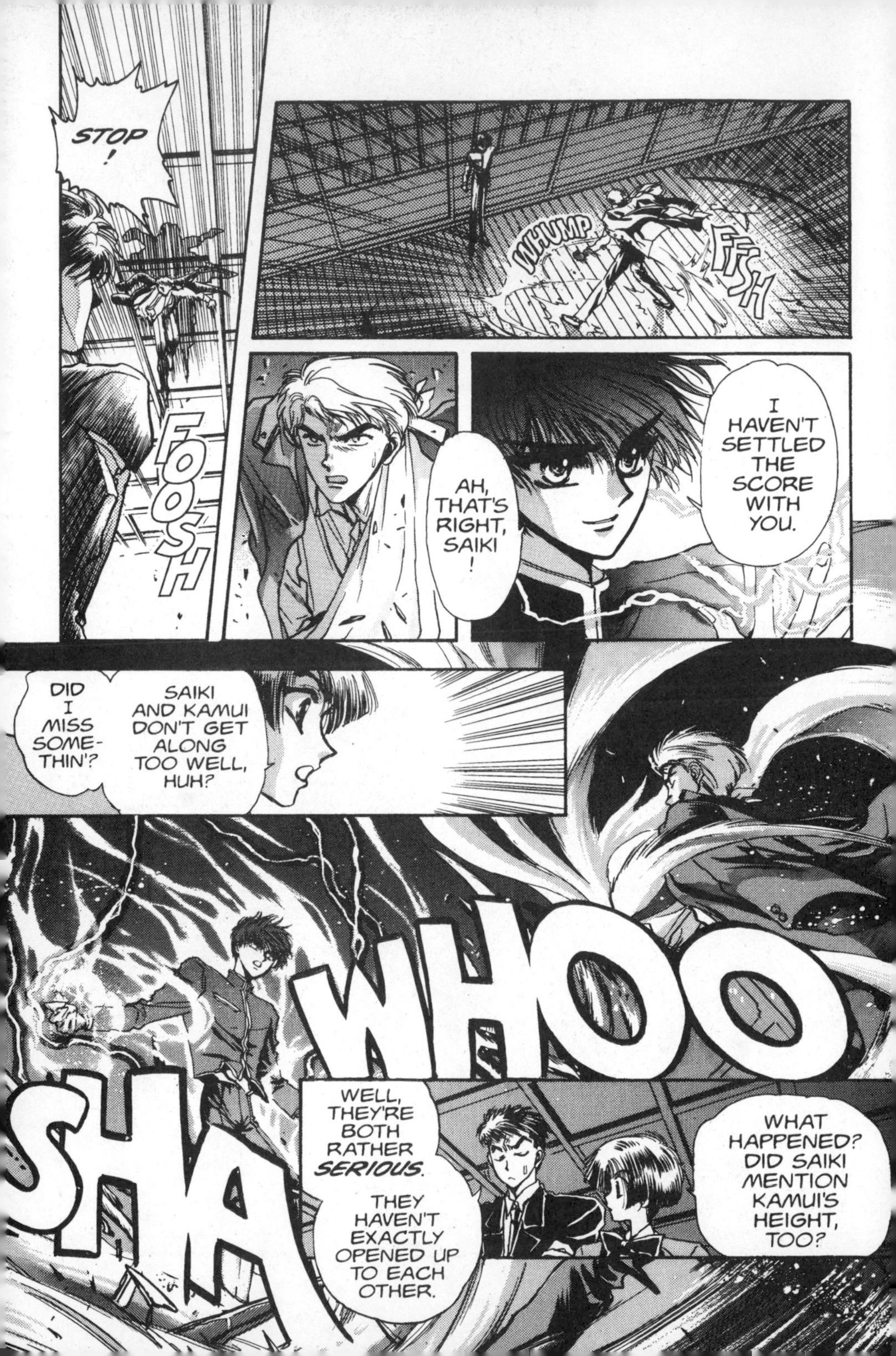
STOP!
FOOSH
WHUMP
FFSH
AH, THAT'S RIGHT, SAIKI!
I HAVEN'T SETTLED THE SCORE WITH YOU.
DID I MISS SOME-THIN'?
SAIKI AND KAMUI DON'T GET ALONG TOO WELL, HUH?
WHOO
SHA
WELL, THEY'RE BOTH RATHER *SERIOUS*.
THEY HAVEN'T EXACTLY OPENED UP TO EACH OTHER.
WHAT HAPPENED? DID SAIKI MENTION KAMUI'S HEIGHT, TOO?

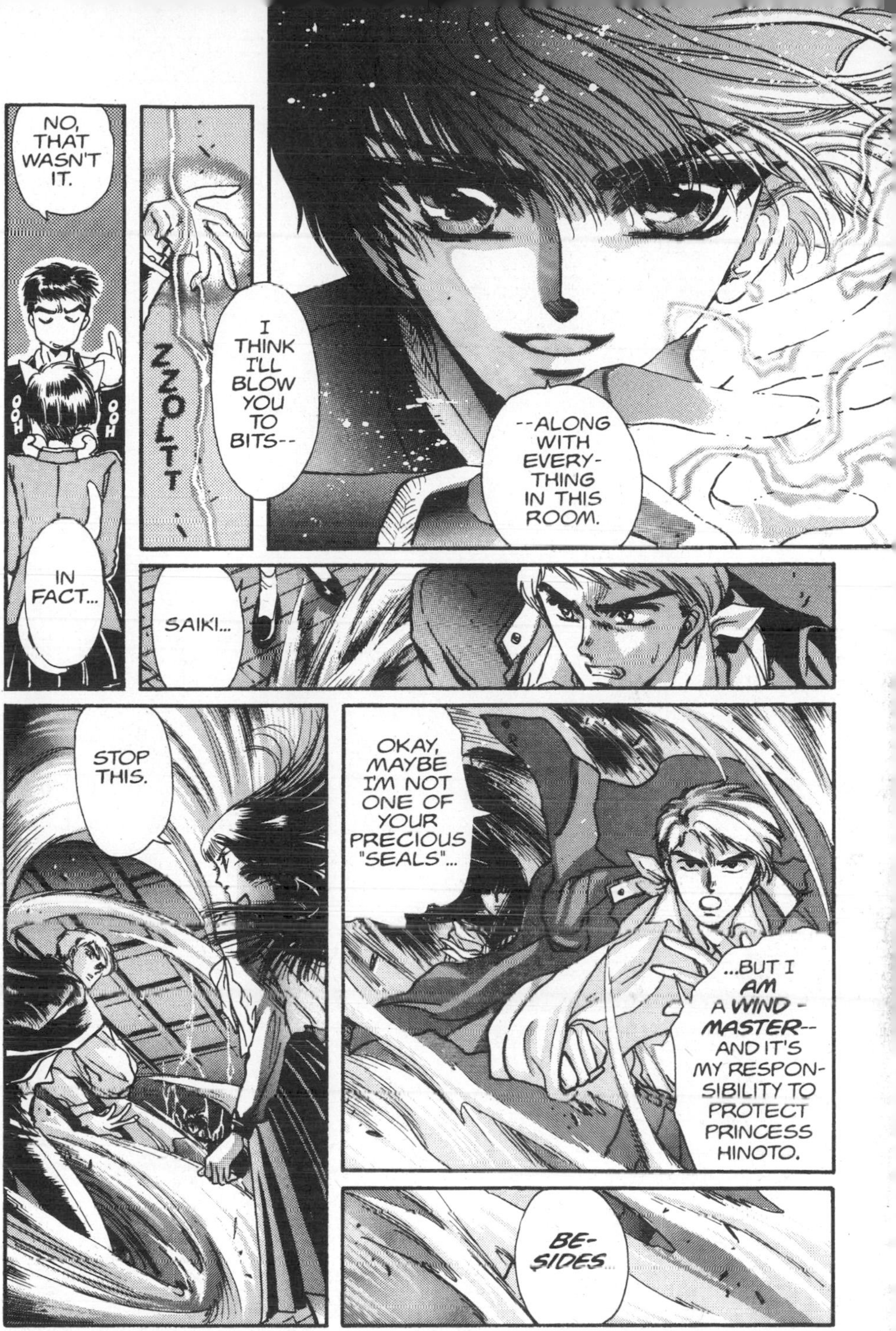
NO, THAT WASN'T IT.
OOH
OOH
IN FACT...
ZZOLTT
I THINK I'LL BLOW YOU TO BITS--
--ALONG WITH EVERY-THING IN THIS ROOM.
SAIKI...
STOP THIS.
OKAY, MAYBE I'M NOT ONE OF YOUR PRECIOUS "SEALS"...
...BUT I AM A WIND-MASTER--AND IT'S MY RESPON-SIBILITY TO PROTECT PRINCESS HINOTO.
BE-SIDES...

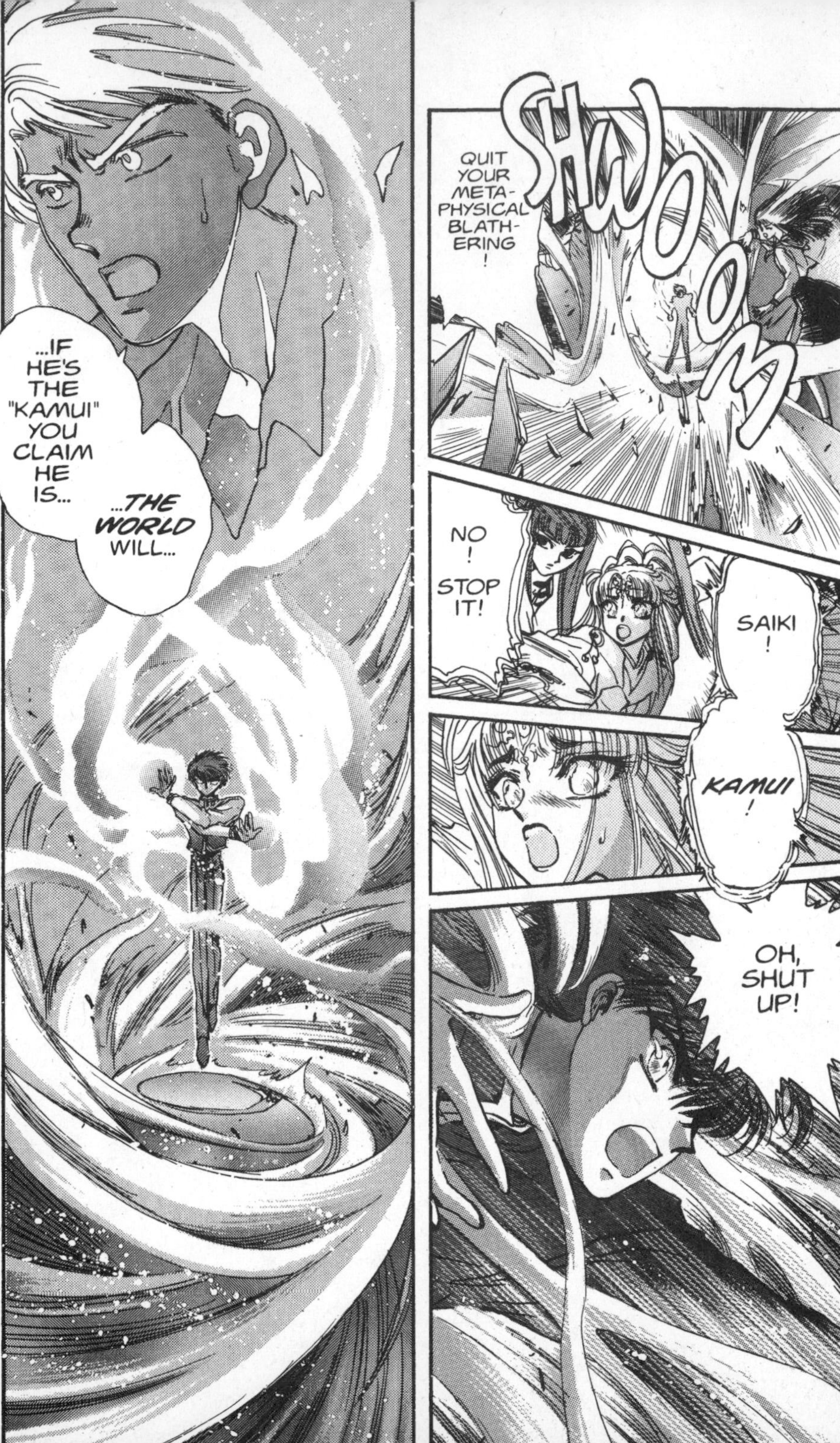
...IF HE'S THE "KAMUI" YOU CLAIM HE IS...
...THE WORLD WILL...
SHWOOOM
QUIT YOUR META-PHYSICAL BLATH-ERING!
NO! STOP IT!
SAIKI!
KAMUI!
OH, SHUT UP!

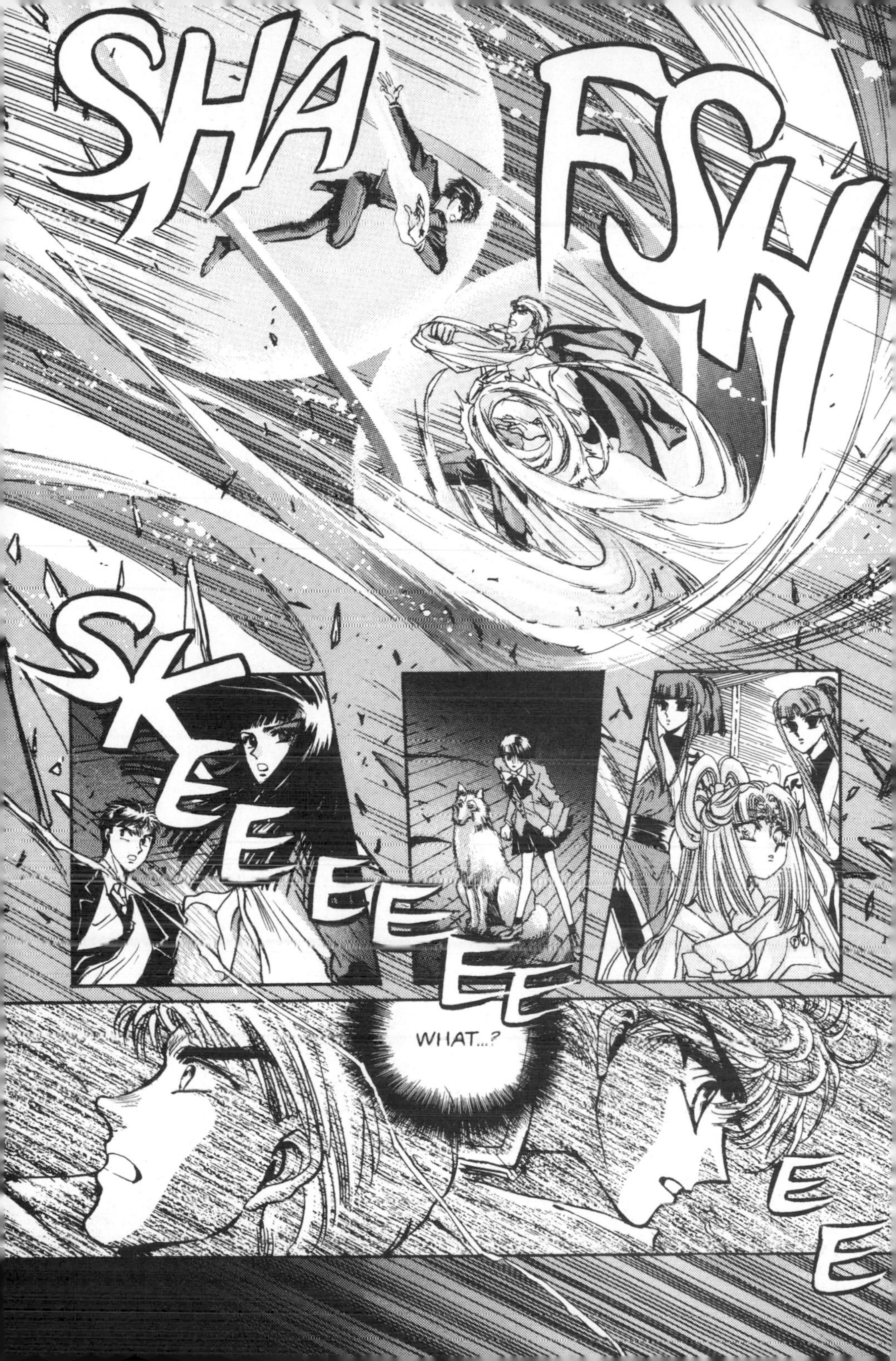
SHA
FSSH
SKEEEEEEE
WHAT...?
EE

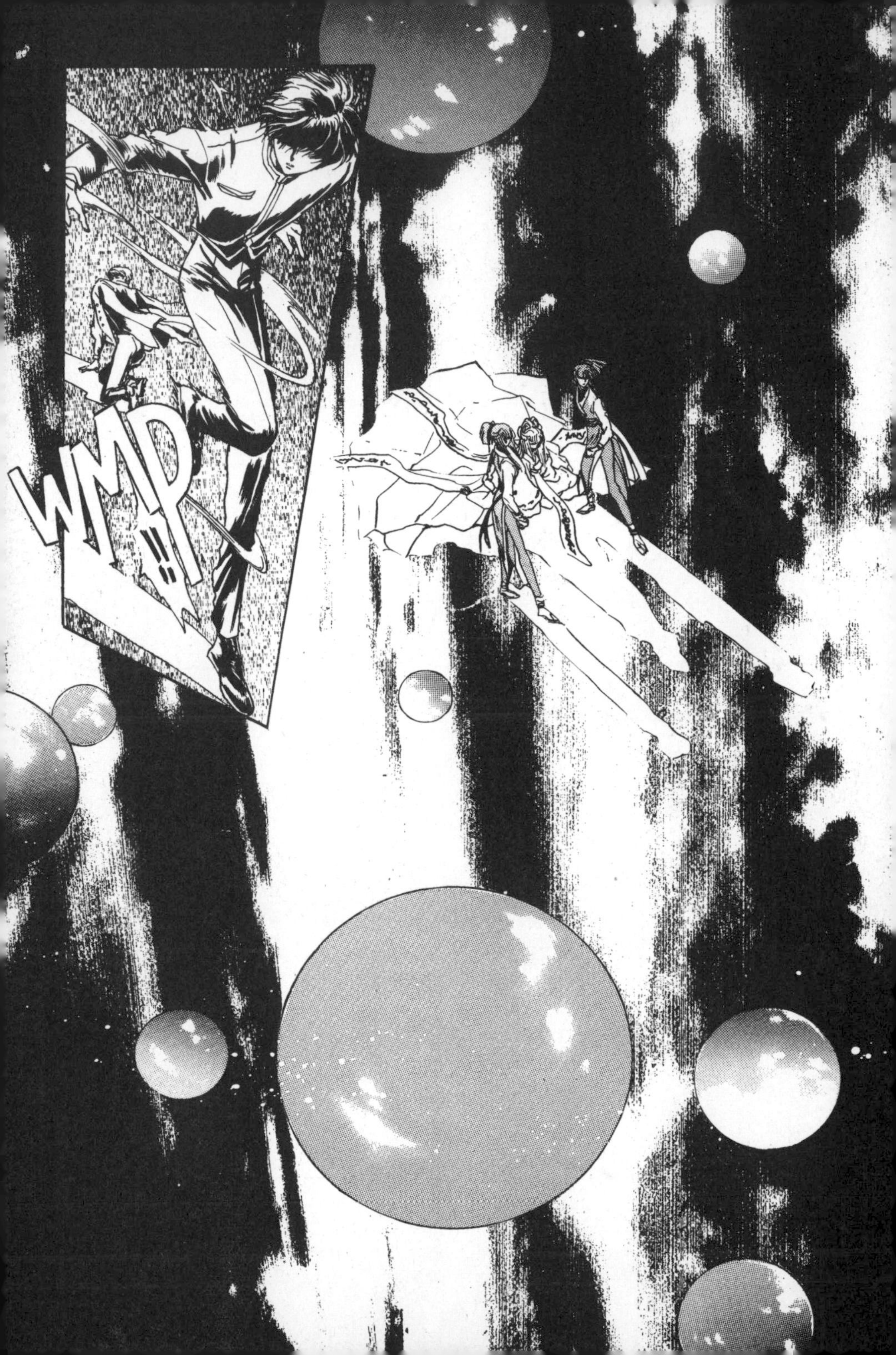
WMP!!

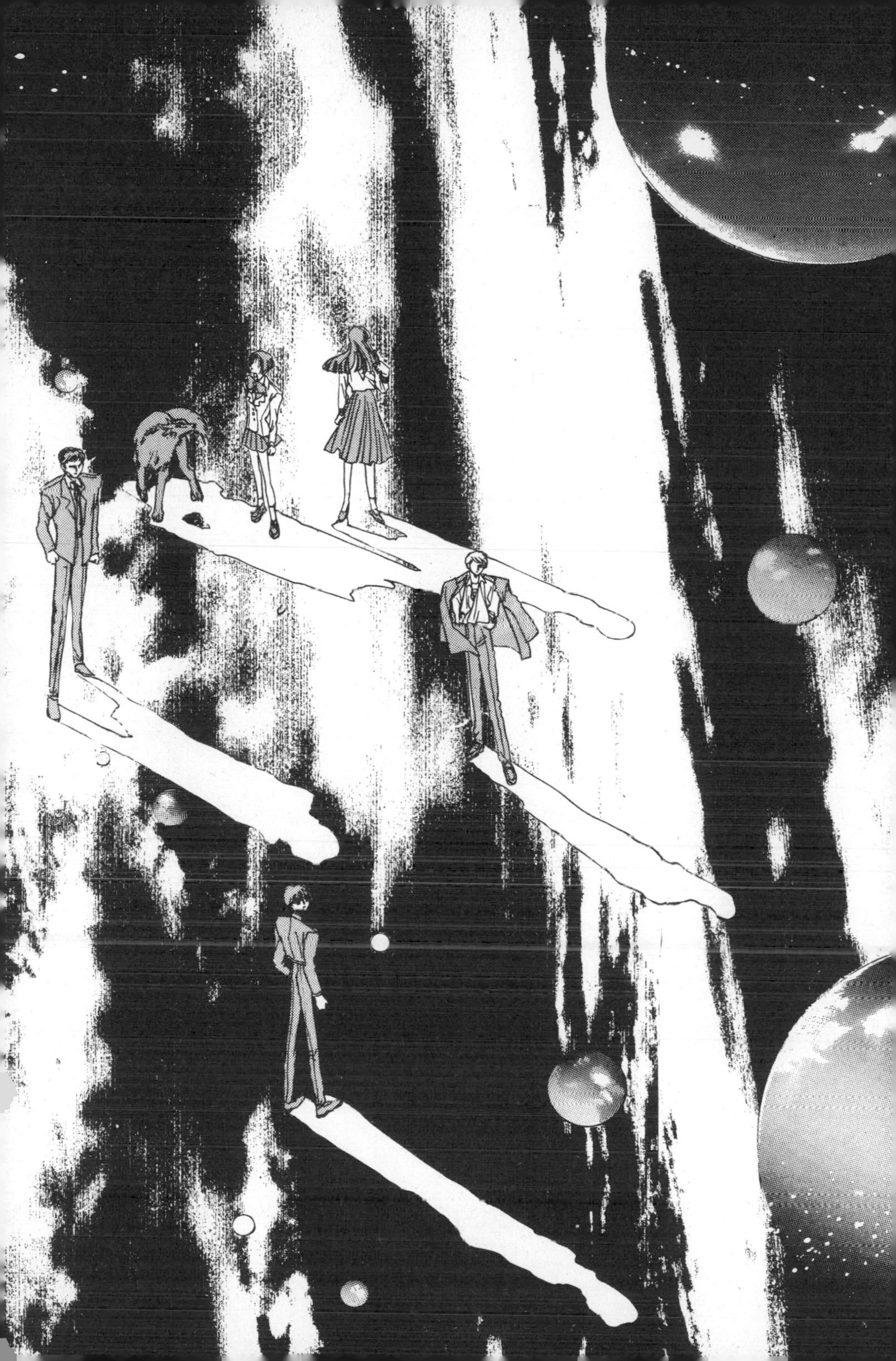

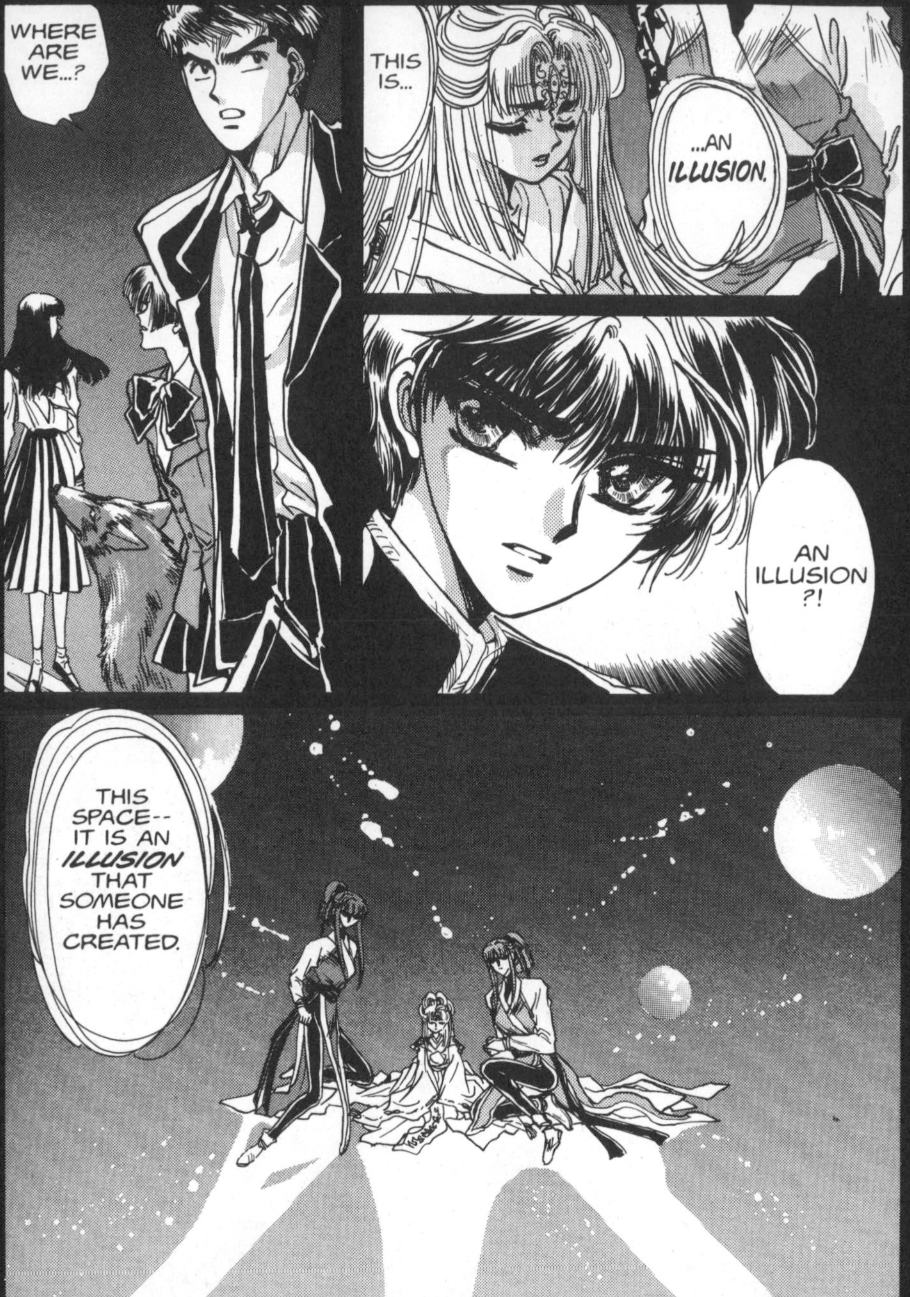
WHERE ARE WE...?
THIS IS...
...AN *ILLUSION.*
AN ILLUSION ?!
THIS SPACE-- IT IS AN *ILLUSION* THAT SOMEONE HAS CREATED.

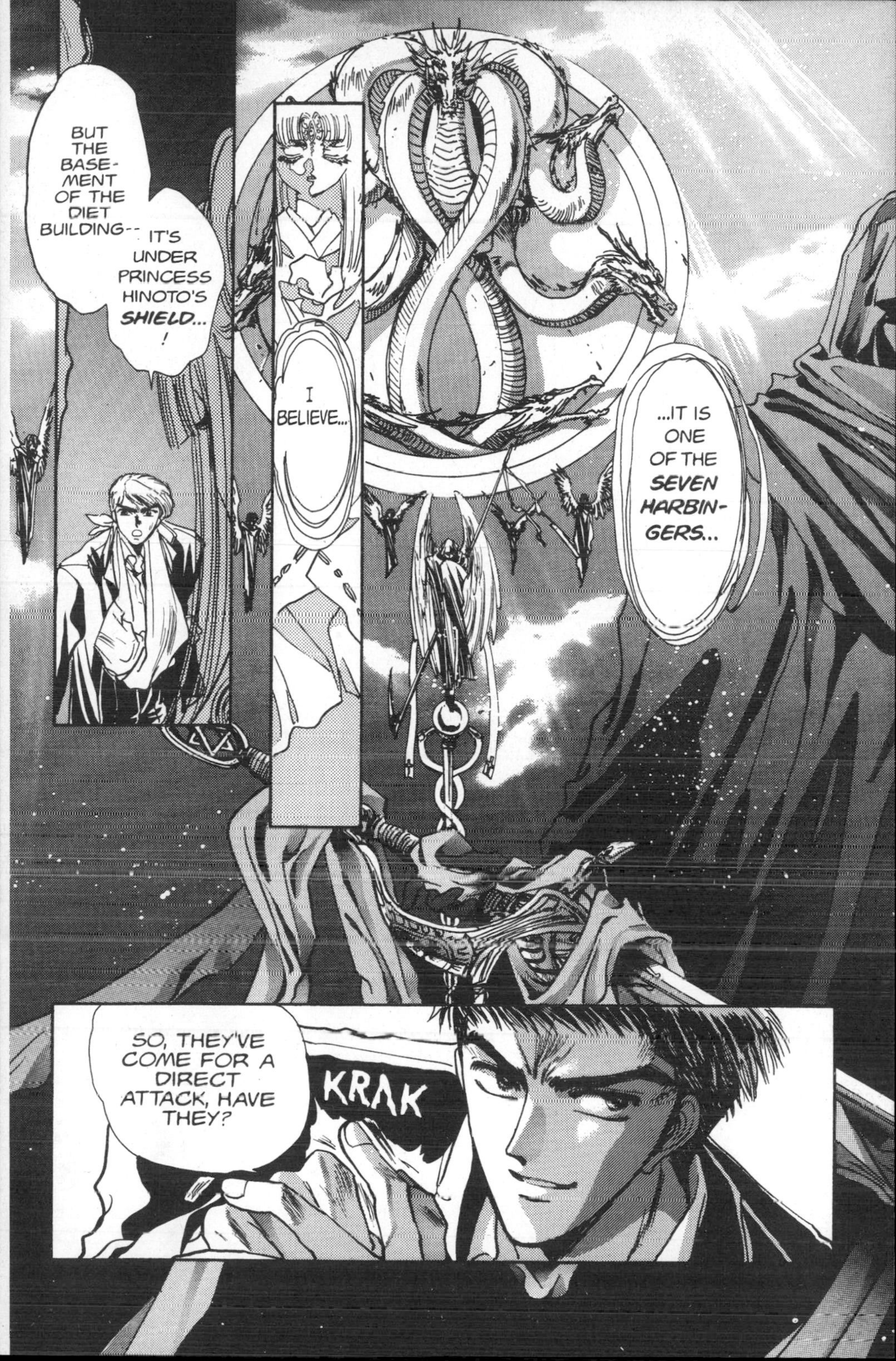
BUT THE BASE-MENT OF THE DIET BUILDING--
IT'S UNDER PRINCESS HINOTO'S SHIELD... !
I BELIEVE...
...IT IS ONE OF THE SEVEN HARBIN-GERS...
SO, THEY'VE COME FOR A DIRECT ATTACK, HAVE THEY?
KRAK

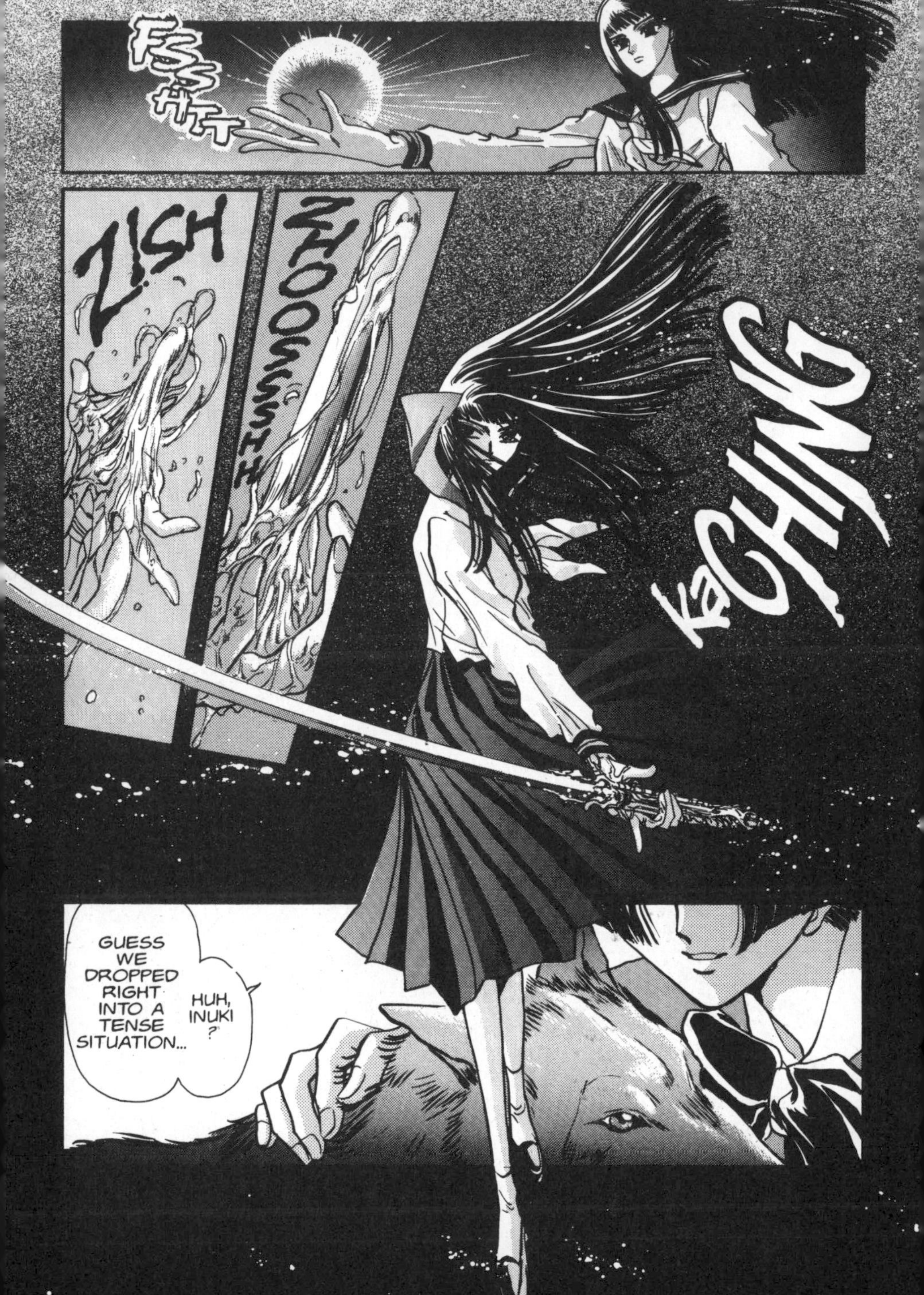
FSSHITT
ZISH
ZHOOSSSHH
KaCHING
GUESS WE DROPPED RIGHT INTO A TENSE SITUATION...
HUH, INUKI?

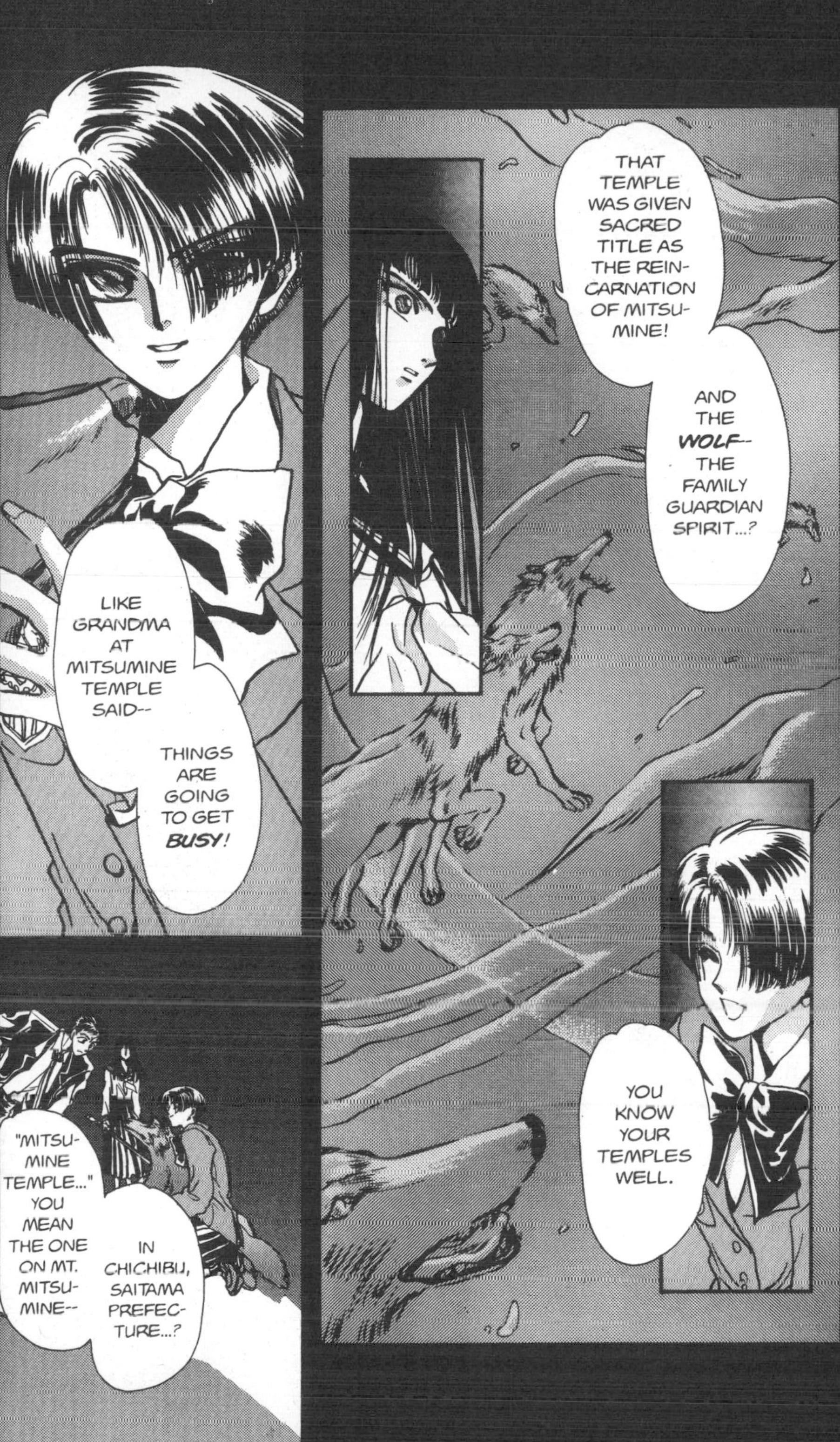
LIKE GRANDMA AT MITSUMINE TEMPLE SAID--
THINGS ARE GOING TO GET ***BUSY***!
"MITSU-MINE TEMPLE..." YOU MEAN THE ONE ON MT. MITSU-MINE--
IN CHICHIBU, SAITAMA PREFEC-TURE...?
THAT TEMPLE WAS GIVEN SACRED TITLE AS THE REIN-CARNATION OF MITSU-MINE!
AND THE ***WOLF***-- THE FAMILY GUARDIAN SPIRIT...?
YOU KNOW YOUR TEMPLES WELL.

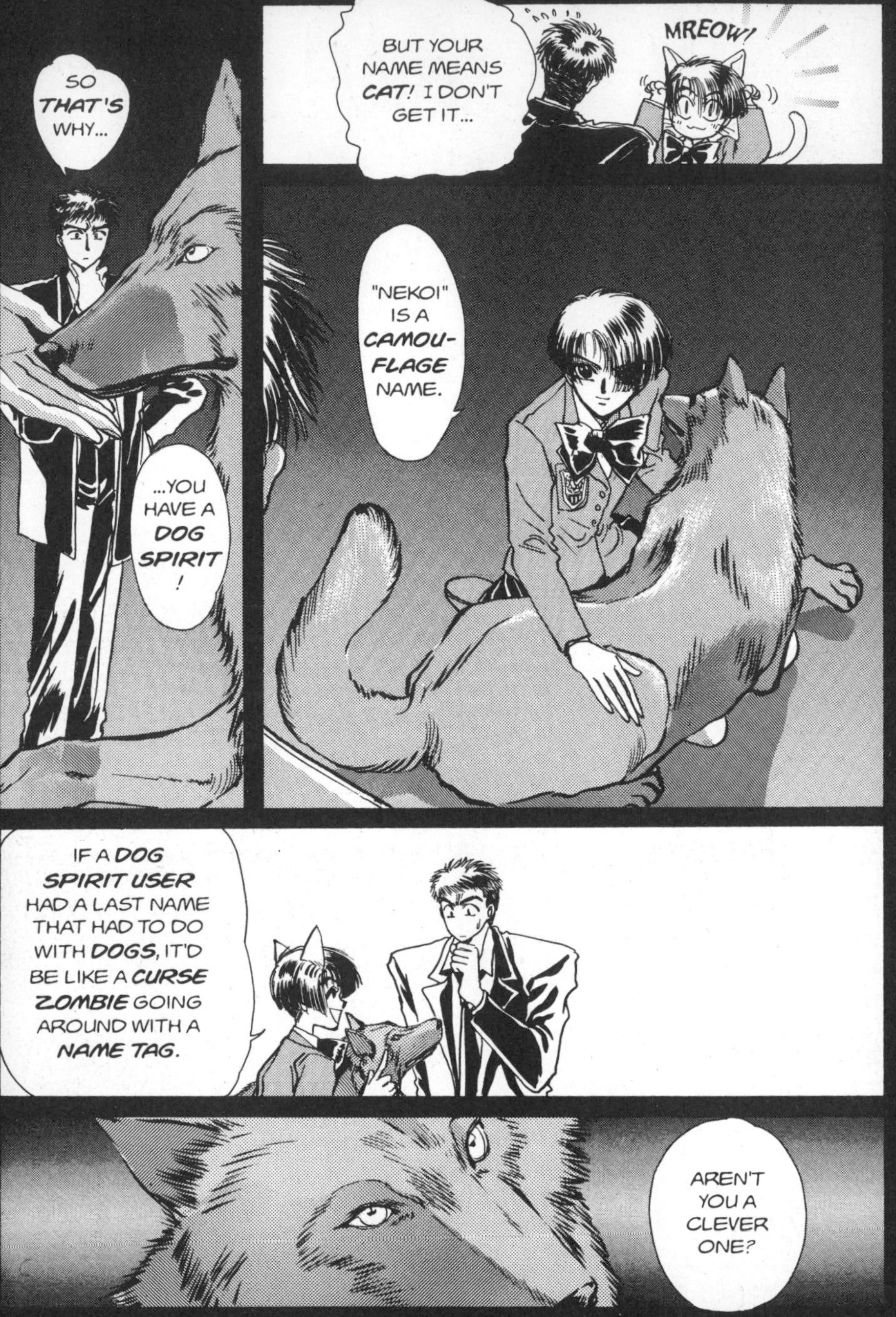
SO THAT'S WHY...
...YOU HAVE A DOG SPIRIT!
BUT YOUR NAME MEANS CAT! I DON'T GET IT...
MREOW!
"NEKOI" IS A CAMOUFLAGE NAME.
IF A DOG SPIRIT USER HAD A LAST NAME THAT HAD TO DO WITH DOGS, IT'D BE LIKE A CURSE ZOMBIE GOING AROUND WITH A NAME TAG.
AREN'T YOU A CLEVER ONE?

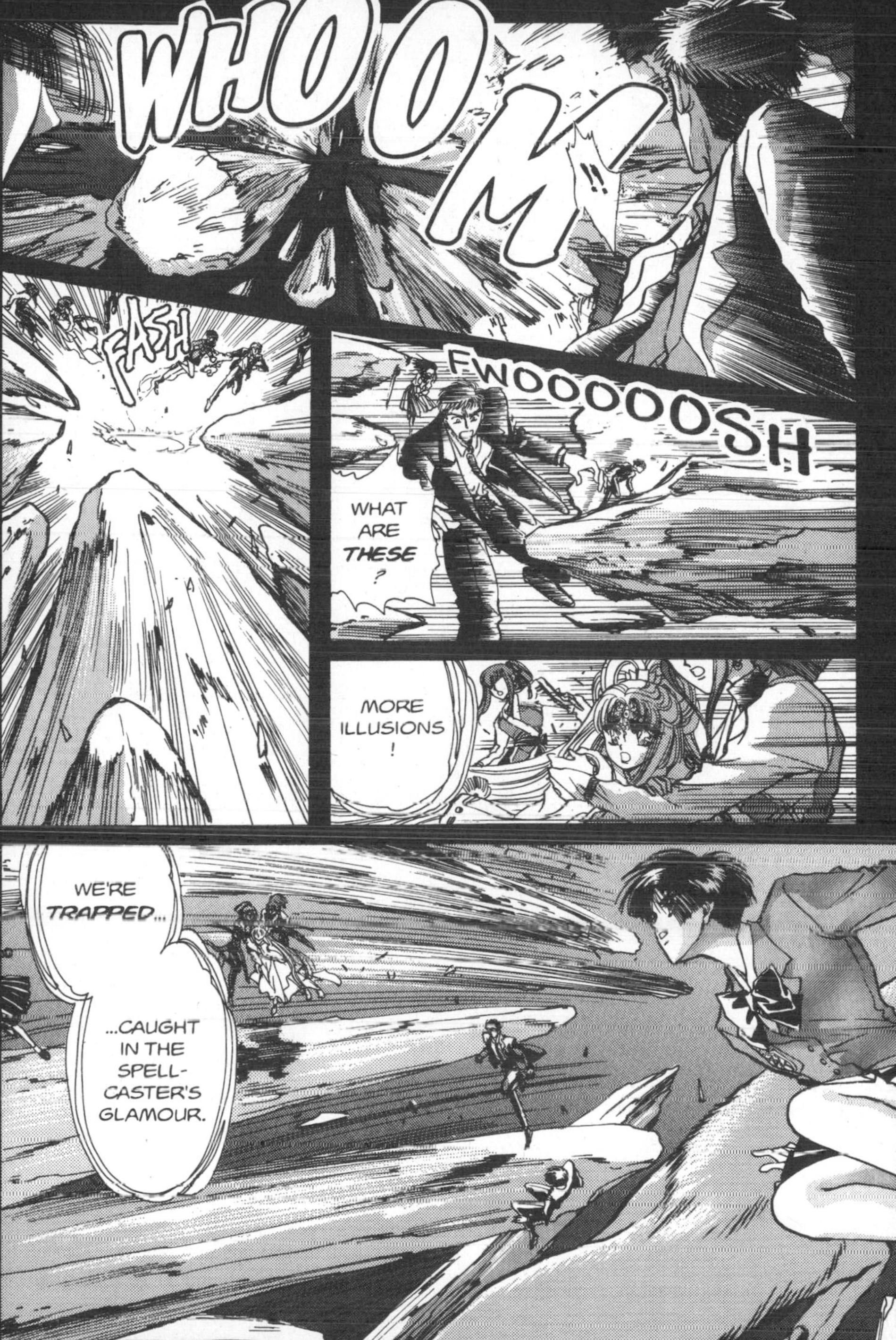
WHOOM
!!
FASH
FWOOOOOOSH
WHAT ARE THESE?
MORE ILLUSIONS!
WE'RE TRAPPED...
...CAUGHT IN THE SPELL-CASTER'S GLAMOUR.

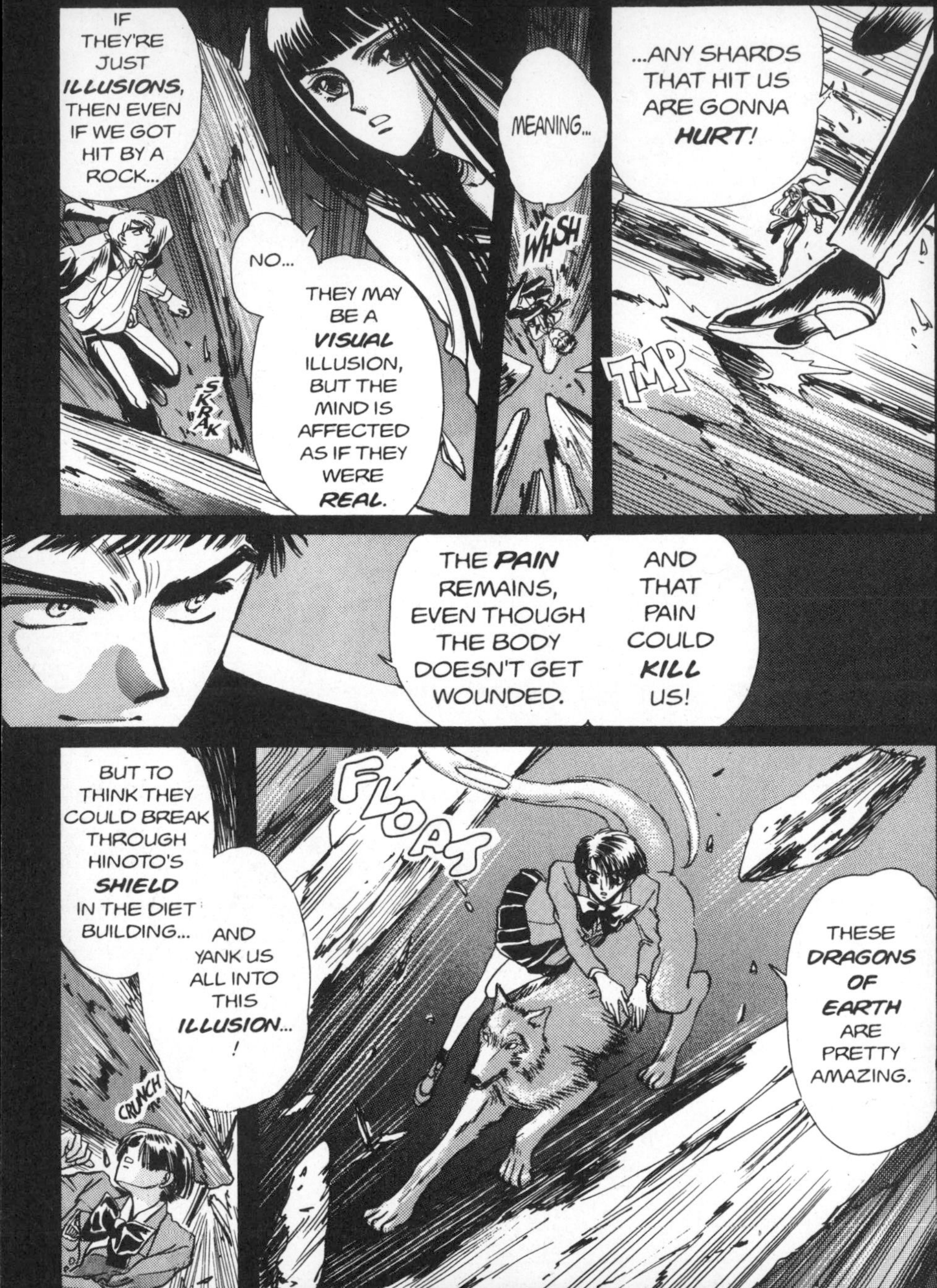
IF THEY'RE JUST ILLUSIONS, THEN EVEN IF WE GOT HIT BY A ROCK...
NO...
THEY MAY BE A VISUAL ILLUSION, BUT THE MIND IS AFFECTED AS IF THEY WERE REAL.
SKRAK
MEANING...
WHSH
...ANY SHARDS THAT HIT US ARE GONNA HURT!
TMP
THE PAIN REMAINS, EVEN THOUGH THE BODY DOESN'T GET WOUNDED.
AND THAT PAIN COULD KILL US!
BUT TO THINK THEY COULD BREAK THROUGH HINOTO'S SHIELD IN THE DIET BUILDING...
AND YANK US ALL INTO THIS ILLUSION...!
CRUNCH
FLOAT
THESE DRAGONS OF EARTH ARE PRETTY AMAZING.

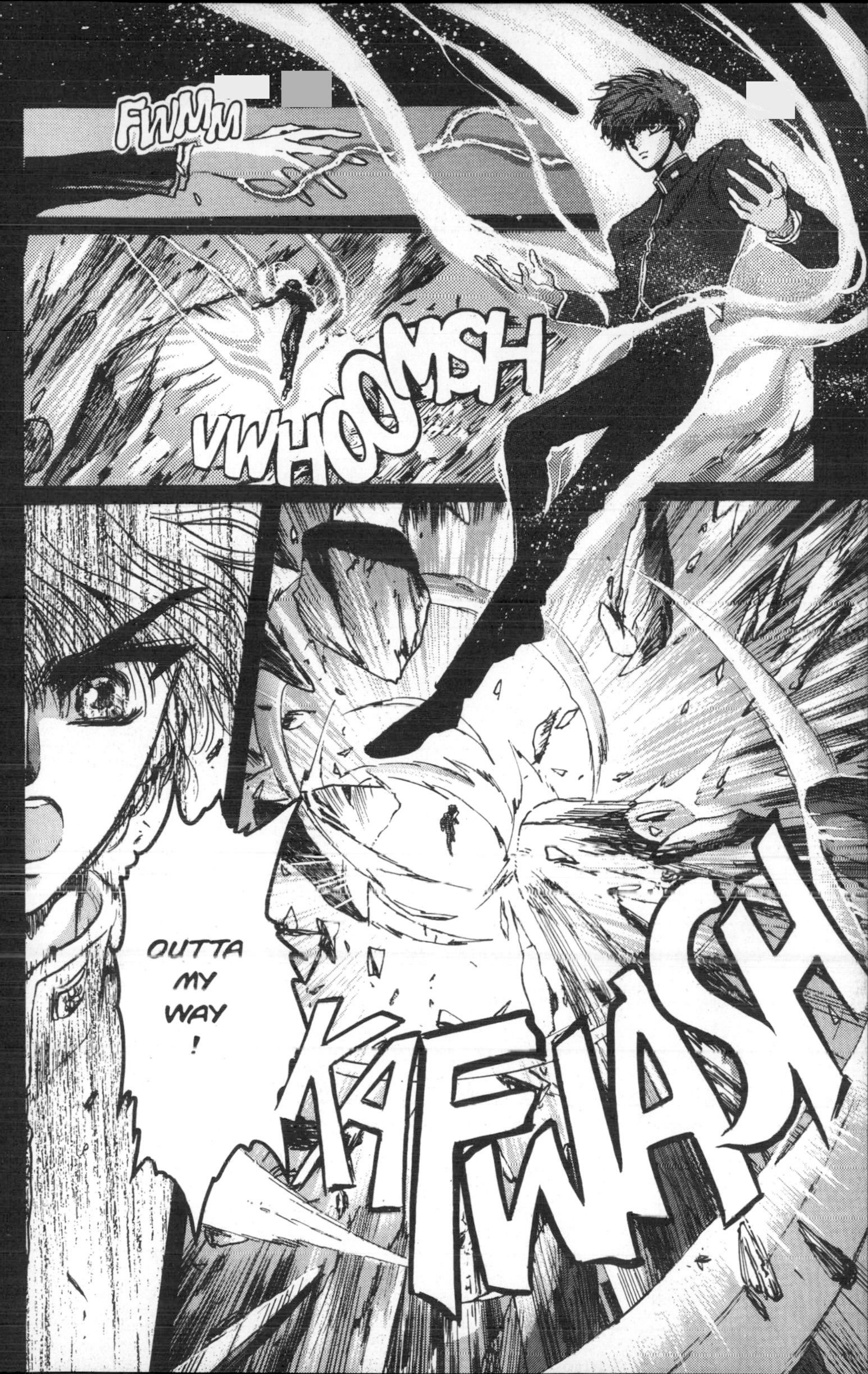
FWMM
VWHOOMSH
OUTTA MY WAY!
KAFWASH

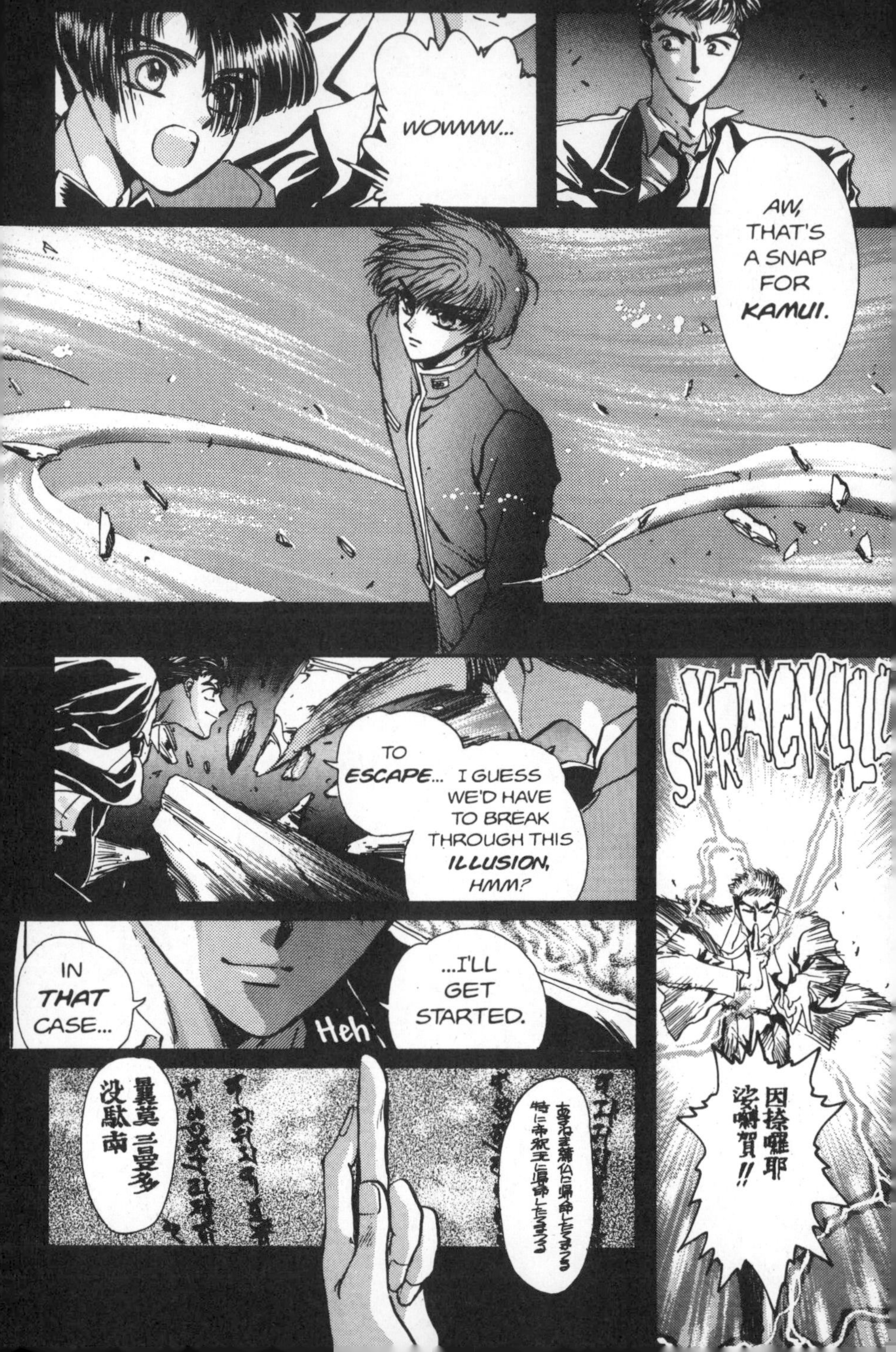
WOWWW...
AW, THAT'S A SNAP FOR **KAMUI.**
TO **ESCAPE**... I GUESS WE'D HAVE TO BREAK THROUGH THIS **ILLUSION,** HMM?
IN **THAT** CASE...
...I'LL GET STARTED.
Heh
あまねき諸仏に帰命したてまつる 特に帝釈天に帰命したてまつる
曩莫三曼多没駄南
SKRACKLLL
因捺囉耶娑嚩賀!!

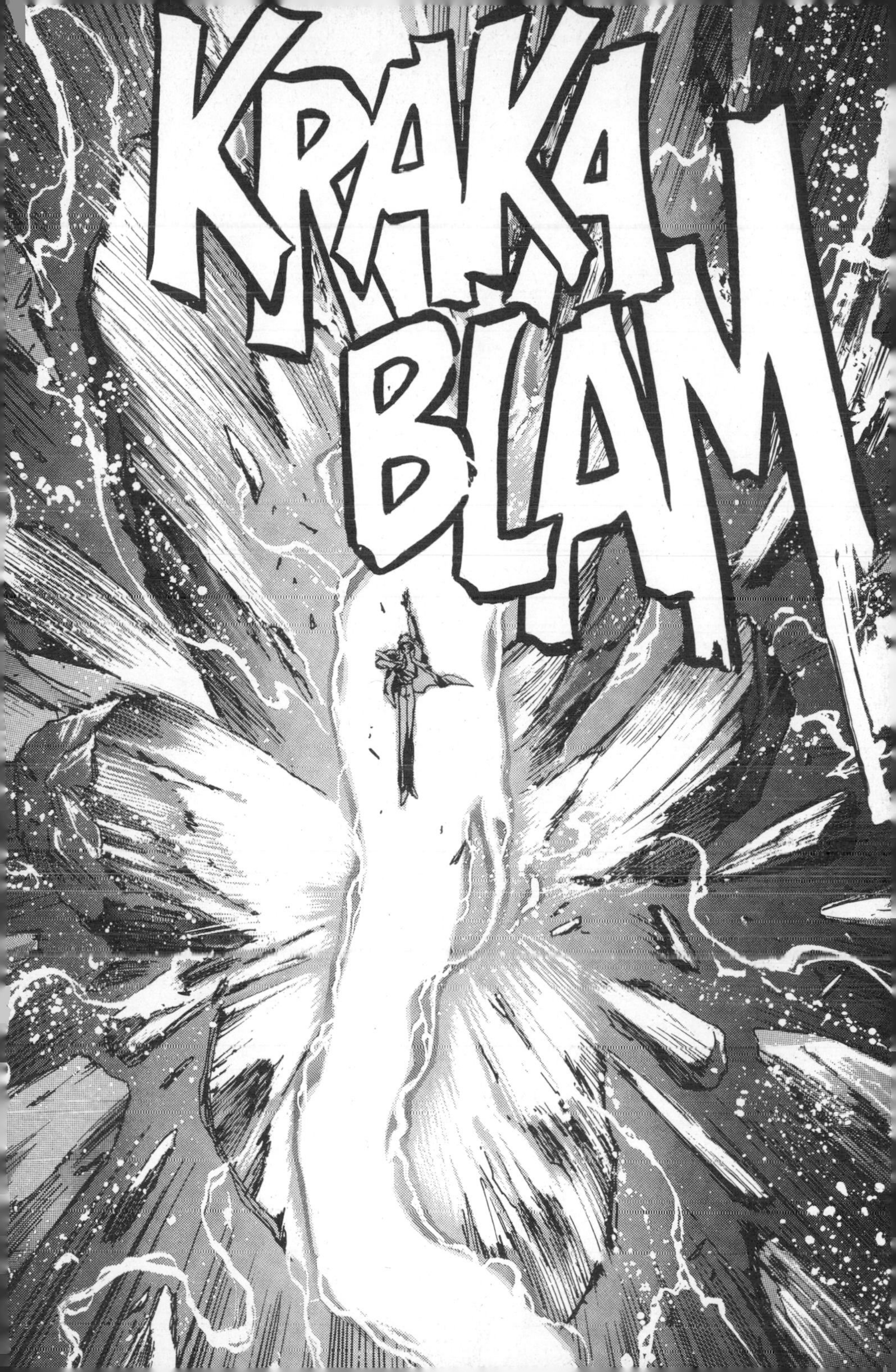
KRAKA
BLAM

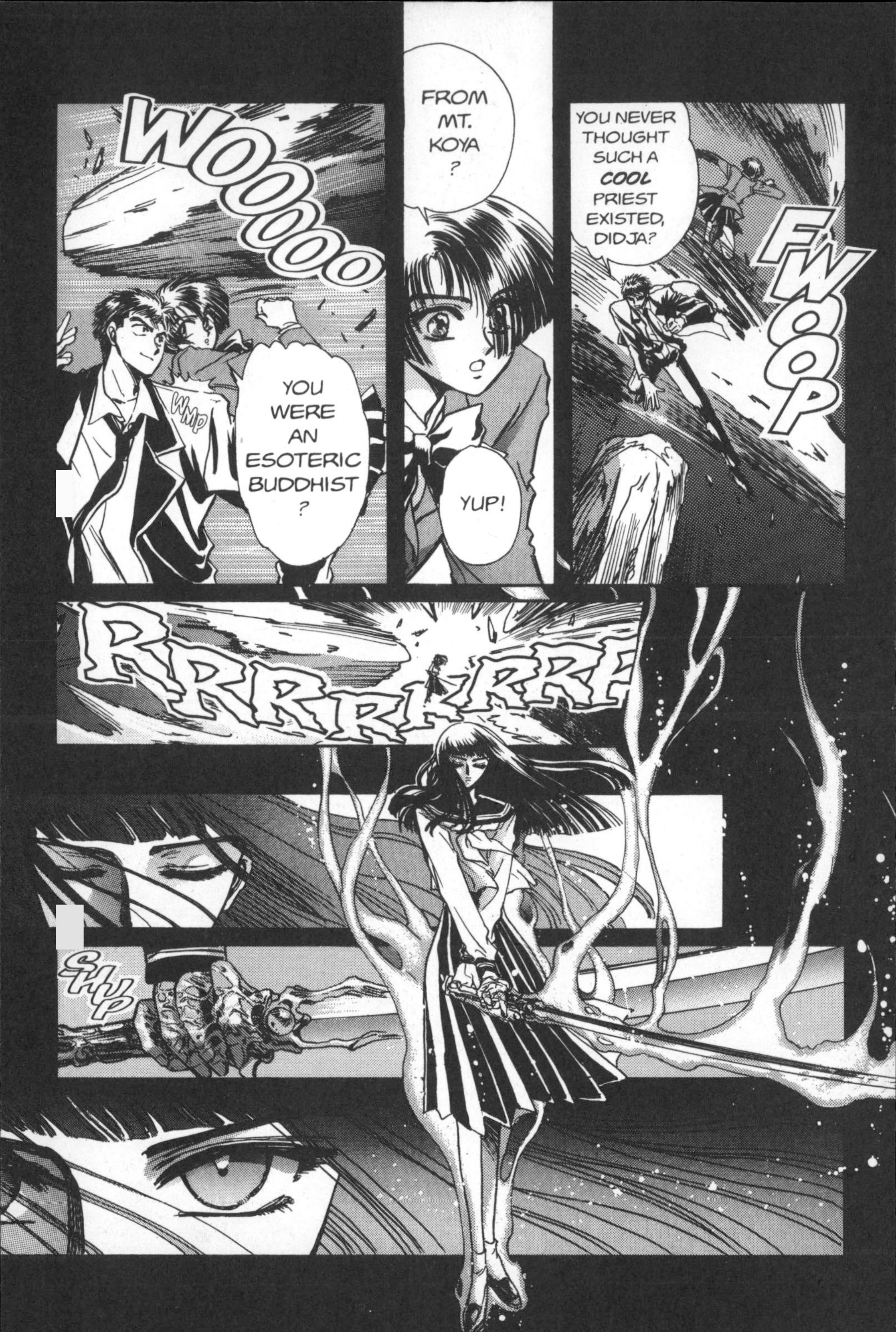
WOOOOOO
WMP
YOU WERE AN ESOTERIC BUDDHIST?
FROM MT. KOYA?
YUP!
YOU NEVER THOUGHT SUCH A **COOL** PRIEST EXISTED, DIDJA?
FWOOOP
SHUP

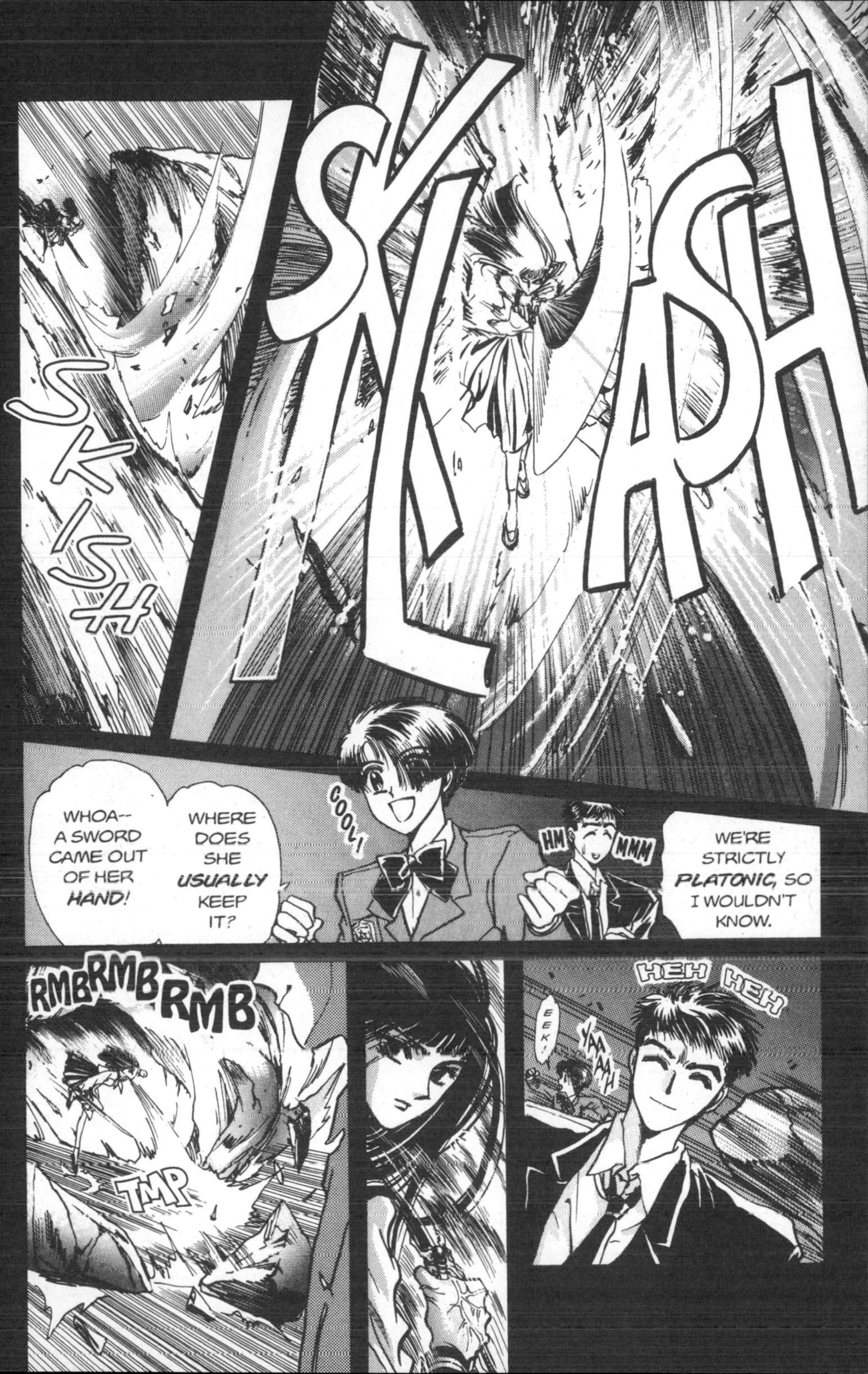
SKISH
SKLASH
WHOA-- A SWORD CAME OUT OF HER ***HAND!***
WHERE DOES SHE ***USUALLY*** KEEP IT?
COOL!
HM MMM
WE'RE STRICTLY ***PLATONIC,*** SO I WOULDN'T KNOW.
RMB RMB RMB
TMP
HEH HEH
EEK!
YAAAAH

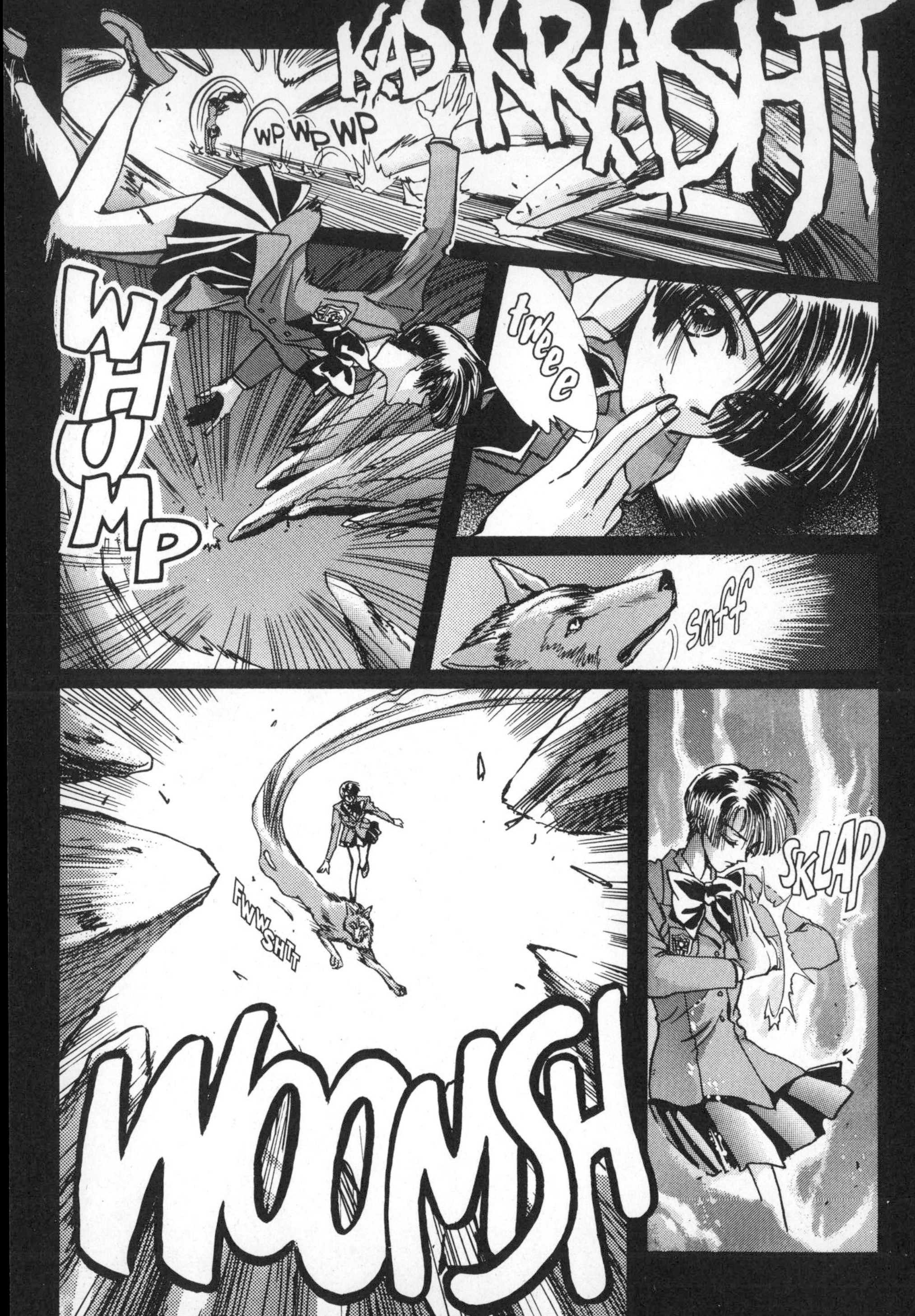
KASKRASHT
WP WP WP
WHUMP
tweee
snff
FWWSHTT
WOOMSH
SKLAP

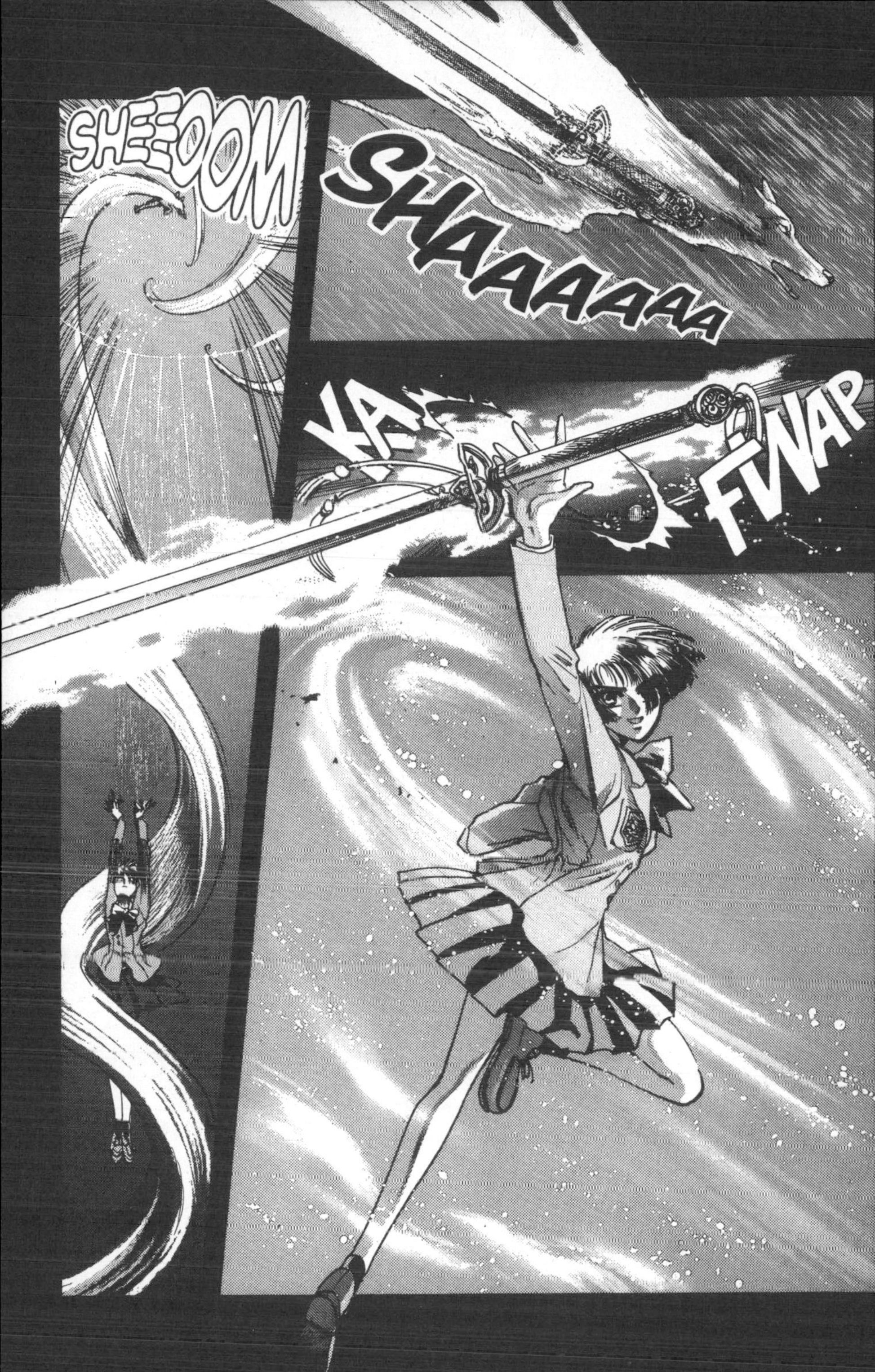
SHEEOOM
SHAAAAAAA
KA
FWAP

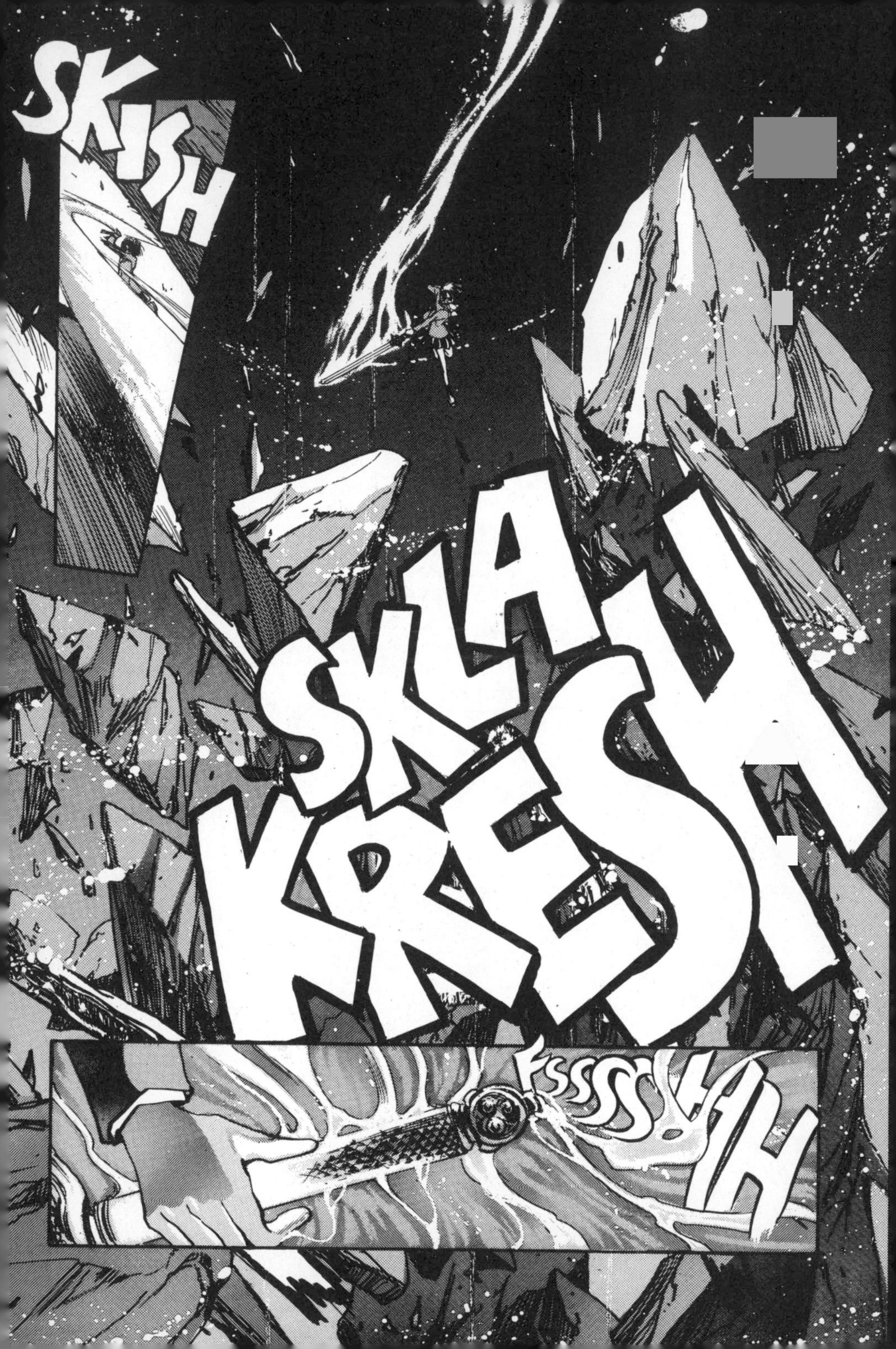
SKISH
SKLA KRESH
FSSSSHHH

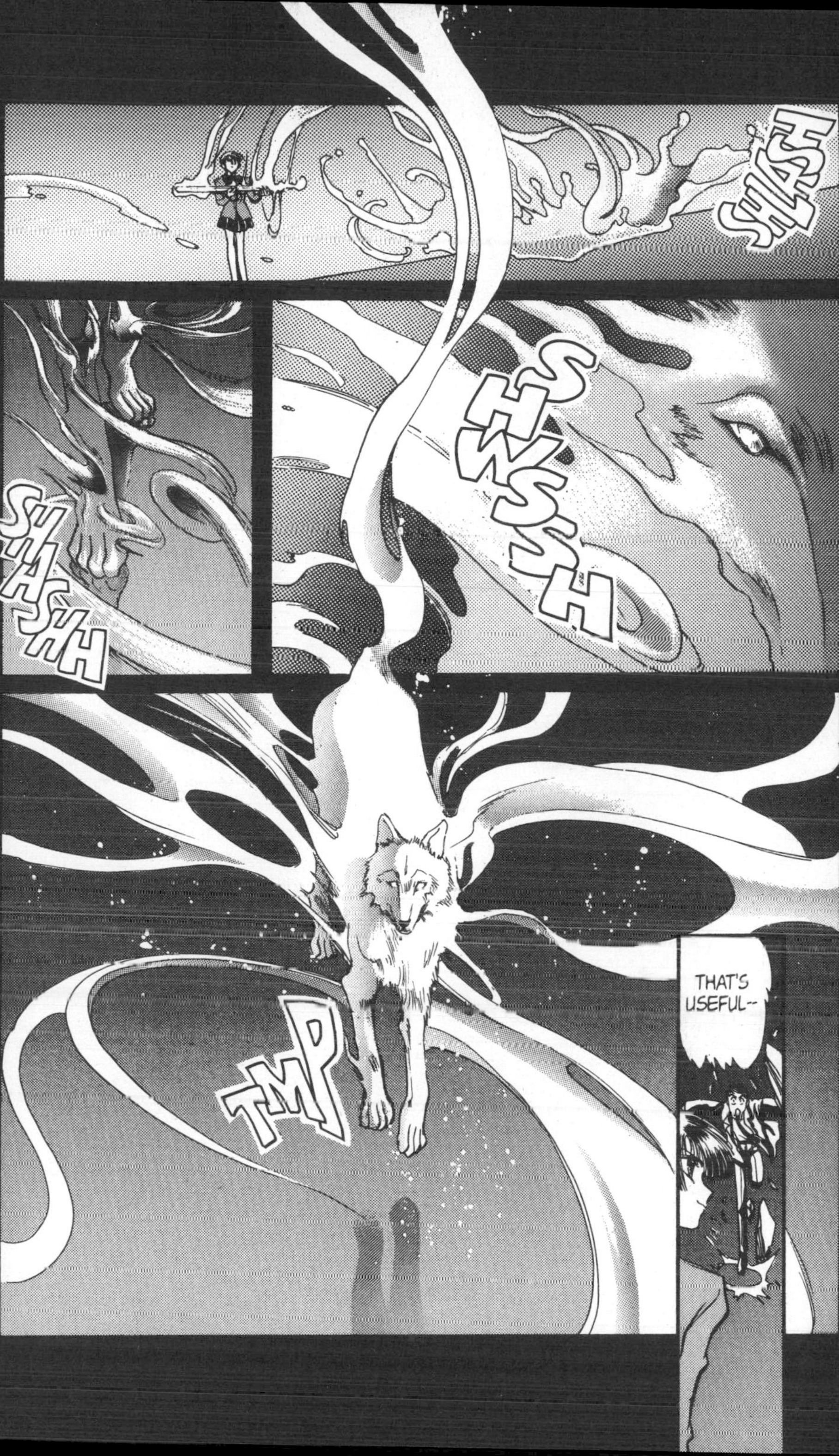
SHASH
SHASHH
SHWSSH
TMP
THAT'S USEFUL--

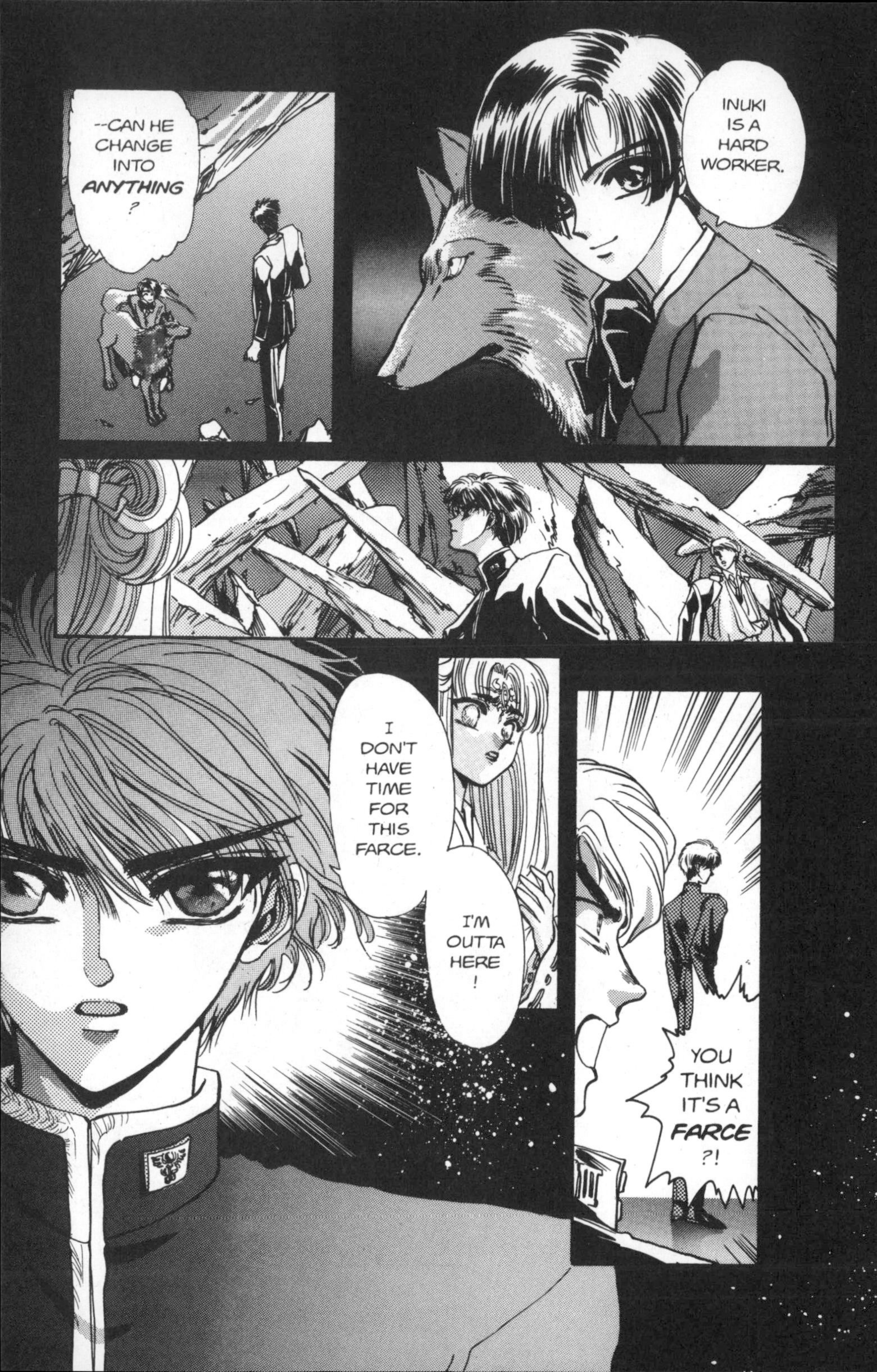
--CAN HE CHANGE INTO ANYTHING ?
INUKI IS A HARD WORKER.
I DON'T HAVE TIME FOR THIS FARCE.
I'M OUTTA HERE !
YOU THINK IT'S A FARCE ?!

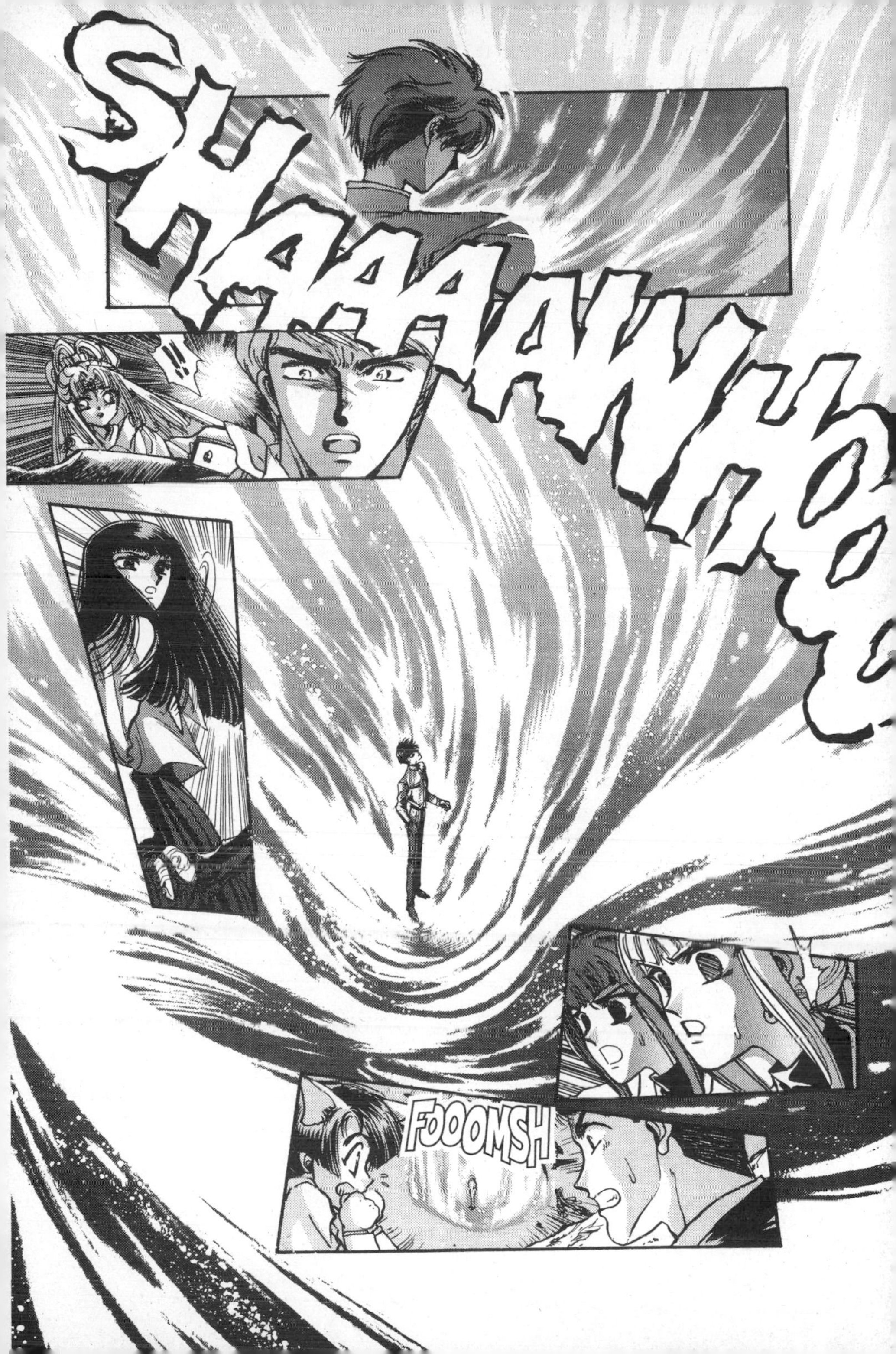
SHAAAAWHOOO
!!
FOOOMSH

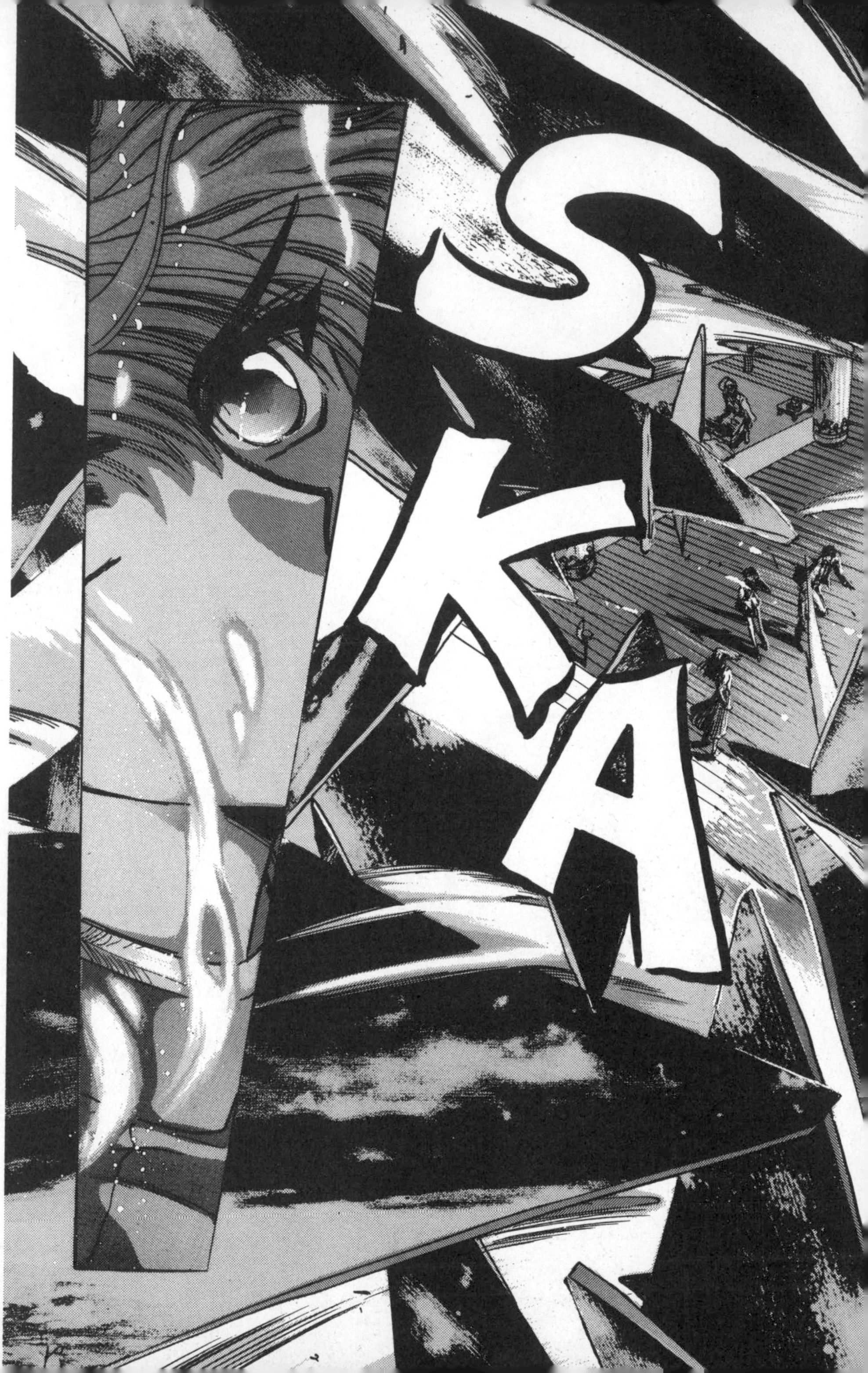
SKA

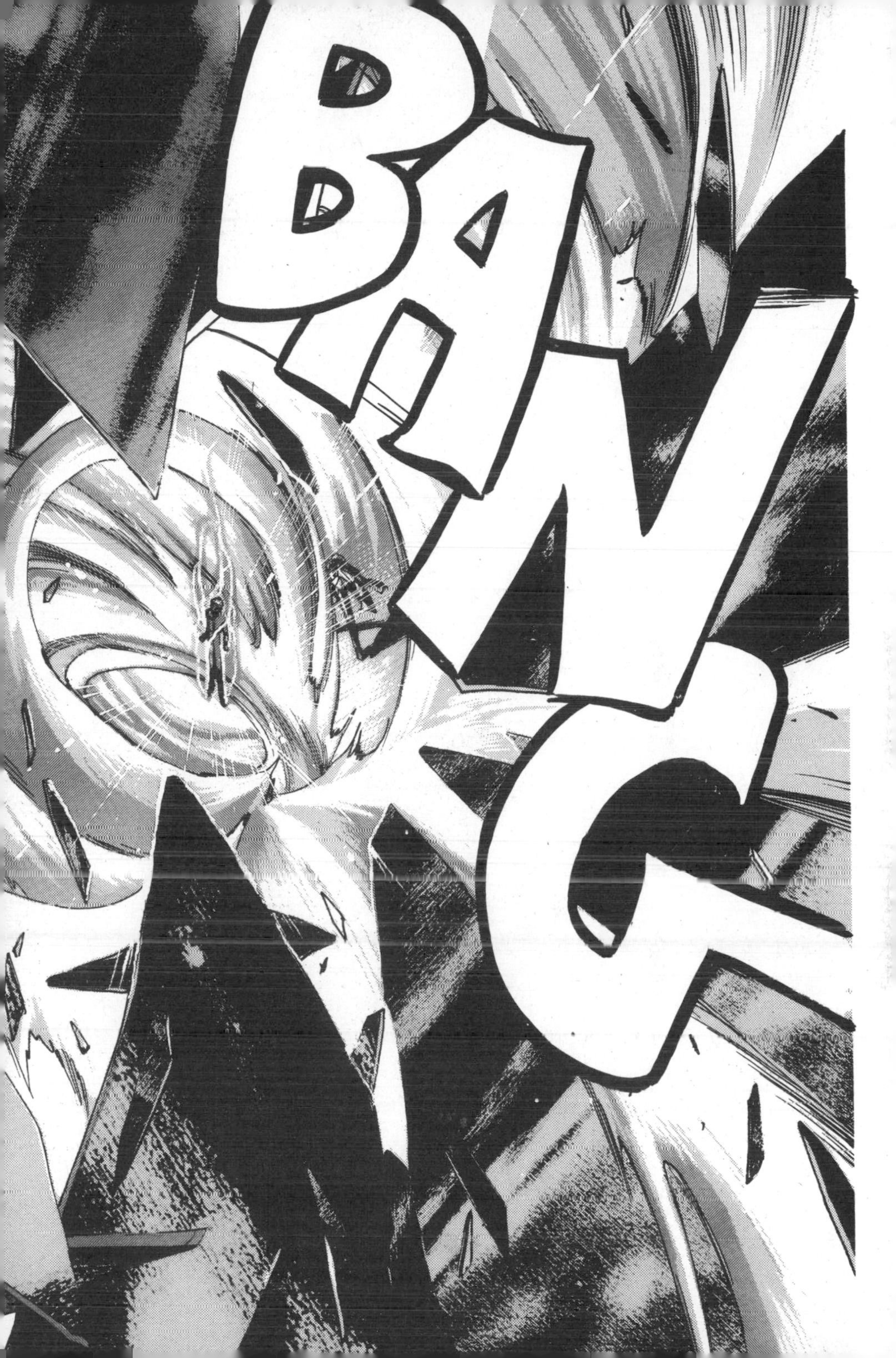
BANG

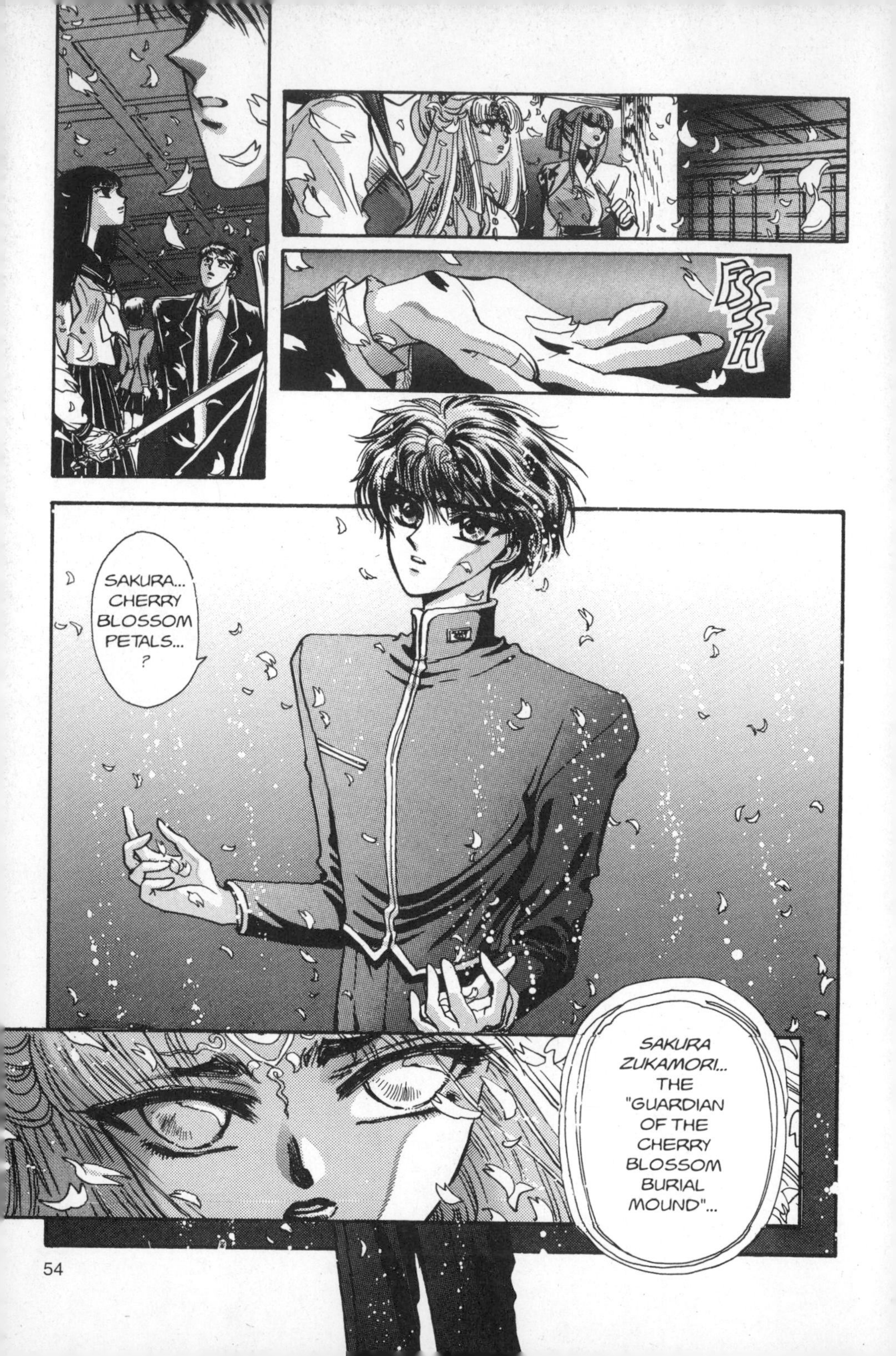
FSSSH
SAKURA... CHERRY BLOSSOM PETALS... ?
SAKURA ZUKAMORI... THE "GUARDIAN OF THE CHERRY BLOSSOM BURIAL MOUND"...

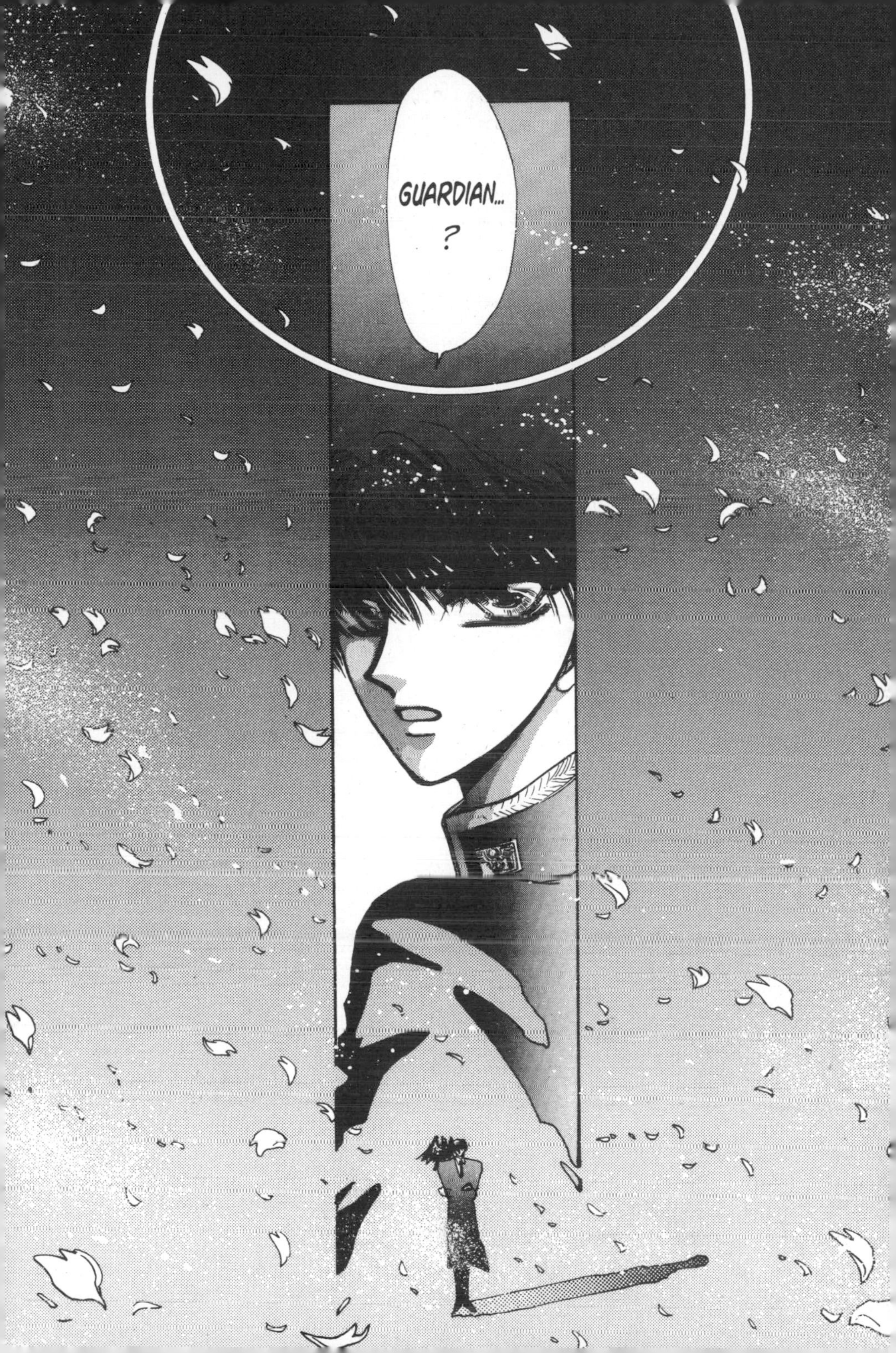
GUARDIAN... ?

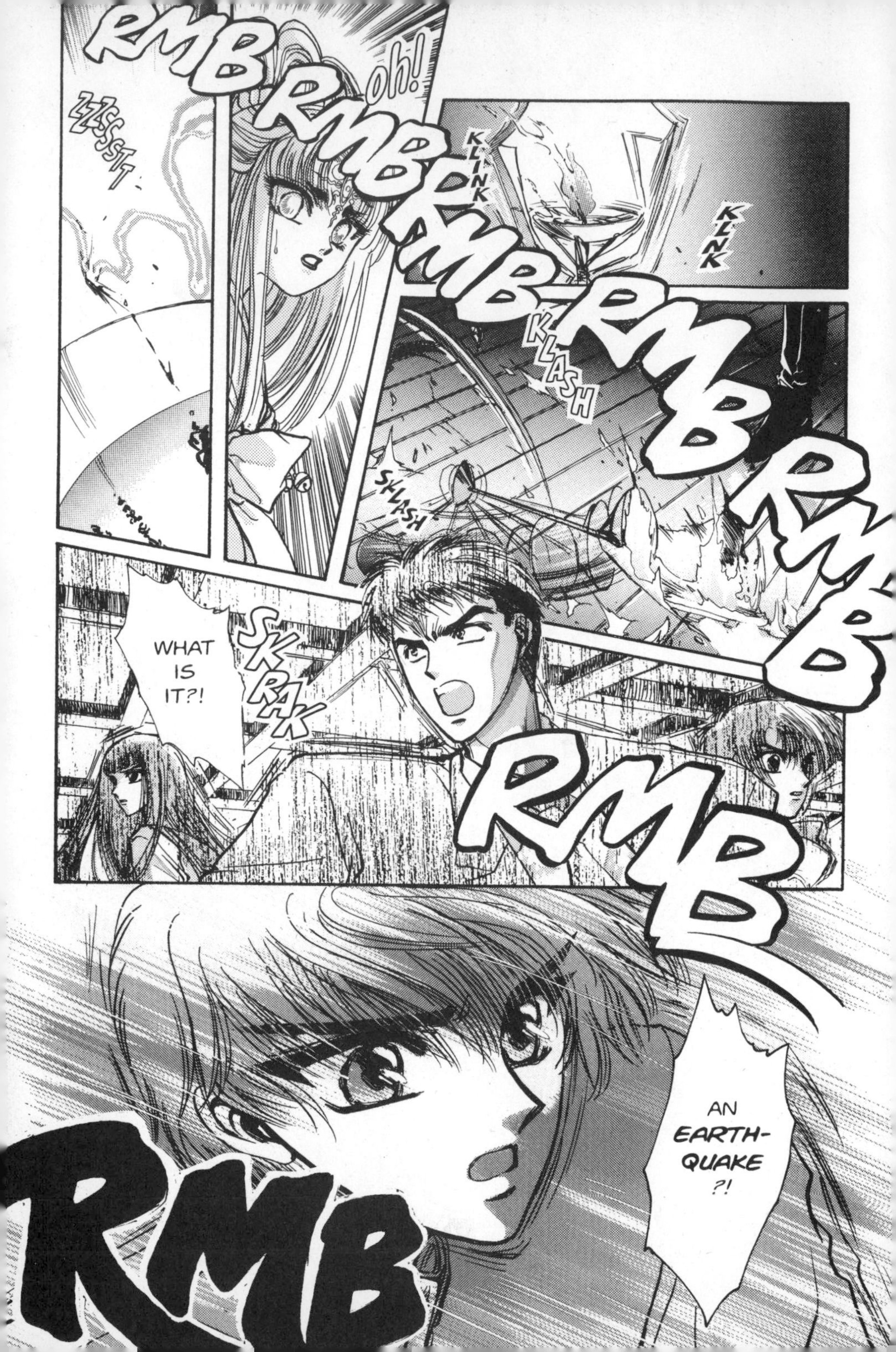
ZZSSSTT
oh!
RMB RMB RMB RMB RMB
KLINK
KLINK
KLASH
SKLASH
WHAT IS IT?!
SKRAK
RMB
RMB
AN EARTH-QUAKE ?!

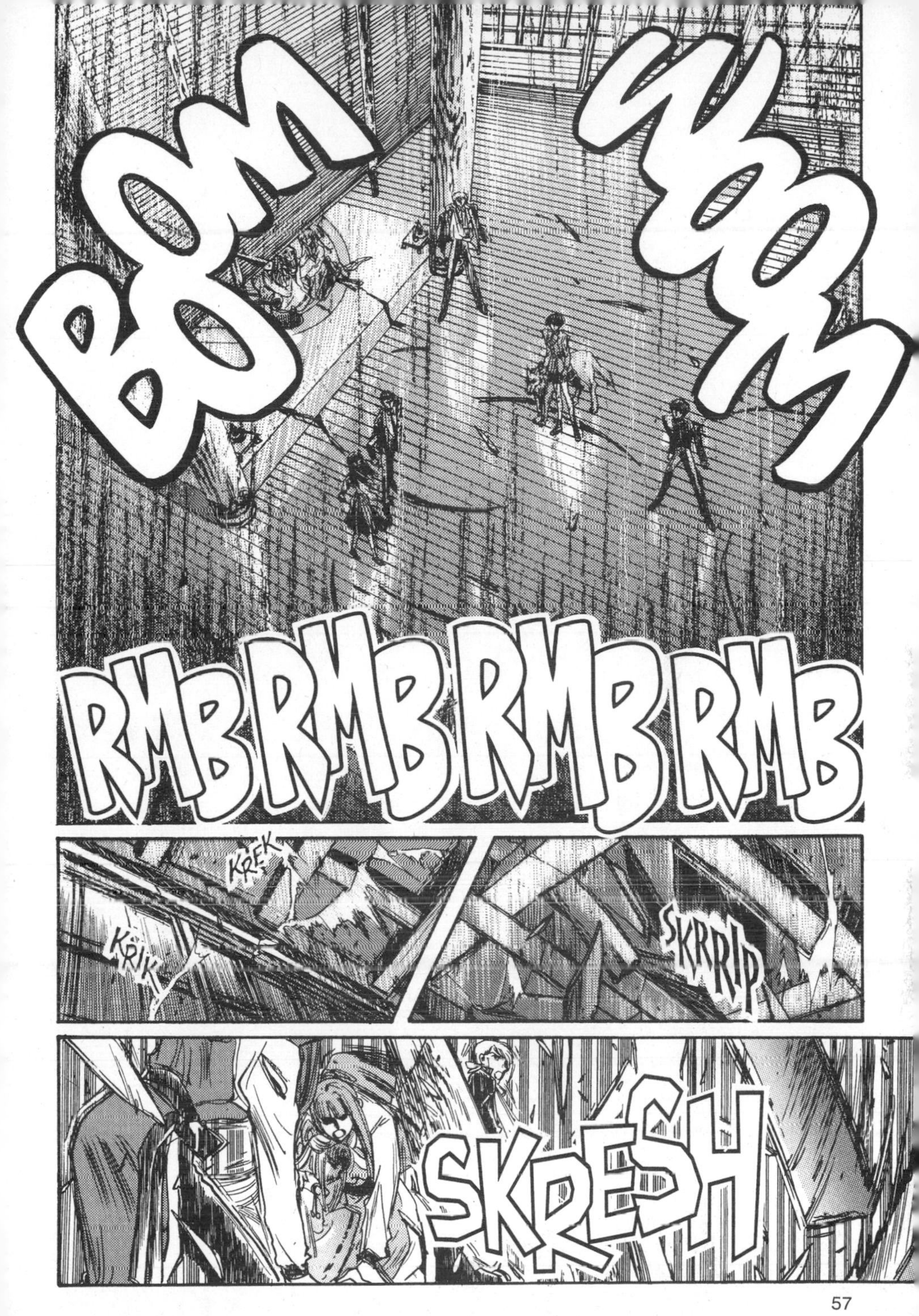
BOOM
BOOM
RMB RMB RMB RMB
KREK
KRIK
SKRRIP
SKRESH

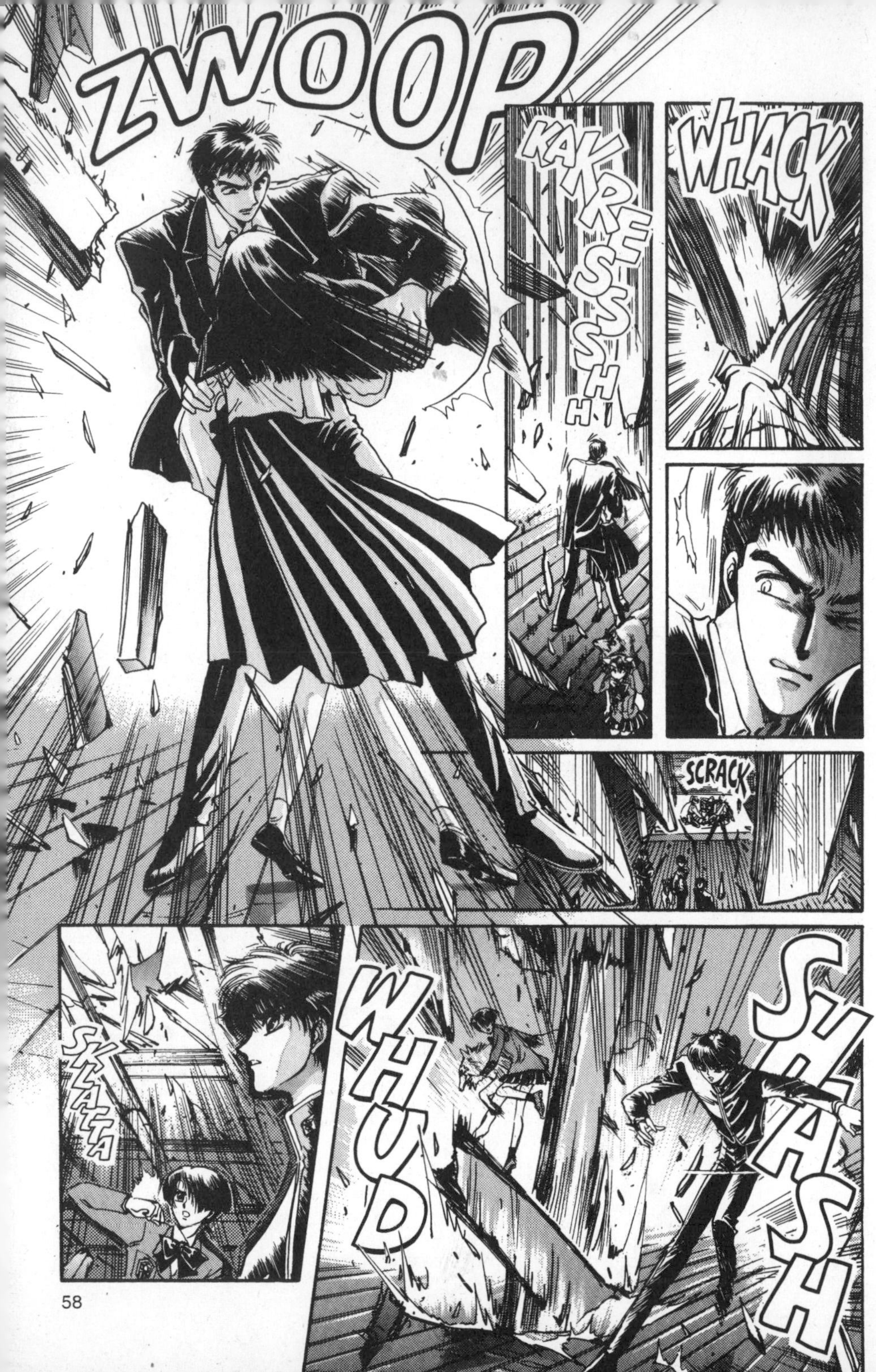
ZWOOP
KAKRESSSHHH
WHACK
SCRACK
SKLATTA
WHUD
SHASH

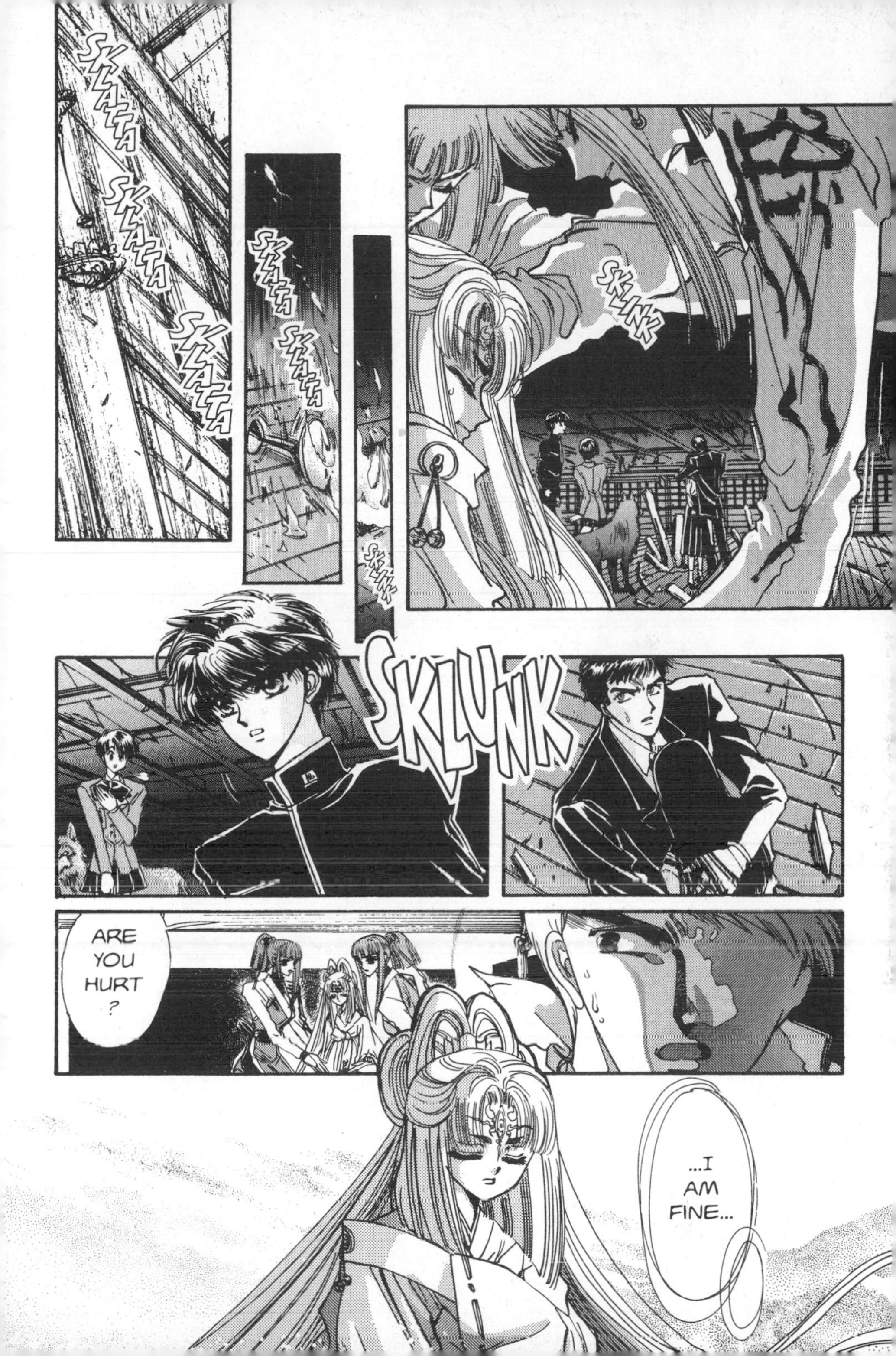
SKLACTA SKLACTA SKLACTA
SKLACTA SKLACTA
SKLUNK
SKLUNK
SKLUNK
ARE YOU HURT?
...I AM FINE...

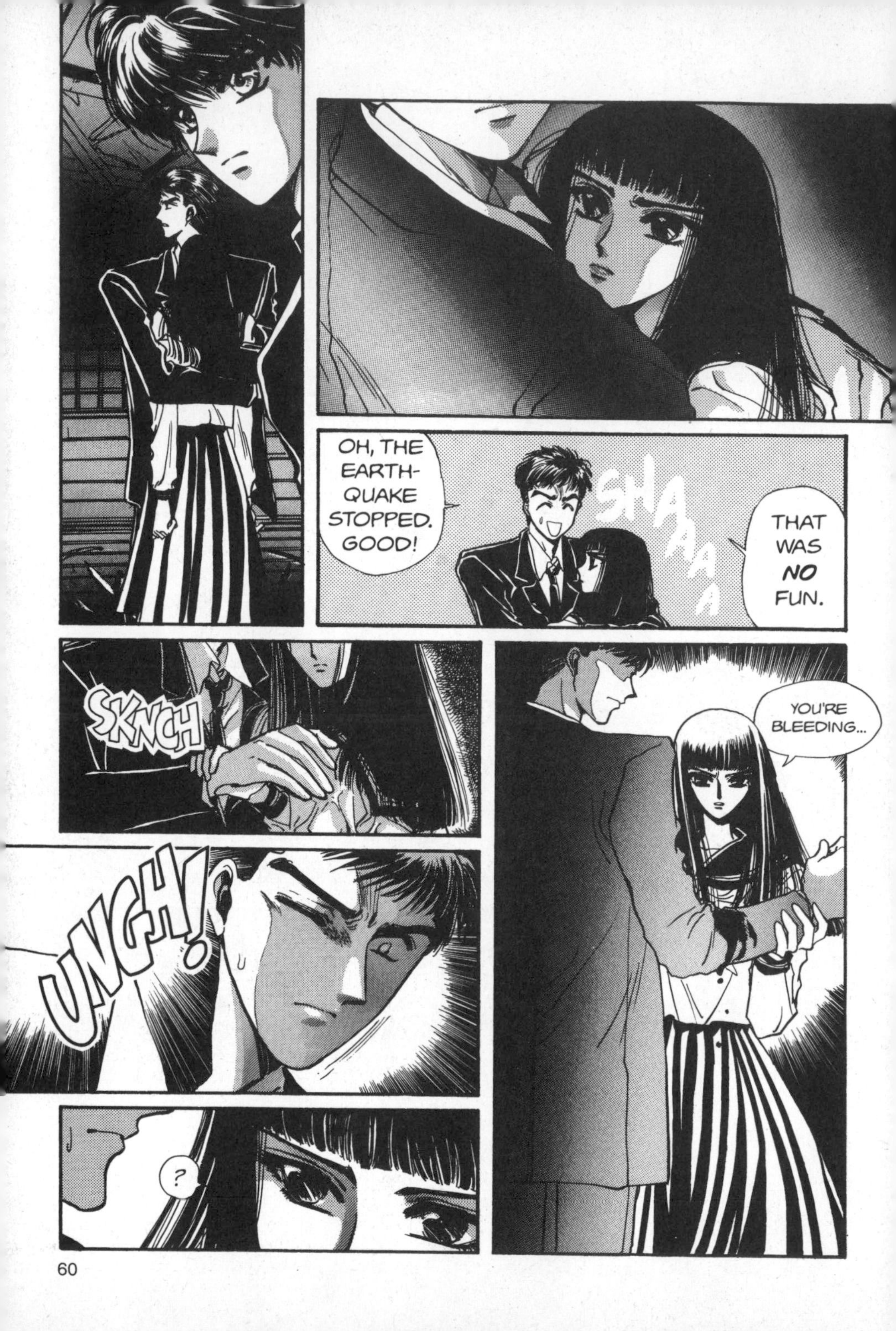
OH, THE EARTH-QUAKE STOPPED. GOOD!
SHAAAAA
THAT WAS NO FUN.
SKNCH
YOU'RE BLEEDING...
UNGH!
?

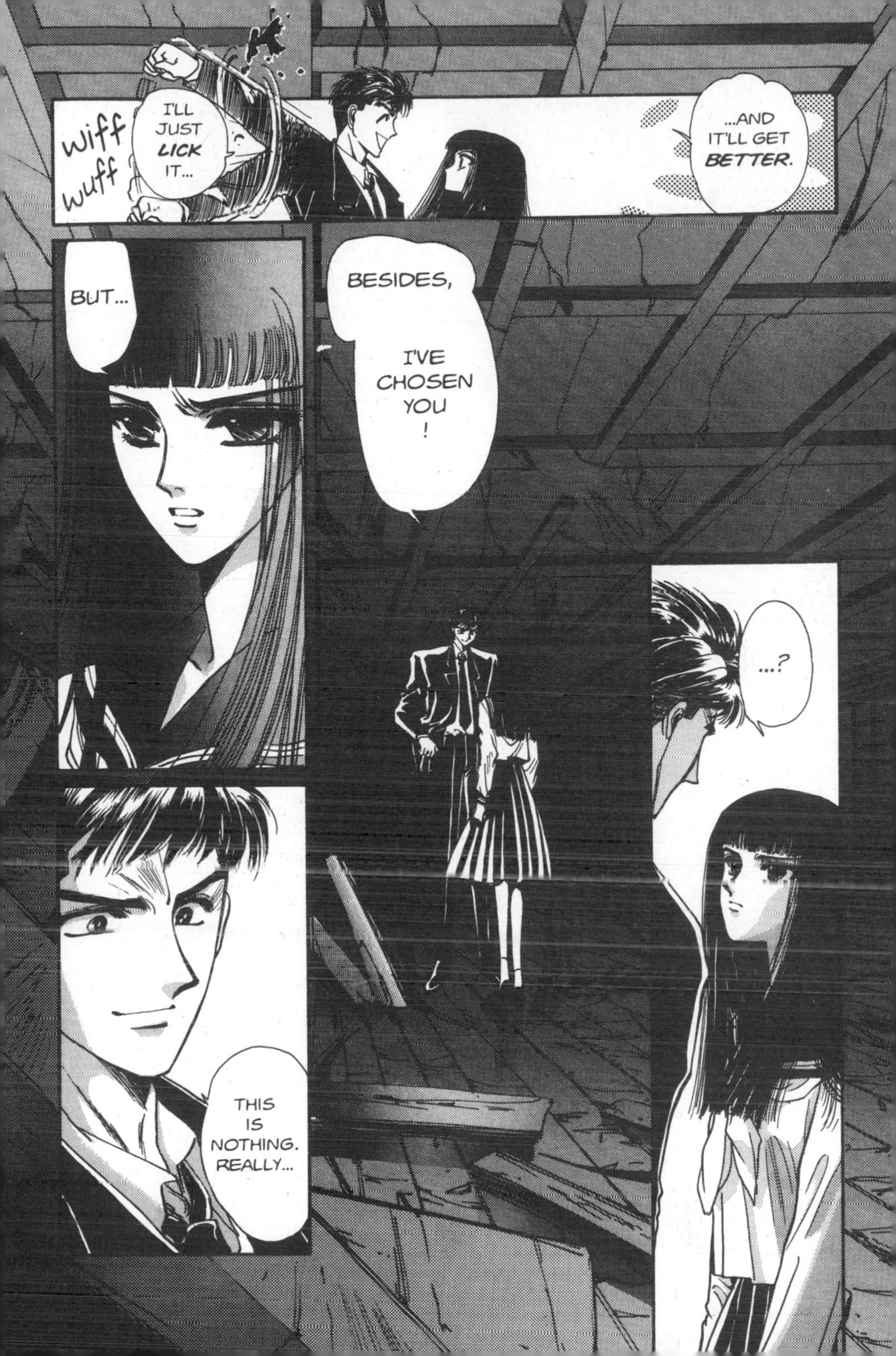
wiff wuff
I'LL JUST LICK IT...
...AND IT'LL GET BETTER.
BUT...
BESIDES,
I'VE CHOSEN YOU!
...?
THIS IS NOTHING. REALLY...

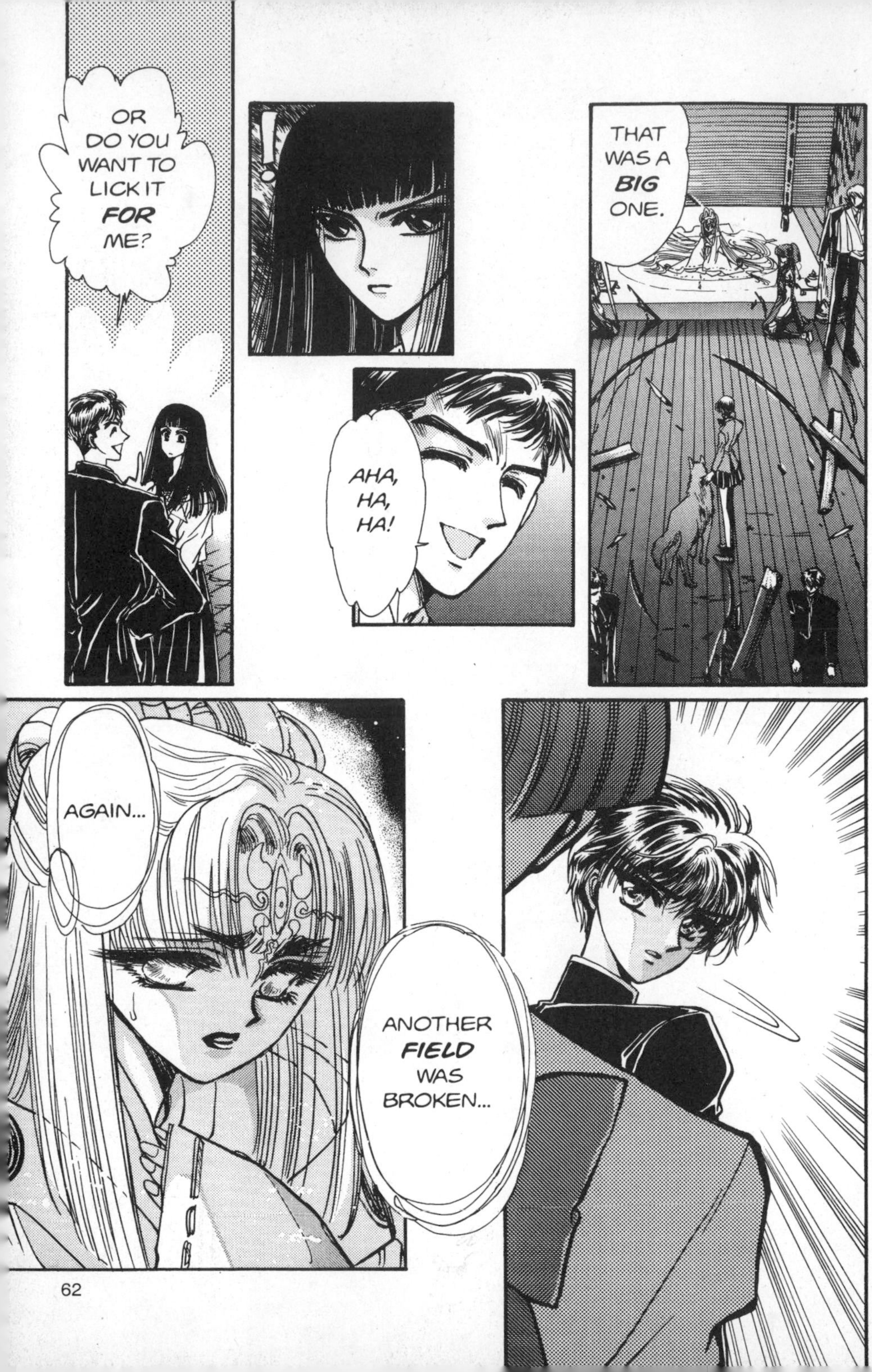
OR DO YOU WANT TO LICK IT ***FOR*** ME?
!
AHA, HA, HA!
THAT WAS A ***BIG*** ONE.
AGAIN...
ANOTHER ***FIELD*** WAS BROKEN...

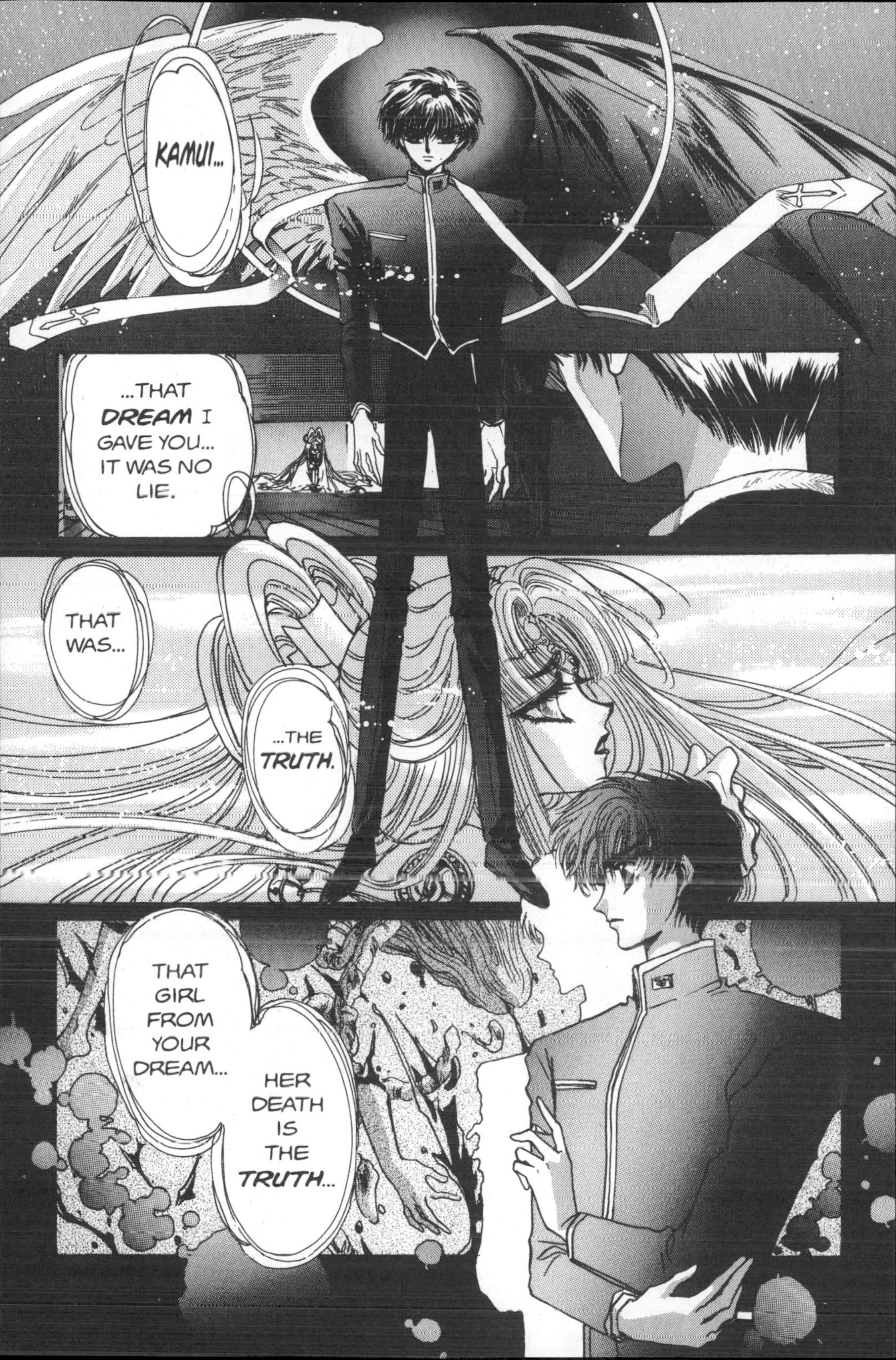
KAMUI...
...THAT DREAM I GAVE YOU... IT WAS NO LIE.
THAT WAS...
...THE TRUTH.
THAT GIRL FROM YOUR DREAM...
HER DEATH IS THE TRUTH...

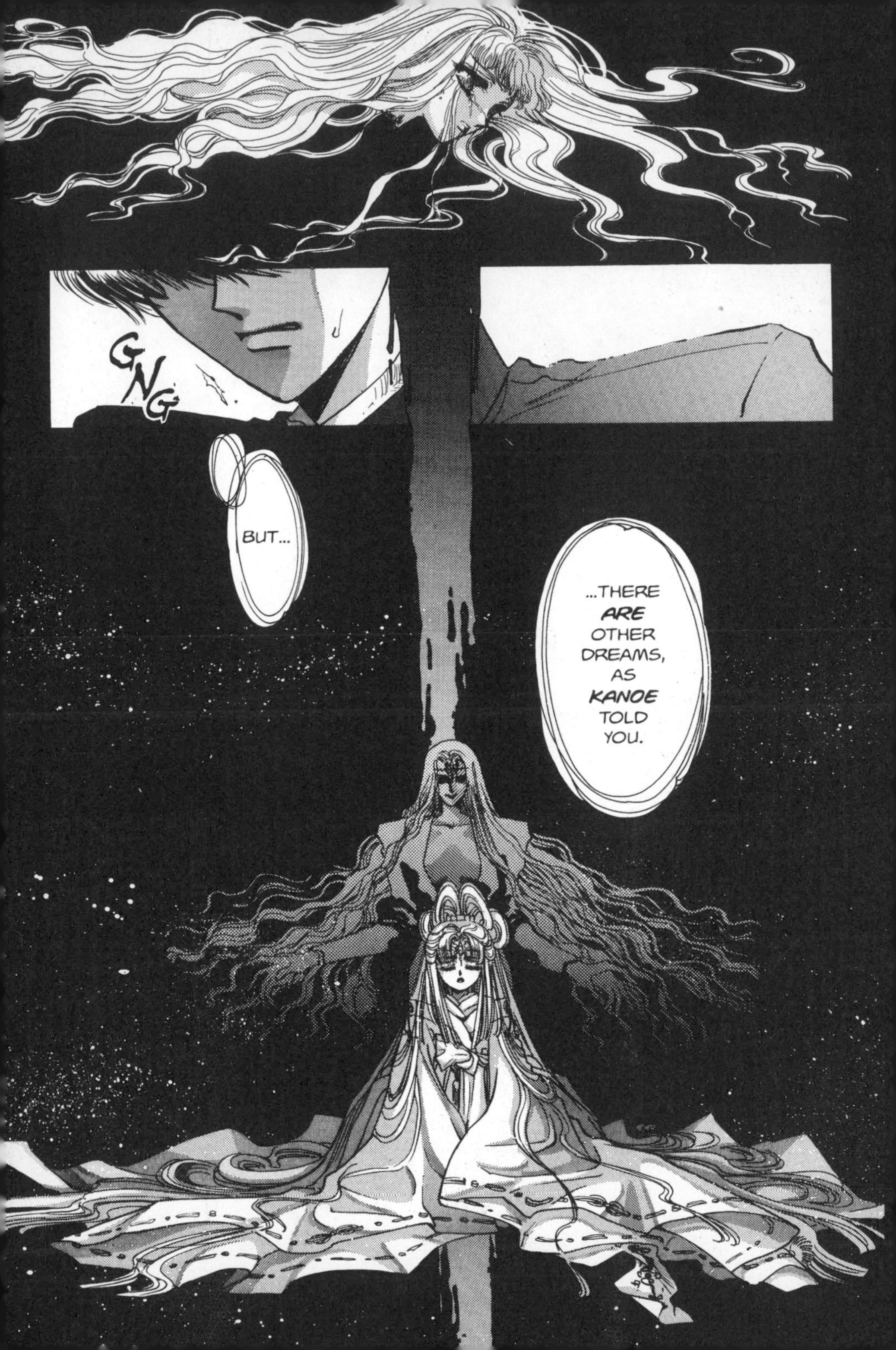
GNG
BUT...
...THERE ARE OTHER DREAMS, AS KANOE TOLD YOU.

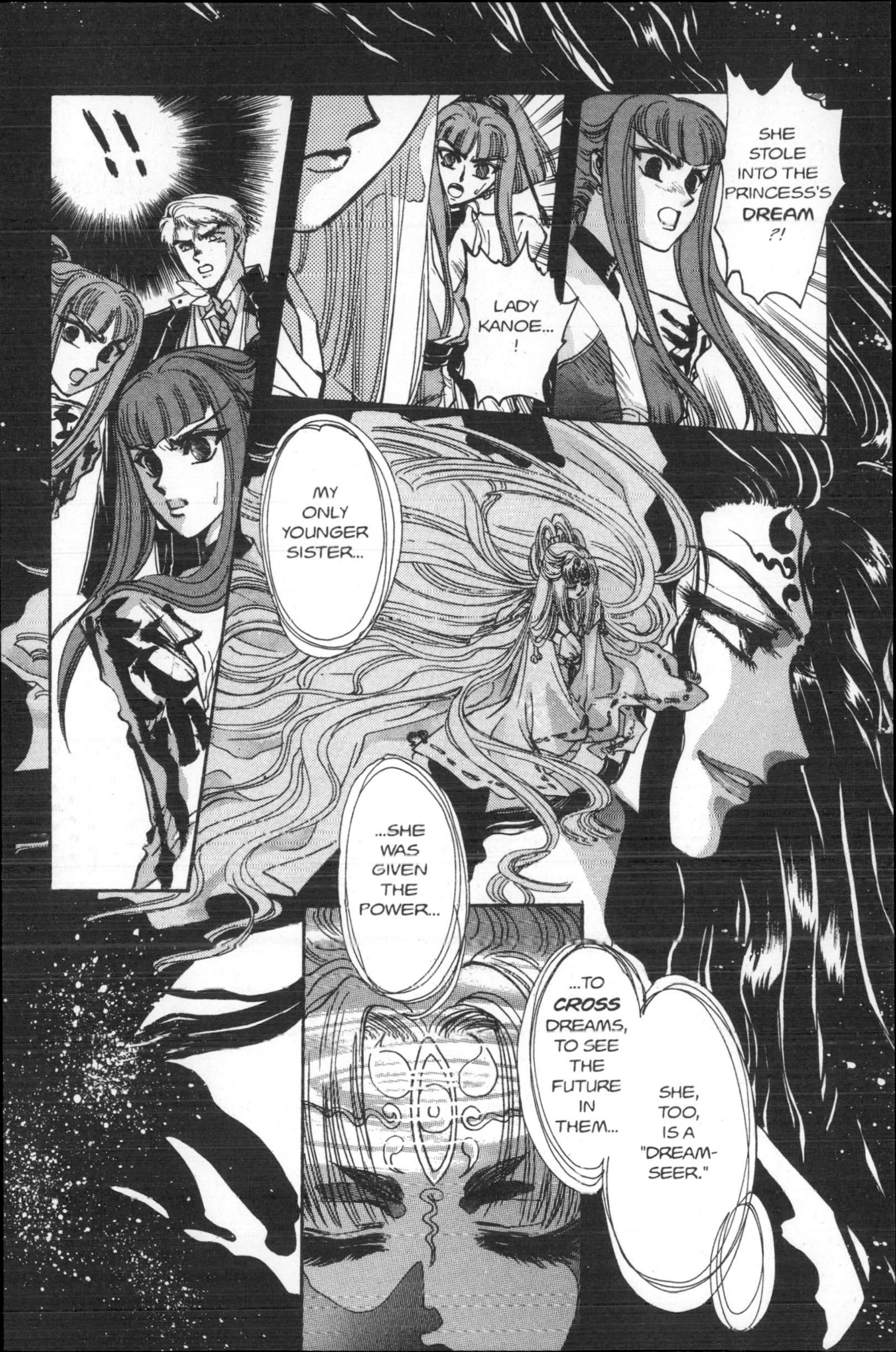
!!
LADY KANOE... !
SHE STOLE INTO THE PRINCESS'S **DREAM** ?!
MY ONLY YOUNGER SISTER...
...SHE WAS GIVEN THE POWER...
...TO **CROSS** DREAMS, TO SEE THE FUTURE IN THEM...
SHE, TOO, IS A "DREAM-SEER."

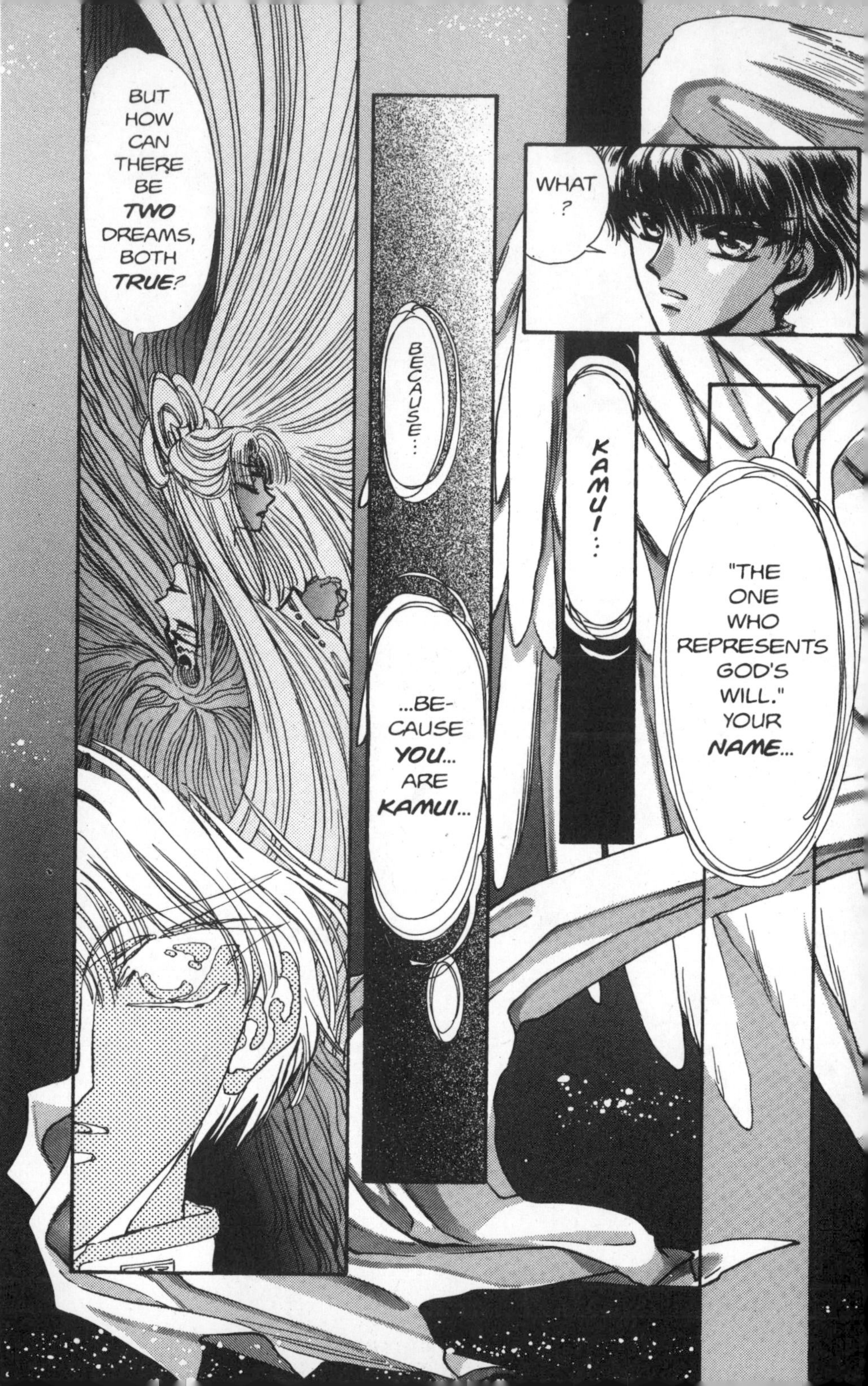
WHAT?
"THE ONE WHO REPRESENTS GOD'S WILL." YOUR NAME...
KAMUI...
BECAUSE...
...BE- CAUSE YOU... ARE KAMUI...
BUT HOW CAN THERE BE TWO DREAMS, BOTH TRUE?

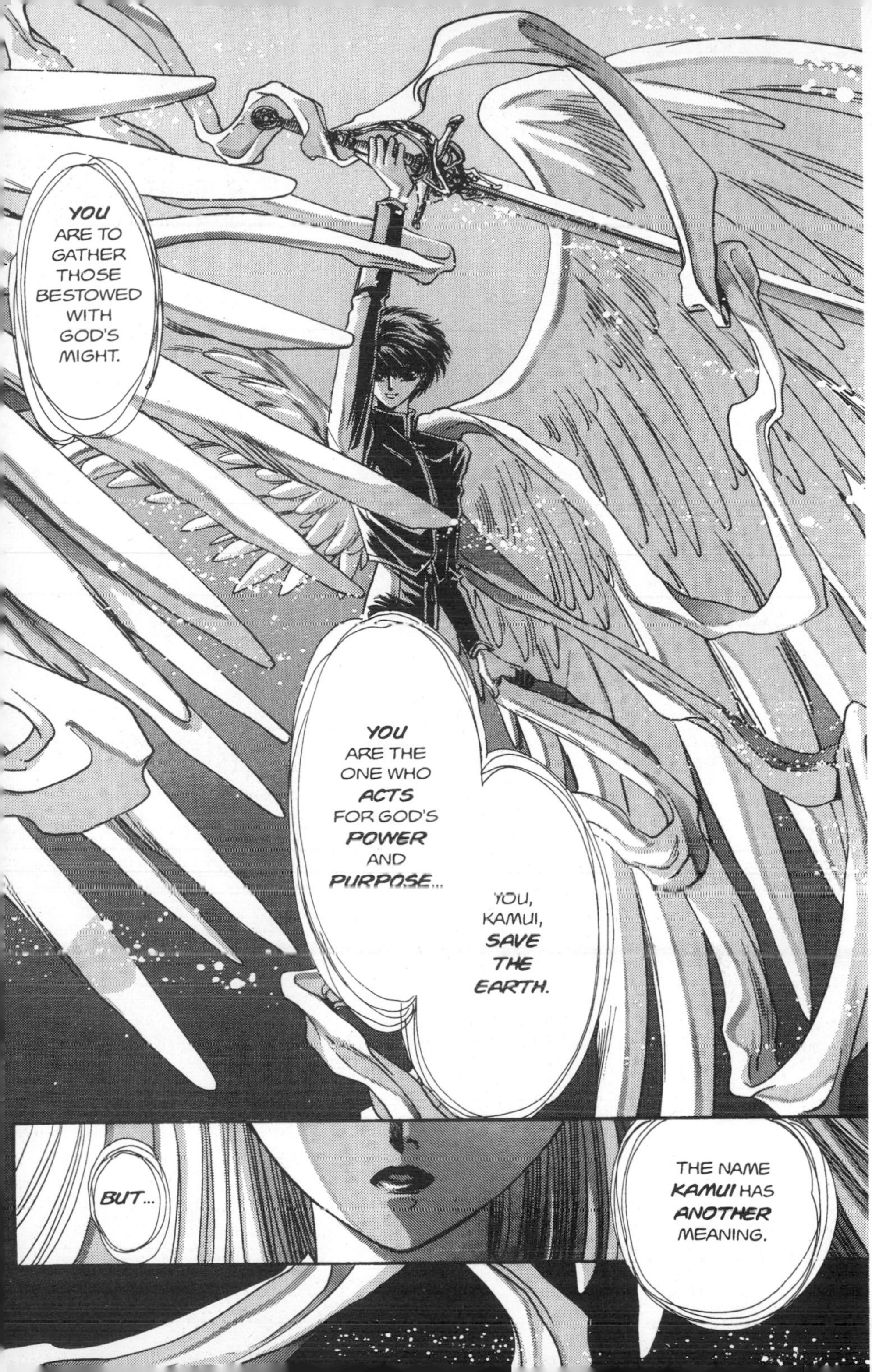
YOU ARE TO GATHER THOSE BESTOWED WITH GOD'S MIGHT.
YOU ARE THE ONE WHO ACTS FOR GOD'S POWER AND PURPOSE...
YOU, KAMUI, SAVE THE EARTH.
BUT...
THE NAME KAMUI HAS ANOTHER MEANING.

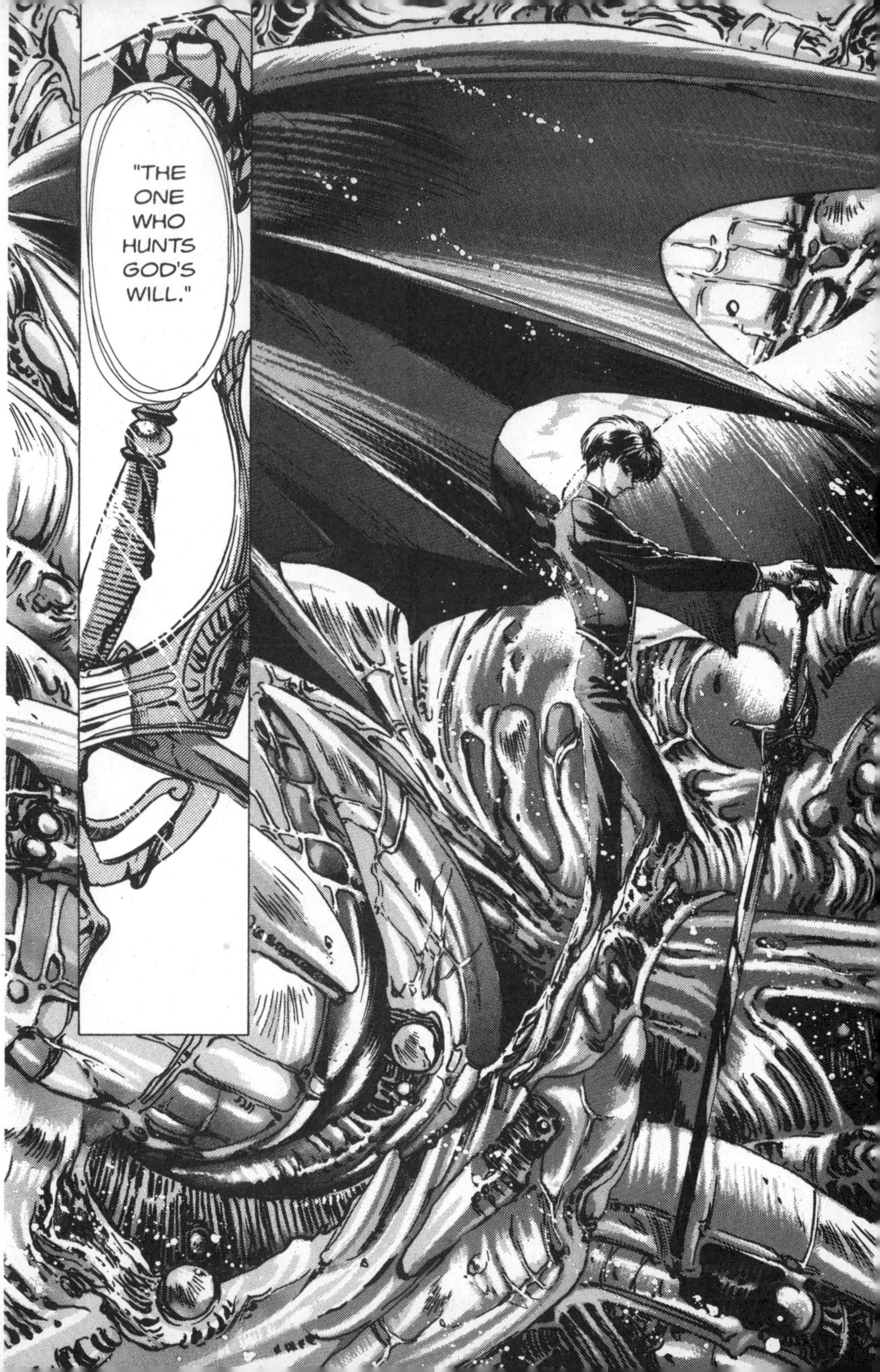
"THE ONE WHO HUNTS GOD'S WILL."

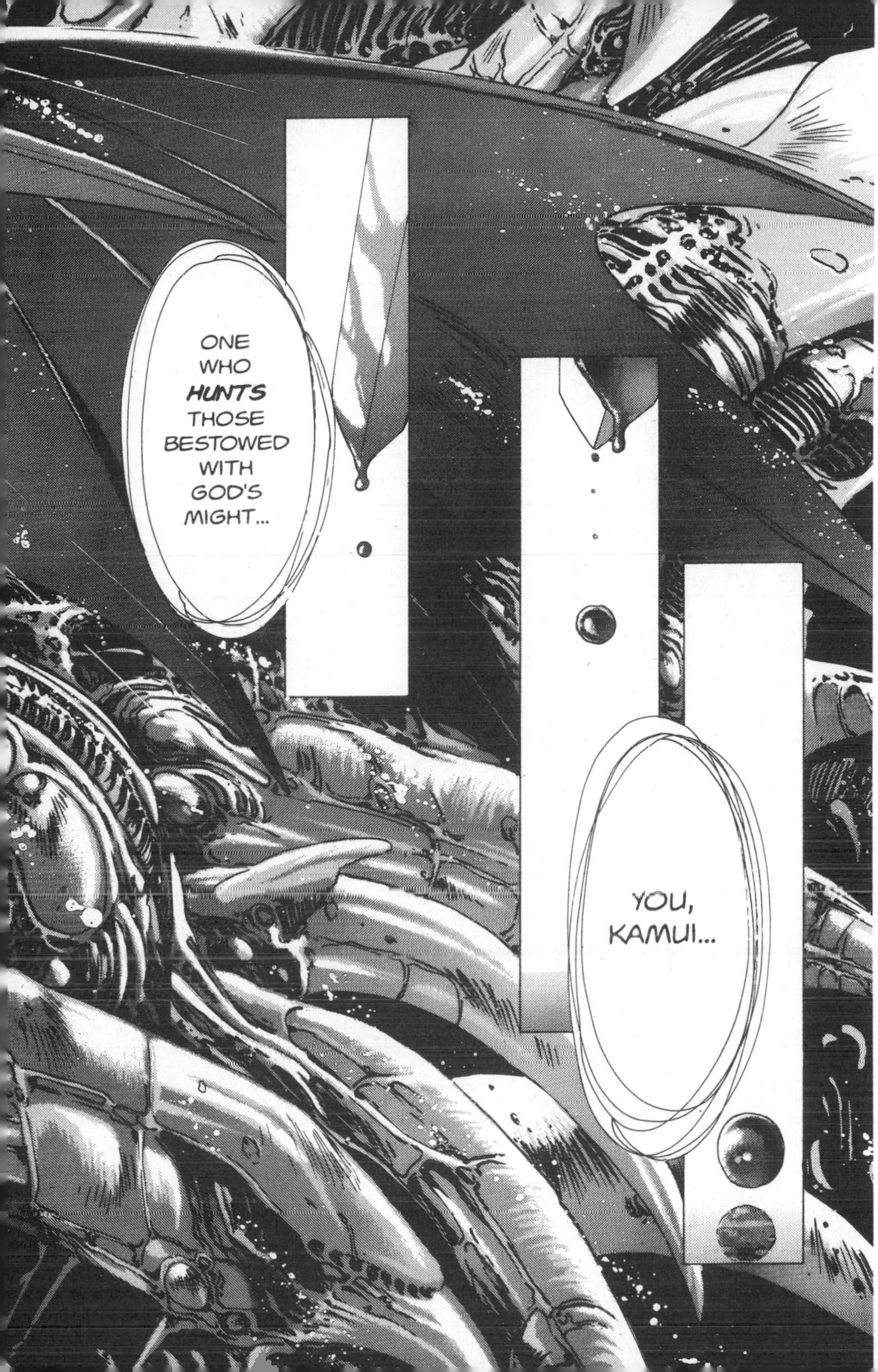
ONE WHO HUNTS THOSE BESTOWED WITH GOD'S MIGHT...
YOU, KAMUI...

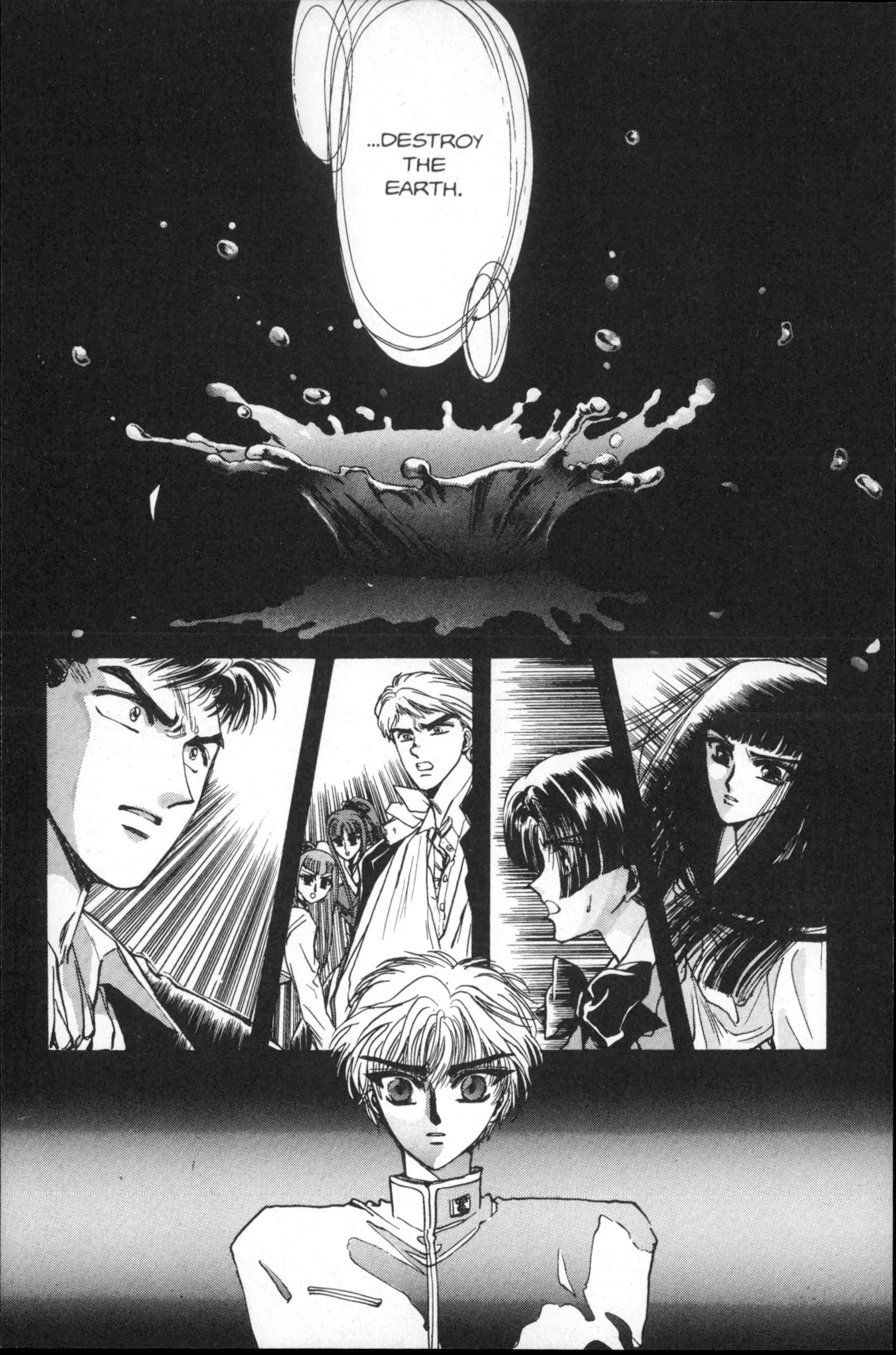
...DESTROY THE EARTH.

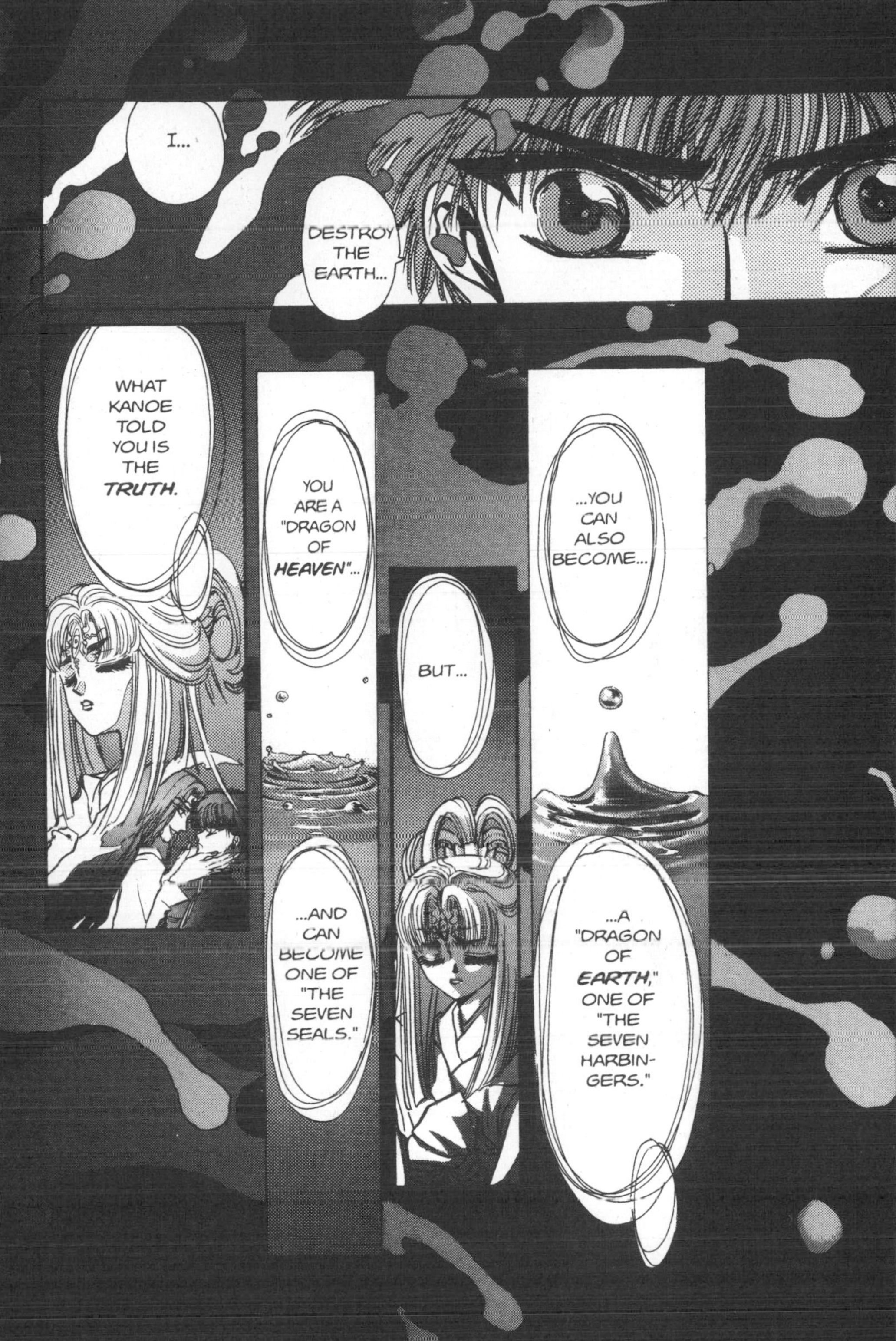
I...
DESTROY THE EARTH...
WHAT KANOE TOLD YOU IS THE *TRUTH*.
YOU ARE A "DRAGON OF *HEAVEN*"...
...AND CAN BECOME ONE OF "THE SEVEN SEALS."
BUT...
...YOU CAN ALSO BECOME...
...A "DRAGON OF *EARTH*," ONE OF "THE SEVEN HARBINGERS."

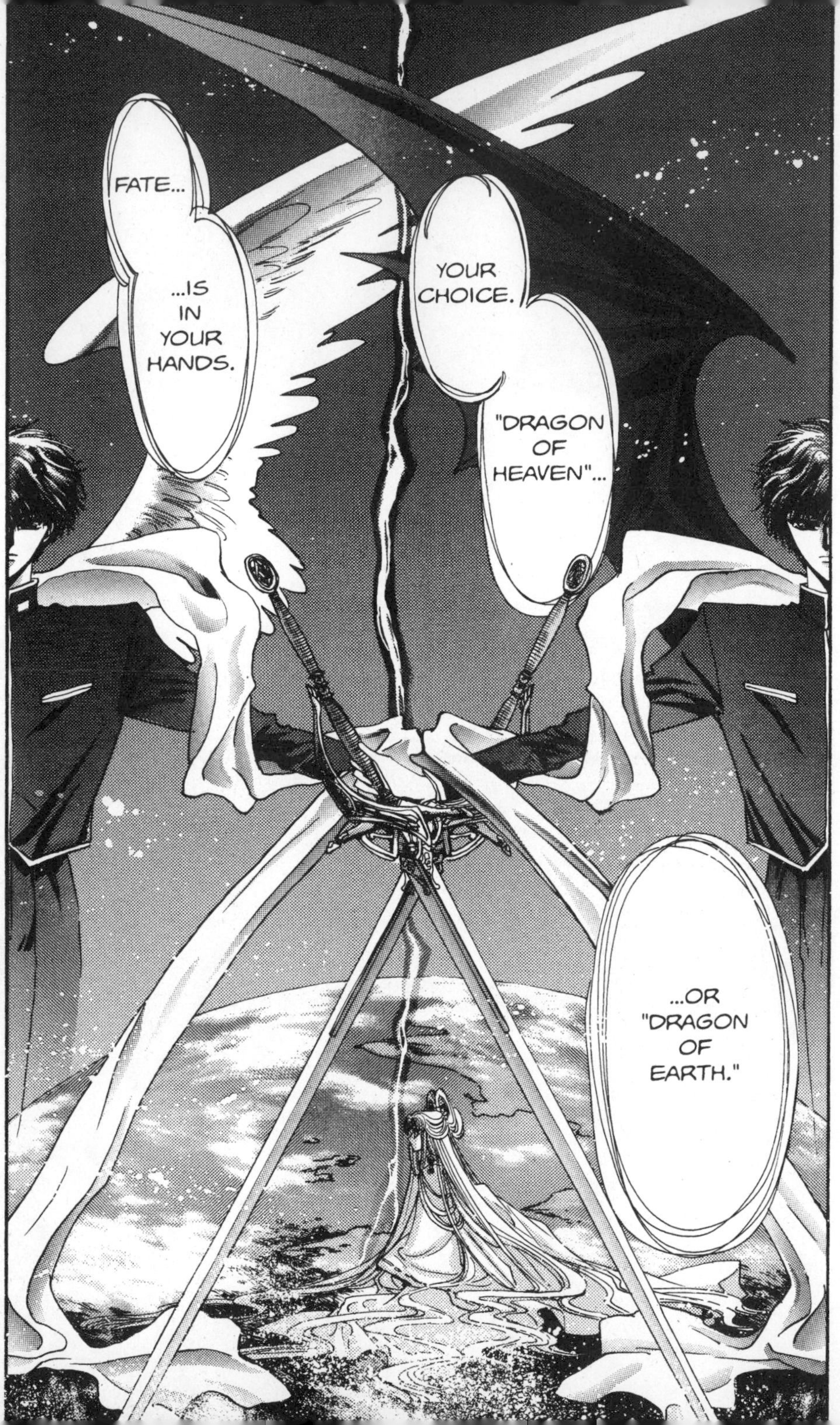
FATE...
...IS IN YOUR HANDS.
YOUR CHOICE.
"DRAGON OF HEAVEN"...
...OR "DRAGON OF EARTH."

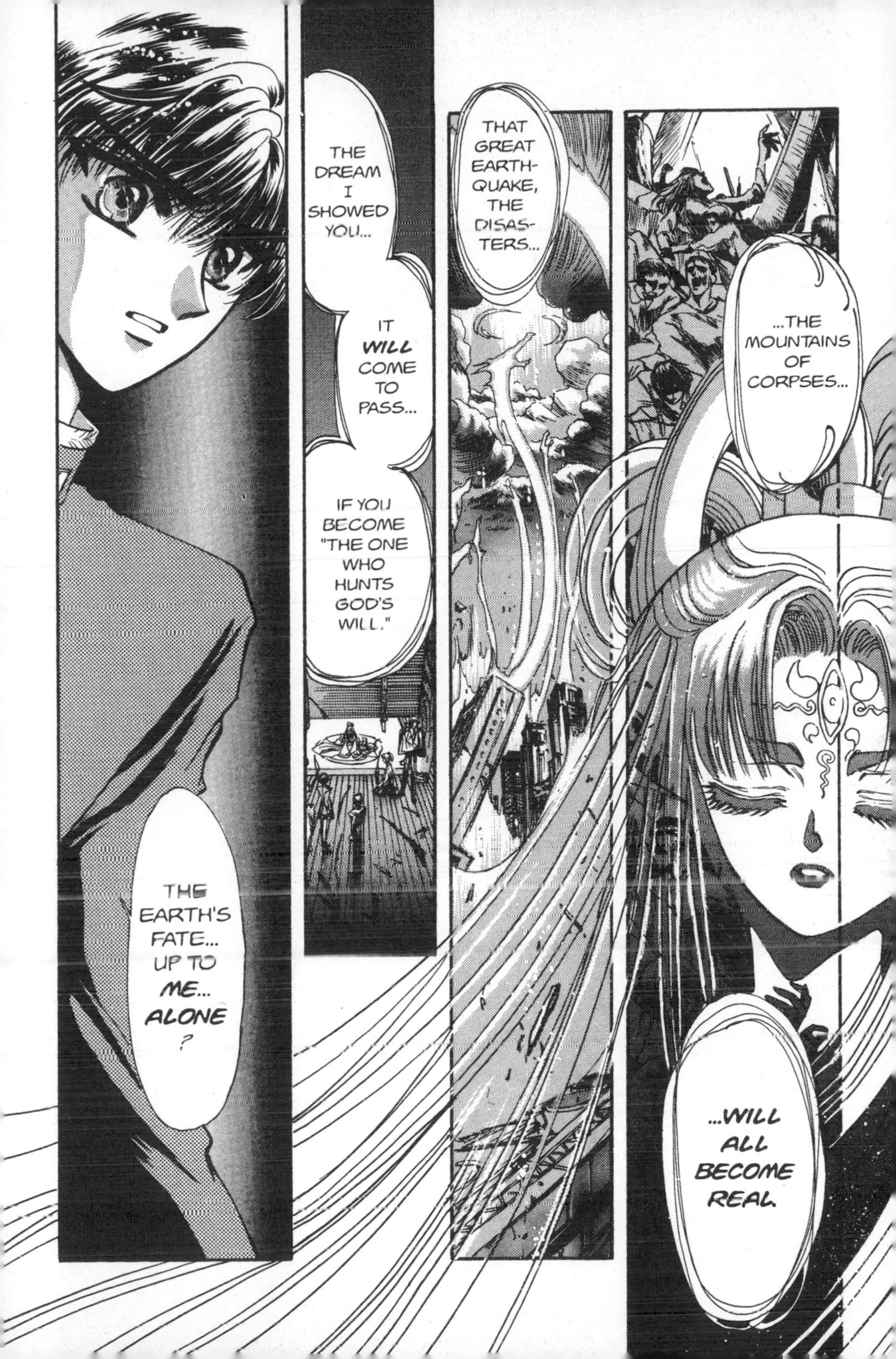
THE DREAM I SHOWED YOU...
THAT GREAT EARTH-QUAKE, THE DISAS-TERS...
...THE MOUNTAINS OF CORPSES...
...WILL ALL BECOME REAL.
IT WILL COME TO PASS...
IF YOU BECOME "THE ONE WHO HUNTS GOD'S WILL."
THE EARTH'S FATE... UP TO ME... ALONE?

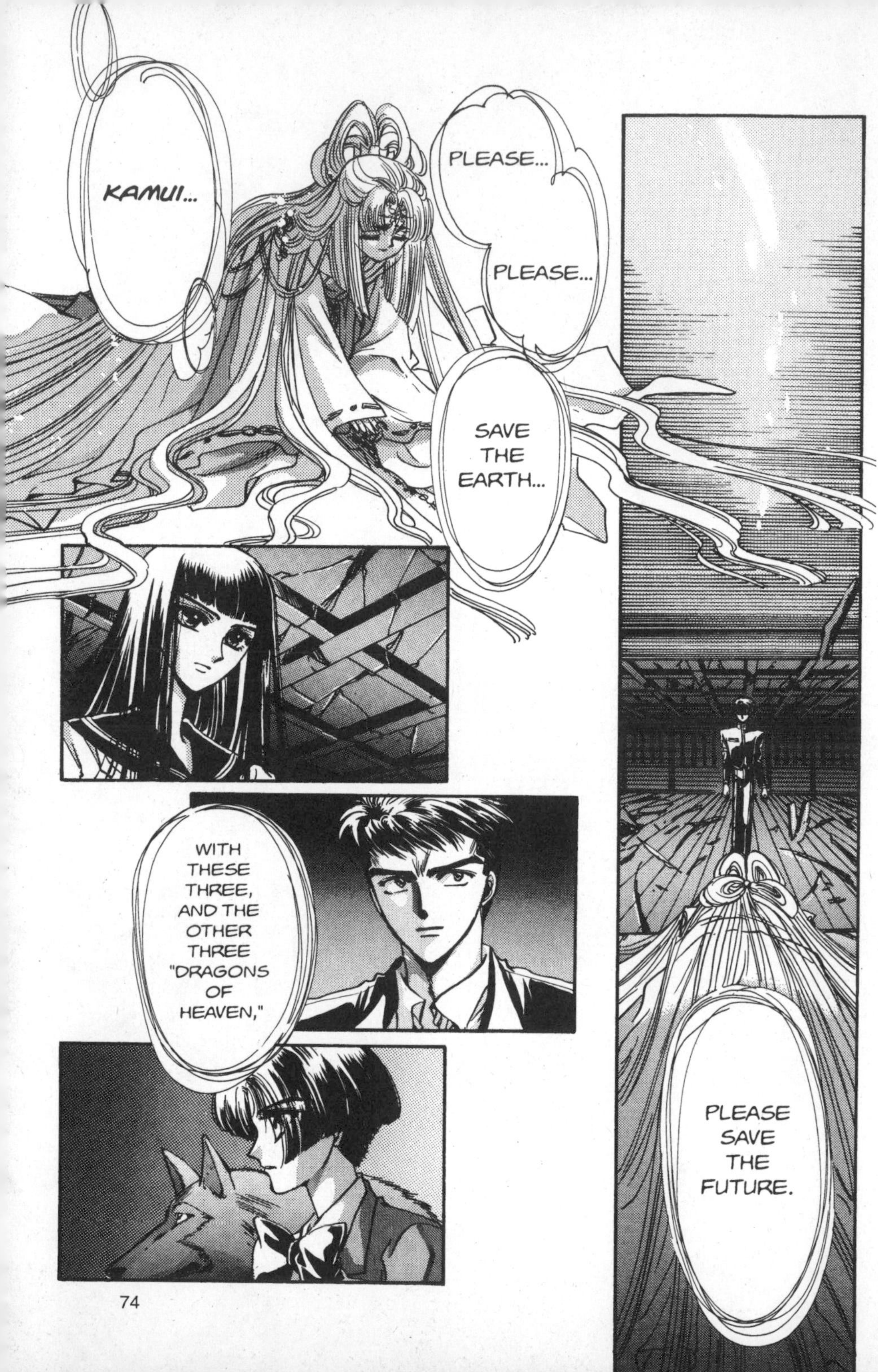
KAMUI...
PLEASE...
PLEASE...
SAVE THE EARTH...
WITH THESE THREE, AND THE OTHER THREE "DRAGONS OF HEAVEN,"
PLEASE SAVE THE FUTURE.

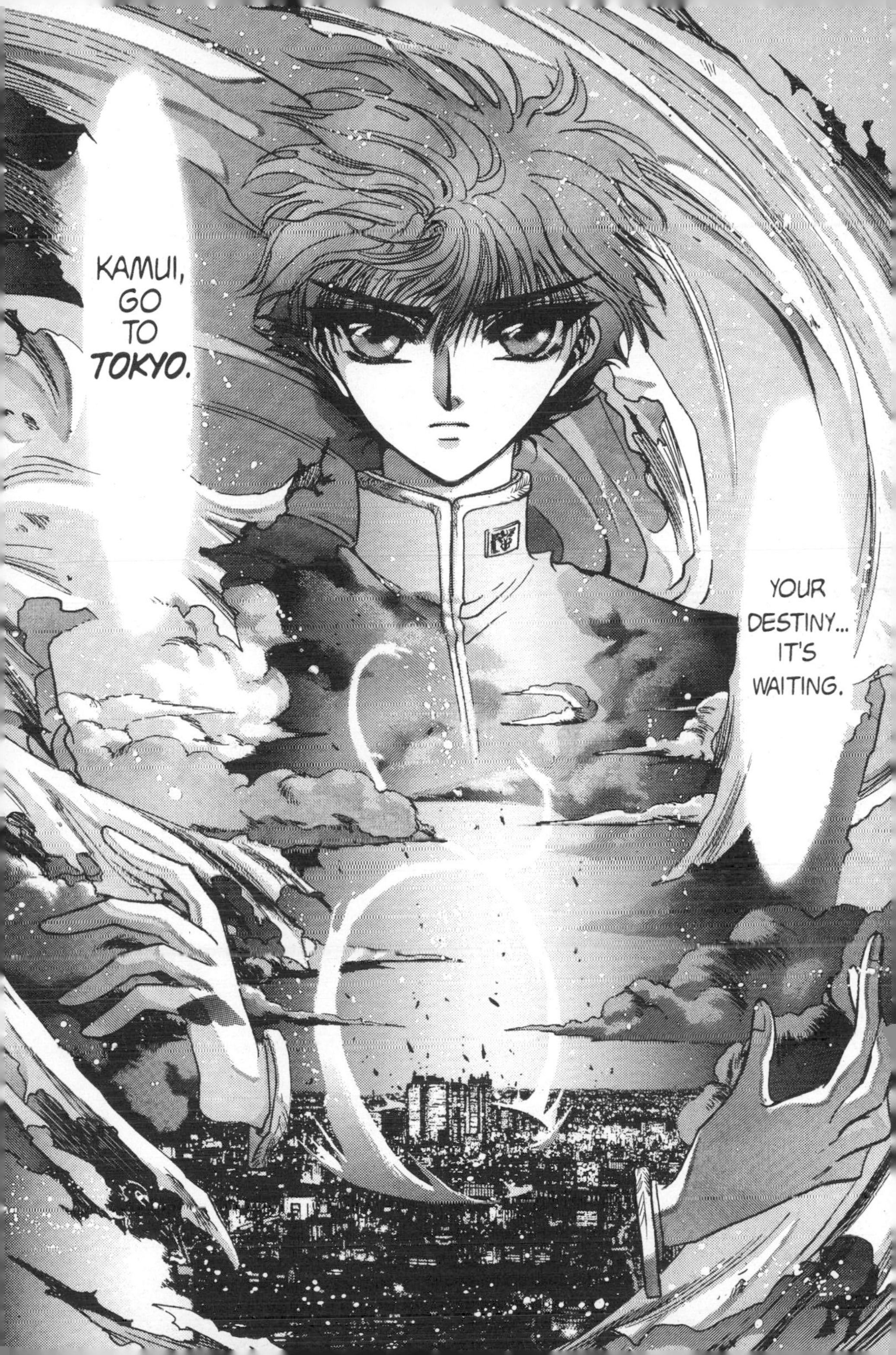
KAMUI, GO TO TOKYO.
YOUR DESTINY... IT'S WAITING.

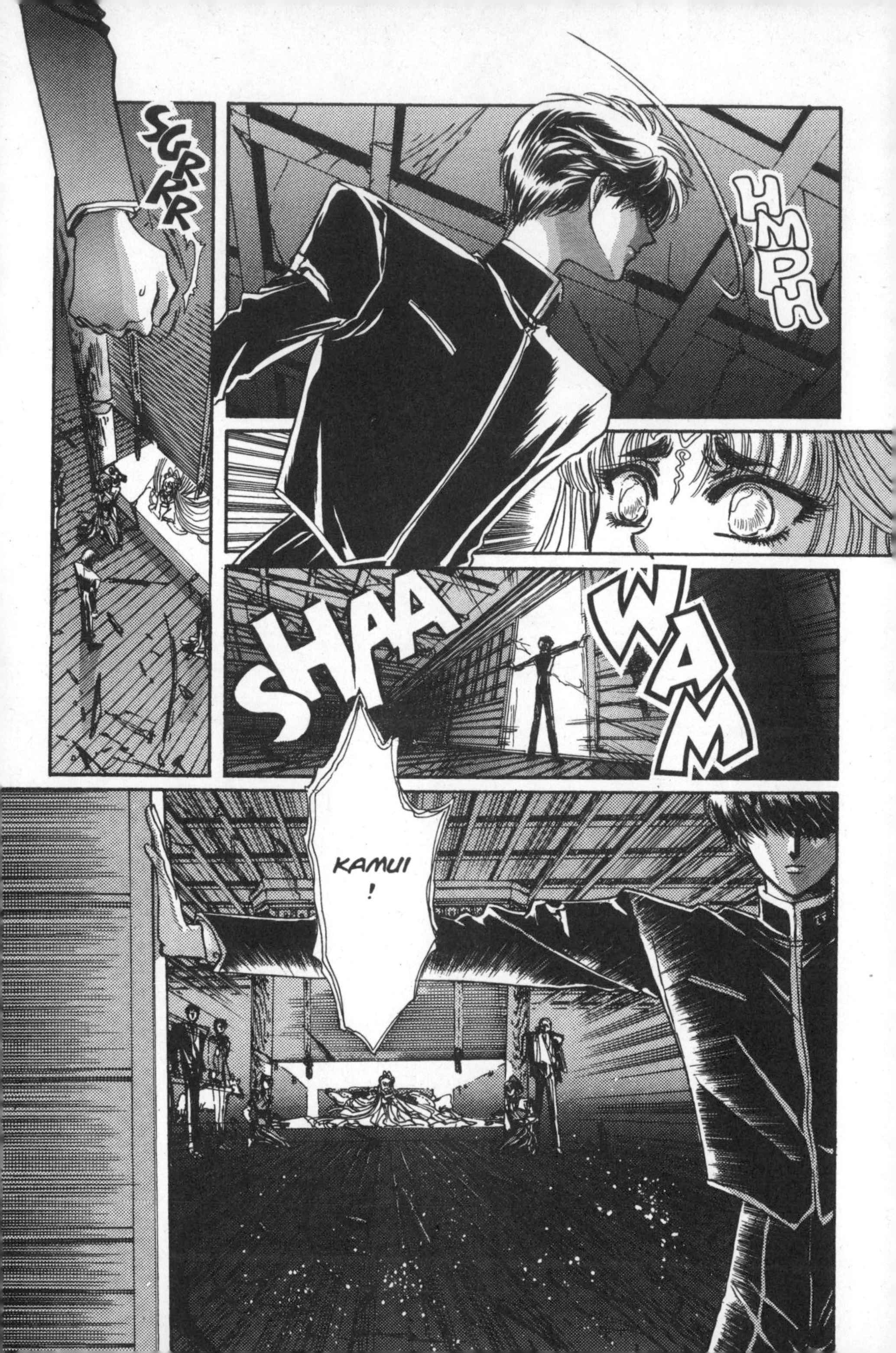
SGRRR
HMPH
SHAA
WAM
KAMUI!

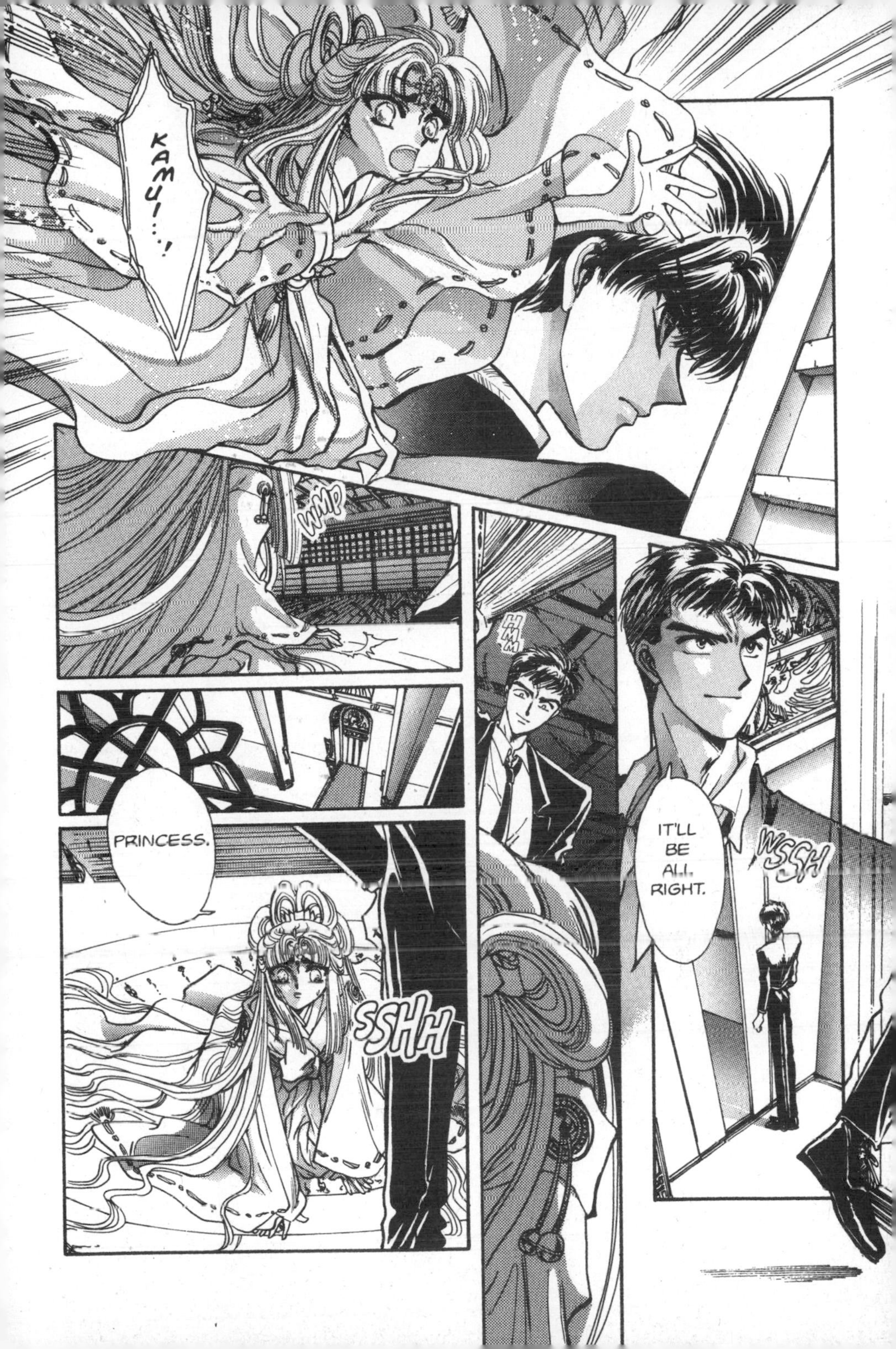
KAMUI...!
WMP
PRINCESS.
SSHH
HMM
IT'LL BE ALL RIGHT.
WSSH

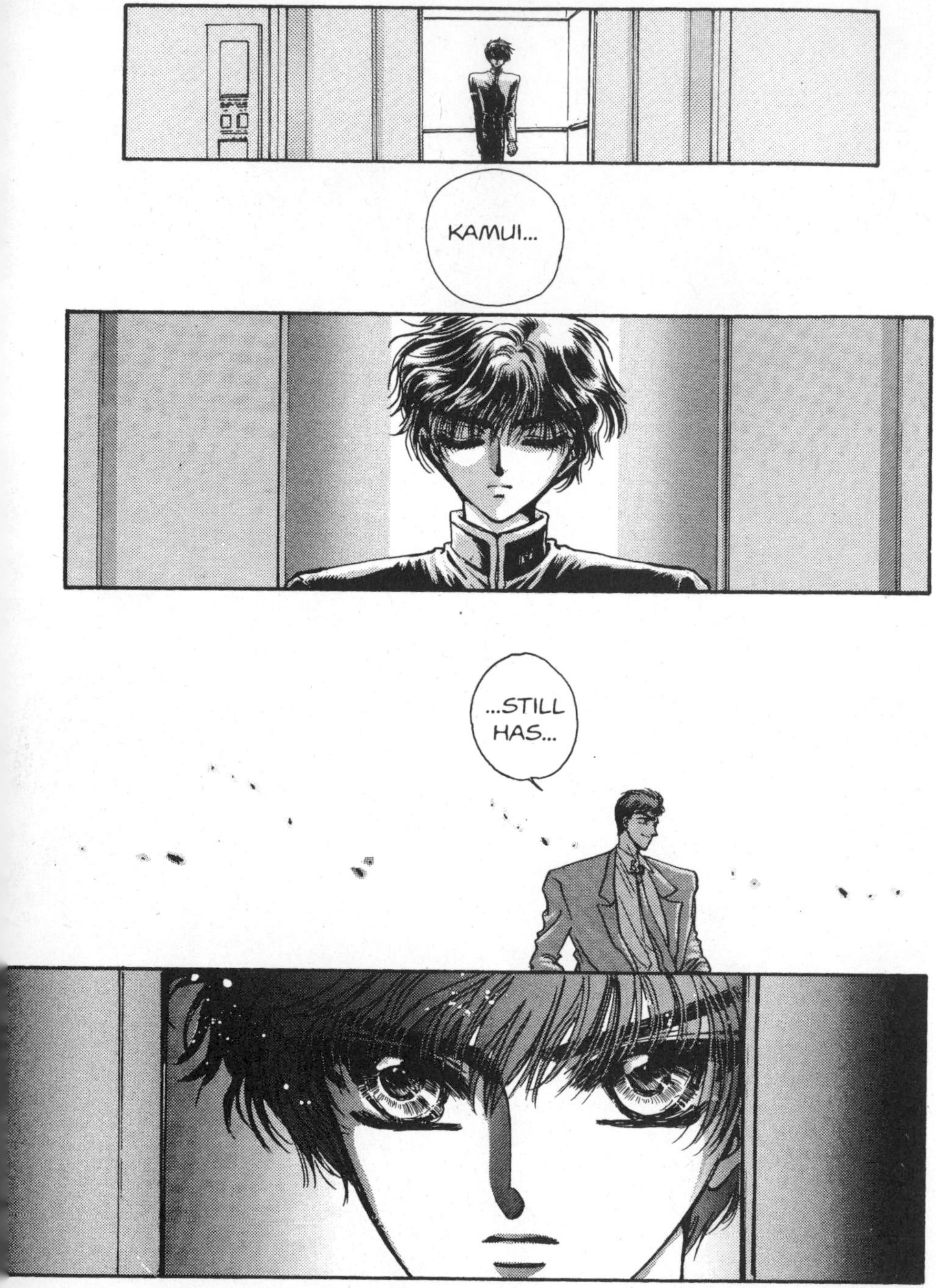
KAMUI...
...STILL HAS...

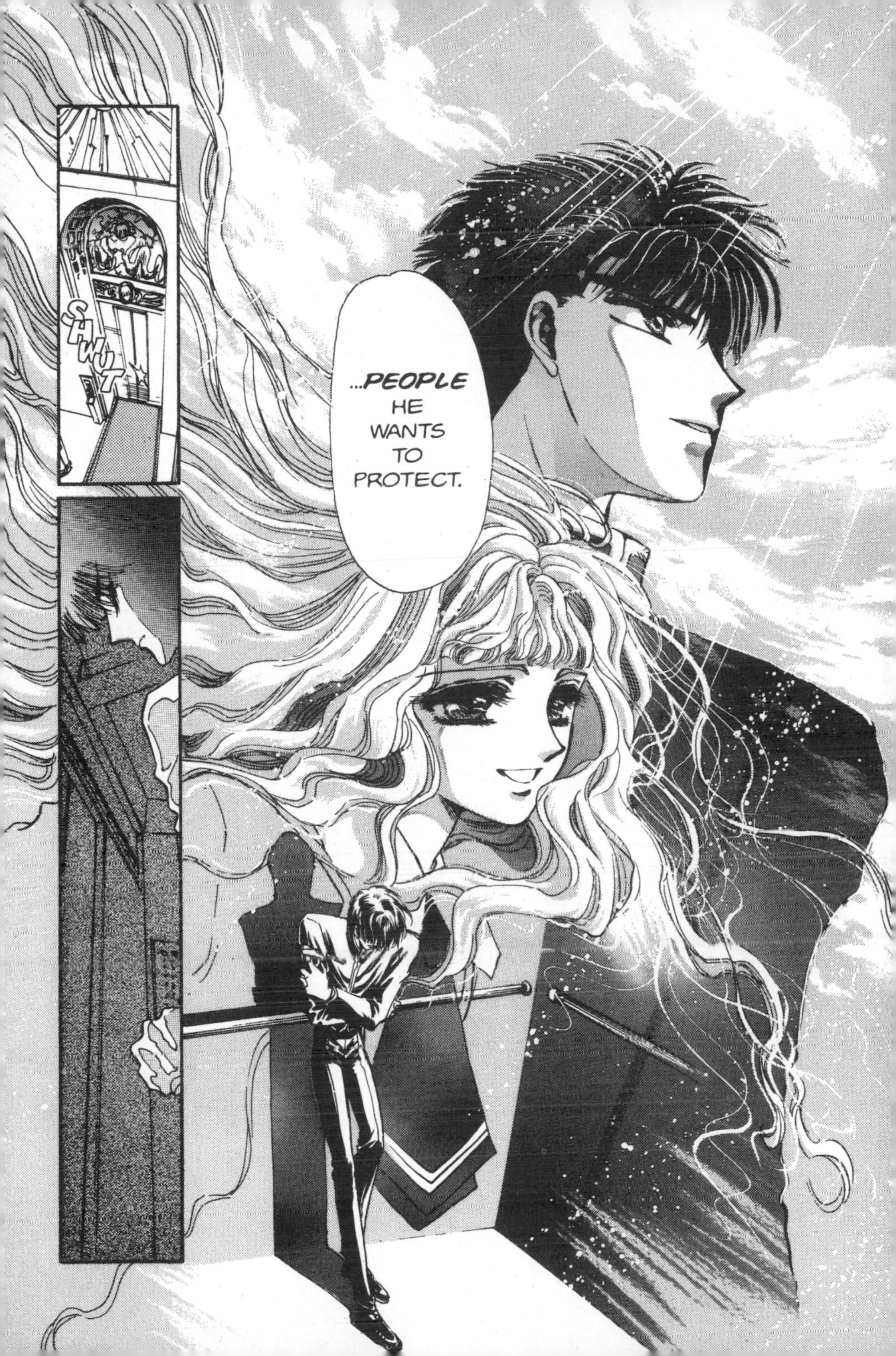
SHWUT
...PEOPLE HE WANTS TO PROTECT.

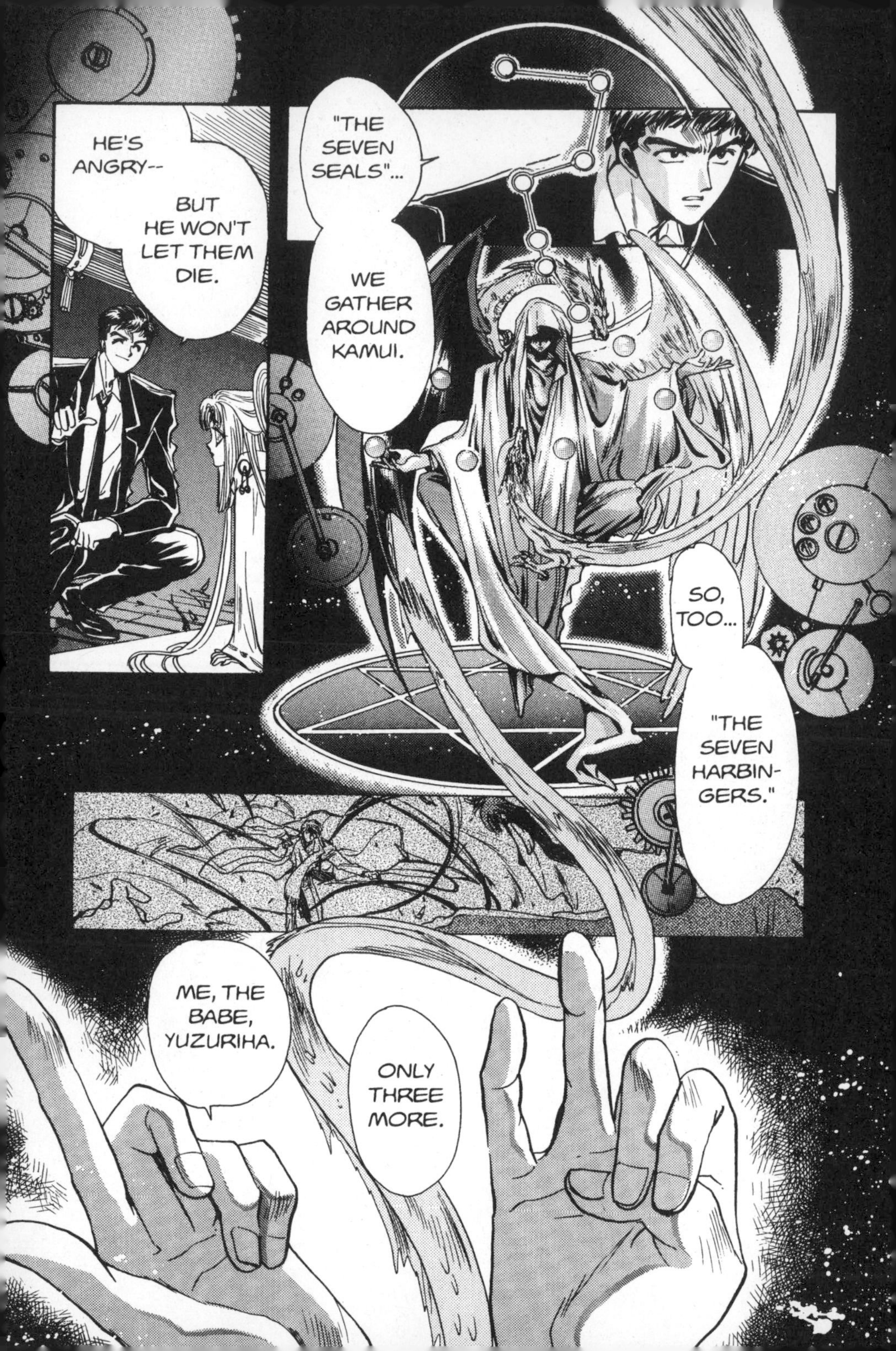
HE'S ANGRY--
BUT HE WON'T LET THEM DIE.
"THE SEVEN SEALS"...
WE GATHER AROUND KAMUI.
SO, TOO...
"THE SEVEN HARBIN-GERS."
ME, THE BABE, YUZURIHA.
ONLY THREE MORE.

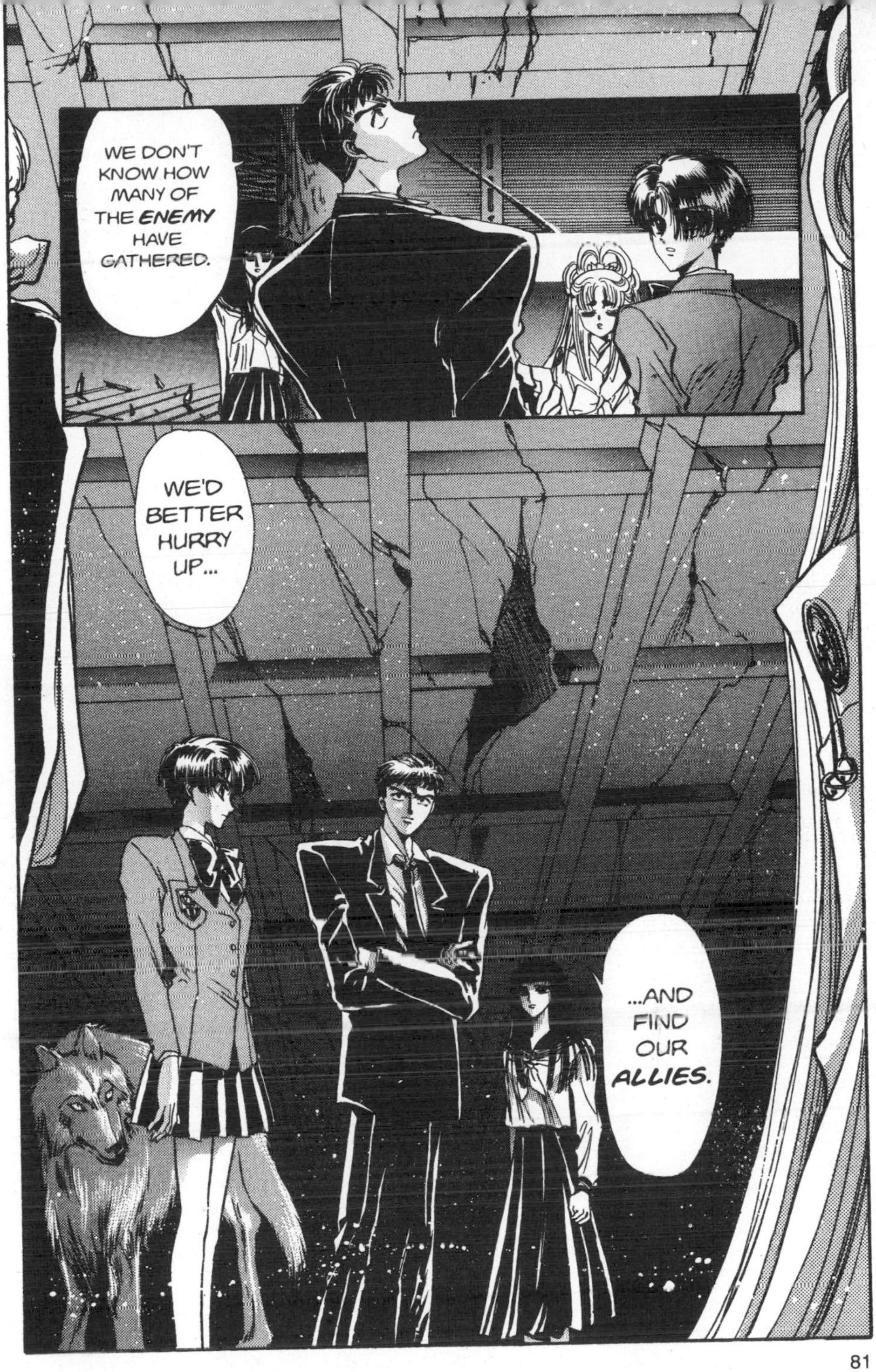
WE DON'T KNOW HOW MANY OF THE ENEMY HAVE GATHERED.
WE'D BETTER HURRY UP...
...AND FIND OUR ALLIES.

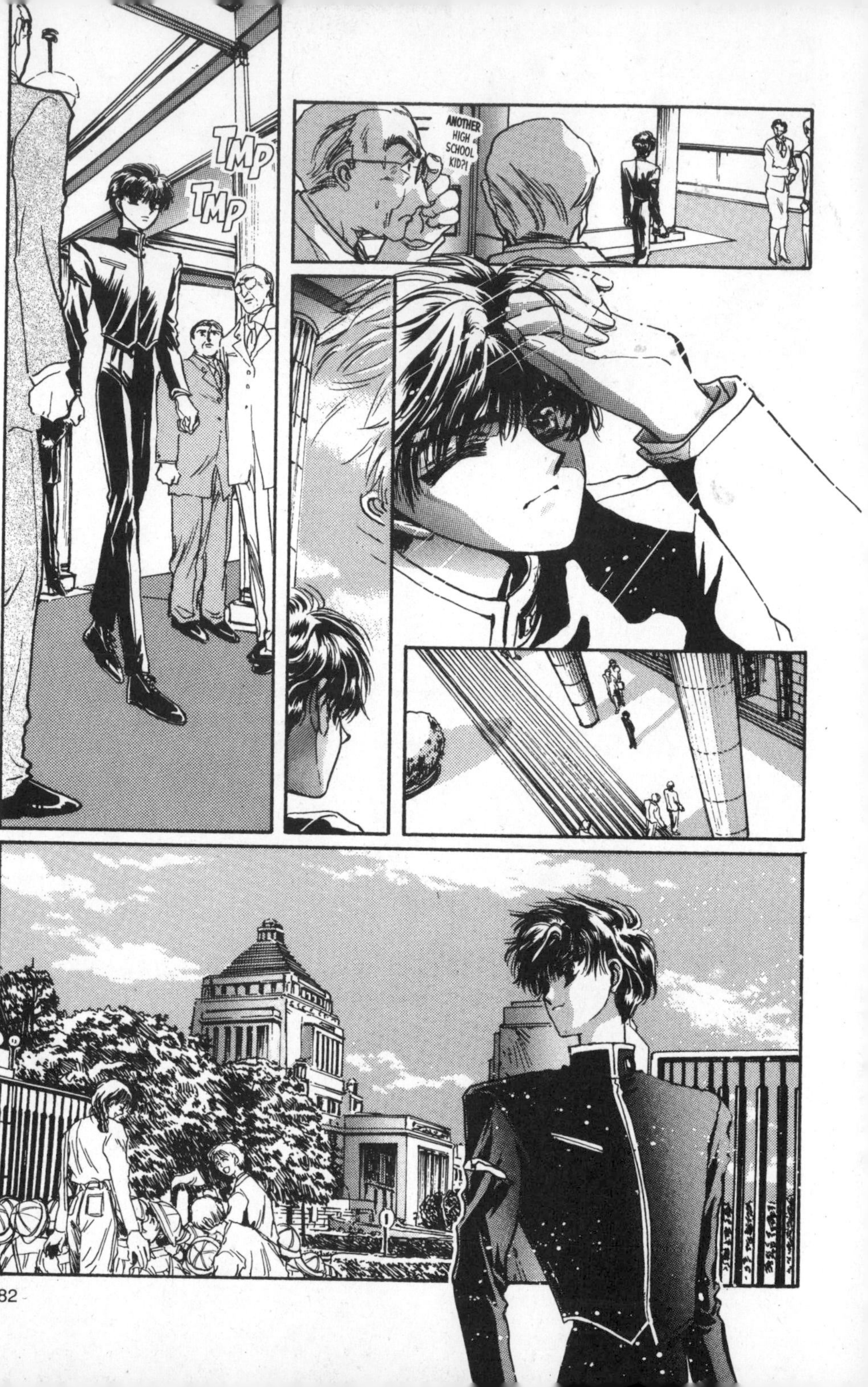
TMP
TMP
ANOTHER HIGH SCHOOL KID?!

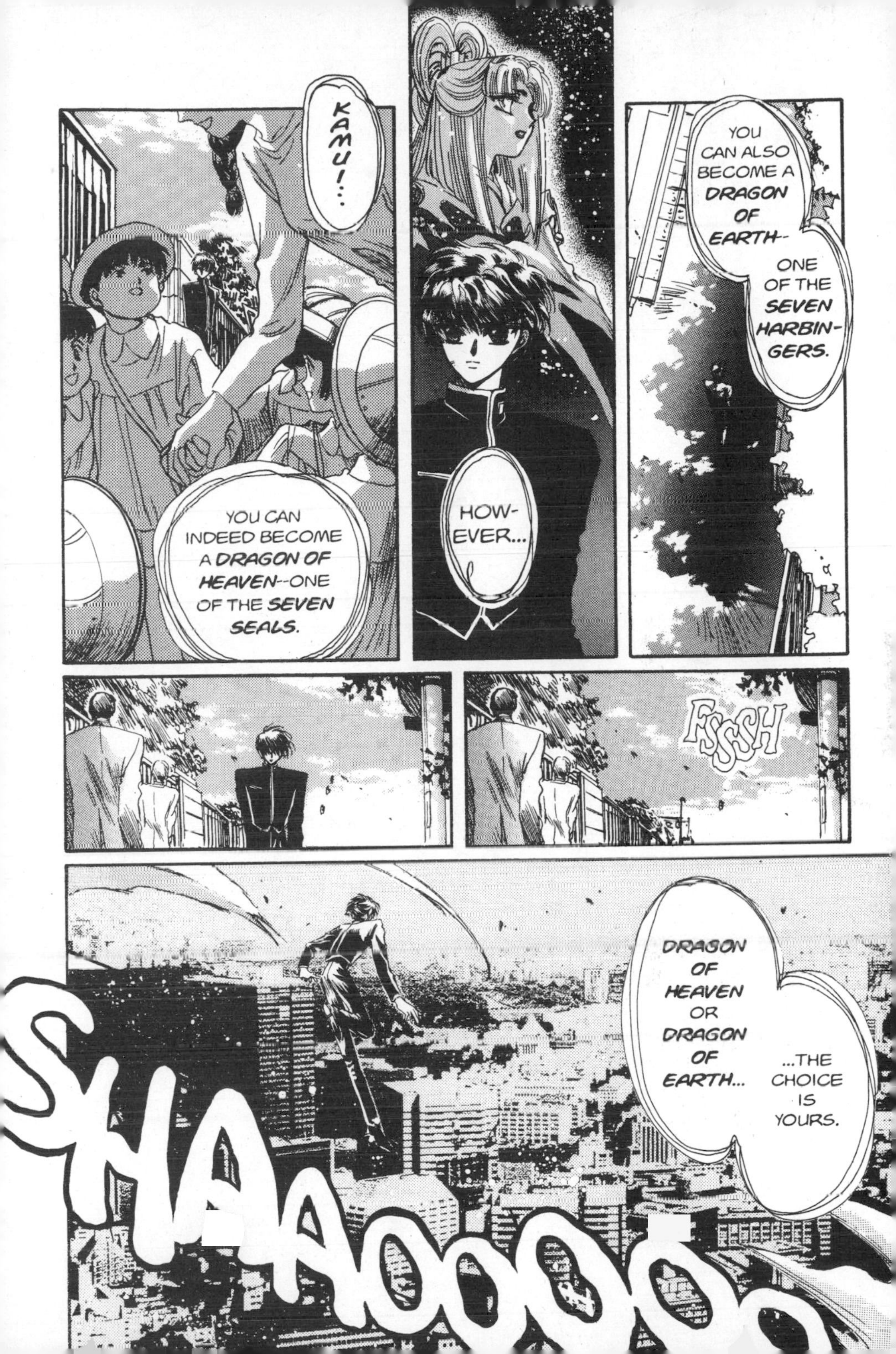
KAMUI...
YOU CAN INDEED BECOME A DRAGON OF HEAVEN--ONE OF THE SEVEN SEALS.
HOW-EVER...
YOU CAN ALSO BECOME A DRAGON OF EARTH--
ONE OF THE SEVEN HARBIN-GERS.
FSSSH
DRAGON OF HEAVEN OR DRAGON OF EARTH...
...THE CHOICE IS YOURS.
SHAAOOOOO

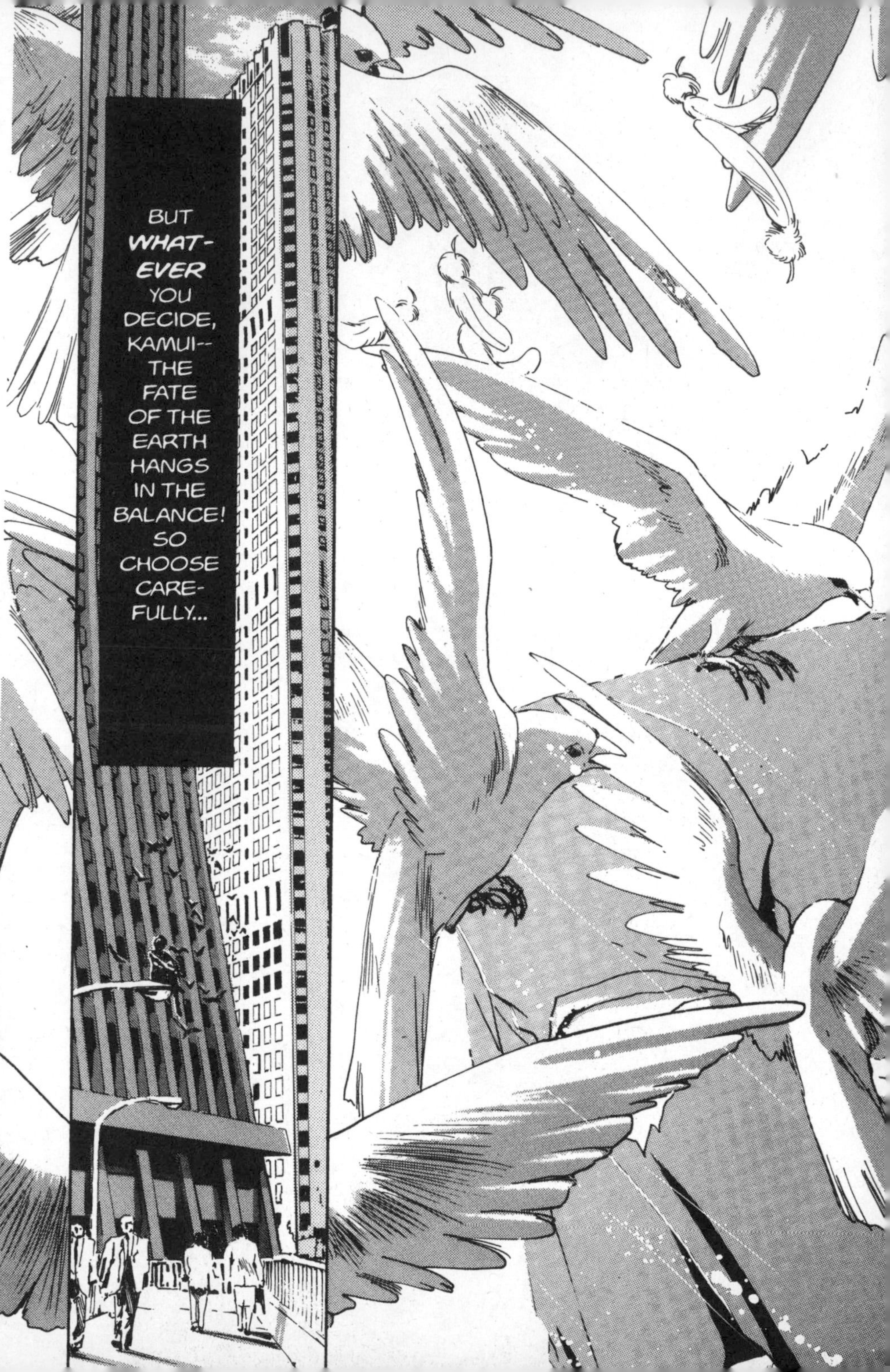
BUT WHATEVER YOU DECIDE, KAMUI-- THE FATE OF THE EARTH HANGS IN THE BALANCE! SO CHOOSE CAREFULLY...

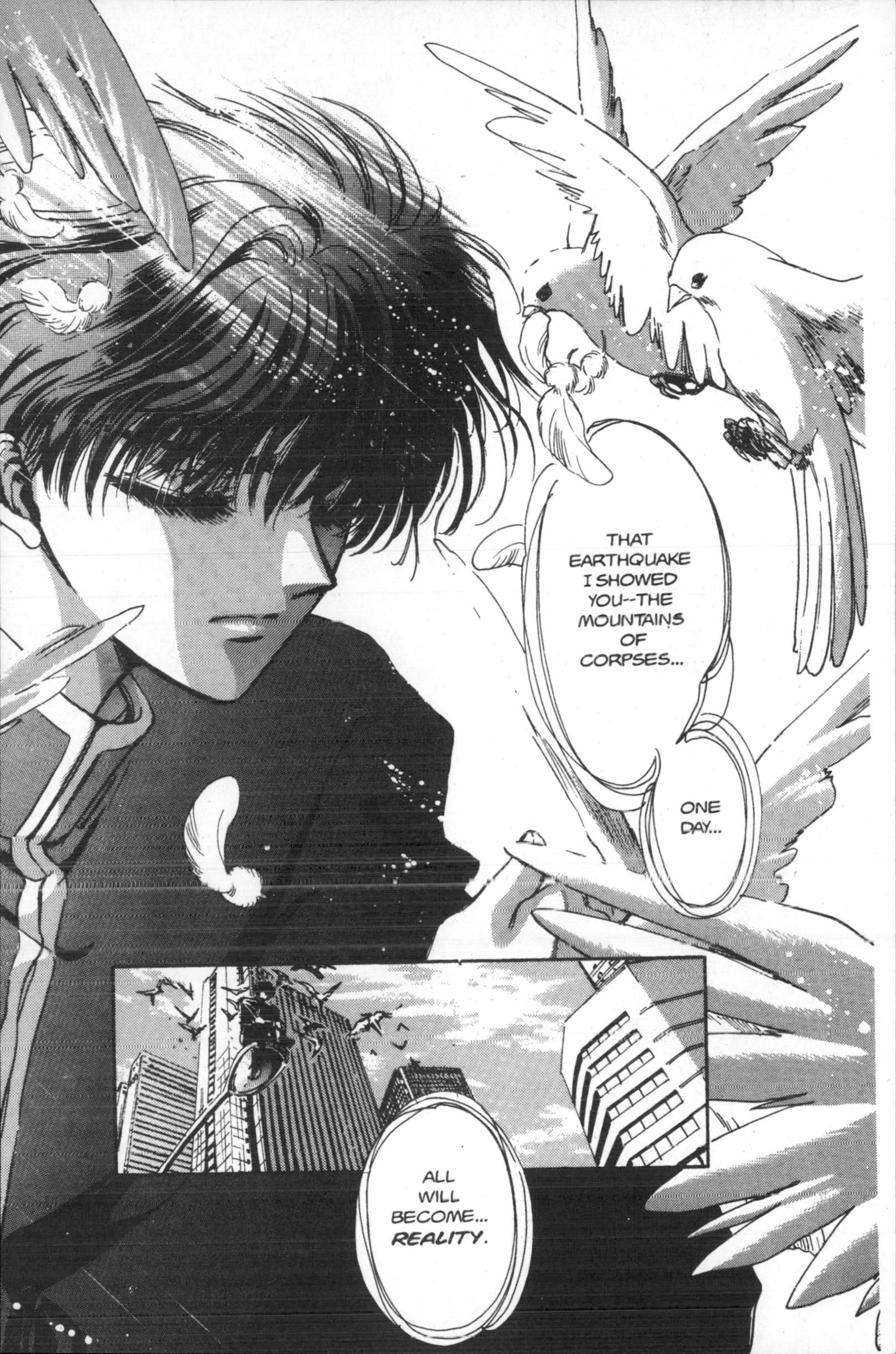
THAT EARTHQUAKE I SHOWED YOU--THE MOUNTAINS OF CORPSES...
ONE DAY...
ALL WILL BECOME... REALITY.

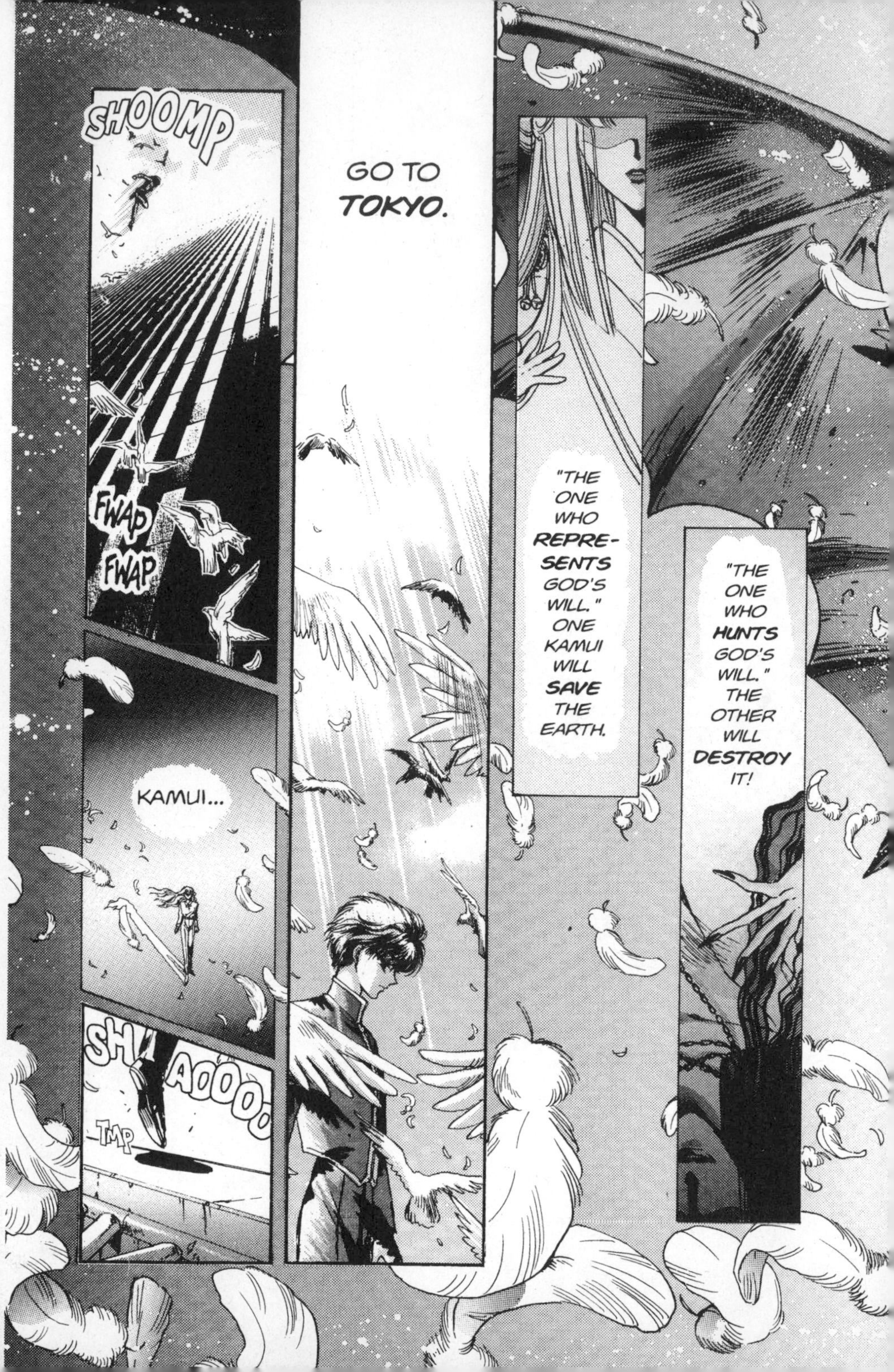
SHOOMP
FWAP
FWAP
KAMUI...
SHAAOOOO
TMP
GO TO TOKYO.
"THE ONE WHO REPRESENTS GOD'S WILL." ONE KAMUI WILL SAVE THE EARTH.
"THE ONE WHO HUNTS GOD'S WILL." THE OTHER WILL DESTROY IT!

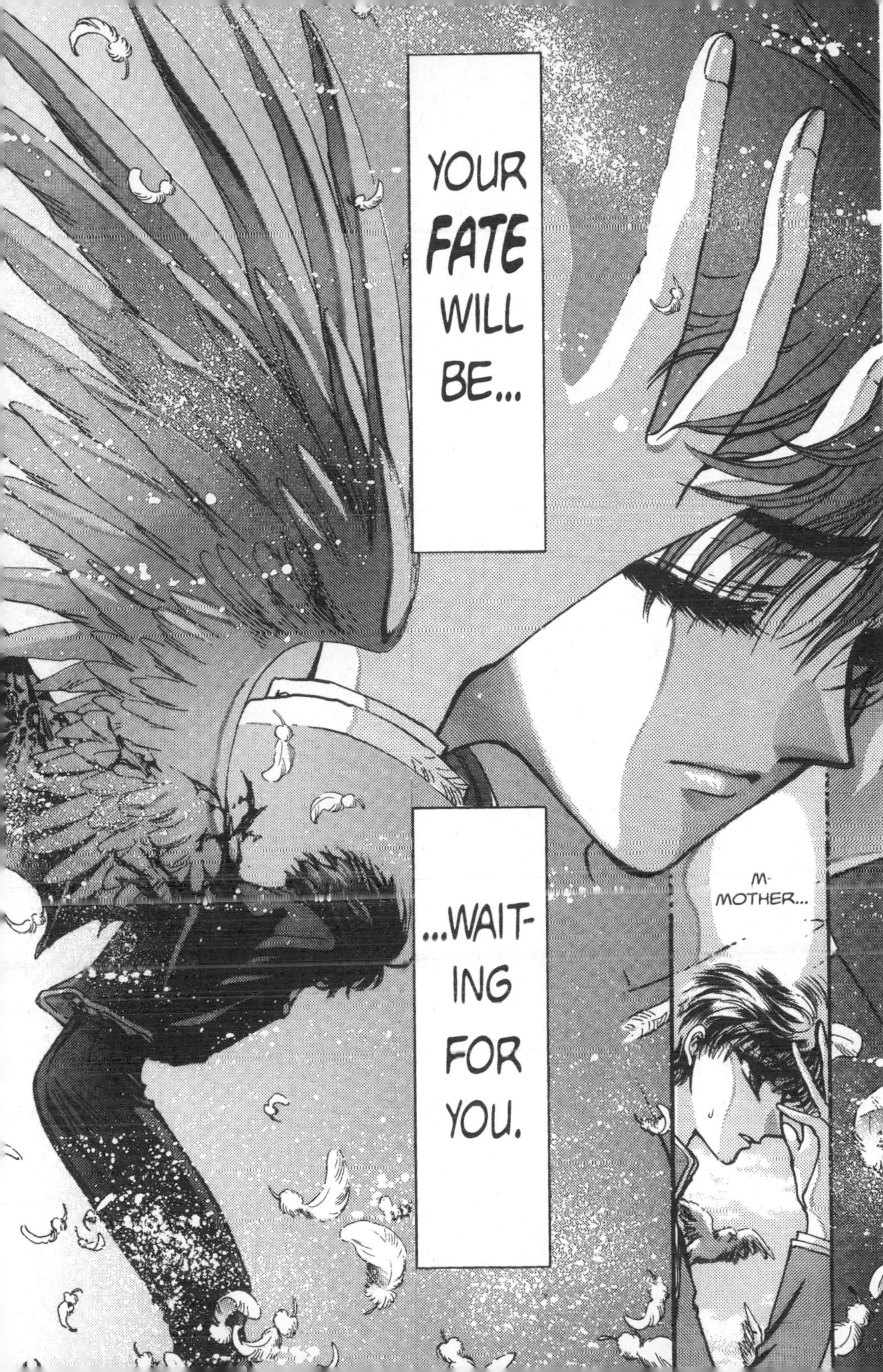
YOUR FATE WILL BE...
...WAIT-ING FOR YOU.
M-MOTHER...

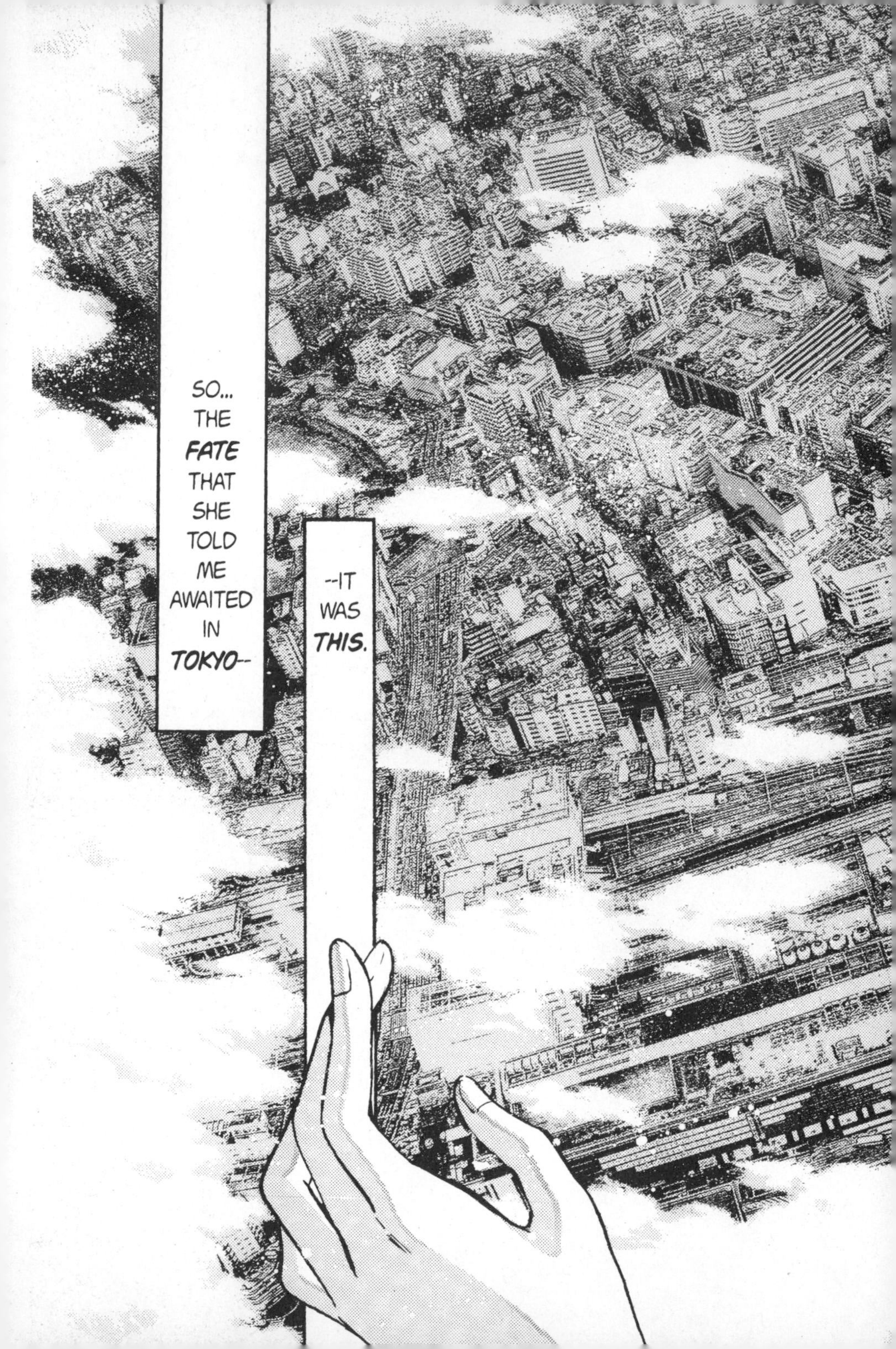
SO... THE *FATE* THAT SHE TOLD ME AWAITED IN *TOKYO*--
--IT WAS *THIS*.

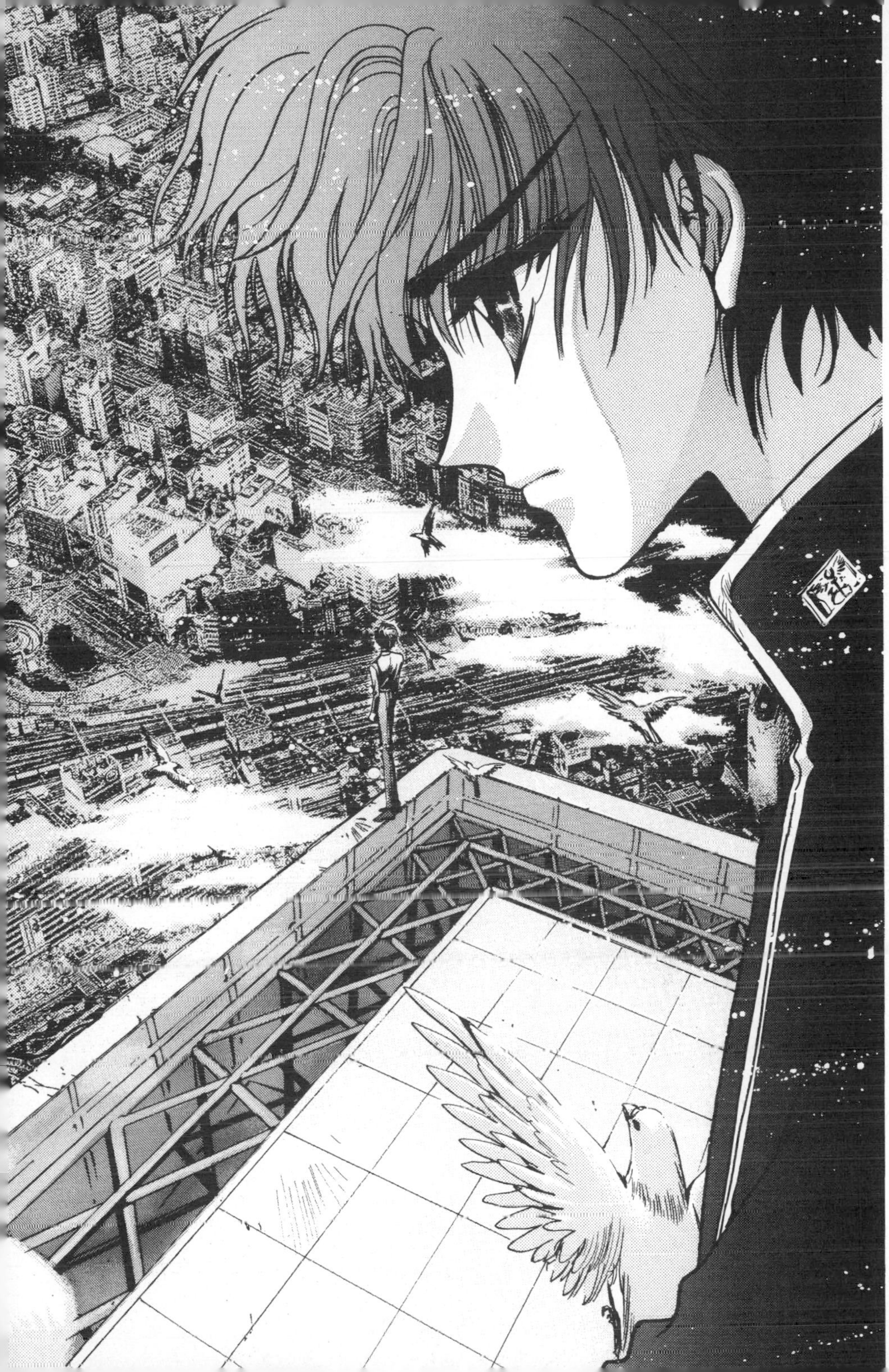

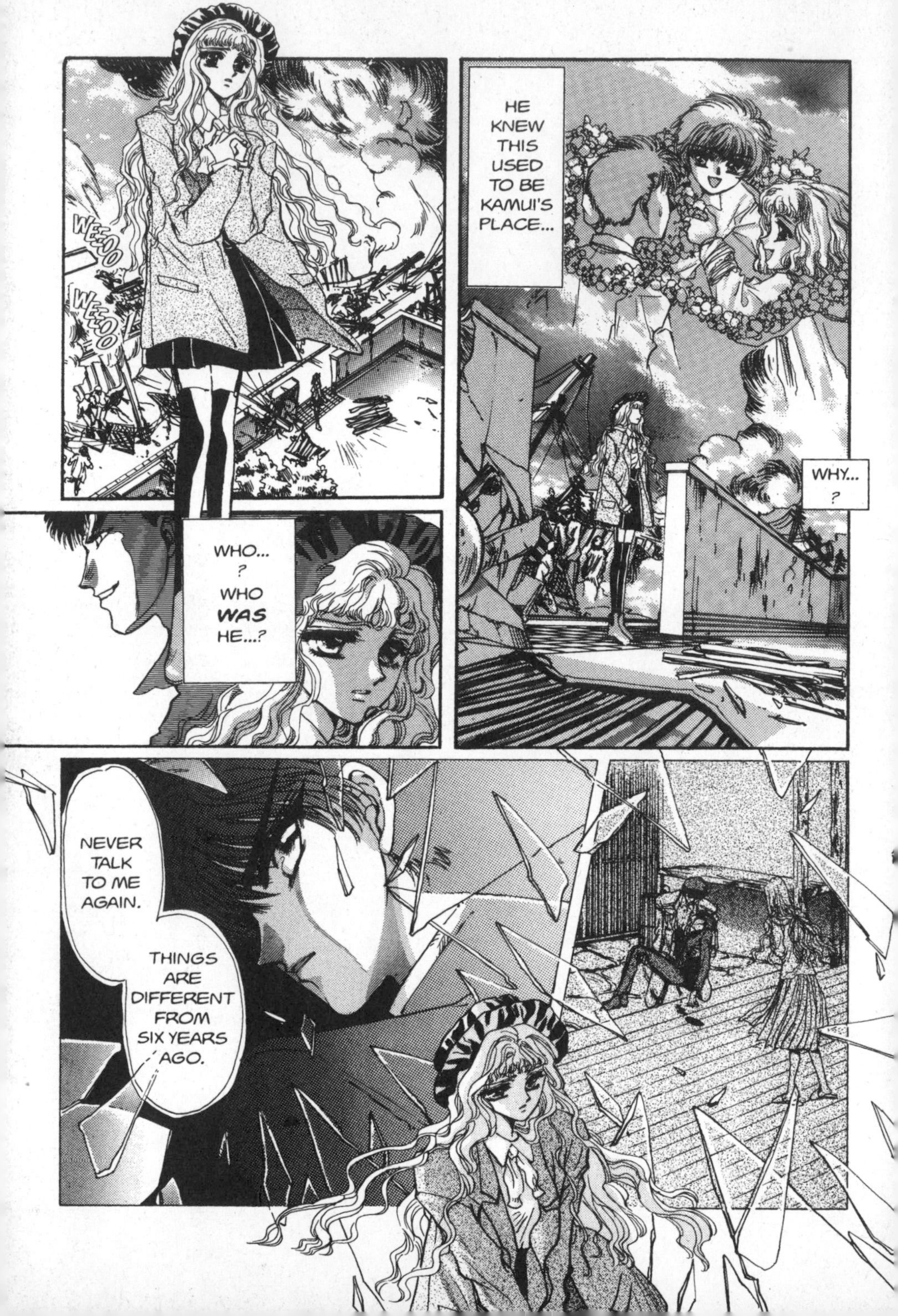
WEEOO
WEEOO
HE KNEW THIS USED TO BE KAMUI'S PLACE...
WHO...? WHO WAS HE...?
WHY...?
NEVER TALK TO ME AGAIN.
THINGS ARE DIFFERENT FROM SIX YEARS AGO.

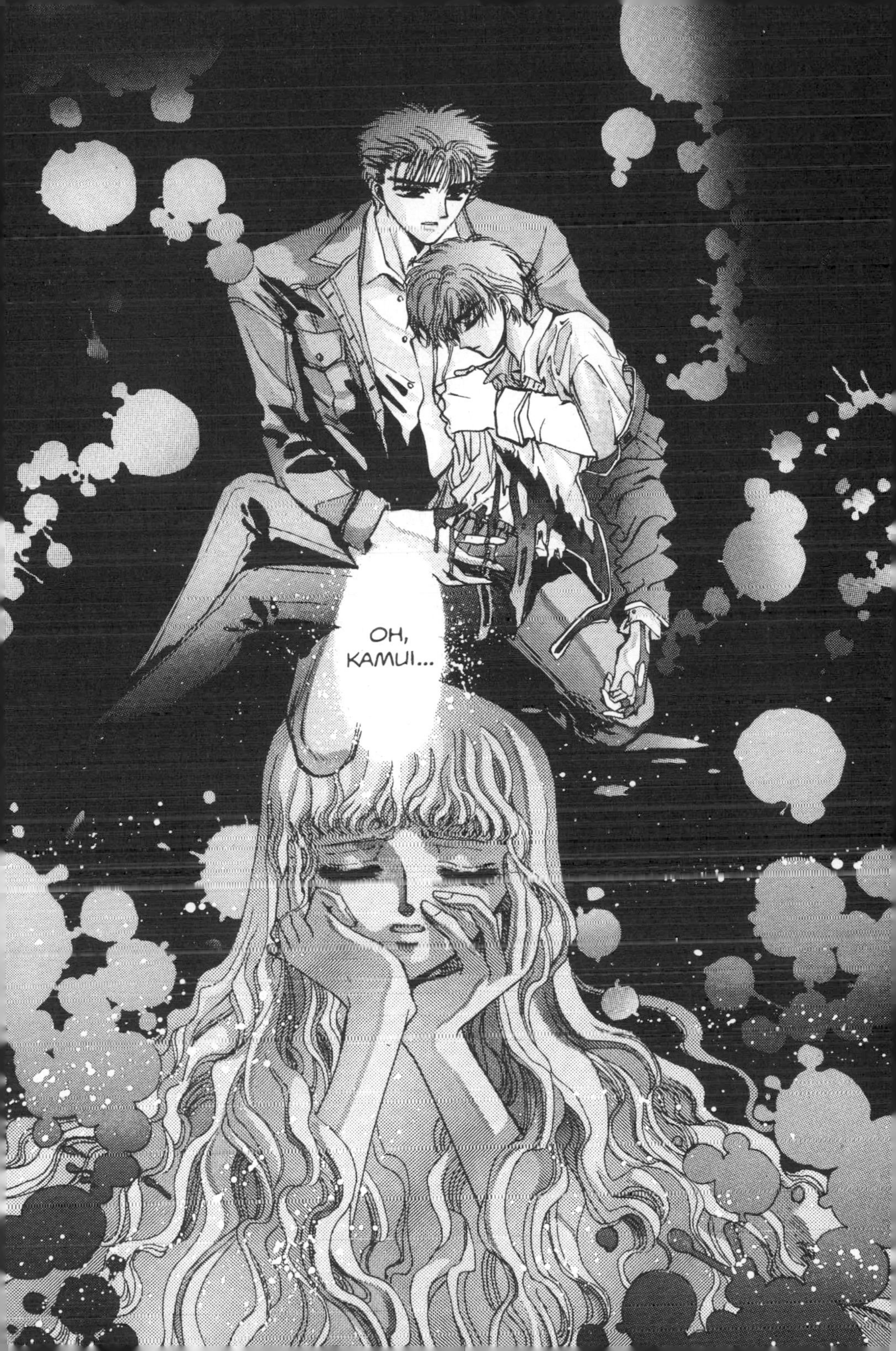
OH, KAMUI...

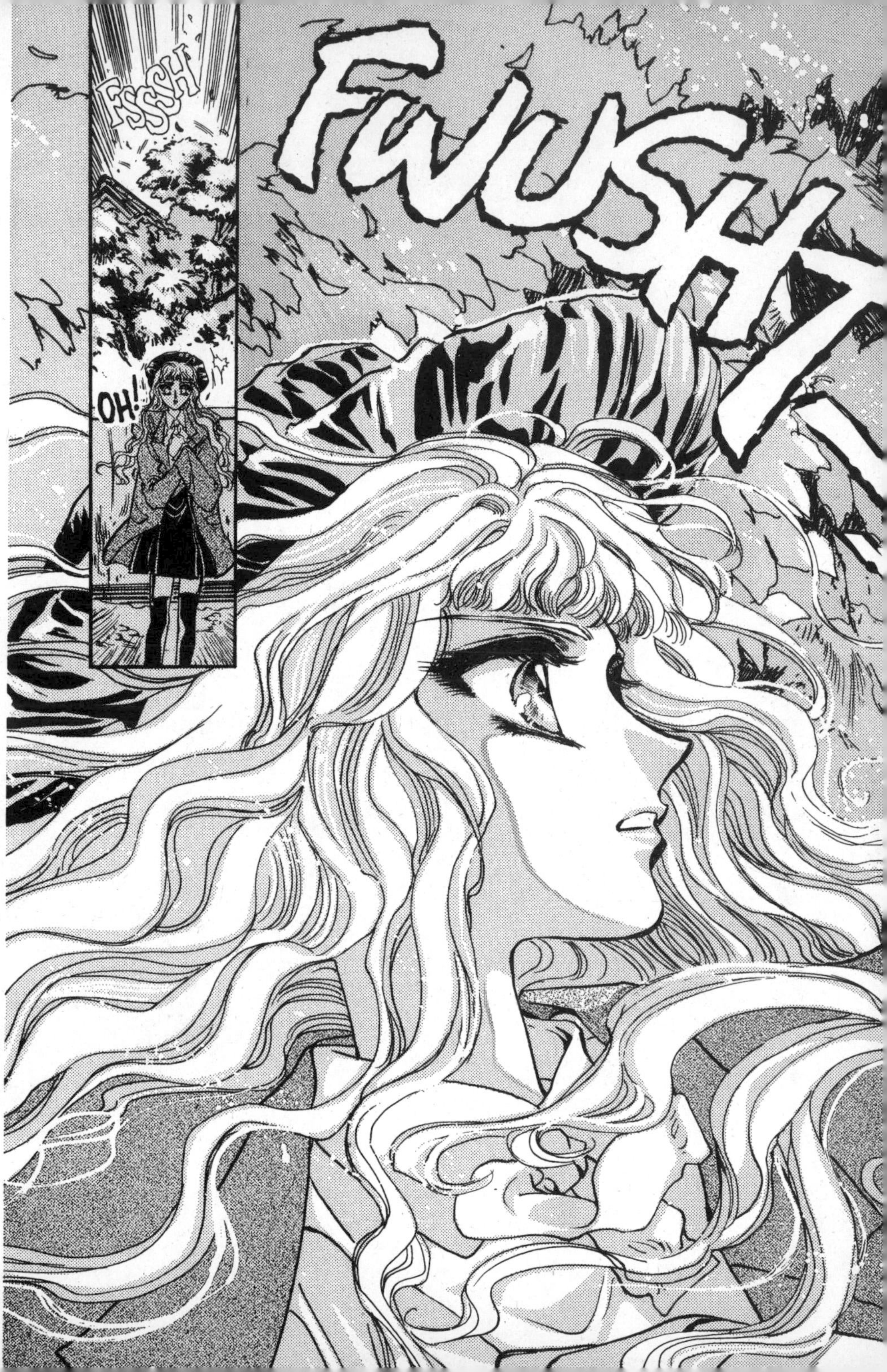
FSSSH
OH!
FWUSH

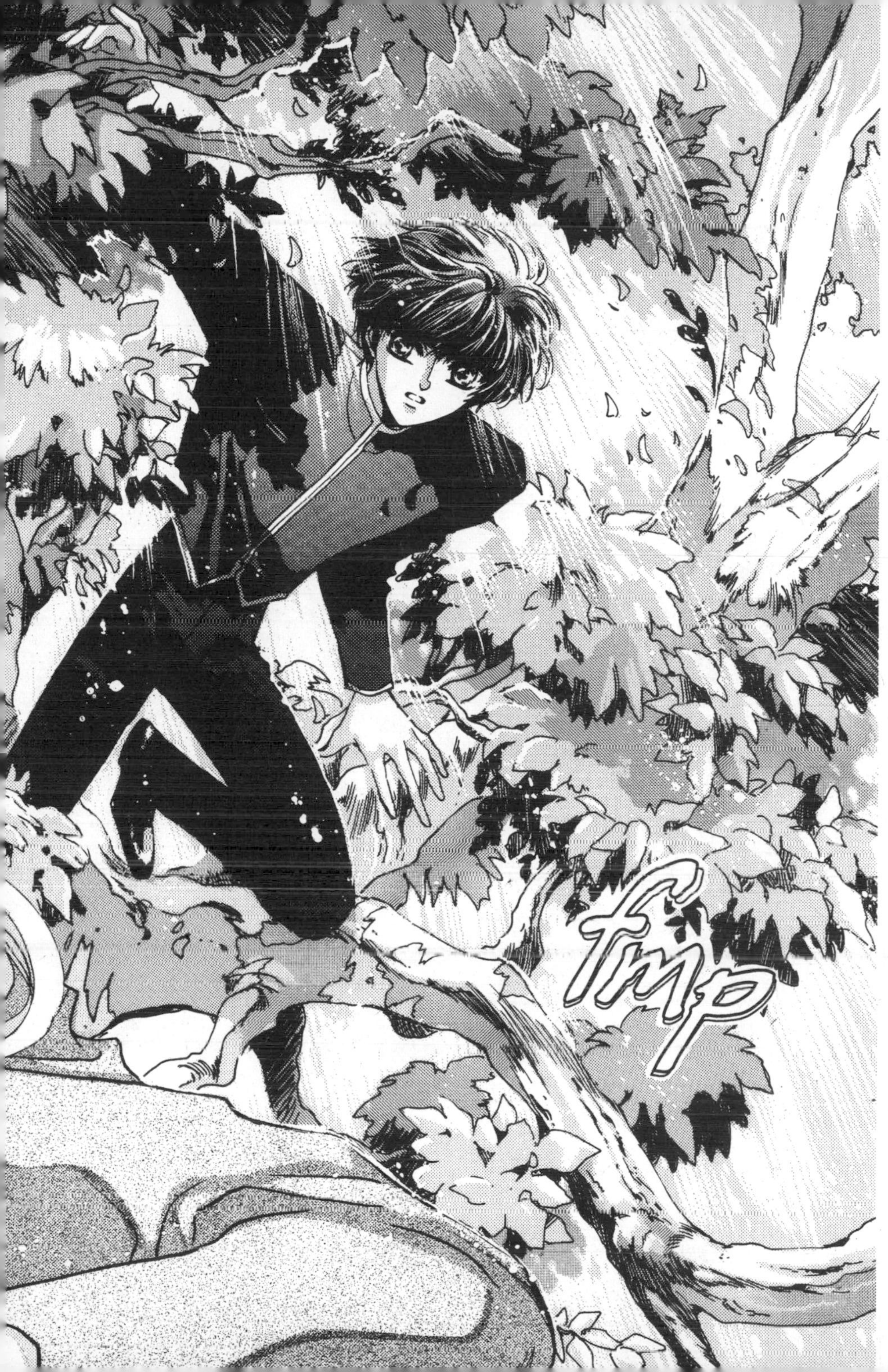
fmp

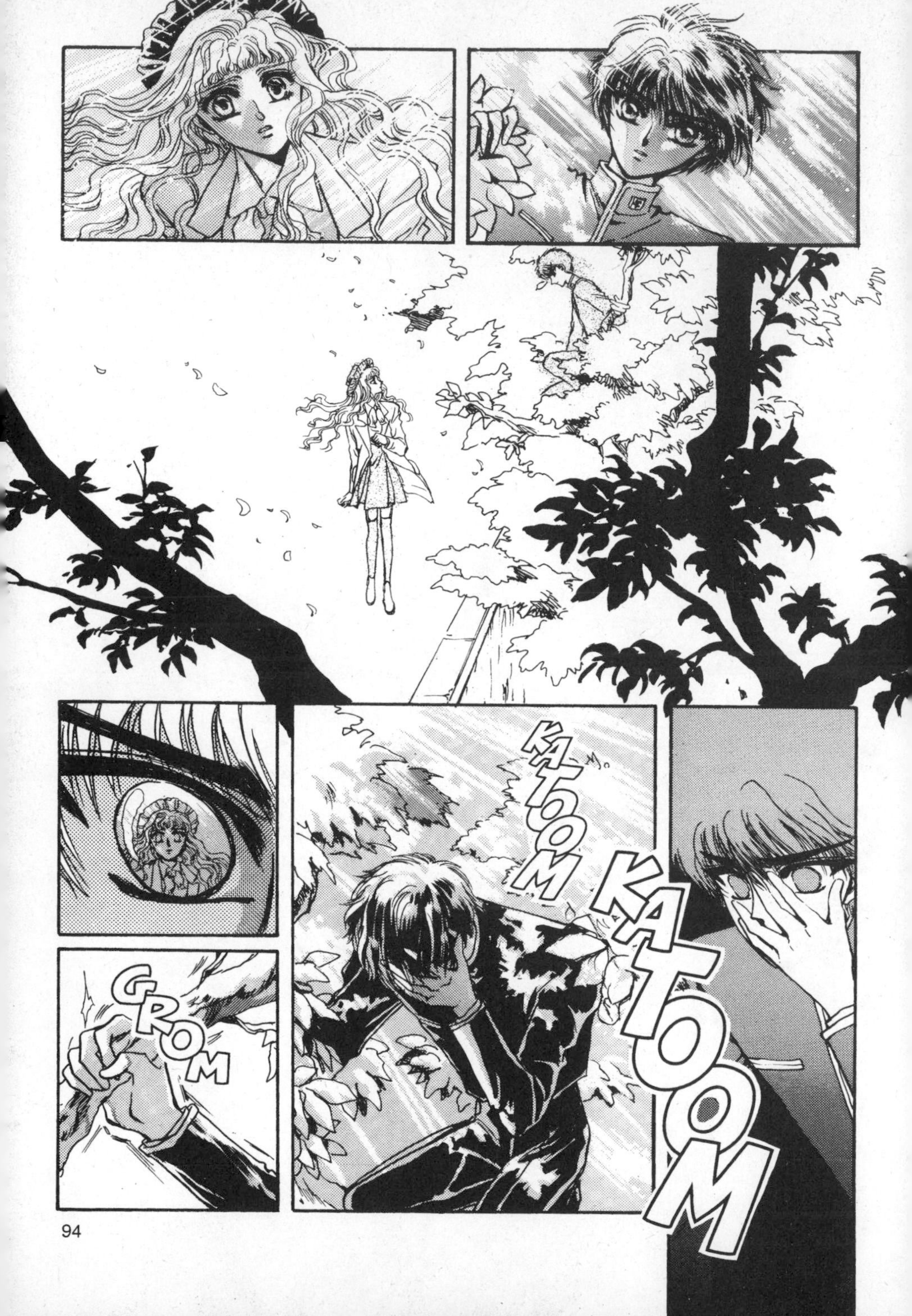
GROM
KATOOM
KATOOM

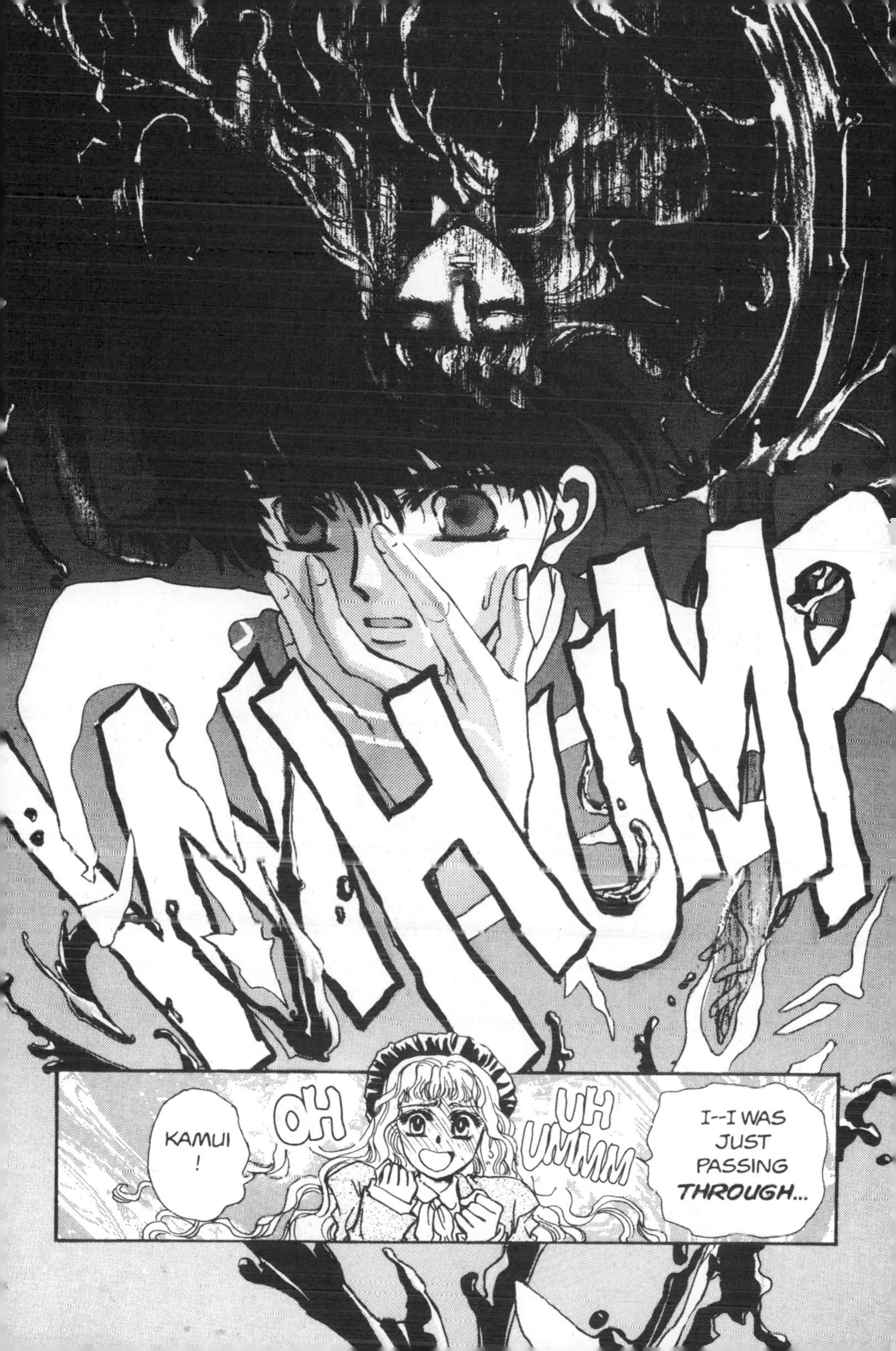
WHUMP
KAMUI!
OH
UH UMMM
I--I WAS JUST PASSING THROUGH...

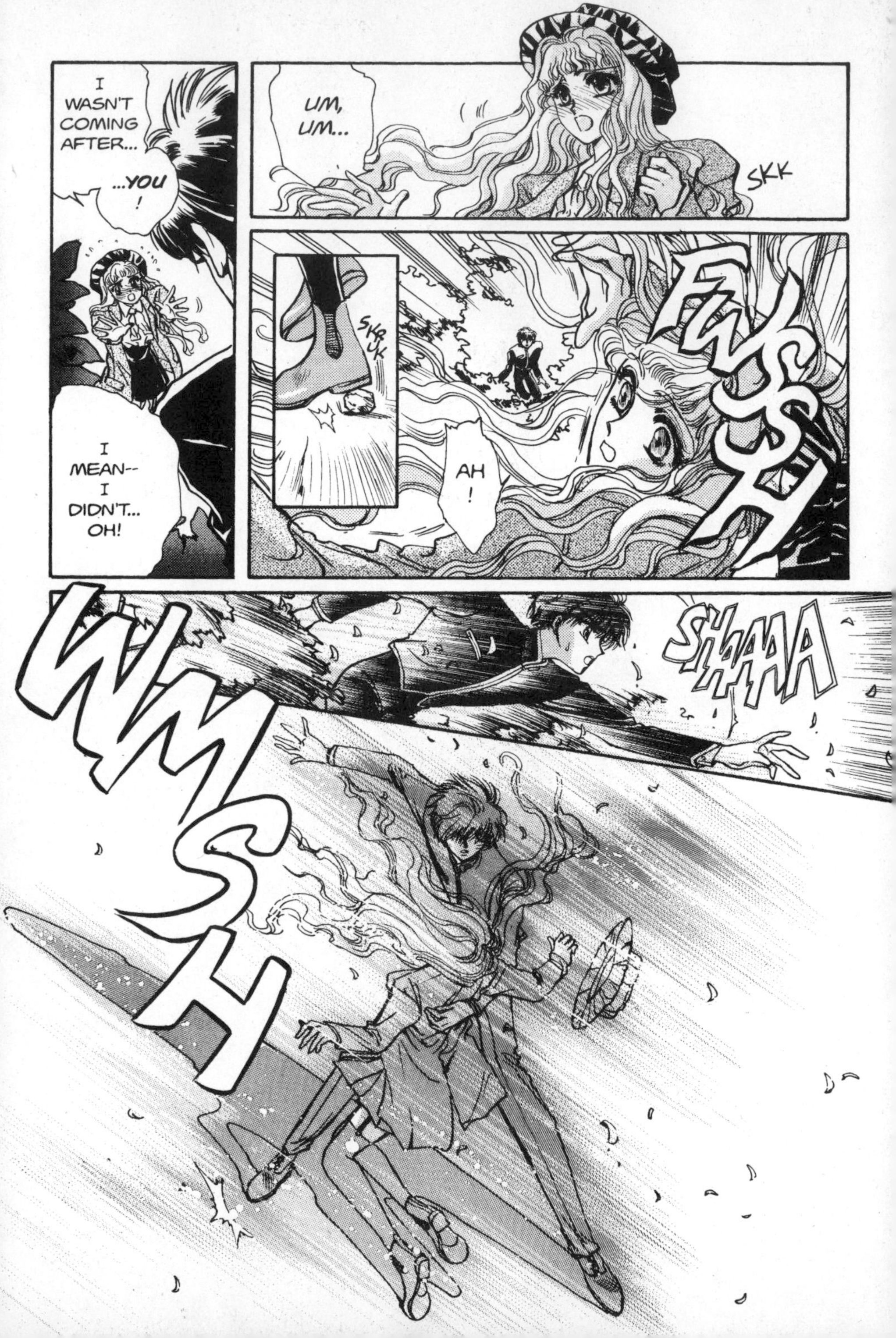
I WASN'T COMING AFTER...
...YOU!
I MEAN-- I DIDN'T... OH!
UM, UM...
SKK
SKRUK
AH!
FWSSH
SHAAA
WMSH

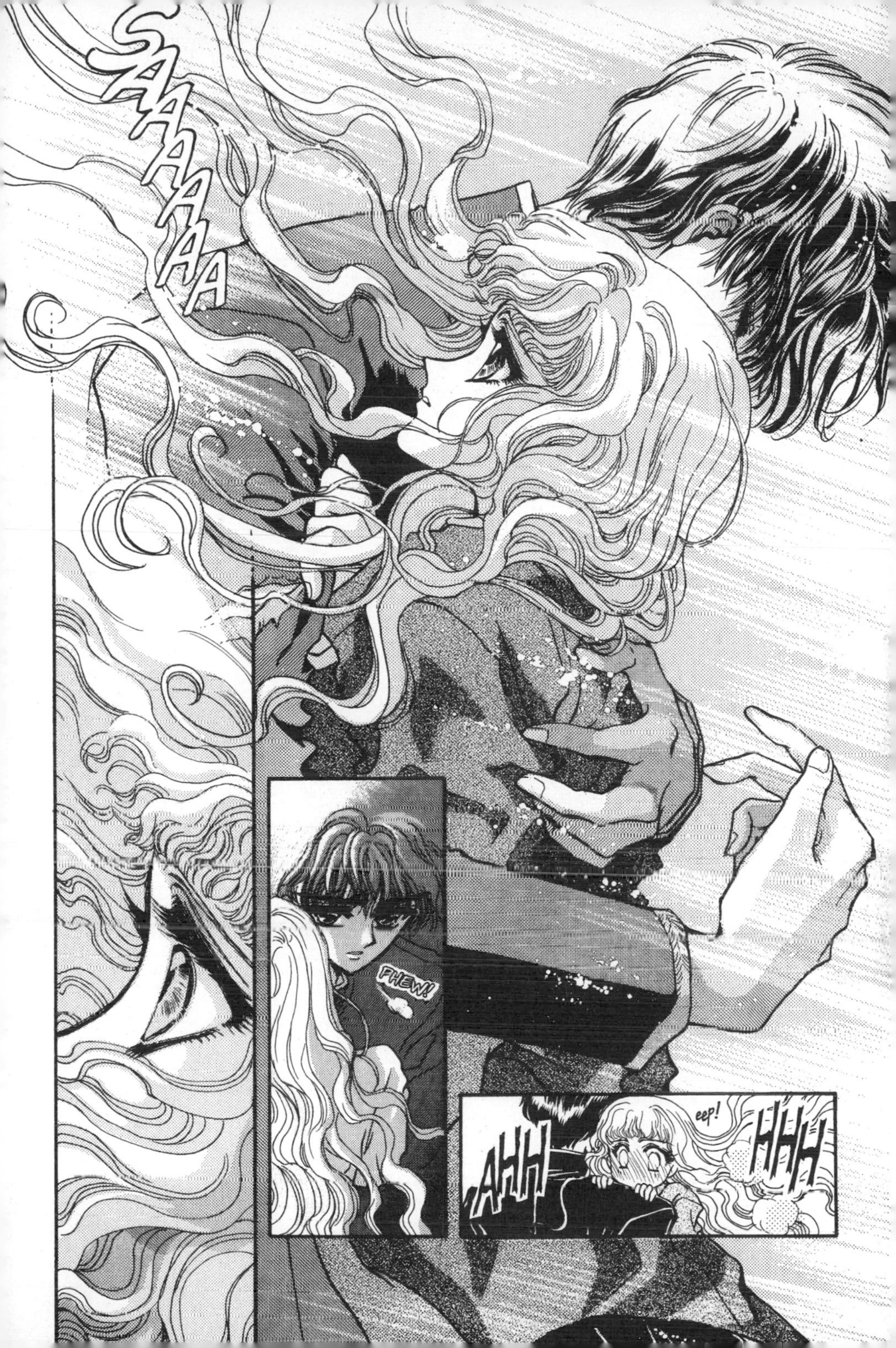
SAAAAAA
FHEW!
AHHHHH
eep!

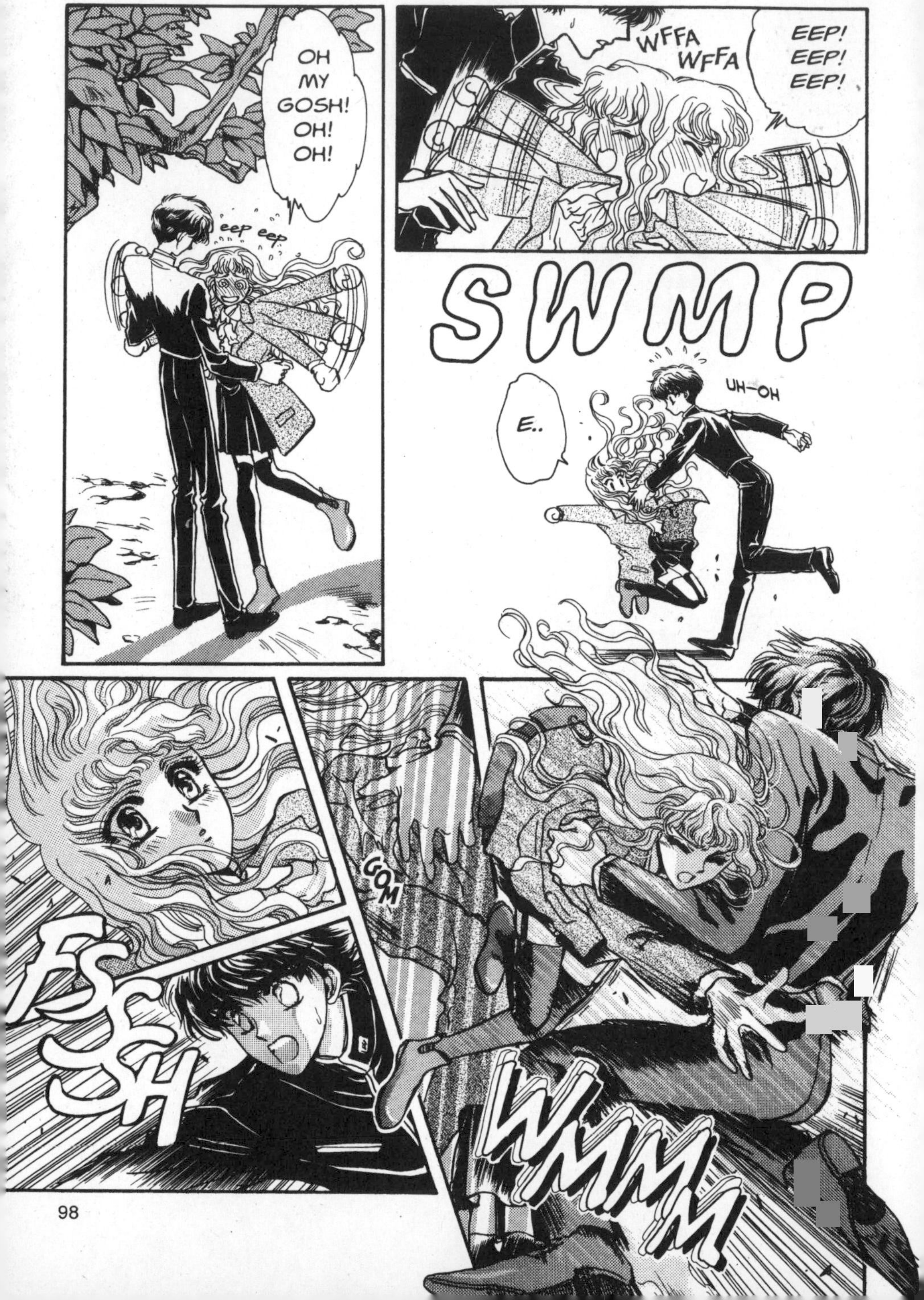
OH MY GOSH! OH! OH!
eep eep
WFFA WFFA
EEP! EEP! EEP!
SWMP
E..
UH-OH
FSSH
GOM
WMMM

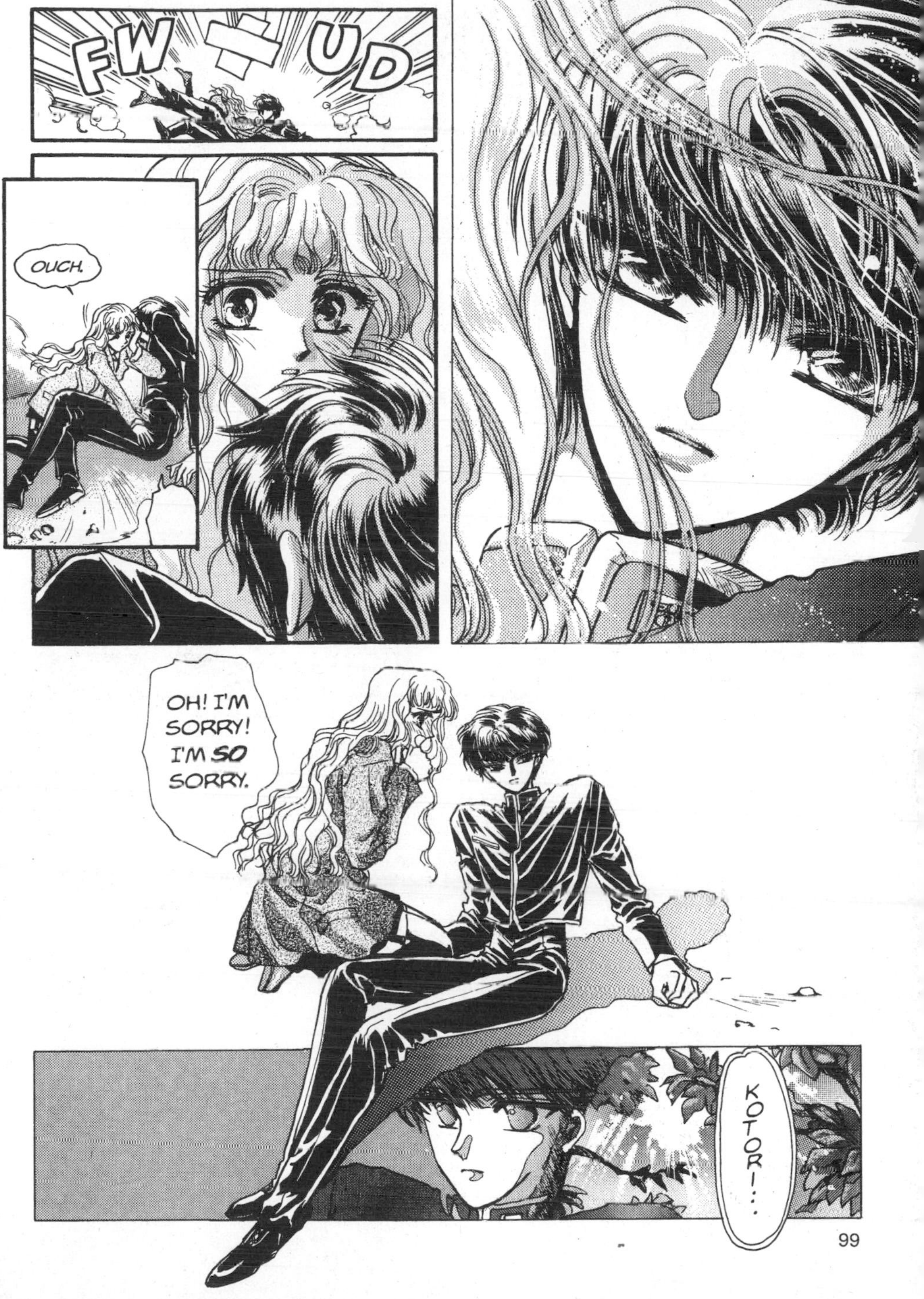
FWUD
OUCH.
OH! I'M SORRY! I'M SO SORRY.
KOTORI!..

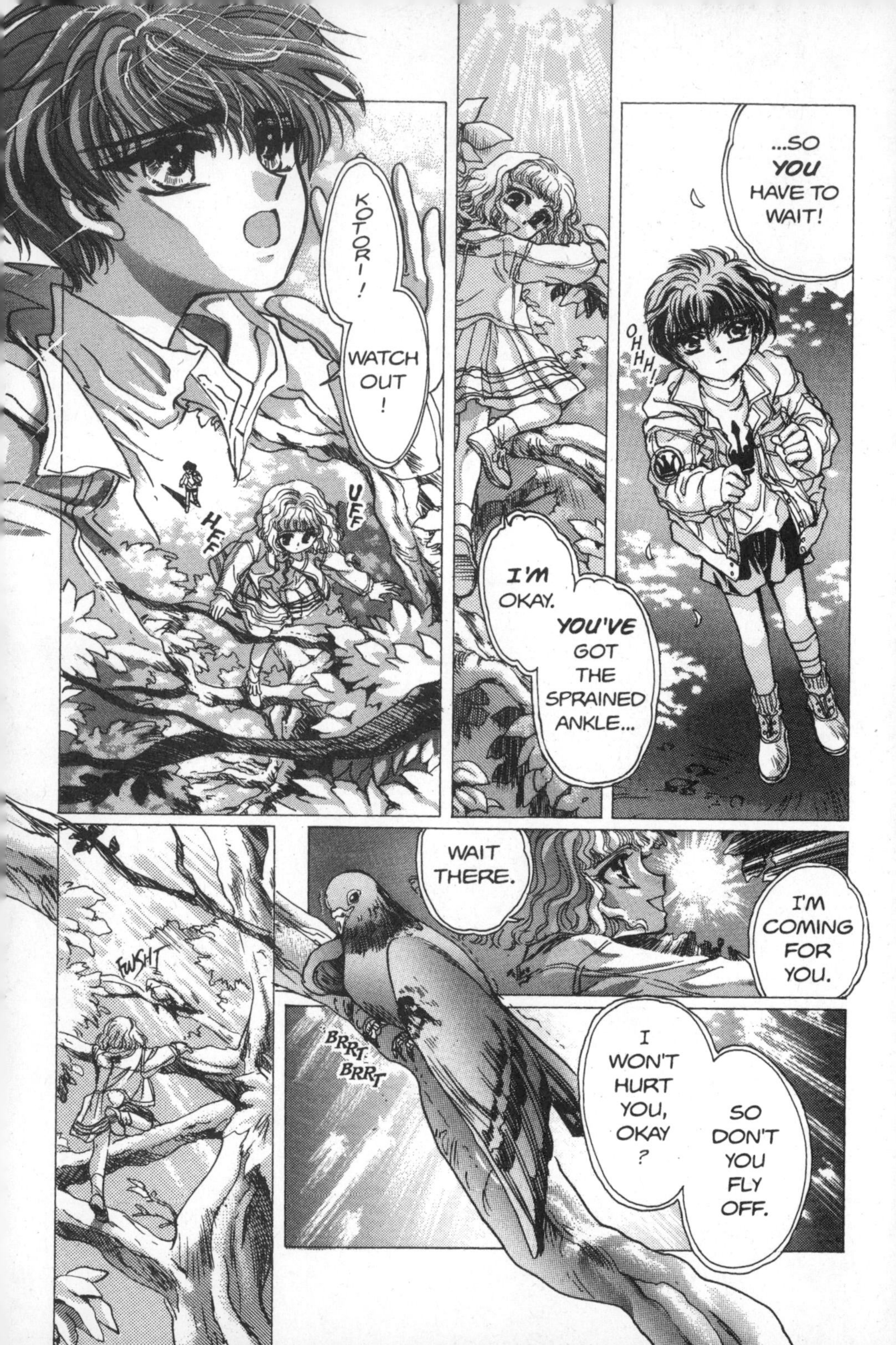
KOTORI! WATCH OUT!
HEF
UFF
I'M OKAY. YOU'VE GOT THE SPRAINED ANKLE...
...SO YOU HAVE TO WAIT!
OHHHH!
FWSHT
WAIT THERE.
I'M COMING FOR YOU.
BRRT BRRT
I WON'T HURT YOU, OKAY?
SO DON'T YOU FLY OFF.

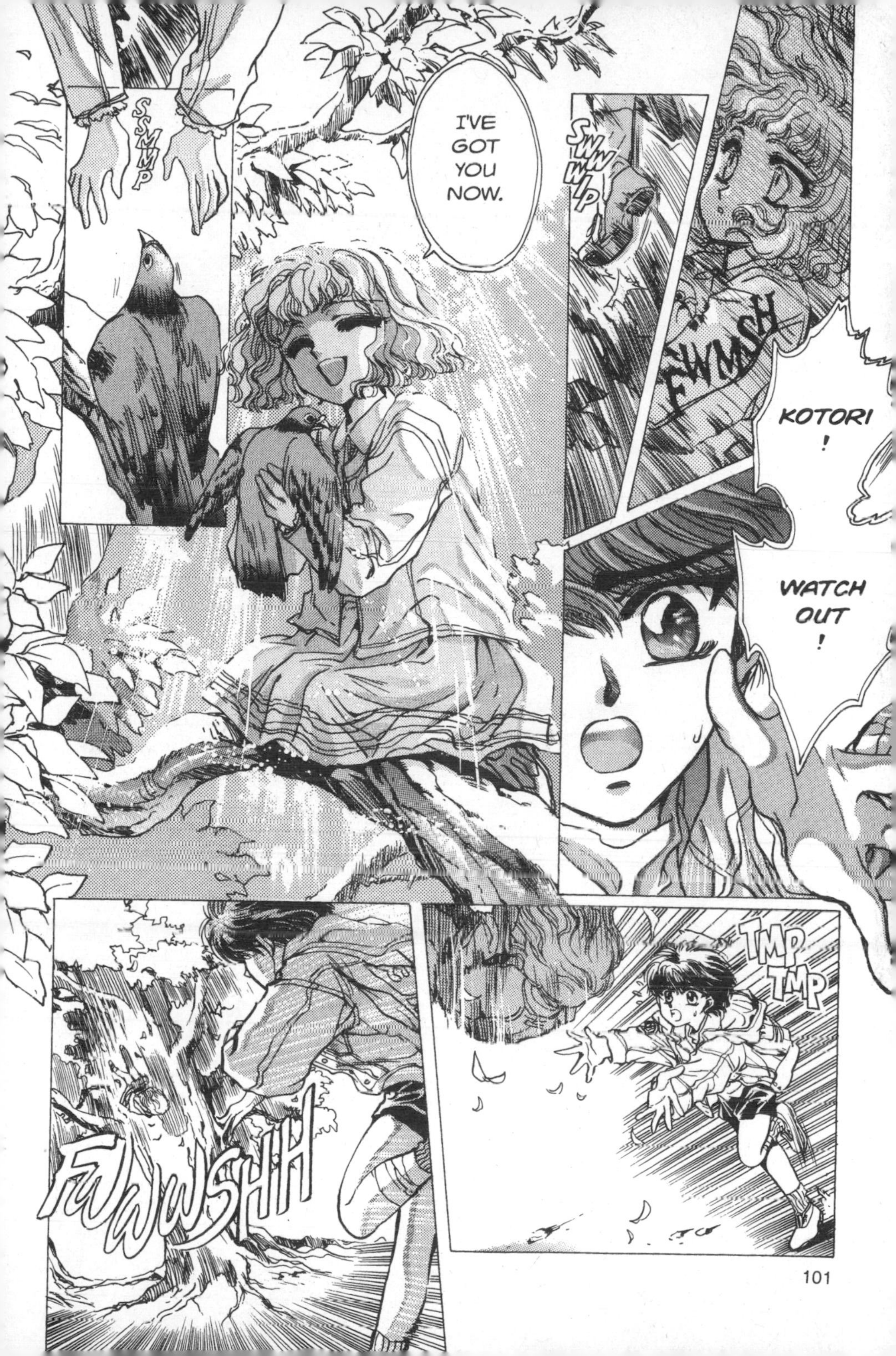
SSMMP
I'VE GOT YOU NOW.
SWWWIP
FWUSH
KOTORI!
WATCH OUT!
FWWSHH
TMP TMP

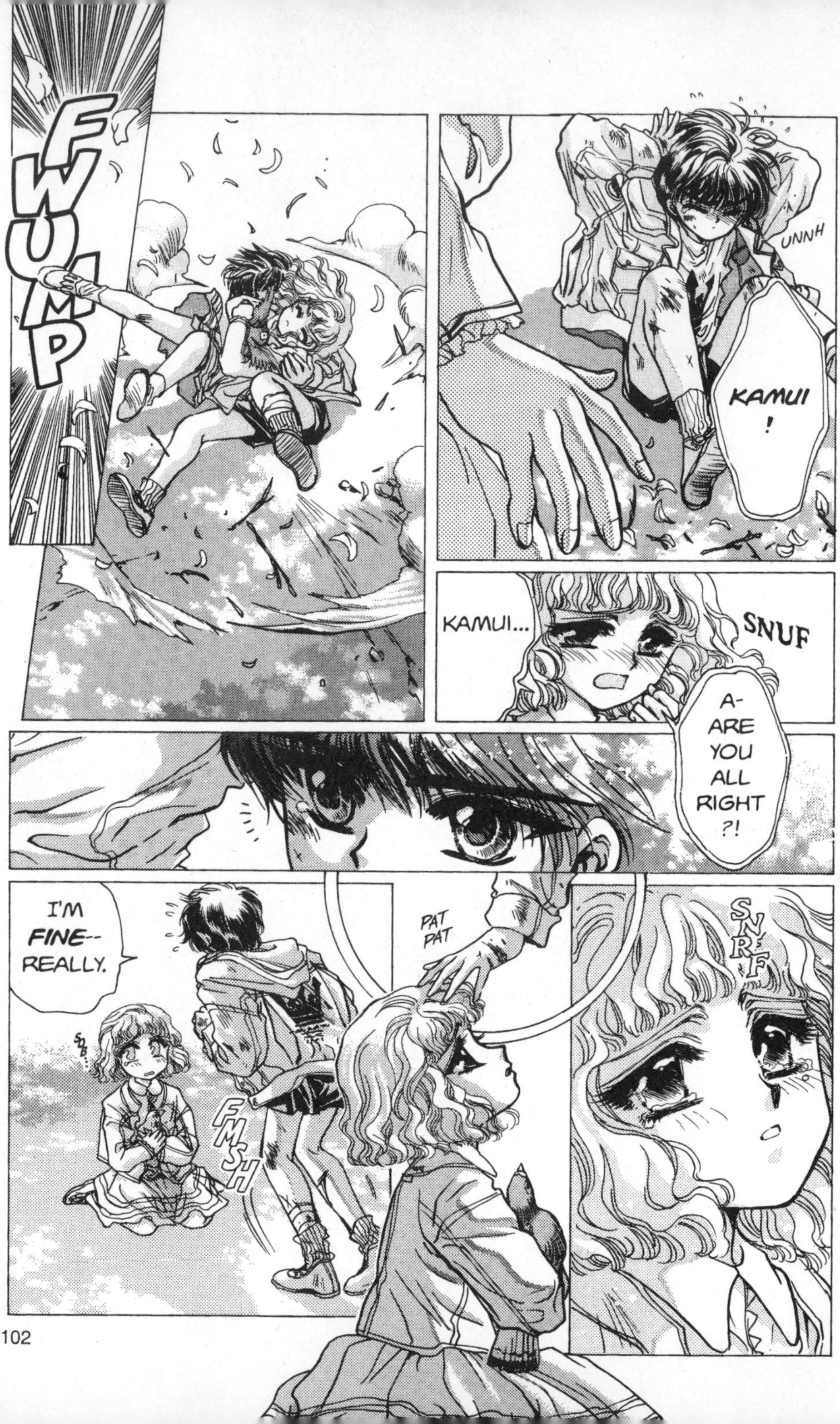
FWUMP
UNNH
KAMUI!
KAMUI...
SNUF
A- ARE YOU ALL RIGHT?!
I'M FINE-- REALLY.
SOB...
FMSH
PAT PAT
SNRF

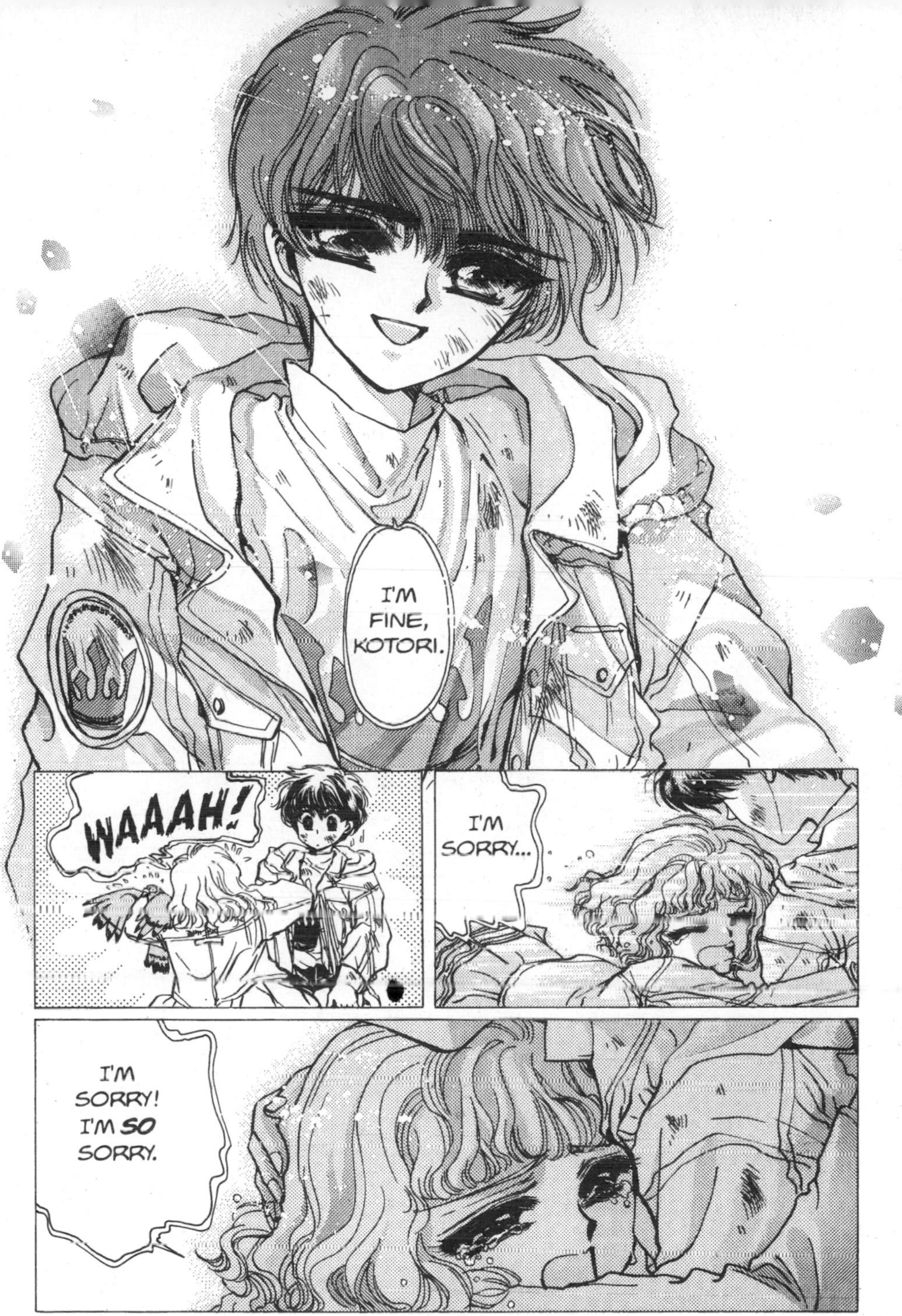
I'M FINE, KOTORI.
WAAAH!
I'M SORRY...
I'M SORRY! I'M *SO* SORRY.

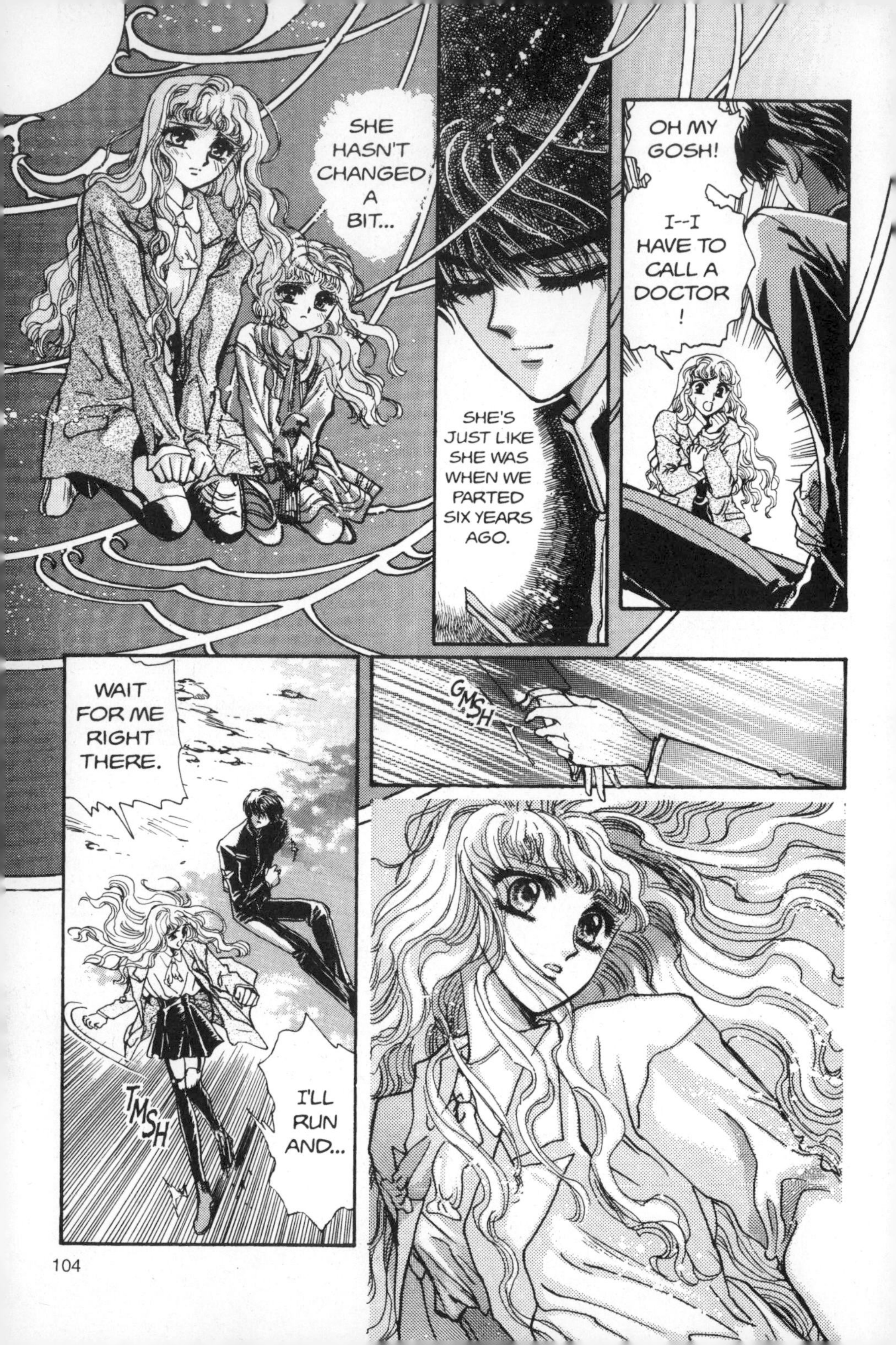
SHE HASN'T CHANGED A BIT...
SHE'S JUST LIKE SHE WAS WHEN WE PARTED SIX YEARS AGO.
OH MY GOSH!
I--I HAVE TO CALL A DOCTOR!
WAIT FOR ME RIGHT THERE.
GMSH
I'LL RUN AND...
TMSH

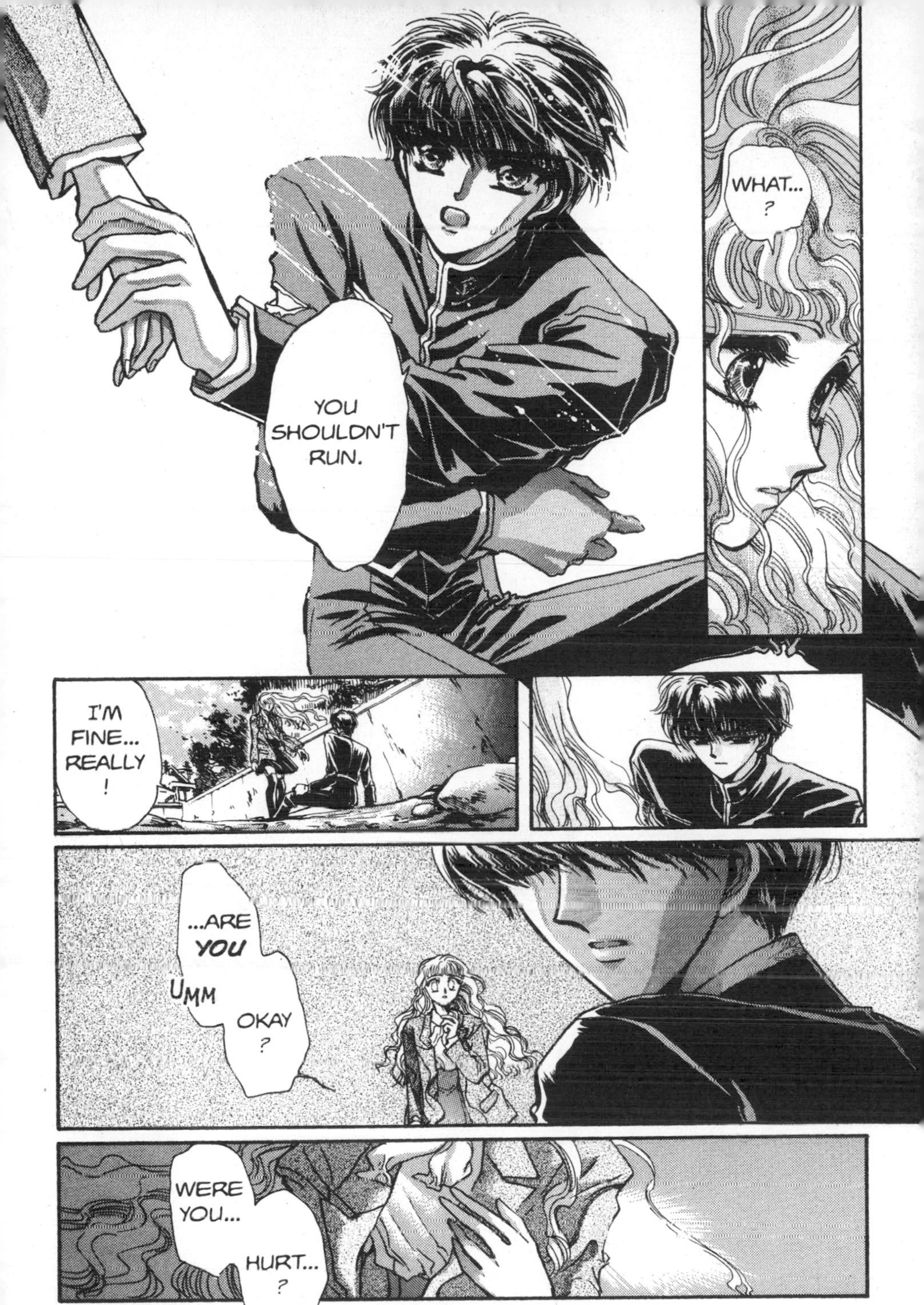
YOU SHOULDN'T RUN.
WHAT... ?
I'M FINE... REALLY !
...ARE YOU
UMM
OKAY ?
WERE YOU...
HURT... ?

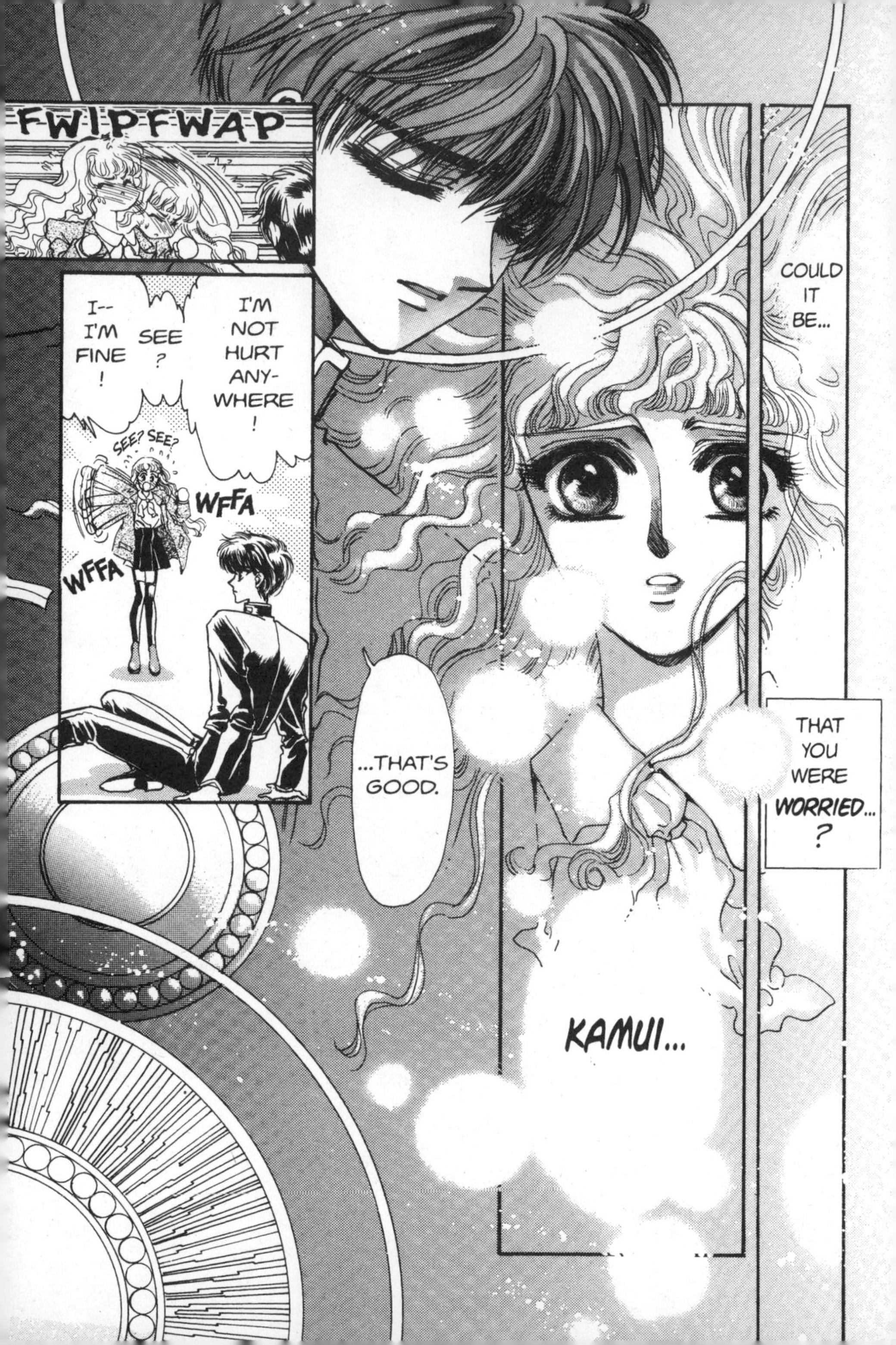

FWIPFWAP
I-- I'M FINE!
SEE?
I'M NOT HURT ANYWHERE!
SEE? SEE?
WFFA
WFFA
...THAT'S GOOD.
COULD IT BE...
THAT YOU WERE **WORRIED...?**
KAMUI...

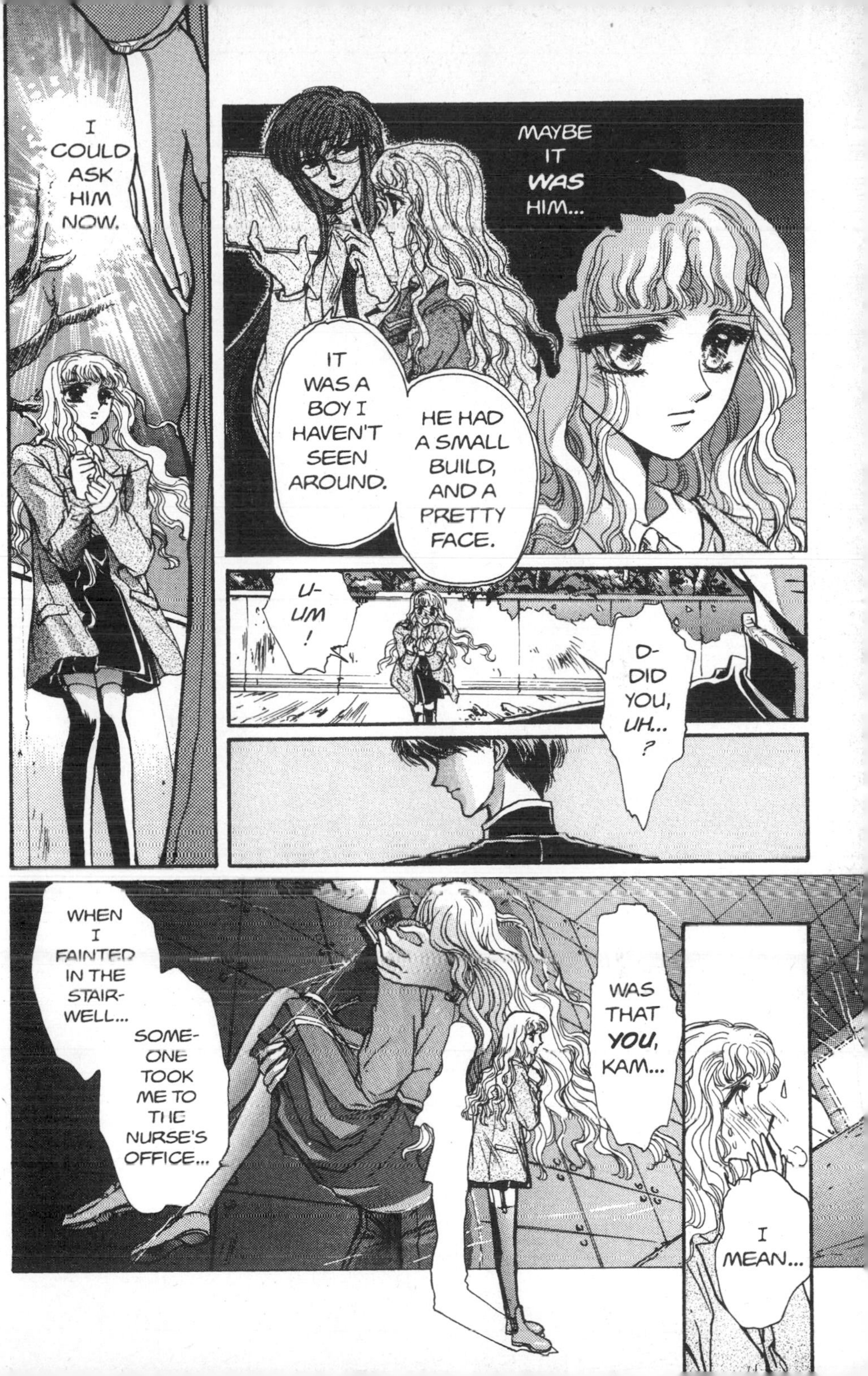
I COULD ASK HIM NOW.
MAYBE IT WAS HIM...
IT WAS A BOY I HAVEN'T SEEN AROUND.
HE HAD A SMALL BUILD, AND A PRETTY FACE.
U-UM!
D-DID YOU, UH...?
WHEN I FAINTED IN THE STAIR-WELL...
SOME-ONE TOOK ME TO THE NURSE'S OFFICE...
WAS THAT YOU, KAM...
I MEAN...

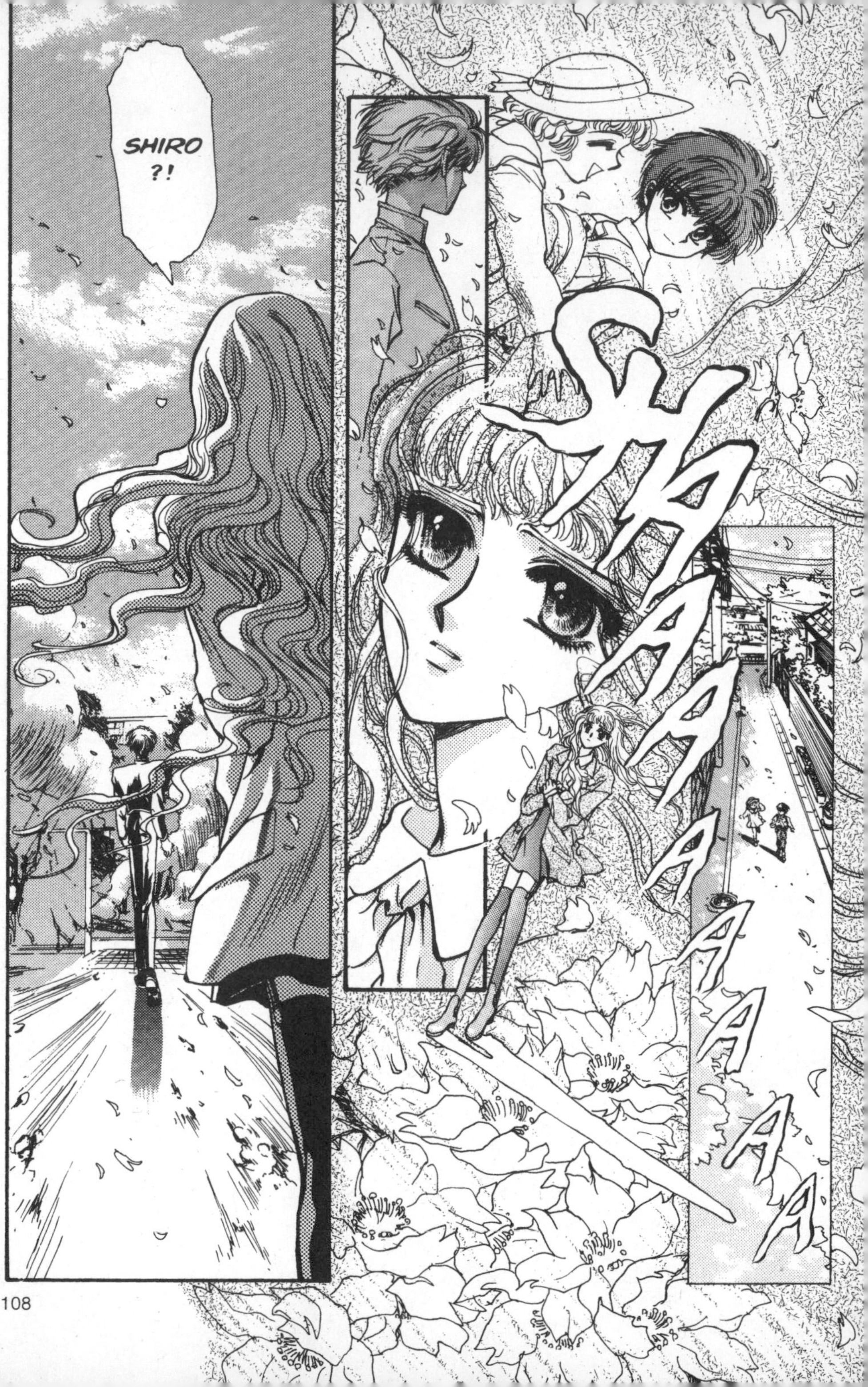
SHIRO ?!
SHAAAAAAAAAA

WHOOSH

WSSSH

AAAH!

FWWT

FWOP

MY HAT...

WMPA WMPA

SHAAA

UMF
UMF

WELL, DUH

BOING

HANG ON! I'LL CLIMB UP.

I-I CAN'T REACH IT.

109

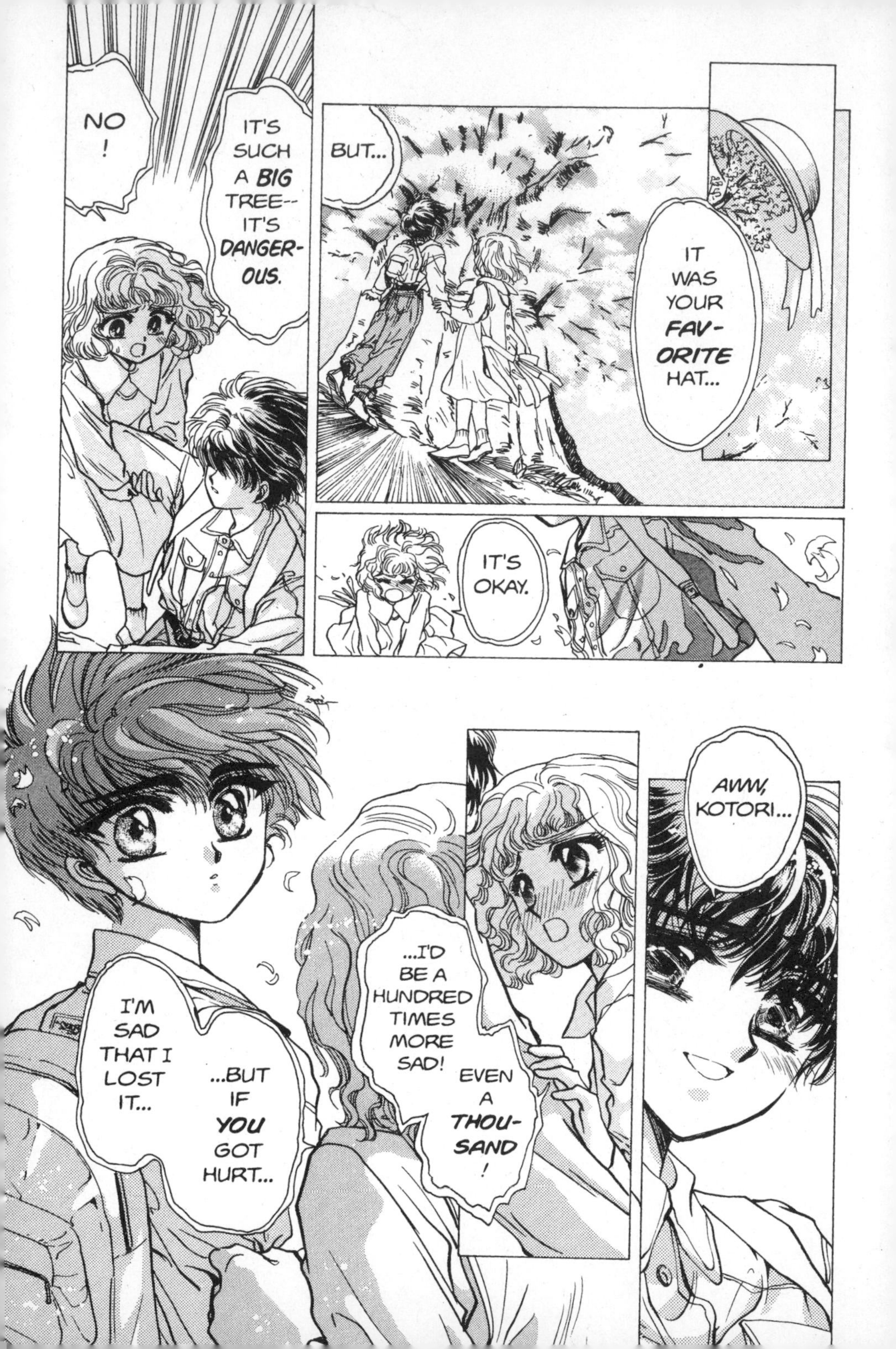
NO!
IT'S SUCH A BIG TREE-- IT'S DANGEROUS.
BUT...
IT WAS YOUR FAVORITE HAT...
IT'S OKAY.
I'M SAD THAT I LOST IT...
...BUT IF YOU GOT HURT...
...I'D BE A HUNDRED TIMES MORE SAD!
EVEN A THOUSAND!
AWW, KOTORI...

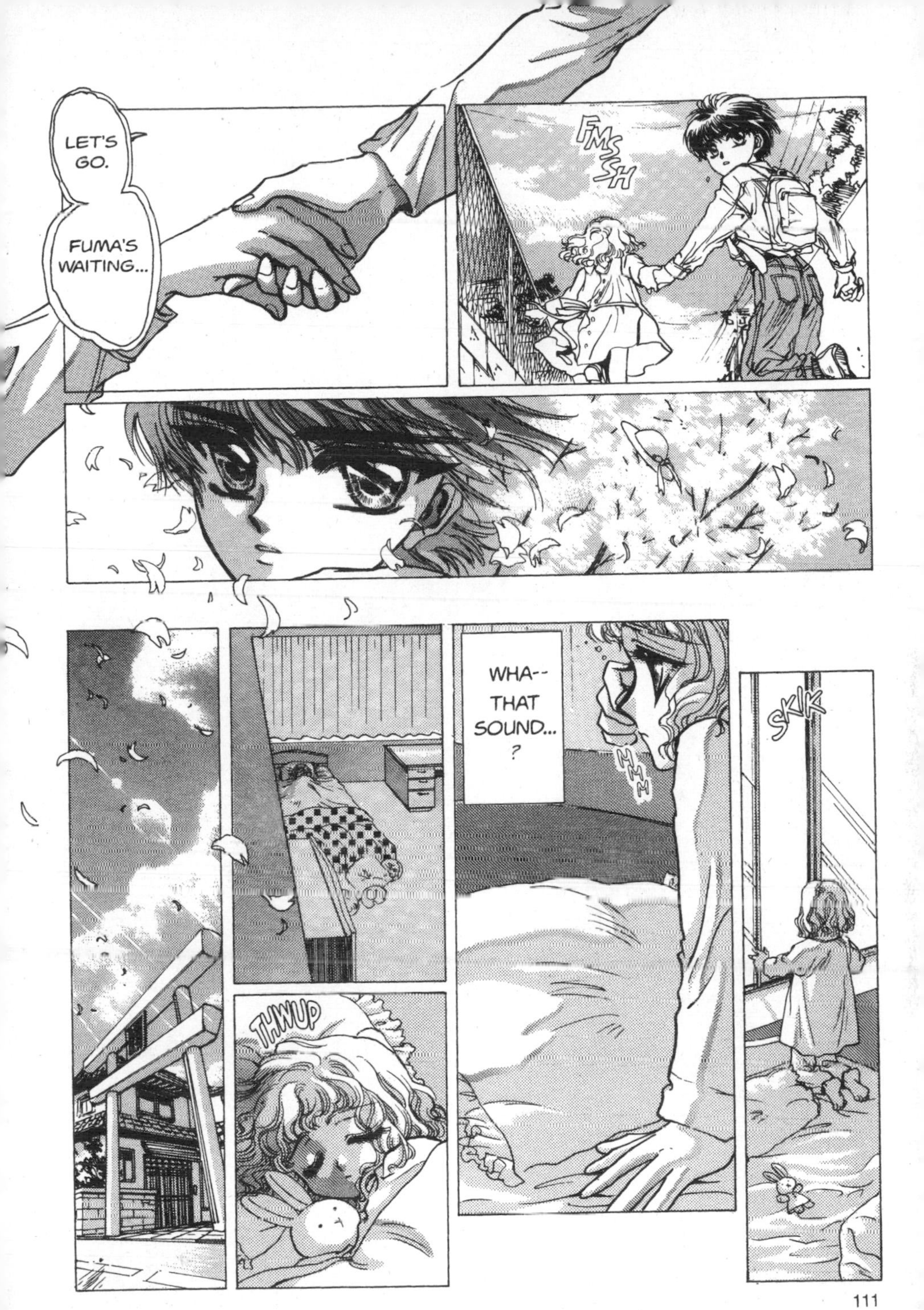

LET'S GO.
FUMA'S WAITING...
FMSSH
THWUP
WHA-- THAT SOUND... ?
HMMM
SKIK

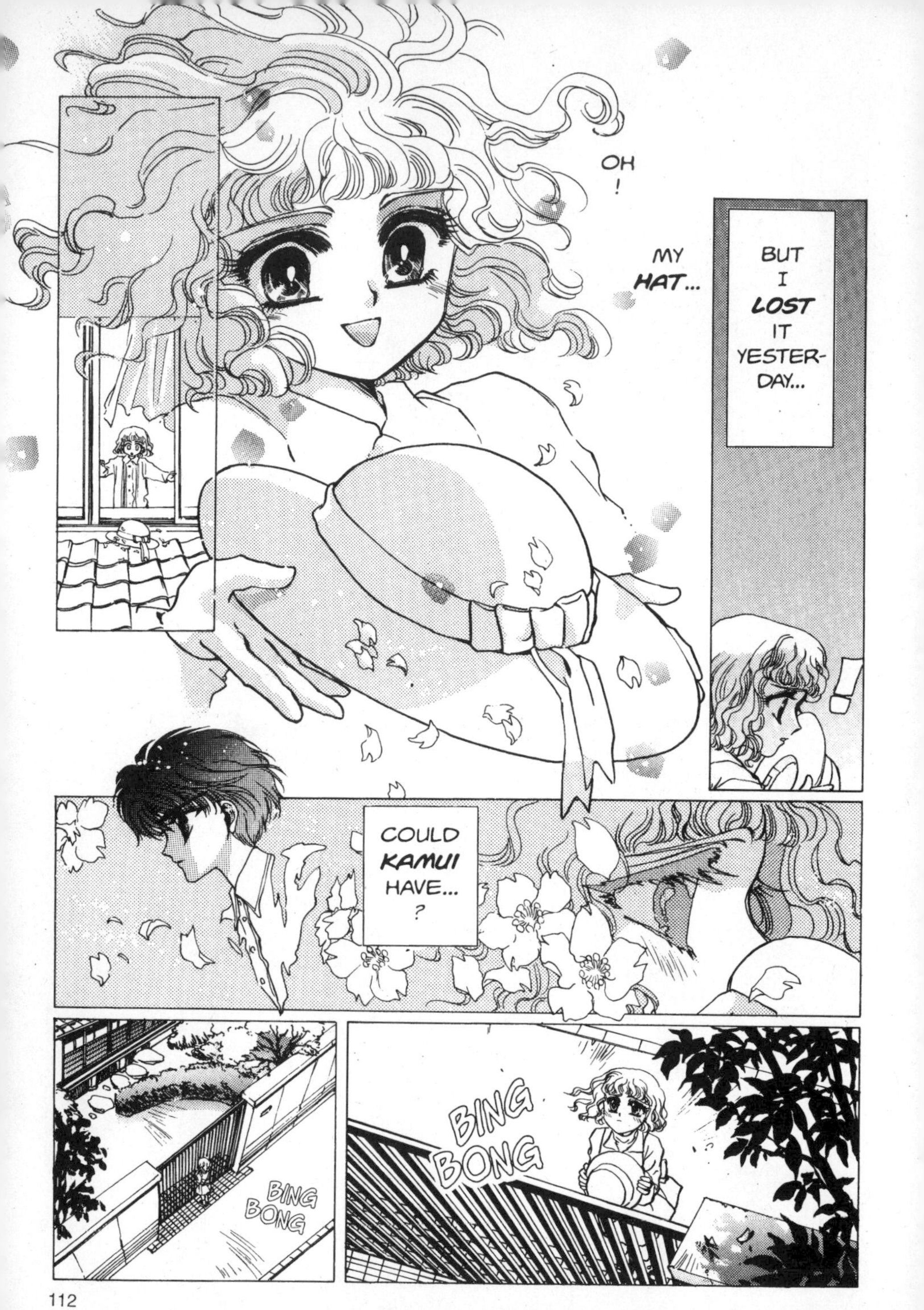
OH !
MY HAT...
BUT I LOST IT YESTERDAY...
COULD KAMUI HAVE... ?
BING BONG
BING BONG

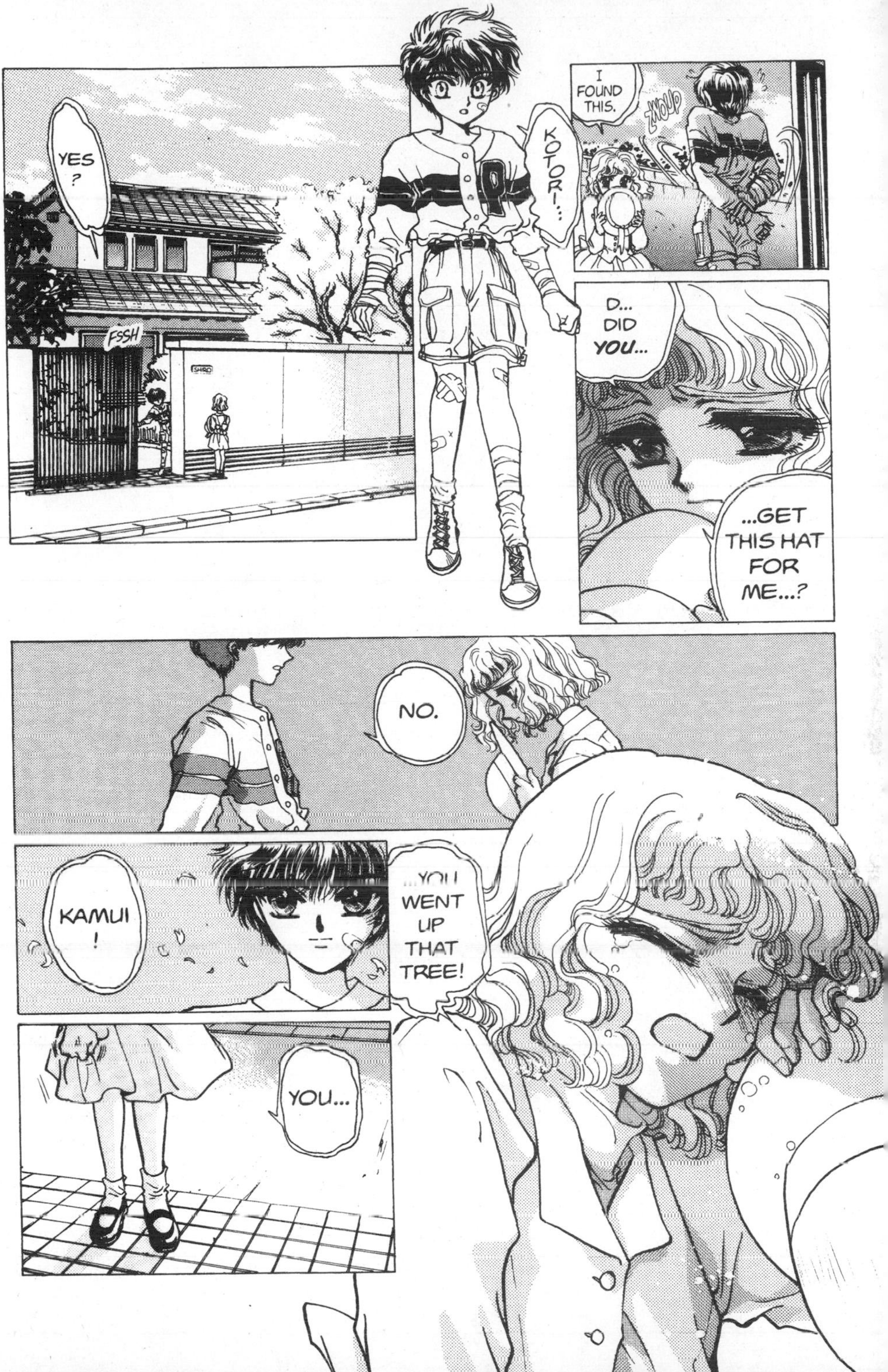
YES ?
FSSH
SHIRO
KOTORI...
I FOUND THIS.
ZWOUP
D... DID YOU...
...GET THIS HAT FOR ME...?
NO.
KAMUI !
...YOU WENT UP THAT TREE!
YOU...

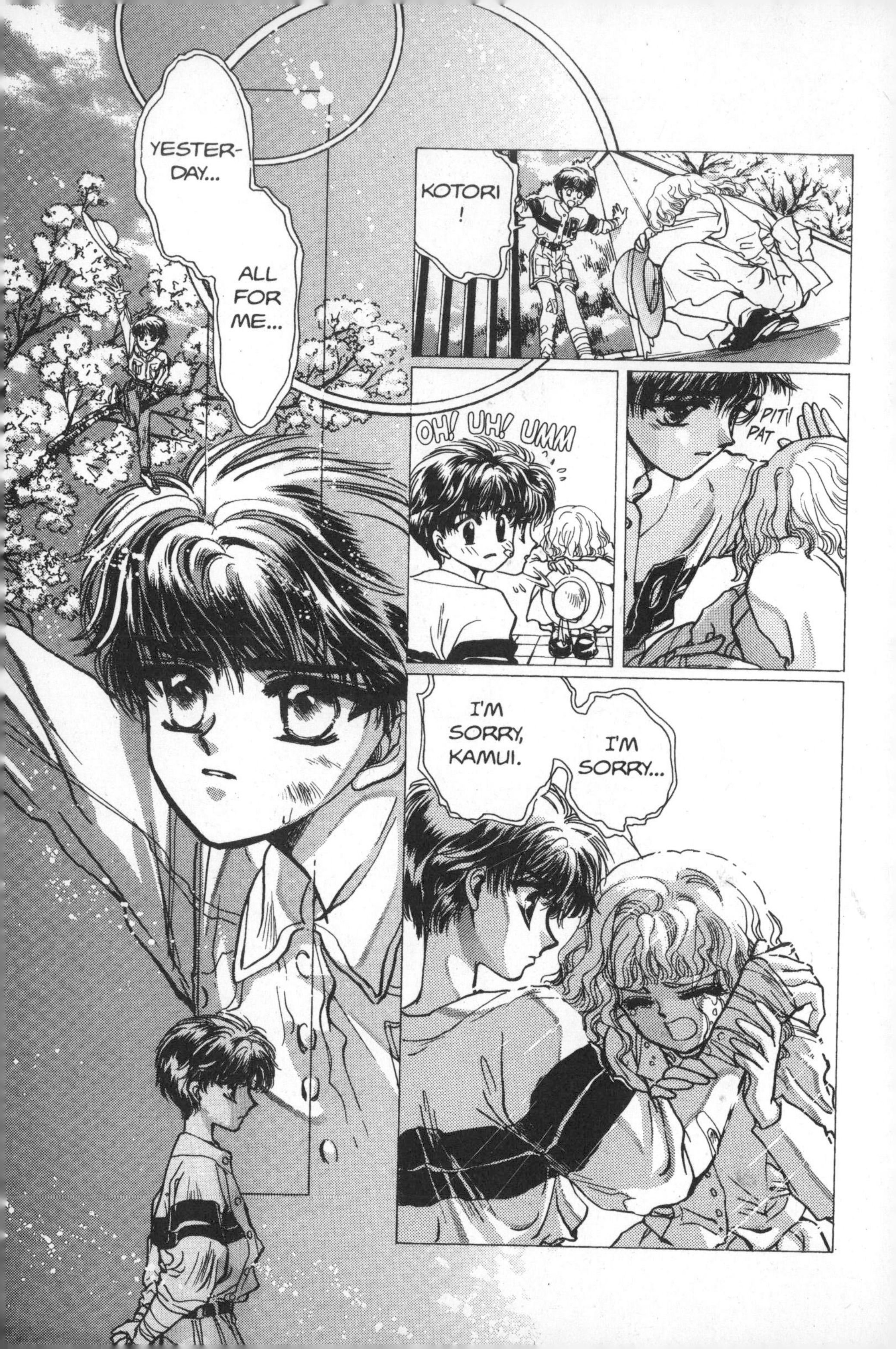
YESTER-DAY...
ALL FOR ME...
KOTORI!
OH! UH! UMM
PIT PAT
I'M SORRY, KAMUI.
I'M SORRY...

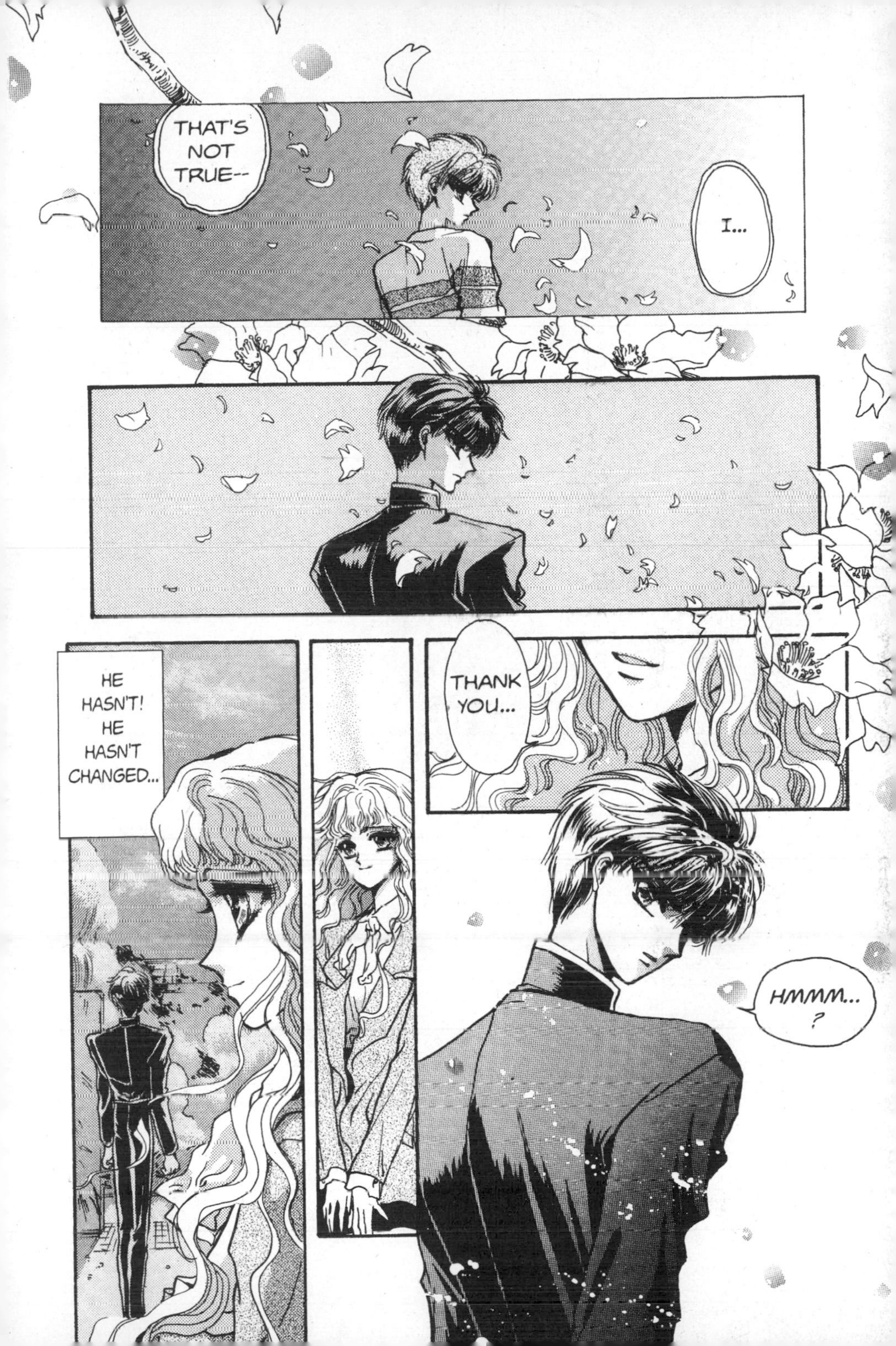
THAT'S NOT TRUE--
I...
HE HASN'T! HE HASN'T CHANGED...
THANK YOU...
HMMM...?

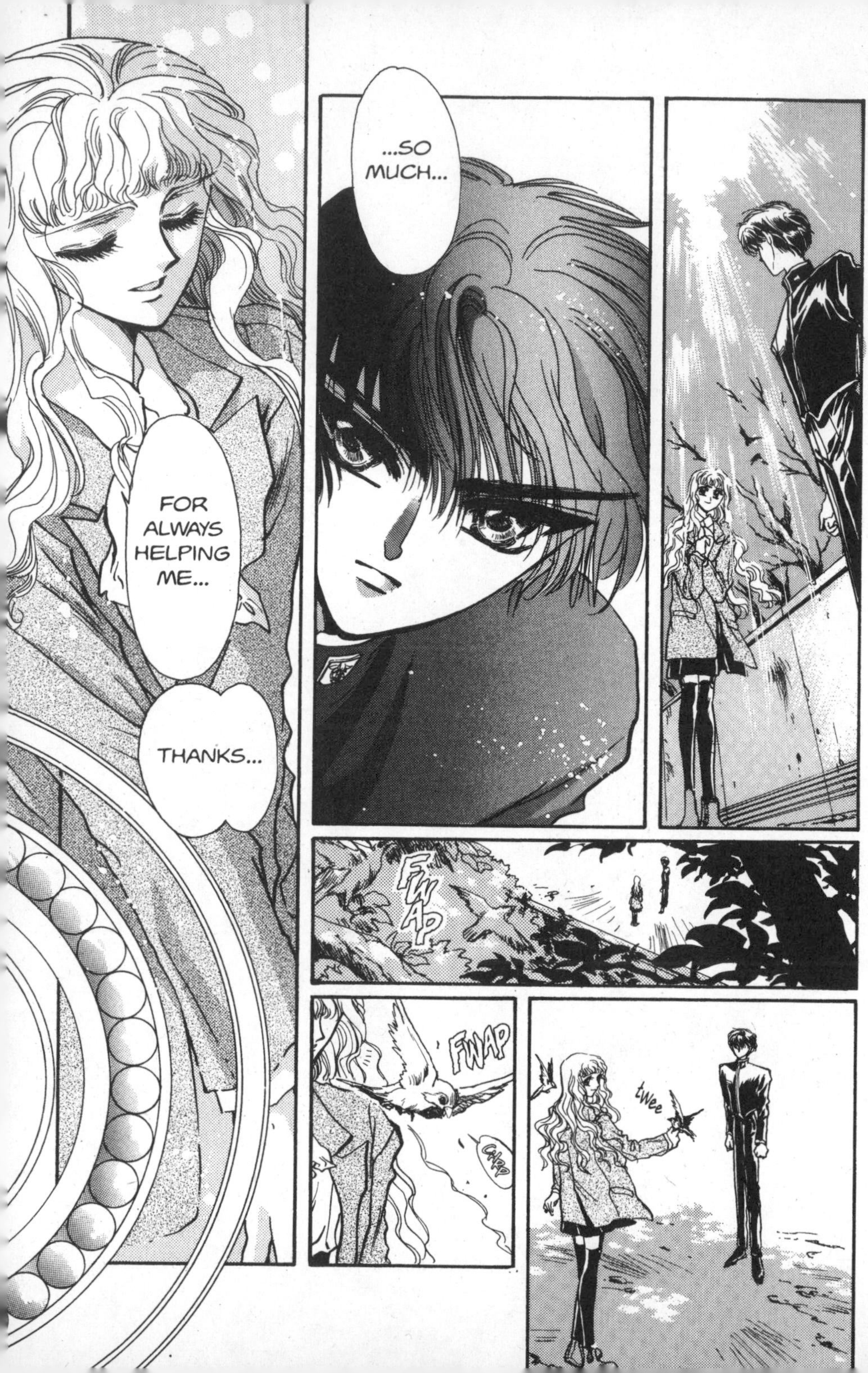
FOR ALWAYS HELPING ME...
THANKS...
...SO MUCH...
FWAP
FWAP
CHIRP
twee

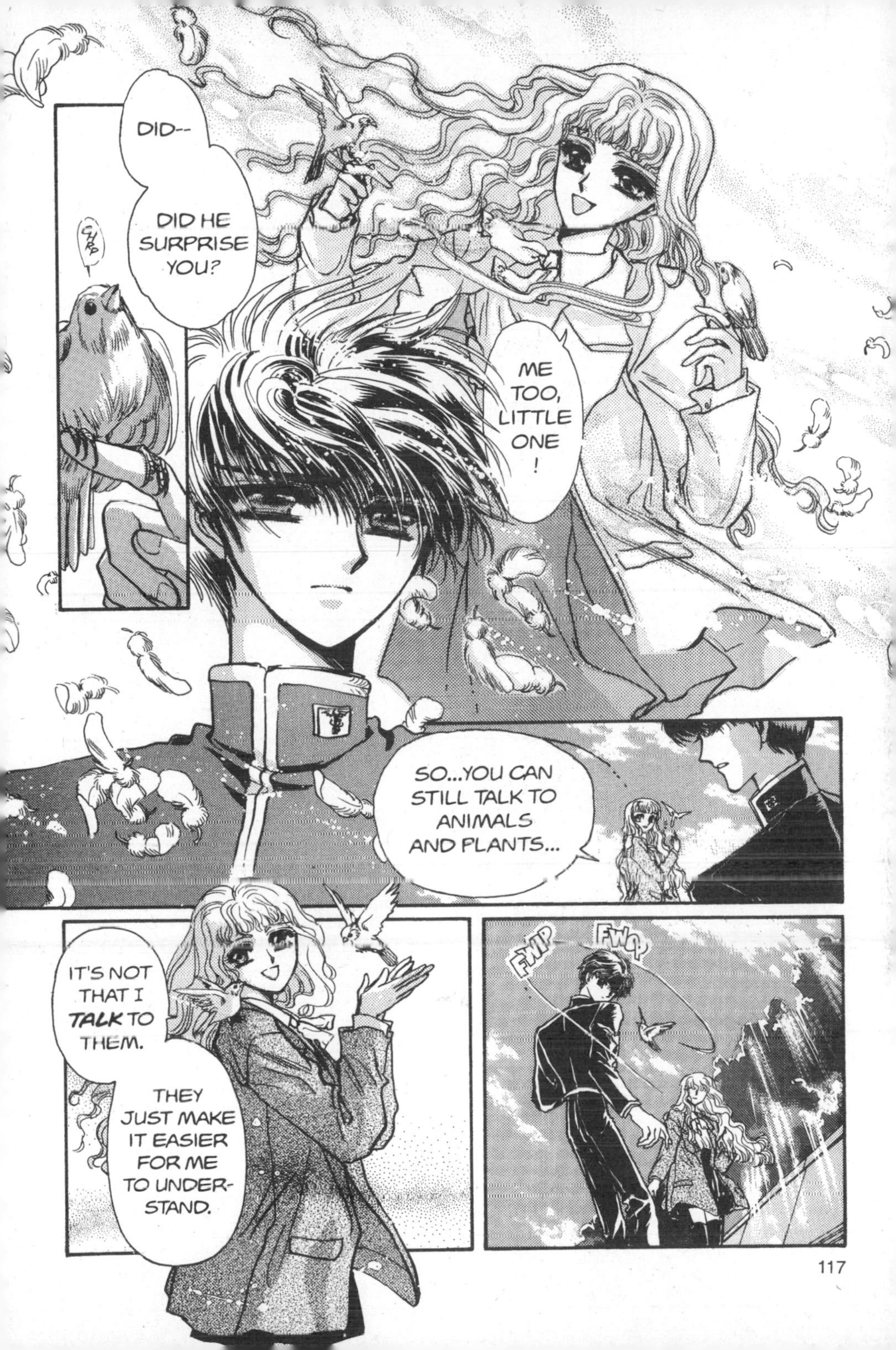
DID--
DID HE SURPRISE YOU?
CHIRP
ME TOO, LITTLE ONE!
SO...YOU CAN STILL TALK TO ANIMALS AND PLANTS...
IT'S NOT THAT I TALK TO THEM.
THEY JUST MAKE IT EASIER FOR ME TO UNDER-STAND.
FWIP

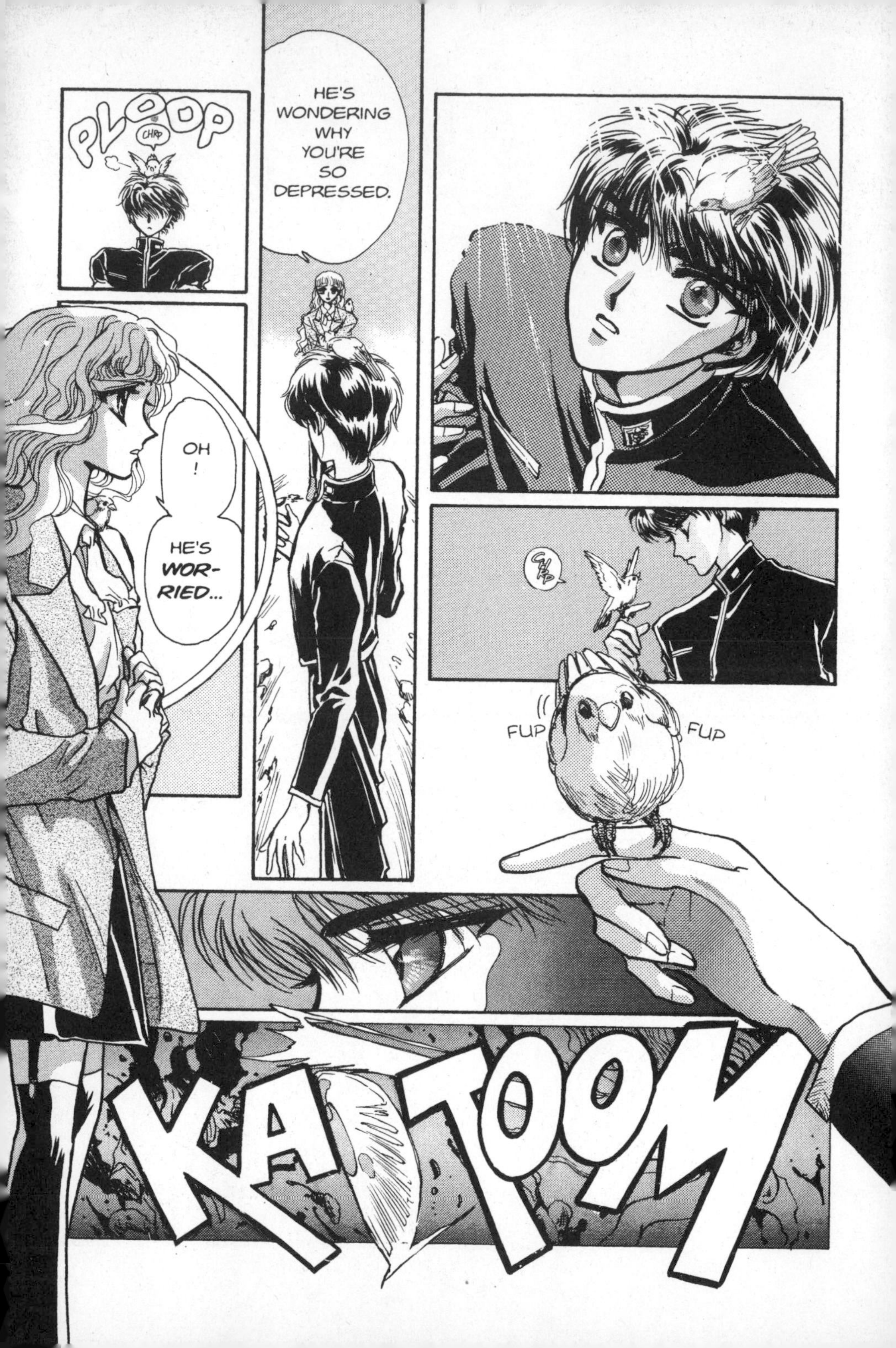
PLOOP
CHRP
HE'S WONDERING WHY YOU'RE SO DEPRESSED.
OH ! HE'S **WORRIED...**
CHRP
FUP
FUP
KATOOM

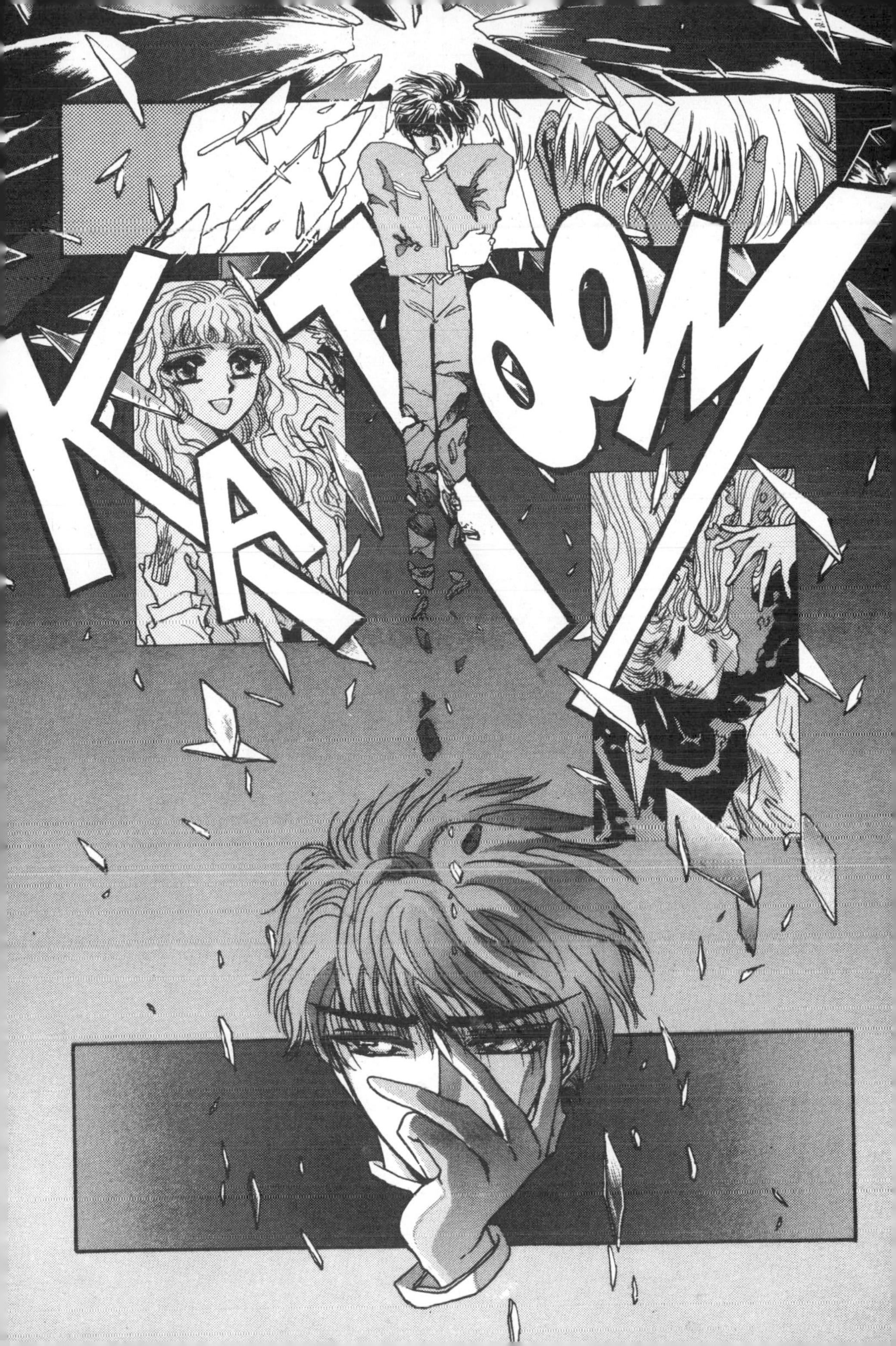
KATOOM

LUCKY...

DAMN LUCKY!

KAMUI'S THE LUCKIEST GUY IN THE WORLD.

HE GETS TO CHAT WITH **SUCH** A CUTE GIRL.

YUP

.....

SHE'S JUST LIKE HER NAME SAYS...

..."A SWEET LITTLE BIRD."

HEY! THAT WAS PRETTY **DEEP**...

A **LITTLE BIRD** WHO TALKS TO LITTLE BIRDS! GOOD, HUH?

120

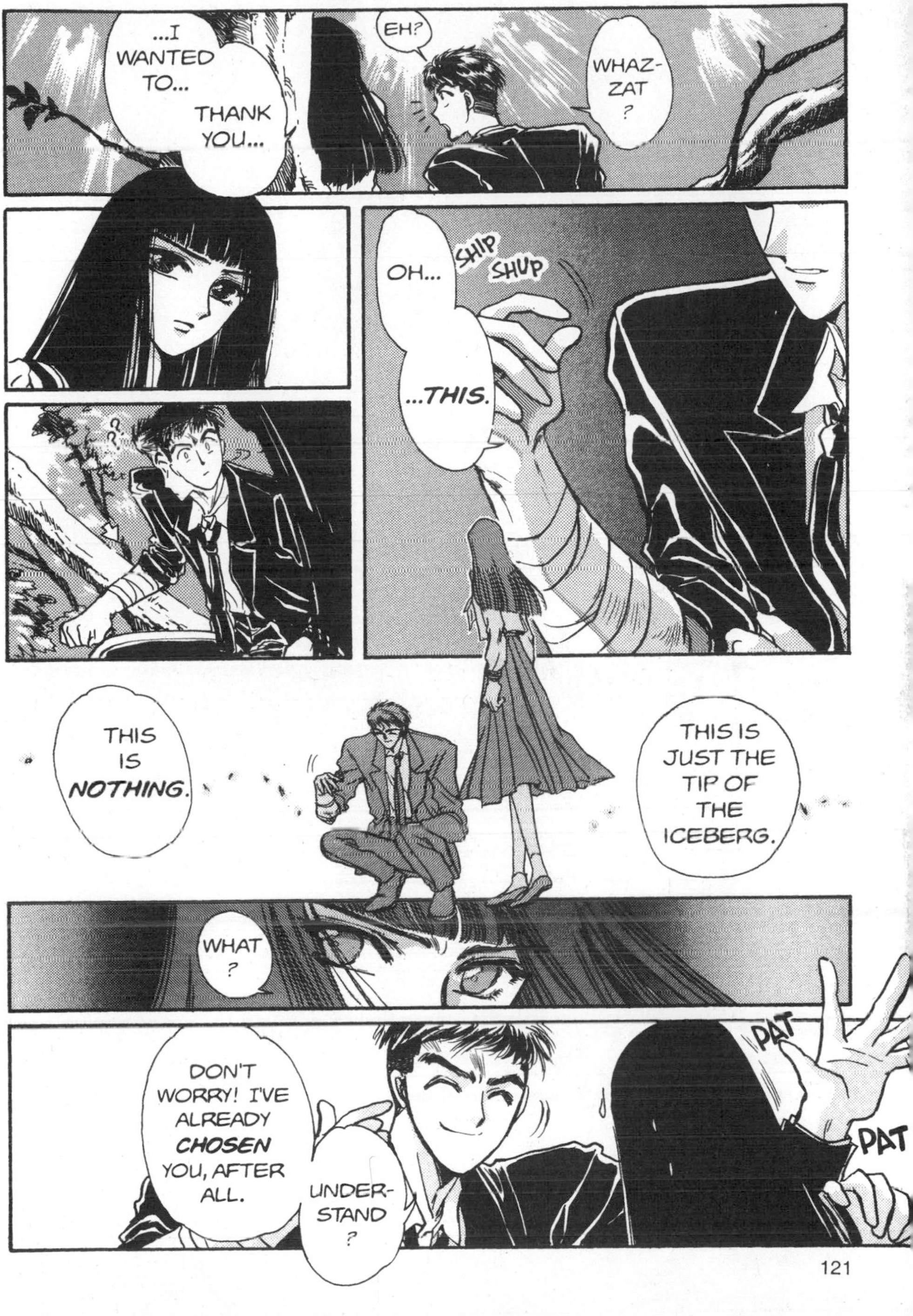
...I WANTED TO... THANK YOU...
EH?
WHAZ-ZAT?
OH...
SHIP
SHUP
...THIS.
THIS IS NOTHING.
THIS IS JUST THE TIP OF THE ICEBERG.
WHAT?
DON'T WORRY! I'VE ALREADY CHOSEN YOU, AFTER ALL.
UNDER-STAND?
PAT
PAT

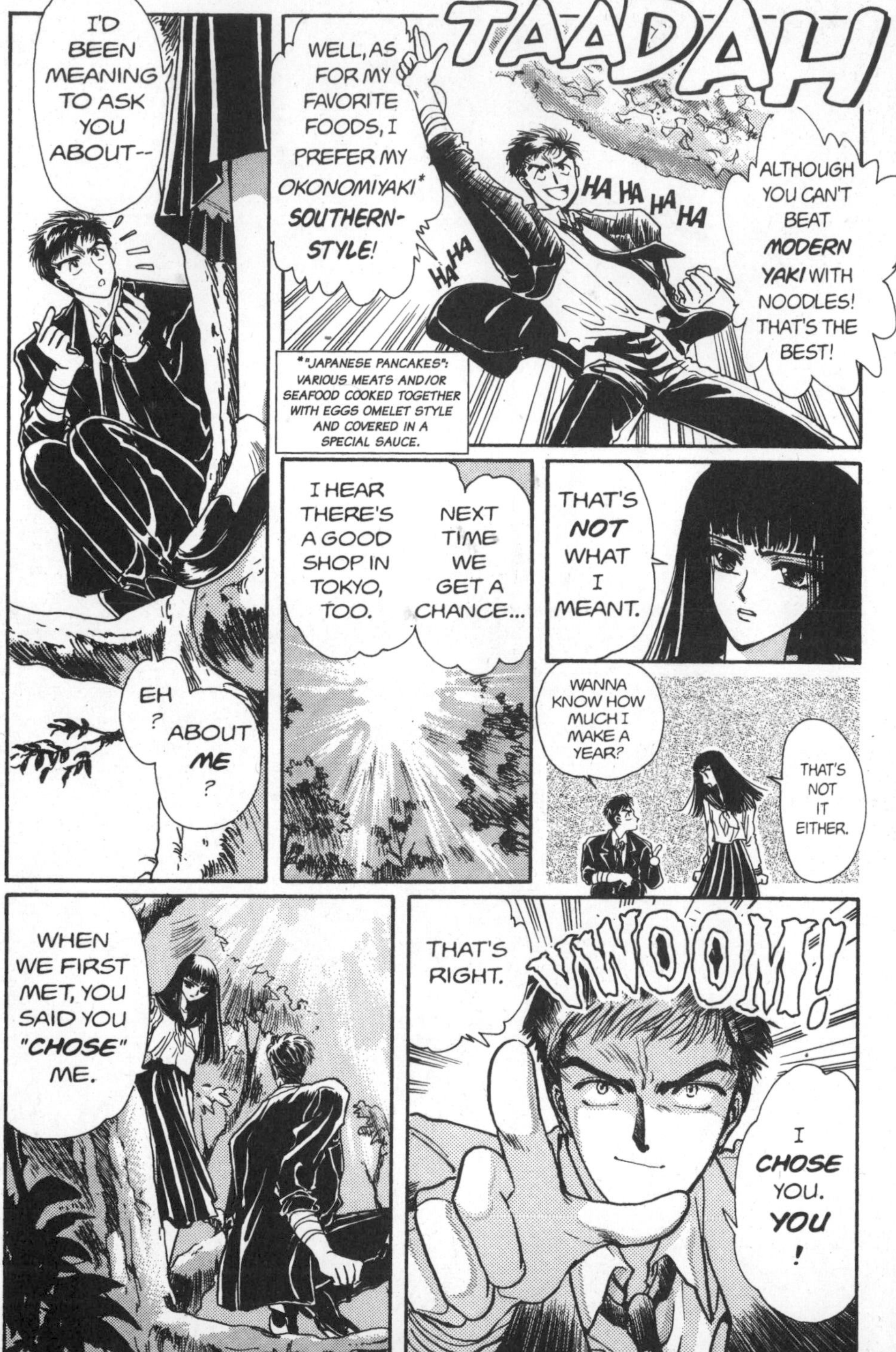
I'D BEEN MEANING TO ASK YOU ABOUT--
EH? ABOUT ME?
WELL, AS FOR MY FAVORITE FOODS, I PREFER MY OKONOMIYAKI* SOUTHERN-STYLE!
TAADAH
HA HA HA HA HA HA
ALTHOUGH YOU CAN'T BEAT MODERN YAKI WITH NOODLES! THAT'S THE BEST!
*"JAPANESE PANCAKES": VARIOUS MEATS AND/OR SEAFOOD COOKED TOGETHER WITH EGGS OMELET STYLE AND COVERED IN A SPECIAL SAUCE.
I HEAR THERE'S A GOOD SHOP IN TOKYO, TOO.
NEXT TIME WE GET A CHANCE...
THAT'S NOT WHAT I MEANT.
WANNA KNOW HOW MUCH I MAKE A YEAR?
THAT'S NOT IT EITHER.
WHEN WE FIRST MET, YOU SAID YOU "CHOSE" ME.
THAT'S RIGHT.
VWOOM!
I CHOSE YOU. YOU!

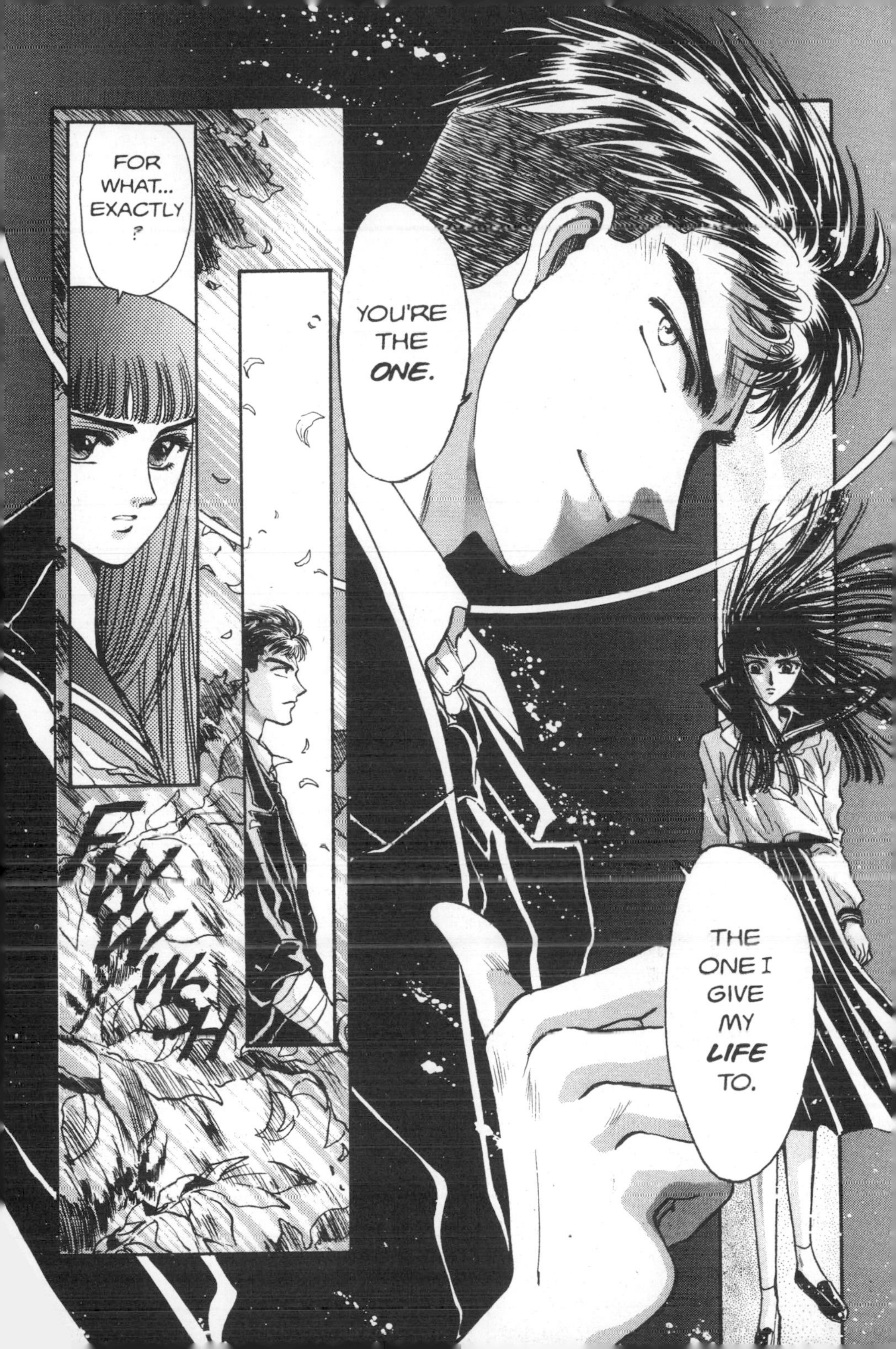
FOR WHAT... EXACTLY ?
FWWSH
YOU'RE THE ONE.
THE ONE I GIVE MY LIFE TO.

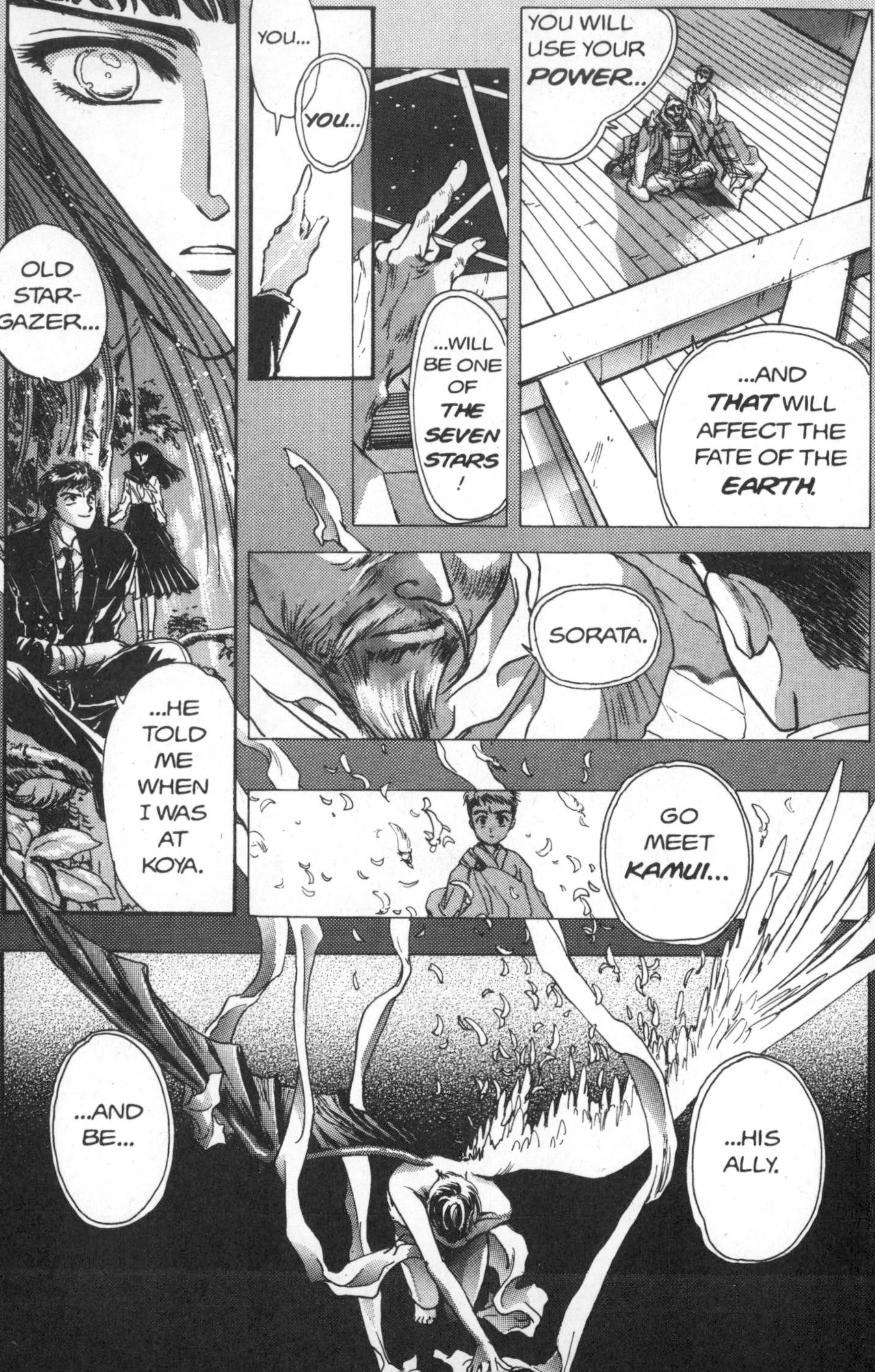
OLD STAR-GAZER...
...HE TOLD ME WHEN I WAS AT KOYA.
YOU...
YOU...
...WILL BE ONE OF THE SEVEN STARS!
YOU WILL USE YOUR POWER...
...AND THAT WILL AFFECT THE FATE OF THE EARTH.
SORATA.
GO MEET KAMUI...
...AND BE...
...HIS ALLY.

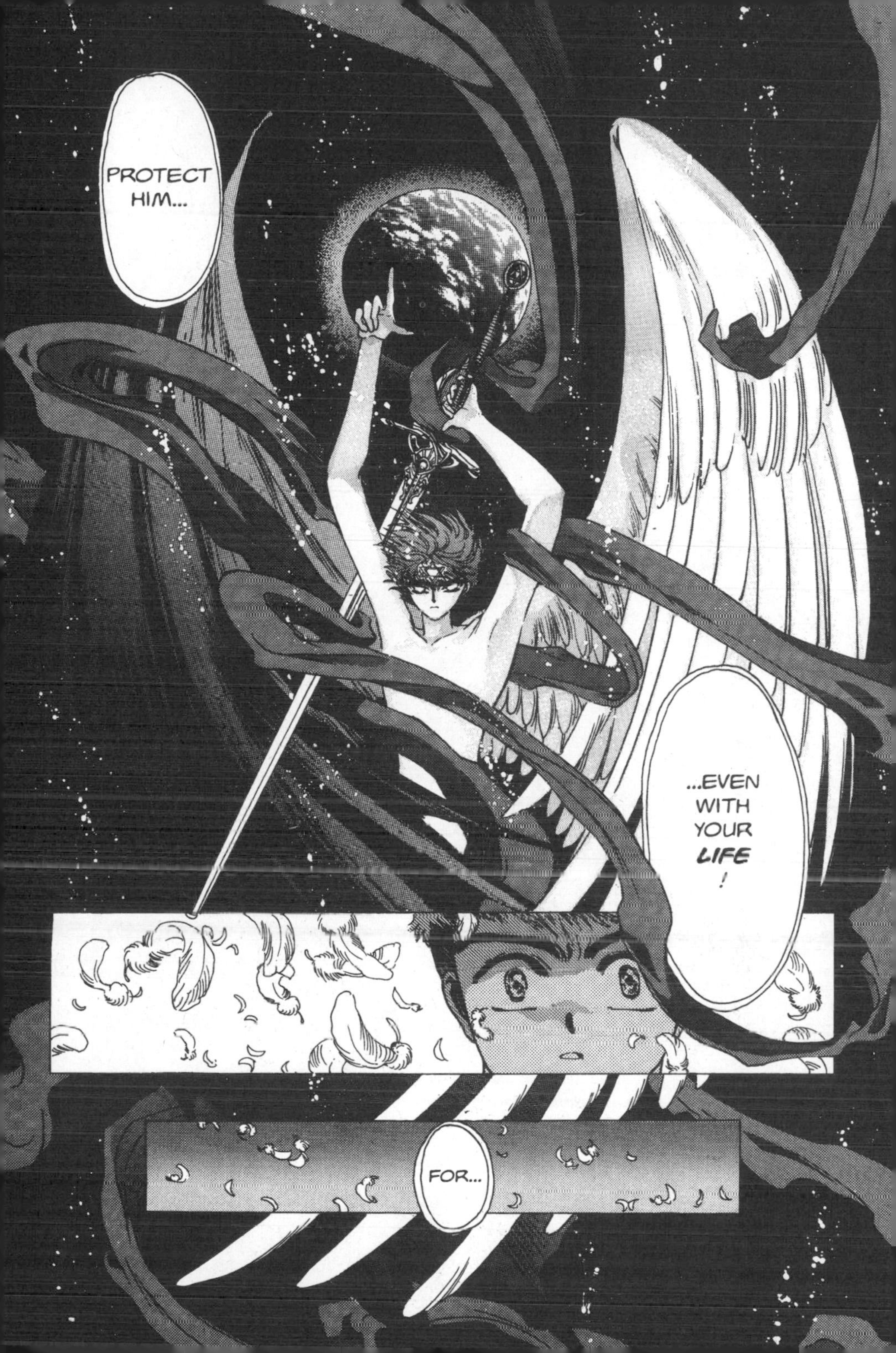
PROTECT HIM...
...EVEN WITH YOUR LIFE!
FOR...

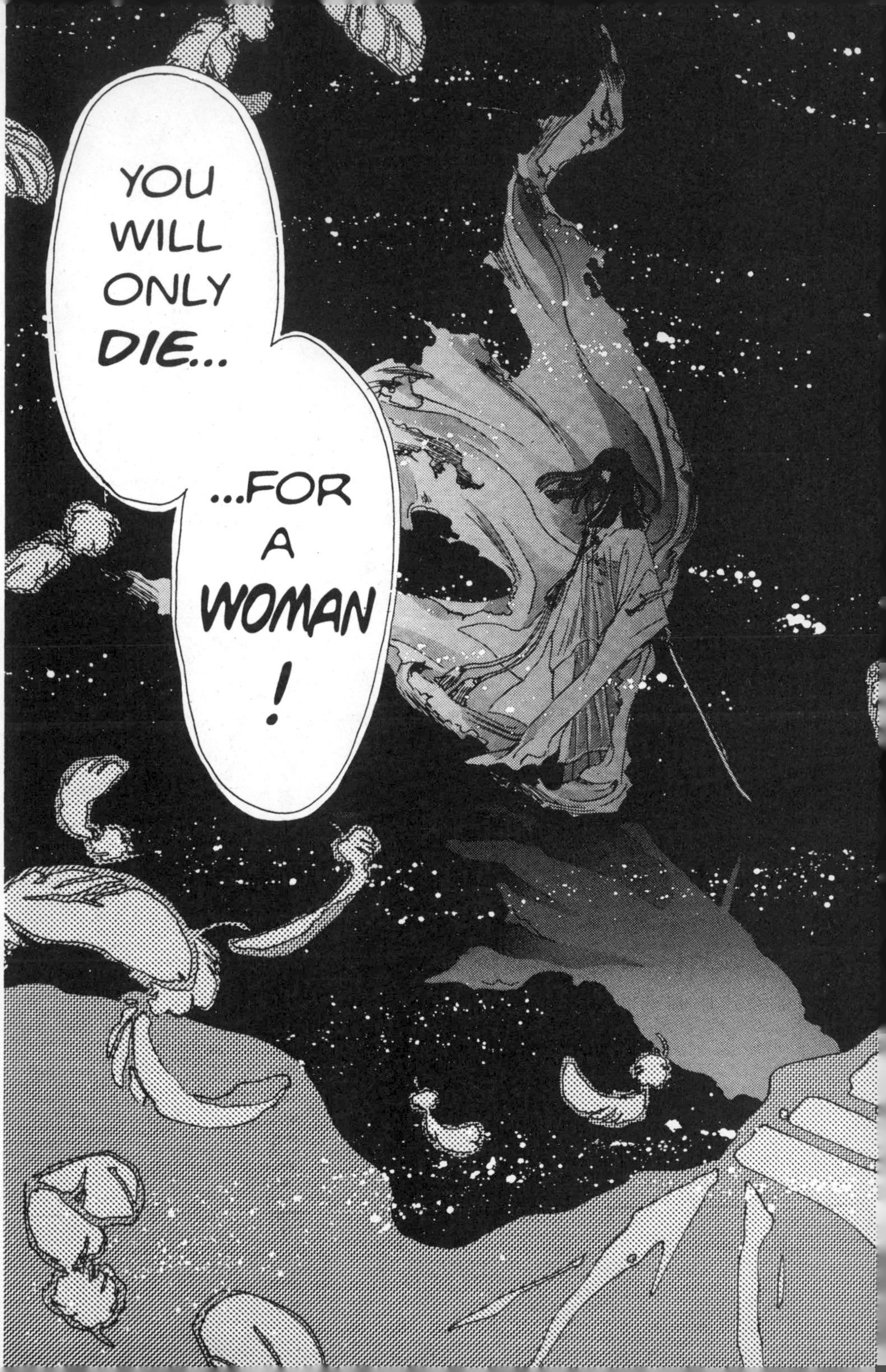
YOU WILL ONLY DIE...
...FOR A WOMAN!

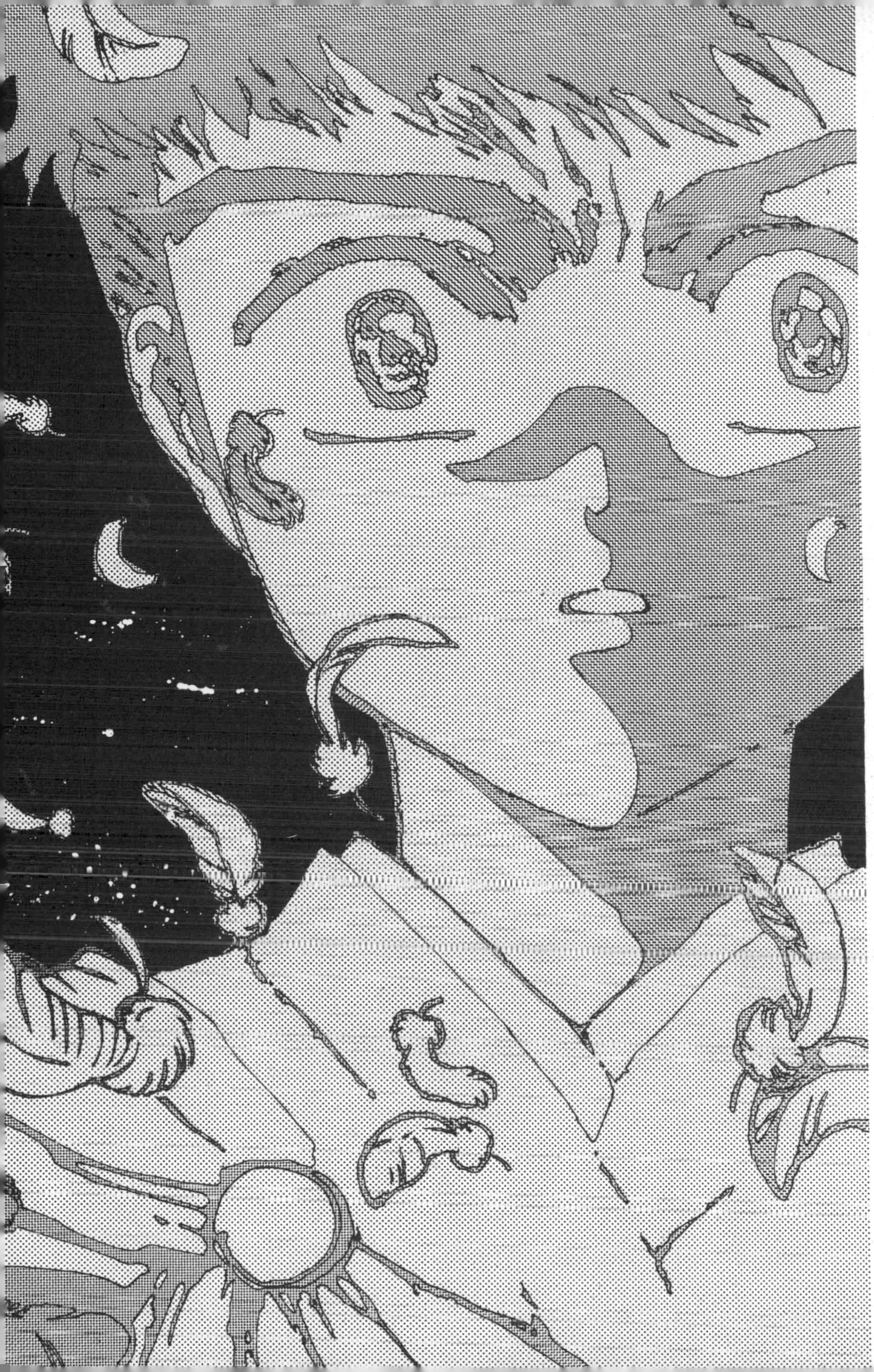

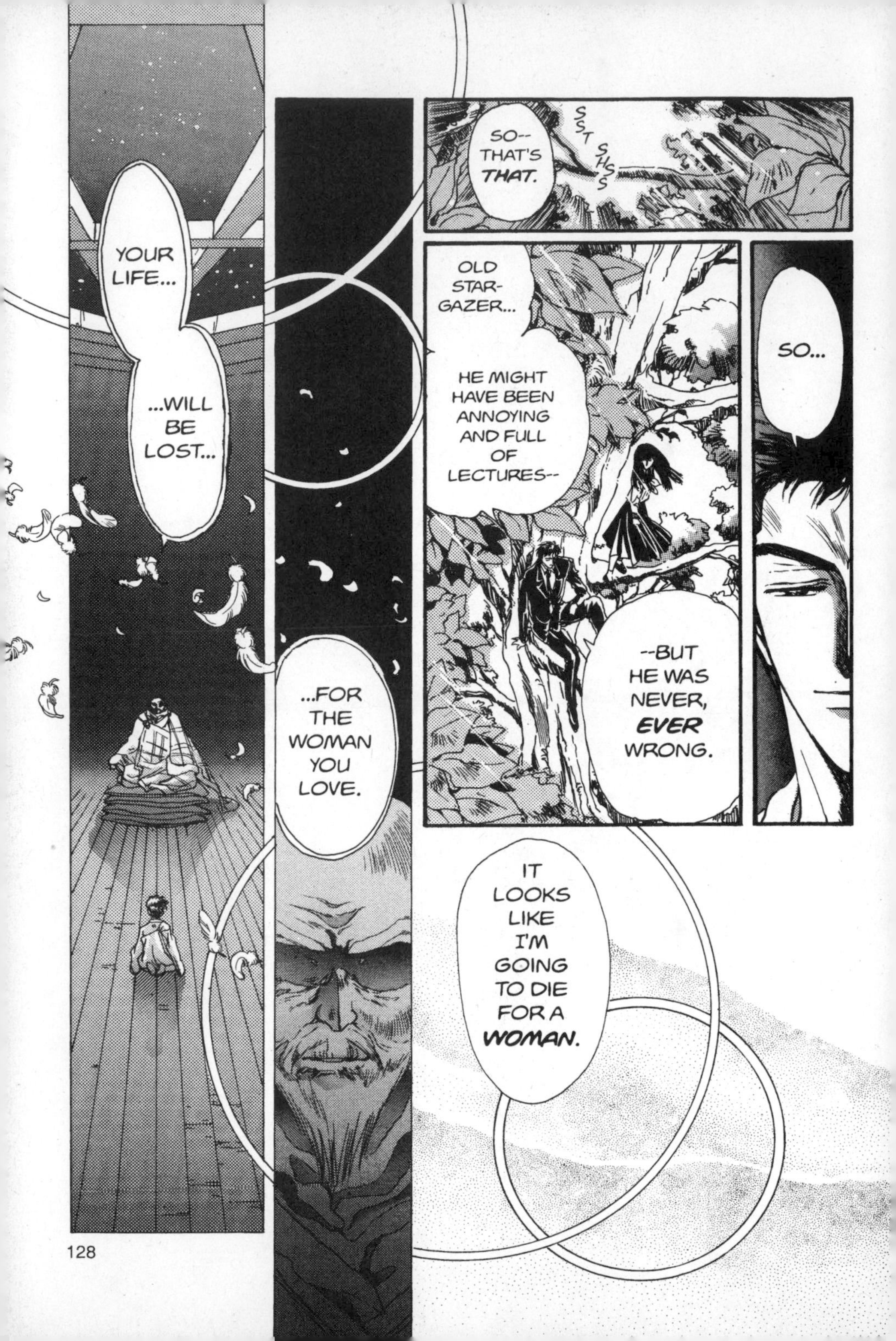
YOUR LIFE...
...WILL BE LOST...
...FOR THE WOMAN YOU LOVE.
SO-- THAT'S THAT.
SST SHSS
OLD STAR-GAZER...
HE MIGHT HAVE BEEN ANNOYING AND FULL OF LECTURES--
--BUT HE WAS NEVER, EVER WRONG.
SO...
IT LOOKS LIKE I'M GOING TO DIE FOR A WOMAN.

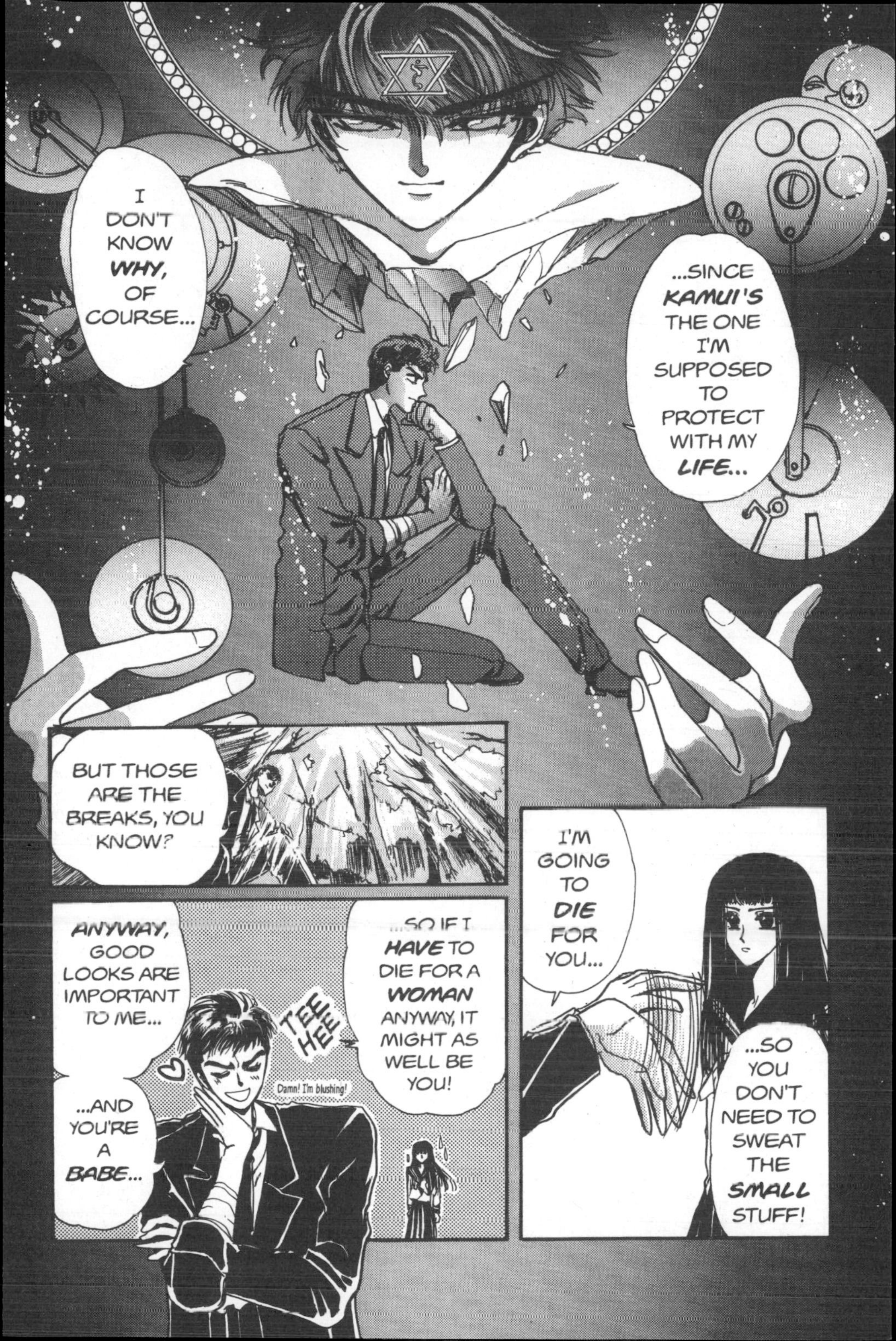
I DON'T KNOW WHY, OF COURSE...
...SINCE KAMUI'S THE ONE I'M SUPPOSED TO PROTECT WITH MY LIFE...
BUT THOSE ARE THE BREAKS, YOU KNOW?
ANYWAY, GOOD LOOKS ARE IMPORTANT TO ME...
...SO IF I HAVE TO DIE FOR A WOMAN ANYWAY, IT MIGHT AS WELL BE YOU!
TEE HEE
Damn! I'm blushing!
...AND YOU'RE A BABE...
I'M GOING TO DIE FOR YOU...
...SO YOU DON'T NEED TO SWEAT THE SMALL STUFF!

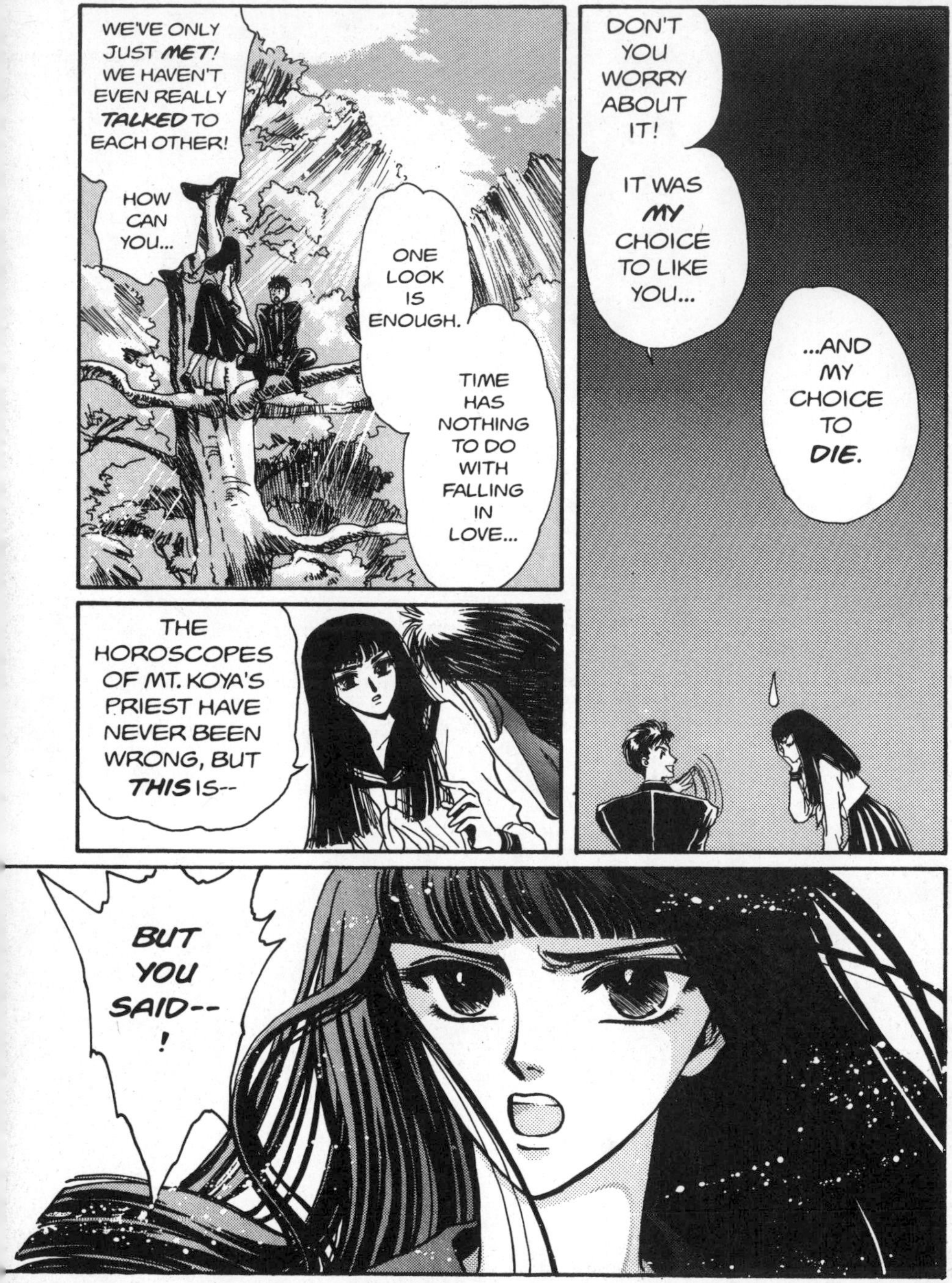
WE'VE ONLY JUST MET! WE HAVEN'T EVEN REALLY TALKED TO EACH OTHER!
HOW CAN YOU...
ONE LOOK IS ENOUGH.
TIME HAS NOTHING TO DO WITH FALLING IN LOVE...
THE HOROSCOPES OF MT. KOYA'S PRIEST HAVE NEVER BEEN WRONG, BUT THIS IS--
DON'T YOU WORRY ABOUT IT!
IT WAS MY CHOICE TO LIKE YOU...
...AND MY CHOICE TO DIE.
BUT YOU SAID--!

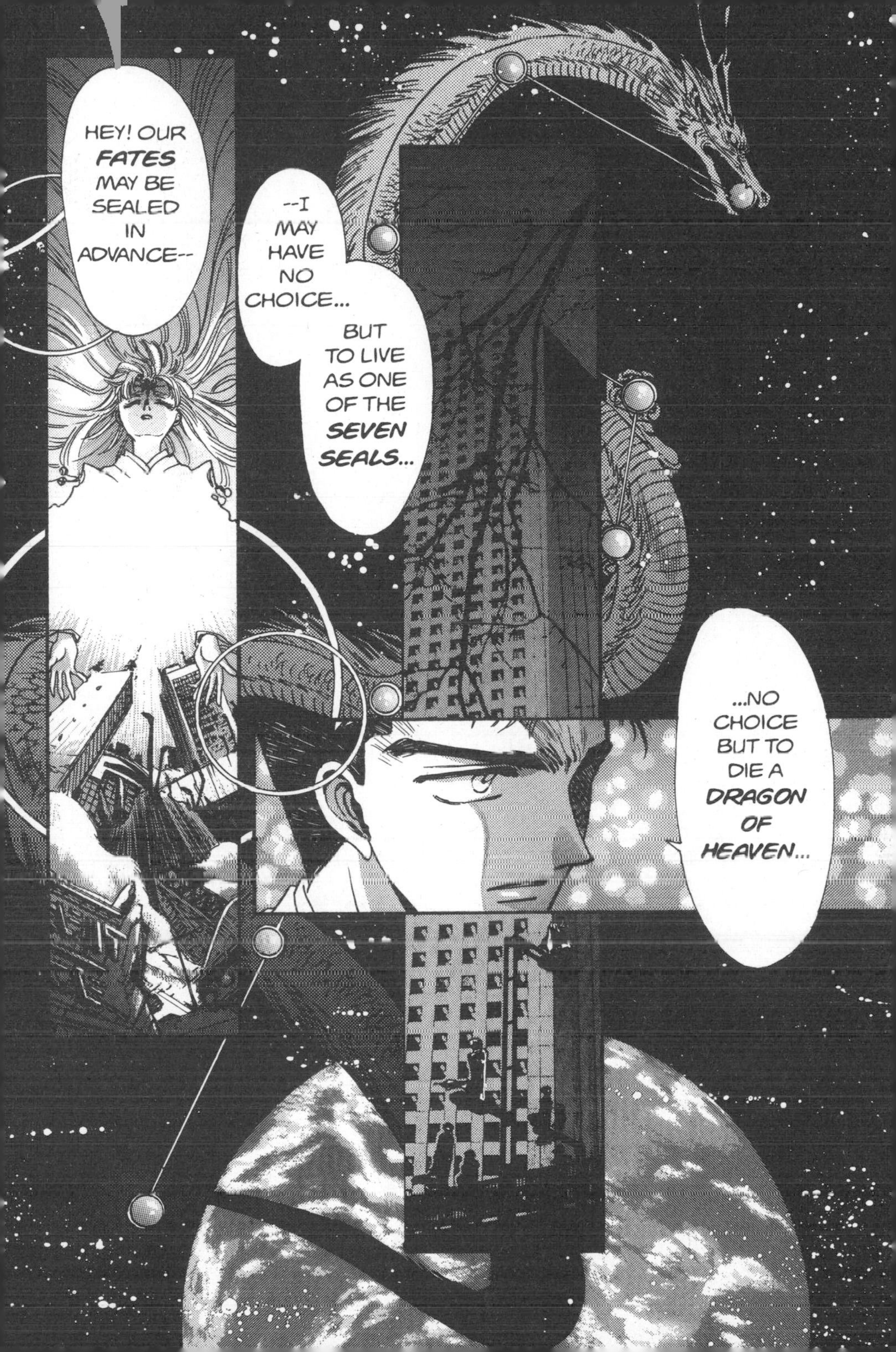
HEY! OUR FATES MAY BE SEALED IN ADVANCE--
--I MAY HAVE NO CHOICE...
BUT TO LIVE AS ONE OF THE SEVEN SEALS...
...NO CHOICE BUT TO DIE A DRAGON OF HEAVEN...

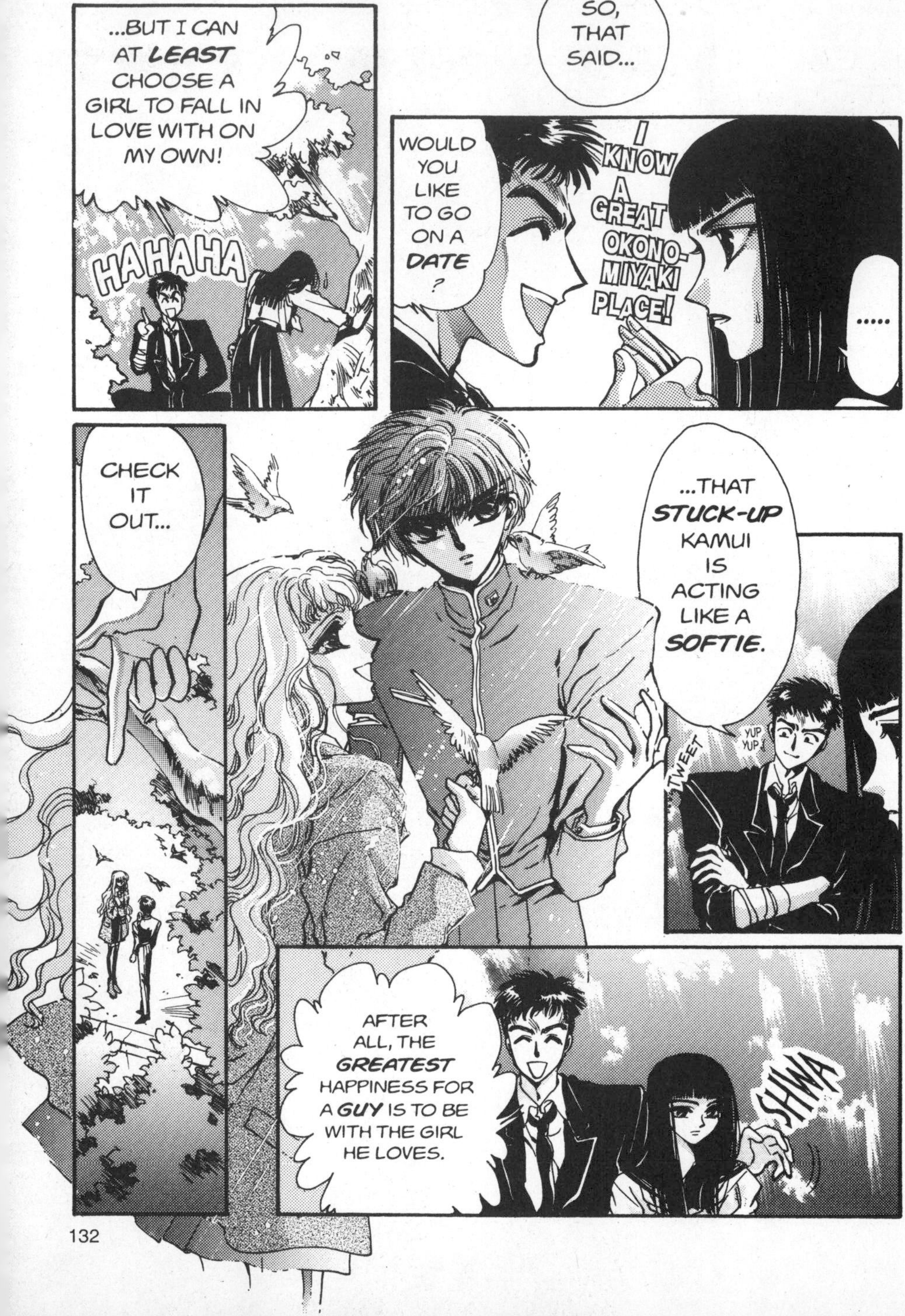
...BUT I CAN AT LEAST CHOOSE A GIRL TO FALL IN LOVE WITH ON MY OWN!
HAHAHA
SO, THAT SAID...
WOULD YOU LIKE TO GO ON A DATE?
I KNOW A GREAT OKONO-MIYAKI PLACE!
.....
CHECK IT OUT...
...THAT STUCK-UP KAMUI IS ACTING LIKE A SOFTIE.
YUP YUP
TWEET
AFTER ALL, THE GREATEST HAPPINESS FOR A GUY IS TO BE WITH THE GIRL HE LOVES.
SHWA

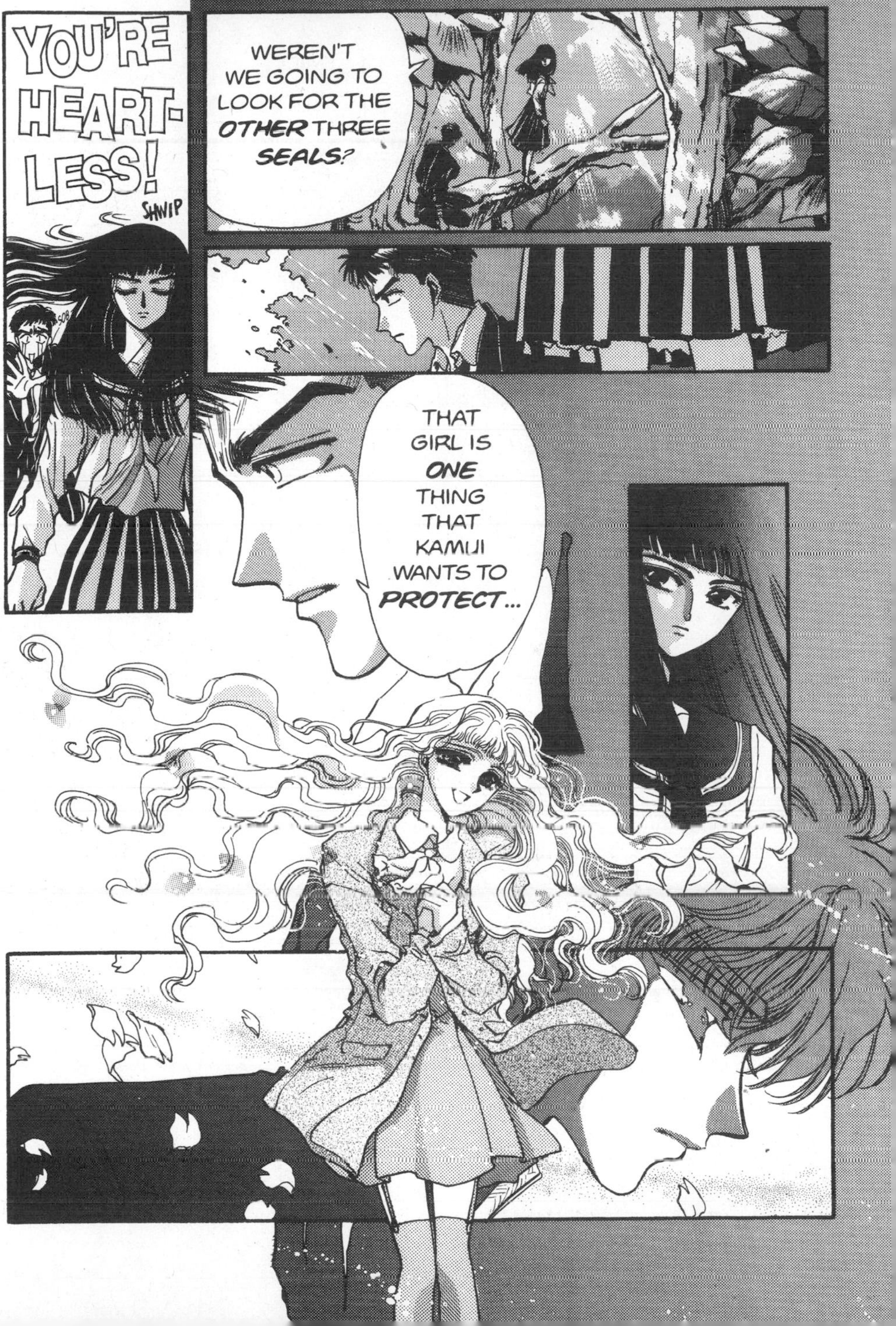
YOU'RE HEART-LESS!
SHWIP
SOB
WEREN'T WE GOING TO LOOK FOR THE *OTHER* THREE *SEALS*?
THAT GIRL IS *ONE* THING THAT KAMUI WANTS TO *PROTECT*...

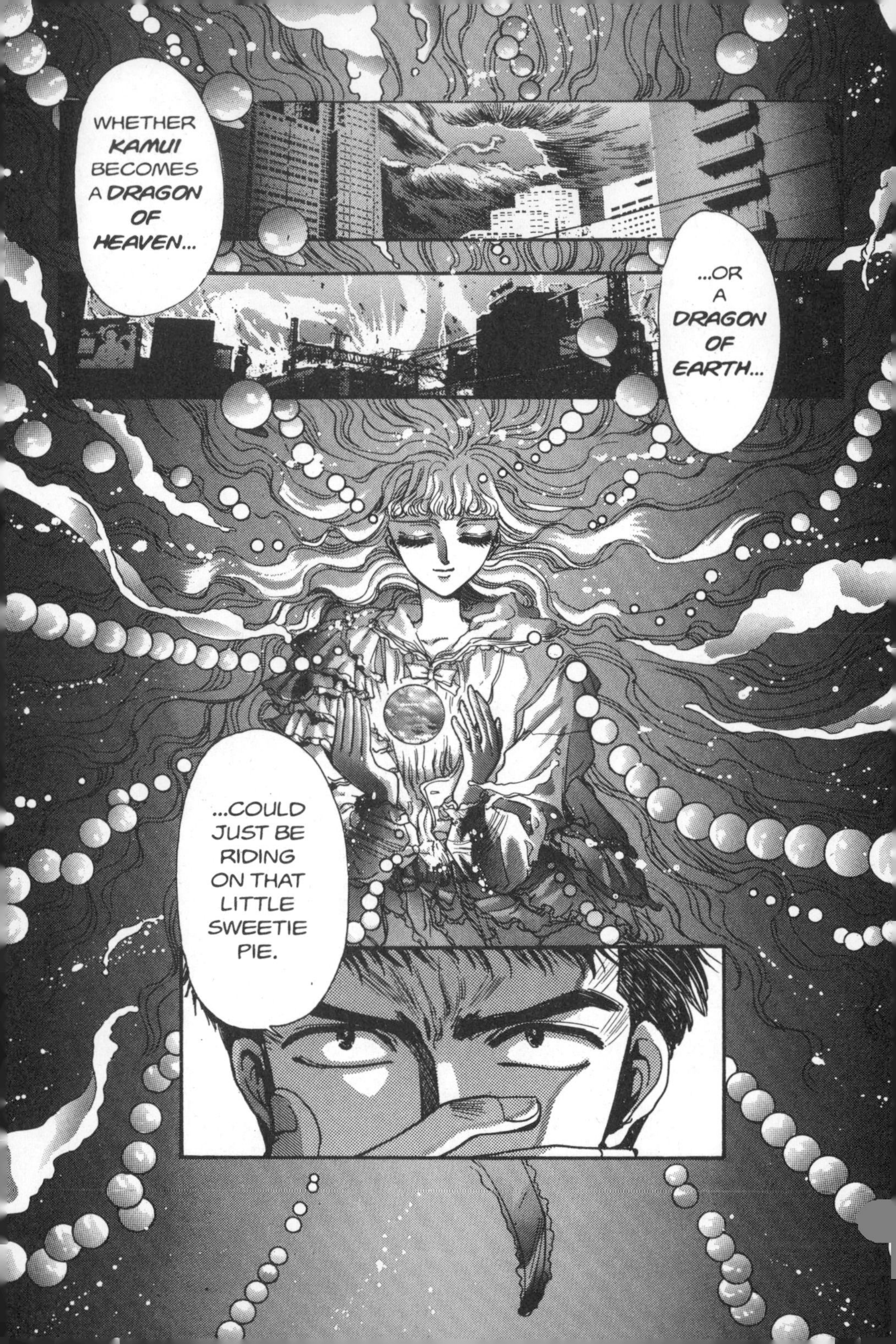
WHETHER KAMUI BECOMES A DRAGON OF HEAVEN...
...OR A DRAGON OF EARTH...
...COULD JUST BE RIDING ON THAT LITTLE SWEETIE PIE.

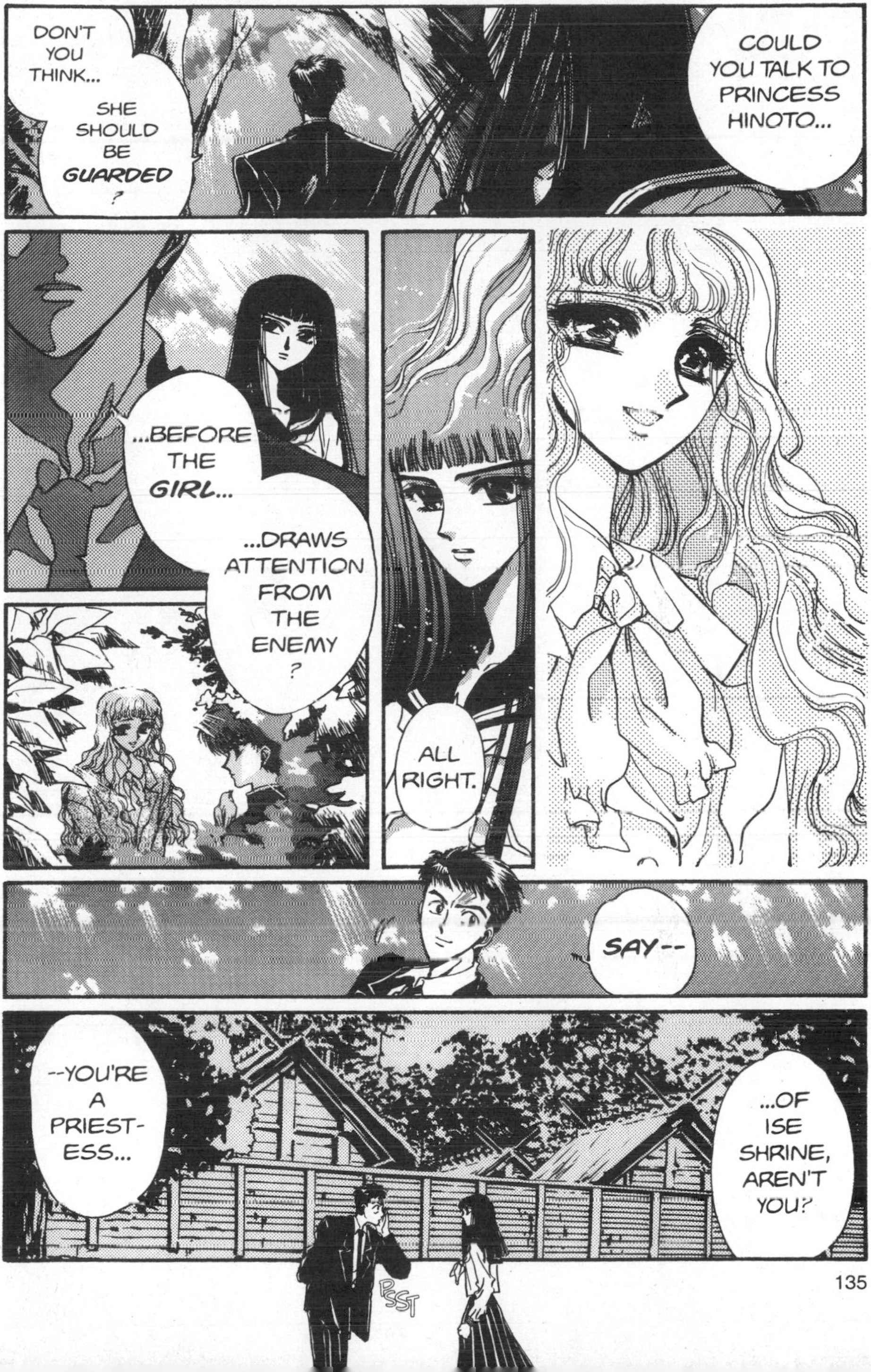
DON'T YOU THINK... SHE SHOULD BE GUARDED?
COULD YOU TALK TO PRINCESS HINOTO...
...BEFORE THE GIRL...
...DRAWS ATTENTION FROM THE ENEMY?
ALL RIGHT.
SAY--
--YOU'RE A PRIEST-ESS...
...OF ISE SHRINE, AREN'T YOU?
PSST

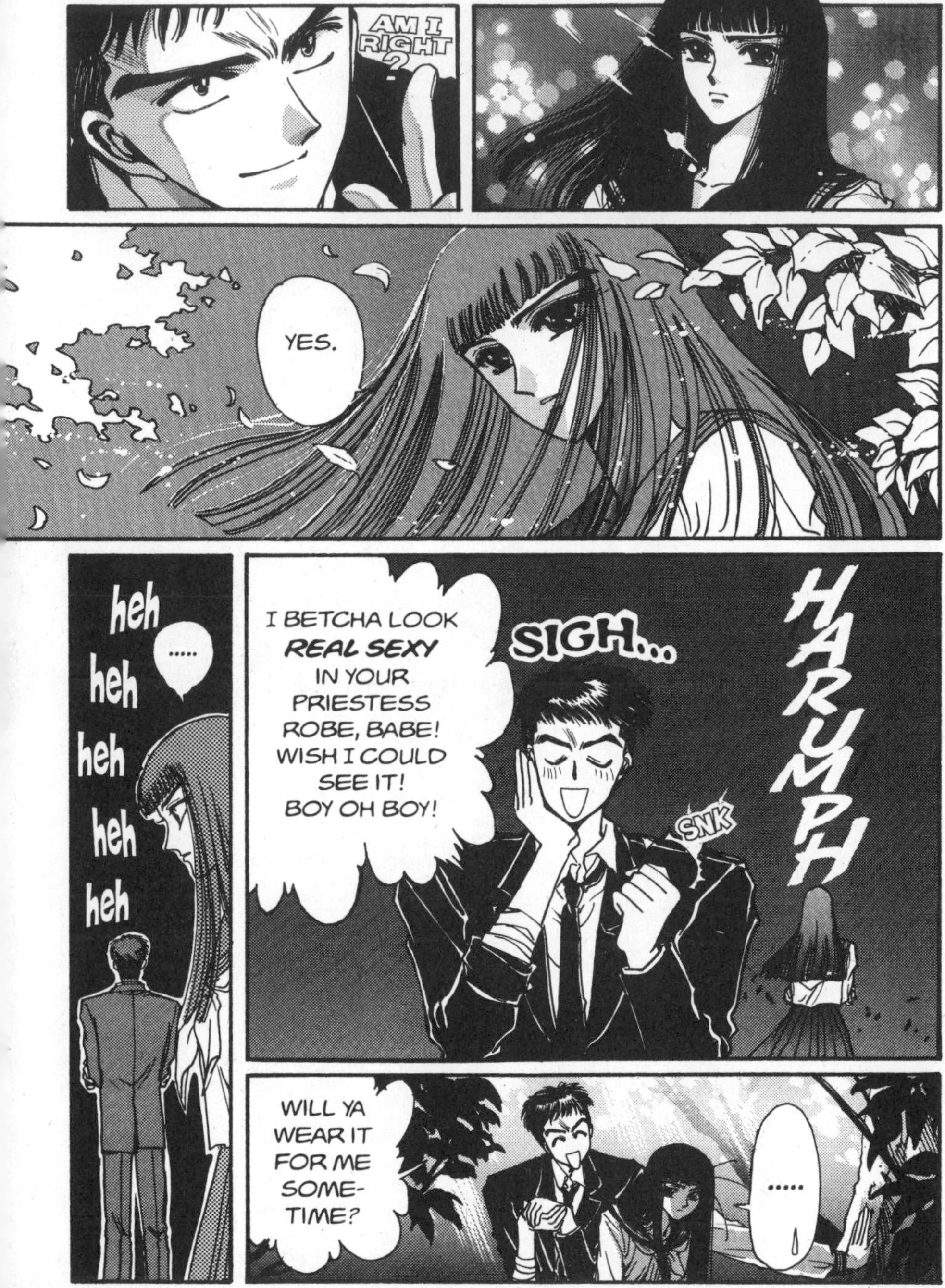
AM I RIGHT?
YES.
heh heh heh heh heh
.....
I BETCHA LOOK **REAL SEXY** IN YOUR PRIESTESS ROBE, BABE! WISH I COULD SEE IT! BOY OH BOY!
SIGH...
SNK
HARUMPH
WILL YA WEAR IT FOR ME SOME-TIME?
.....

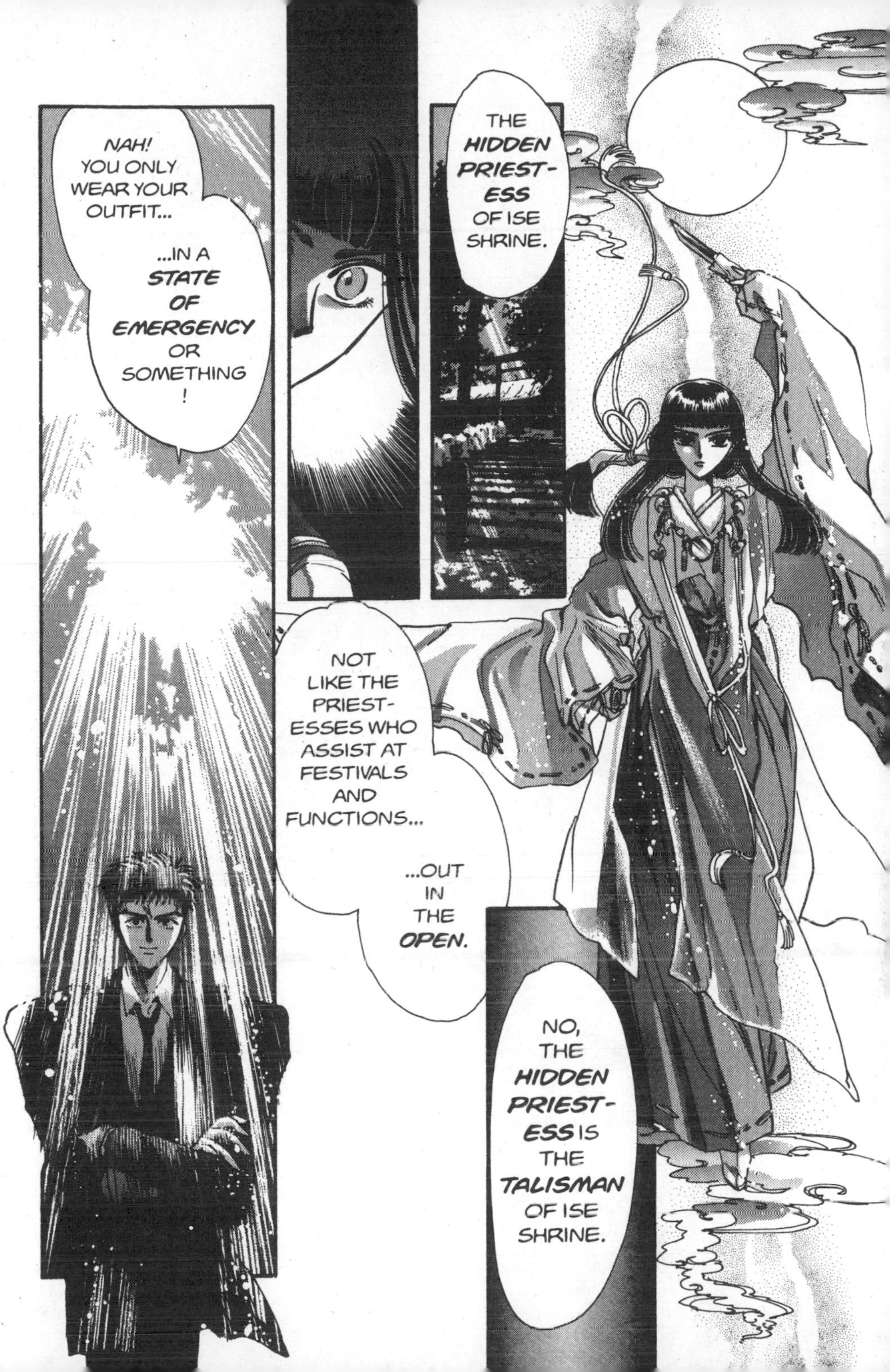
NAH! YOU ONLY WEAR YOUR OUTFIT...
...IN A *STATE OF EMERGENCY* OR SOMETHING!
THE *HIDDEN PRIEST-ESS* OF ISE SHRINE.
NOT LIKE THE PRIEST-ESSES WHO ASSIST AT FESTIVALS AND FUNCTIONS...
...OUT IN THE *OPEN*.
NO, THE *HIDDEN PRIEST-ESS* IS THE *TALISMAN* OF ISE SHRINE.

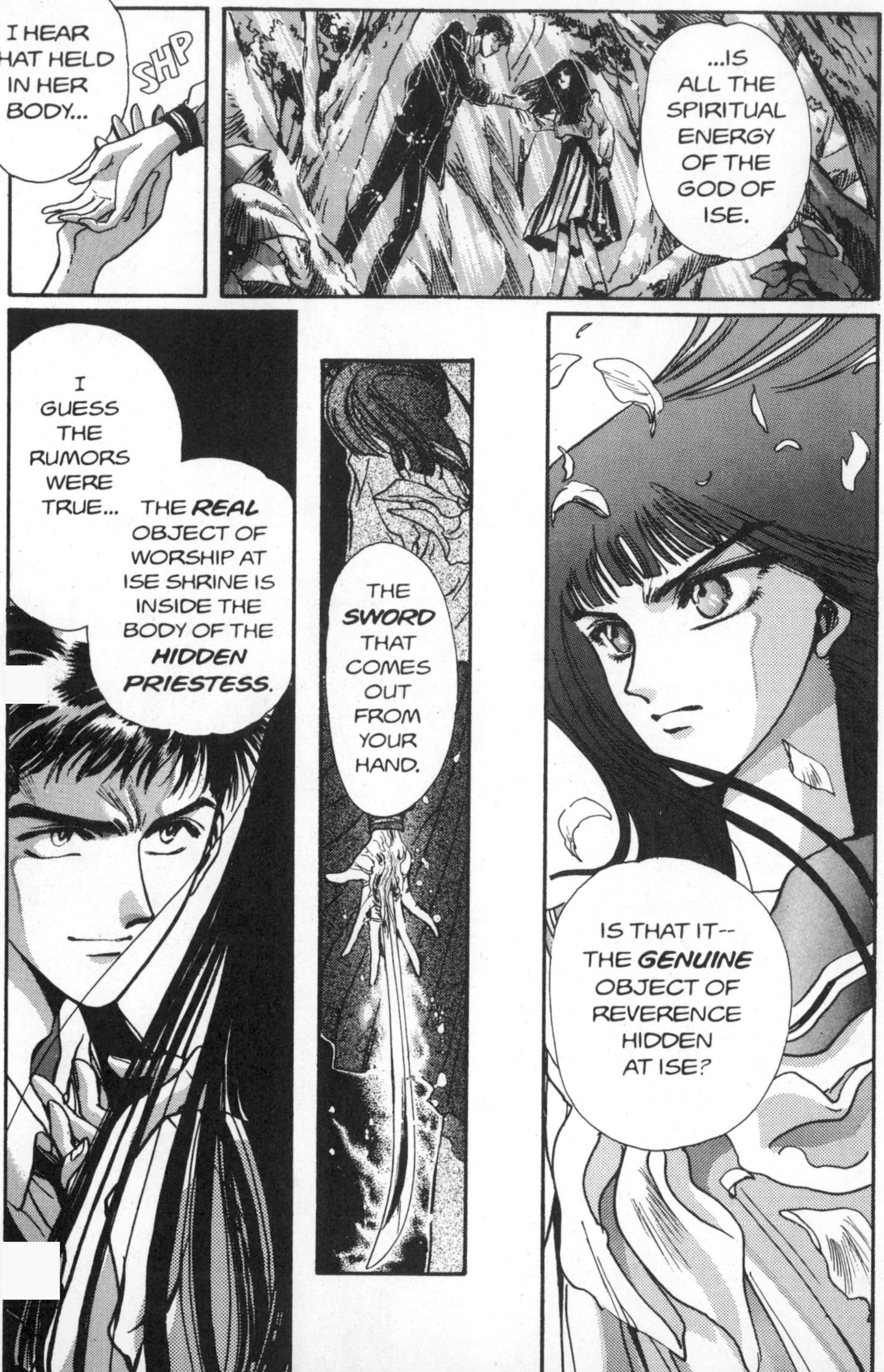
I HEAR THAT HELD IN HER BODY...
SHP
...IS ALL THE SPIRITUAL ENERGY OF THE GOD OF ISE.
I GUESS THE RUMORS WERE TRUE...
THE *REAL* OBJECT OF WORSHIP AT ISE SHRINE IS INSIDE THE BODY OF THE *HIDDEN PRIESTESS*.
THE *SWORD* THAT COMES OUT FROM YOUR HAND.
IS THAT IT-- THE *GENUINE* OBJECT OF REVERENCE HIDDEN AT ISE?

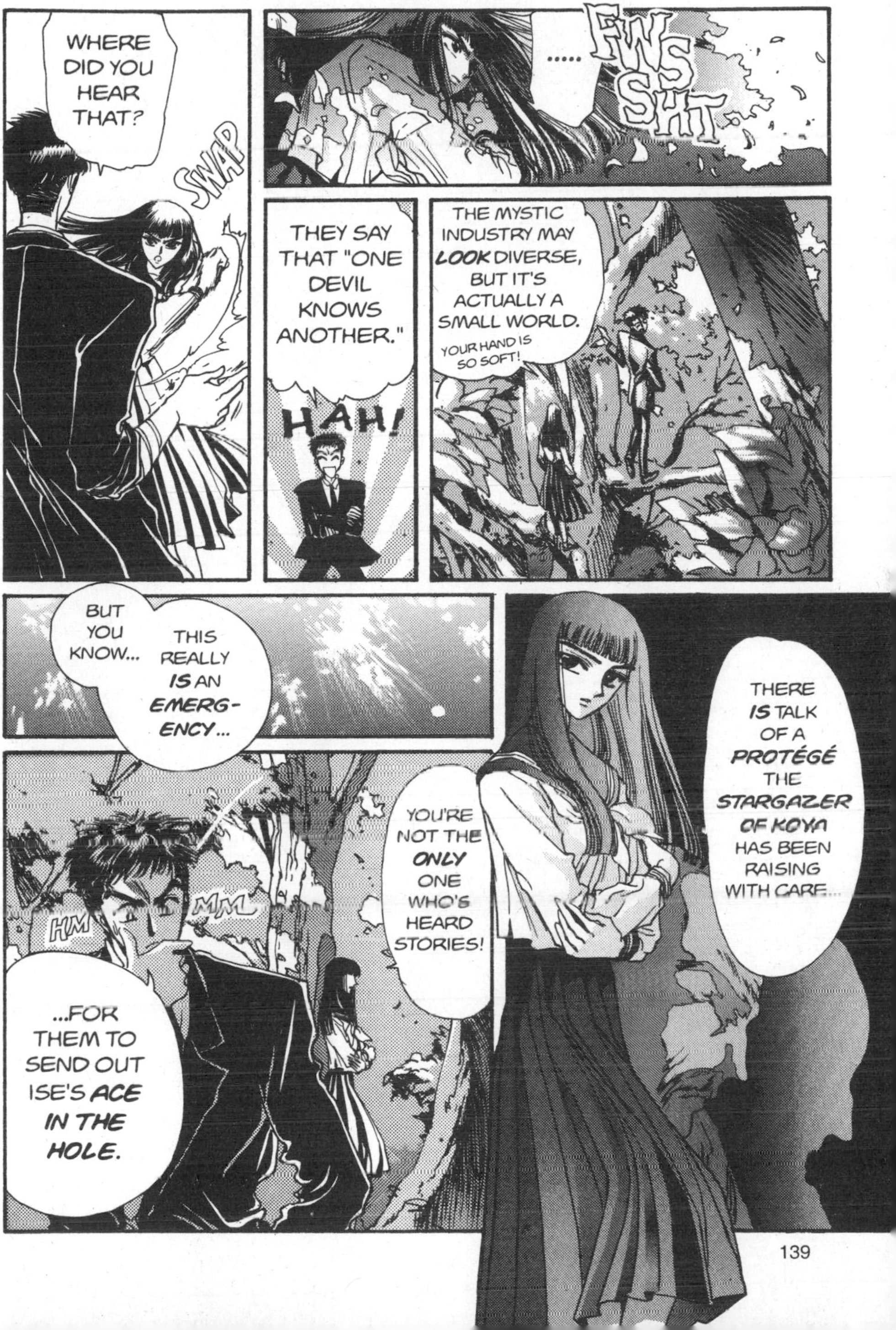
WHERE DID YOU HEAR THAT?
SWAP
.....
FWS SHT
THEY SAY THAT "ONE DEVIL KNOWS ANOTHER."
HAH!
THE MYSTIC INDUSTRY MAY LOOK DIVERSE, BUT IT'S ACTUALLY A SMALL WORLD.
YOUR HAND IS SO SOFT!
BUT YOU KNOW...
THIS REALLY IS AN EMERG-ENCY...
THERE IS TALK OF A PROTÉGÉ THE STARGAZER OF KOYA HAS BEEN RAISING WITH CARE...
SWAP
HM
MM
YOU'RE NOT THE ONLY ONE WHO'S HEARD STORIES!
...FOR THEM TO SEND OUT ISE'S ACE IN THE HOLE.

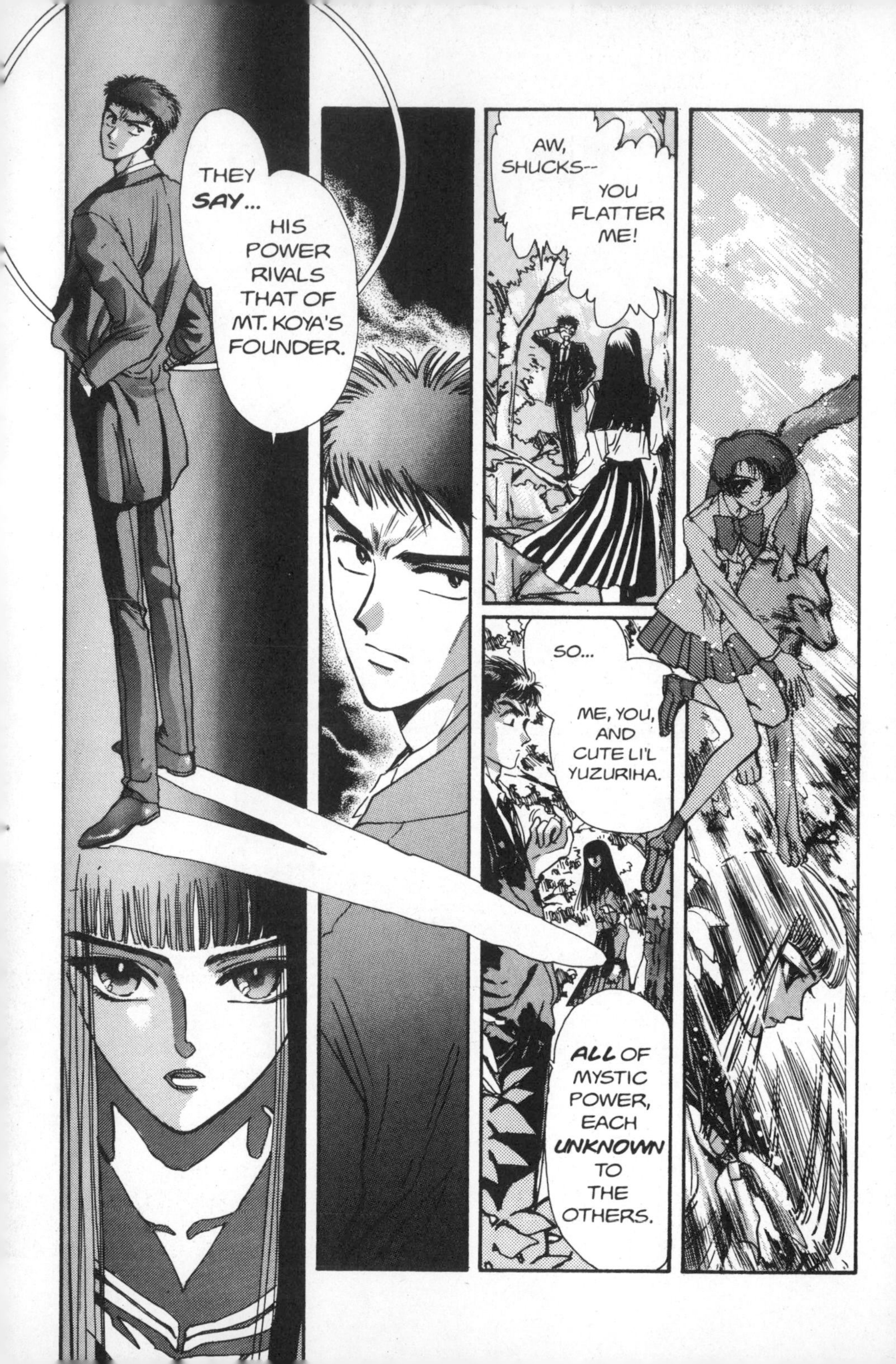
THEY SAY... HIS POWER RIVALS THAT OF MT. KOYA'S FOUNDER.
AW, SHUCKS-- YOU FLATTER ME!
SO... ME, YOU, AND CUTE LI'L YUZURIHA.
ALL OF MYSTIC POWER, EACH UNKNOWN TO THE OTHERS.

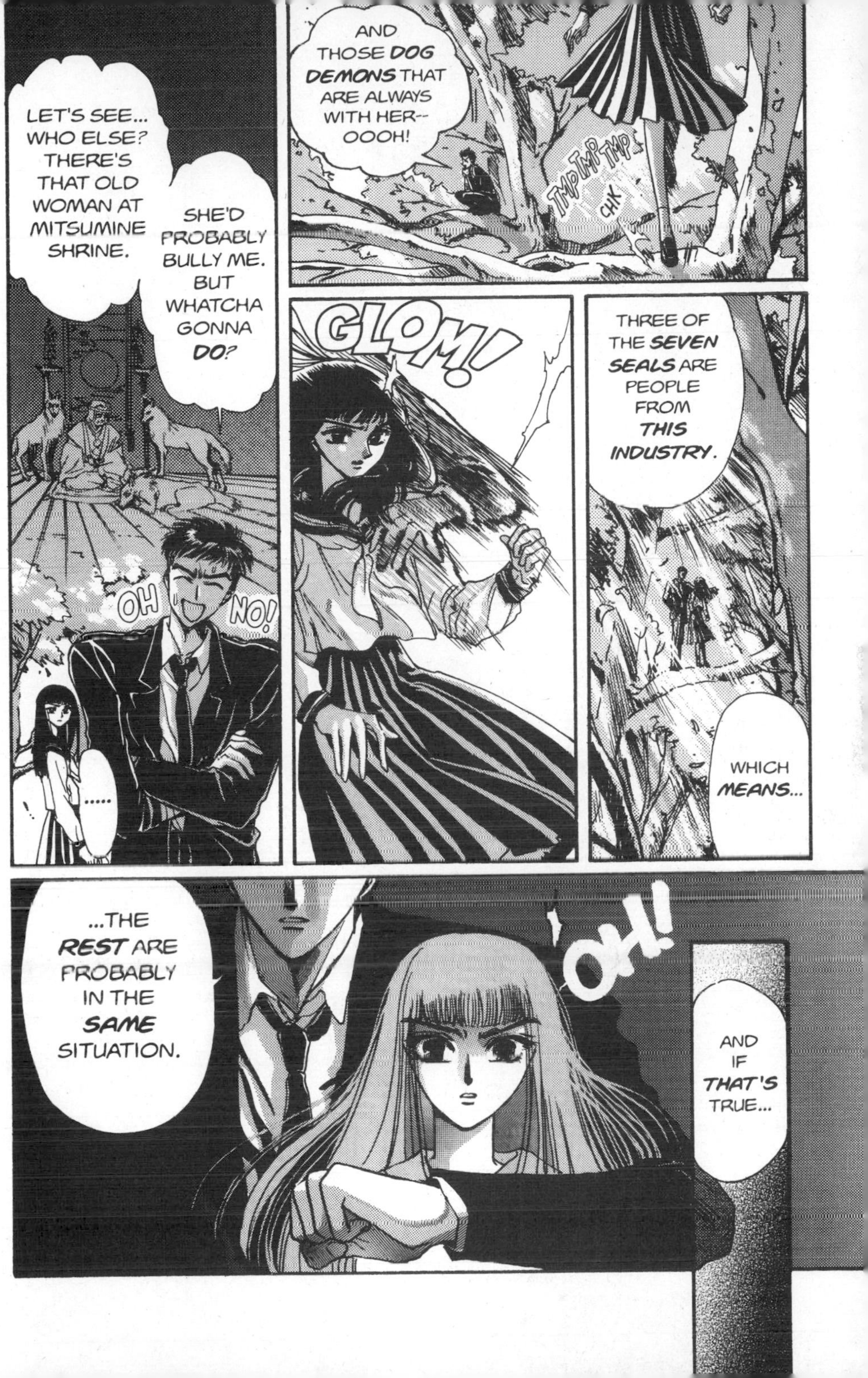
LET'S SEE... WHO ELSE? THERE'S THAT OLD WOMAN AT MITSUMINE SHRINE.
SHE'D PROBABLY BULLY ME. BUT WHATCHA GONNA DO?
OH NO!
.....
AND THOSE DOG DEMONS THAT ARE ALWAYS WITH HER-- OOOH!
TMP TMP TMP
CHK
GLOM!
THREE OF THE SEVEN SEALS ARE PEOPLE FROM THIS INDUSTRY.
WHICH MEANS...
...THE REST ARE PROBABLY IN THE SAME SITUATION.
OH!
AND IF THAT'S TRUE...

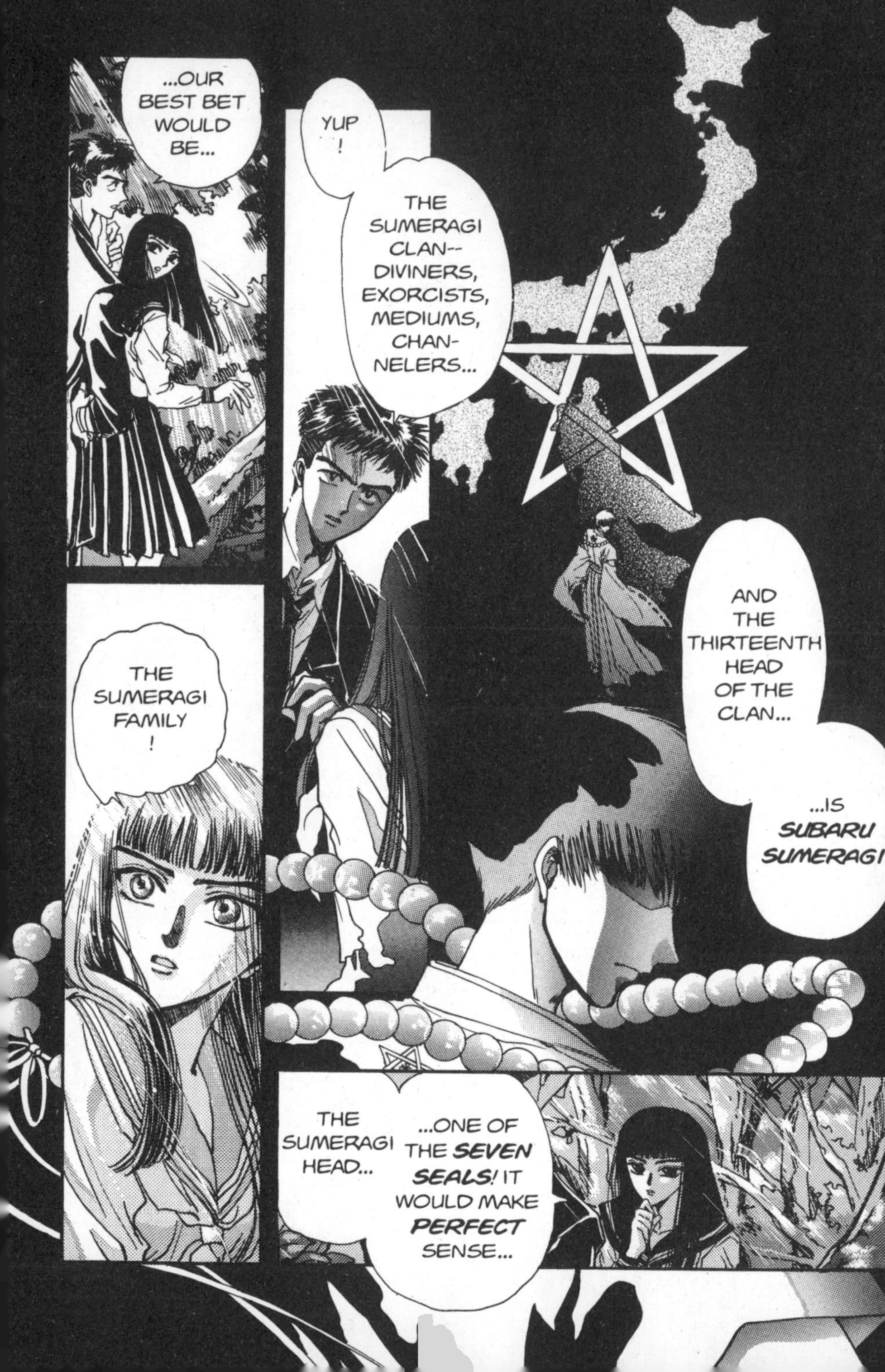
...OUR BEST BET WOULD BE...
THE SUMERAGI FAMILY !
YUP !
THE SUMERAGI CLAN-- DIVINERS, EXORCISTS, MEDIUMS, CHAN-NELERS...
AND THE THIRTEENTH HEAD OF THE CLAN...
...IS *SUBARU SUMERAGI*.
THE SUMERAGI HEAD...
...ONE OF THE *SEVEN SEALS*! IT WOULD MAKE *PERFECT* SENSE...

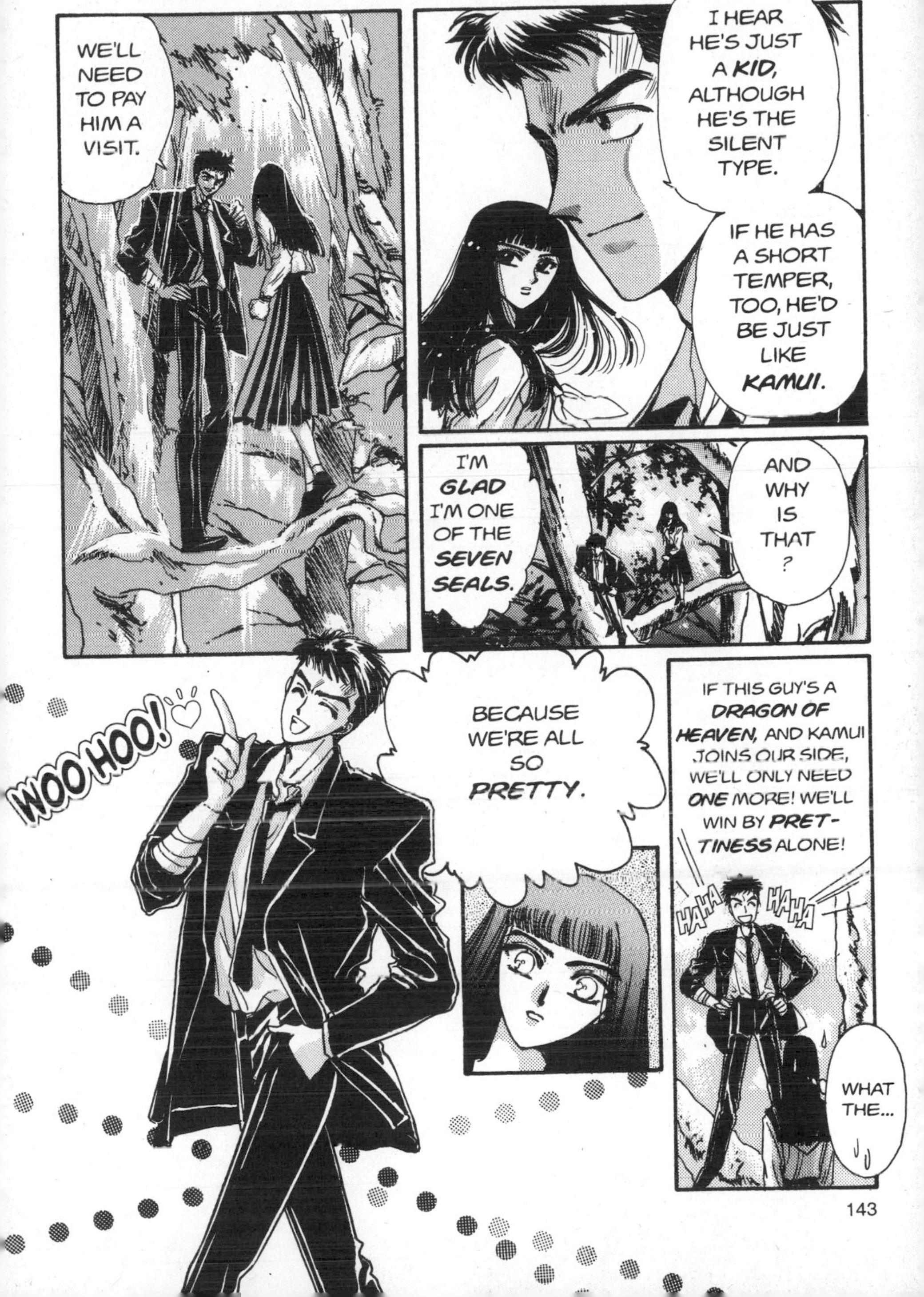
WE'LL NEED TO PAY HIM A VISIT.
I HEAR HE'S JUST A KID, ALTHOUGH HE'S THE SILENT TYPE.
IF HE HAS A SHORT TEMPER, TOO, HE'D BE JUST LIKE KAMUI.
I'M GLAD I'M ONE OF THE SEVEN SEALS.
AND WHY IS THAT ?
WOO HOO!
BECAUSE WE'RE ALL SO PRETTY.
IF THIS GUY'S A DRAGON OF HEAVEN, AND KAMUI JOINS OUR SIDE, WE'LL ONLY NEED ONE MORE! WE'LL WIN BY PRETTINESS ALONE!
HAHA
HAHA
WHAT THE...

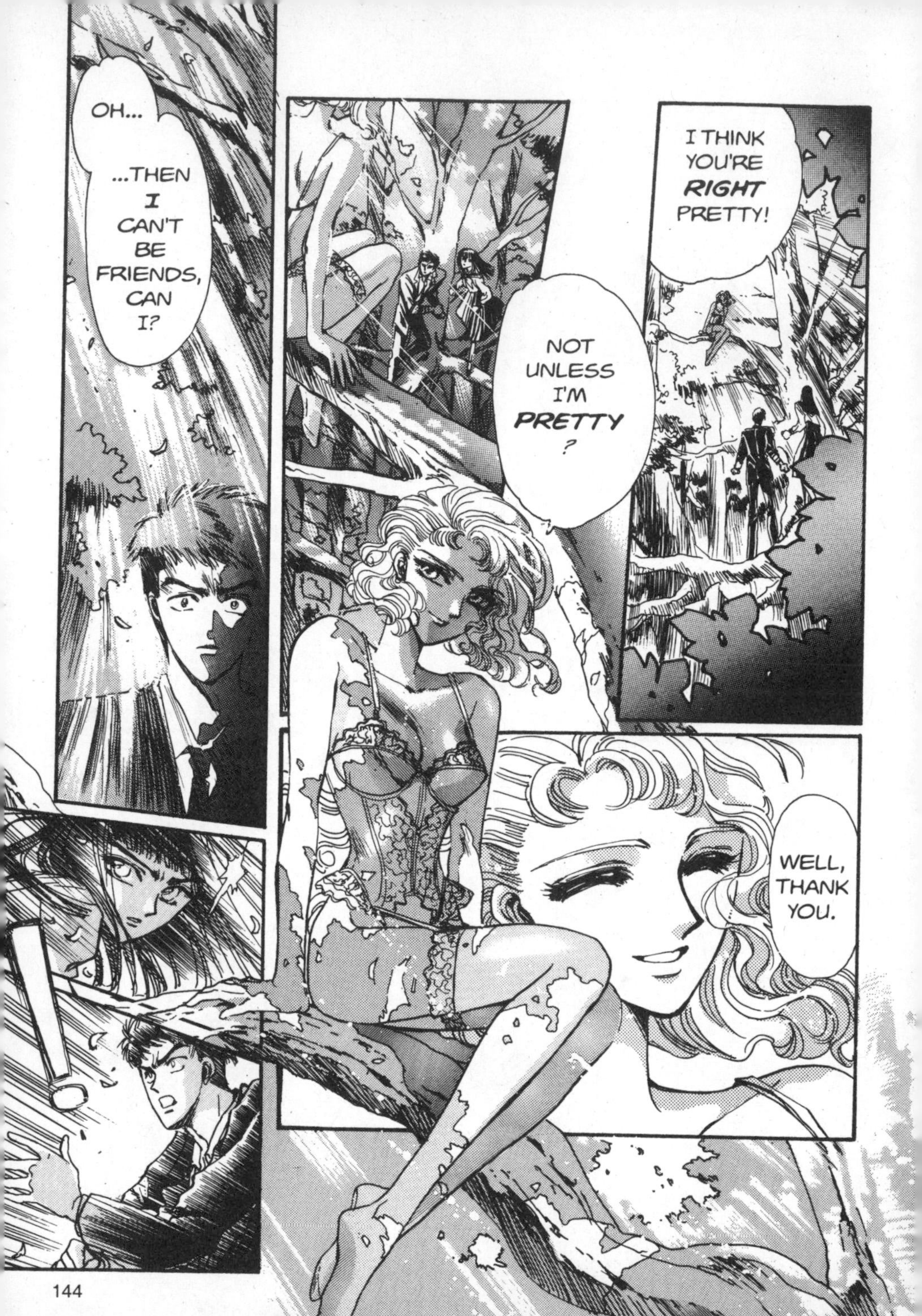
OH...
...THEN I CAN'T BE FRIENDS, CAN I?
NOT UNLESS I'M PRETTY?
I THINK YOU'RE RIGHT PRETTY!
WELL, THANK YOU.

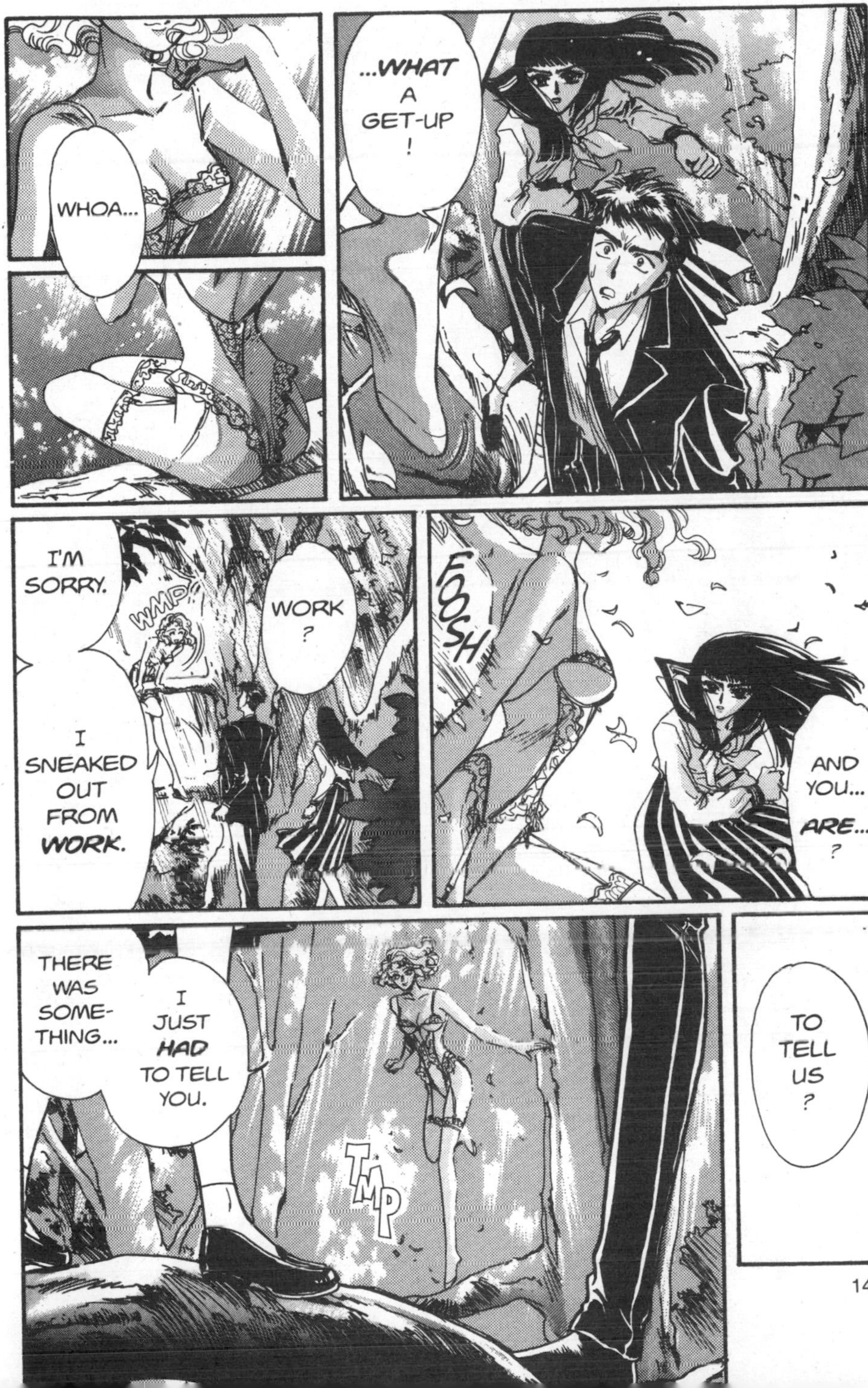
WHOA...
...WHAT A GET-UP !
I'M SORRY.
WMP
WORK ?
I SNEAKED OUT FROM WORK.
FOOSH
AND YOU... ARE... ?
THERE WAS SOME-THING...
I JUST HAD TO TELL YOU.
TMP
TO TELL US ?

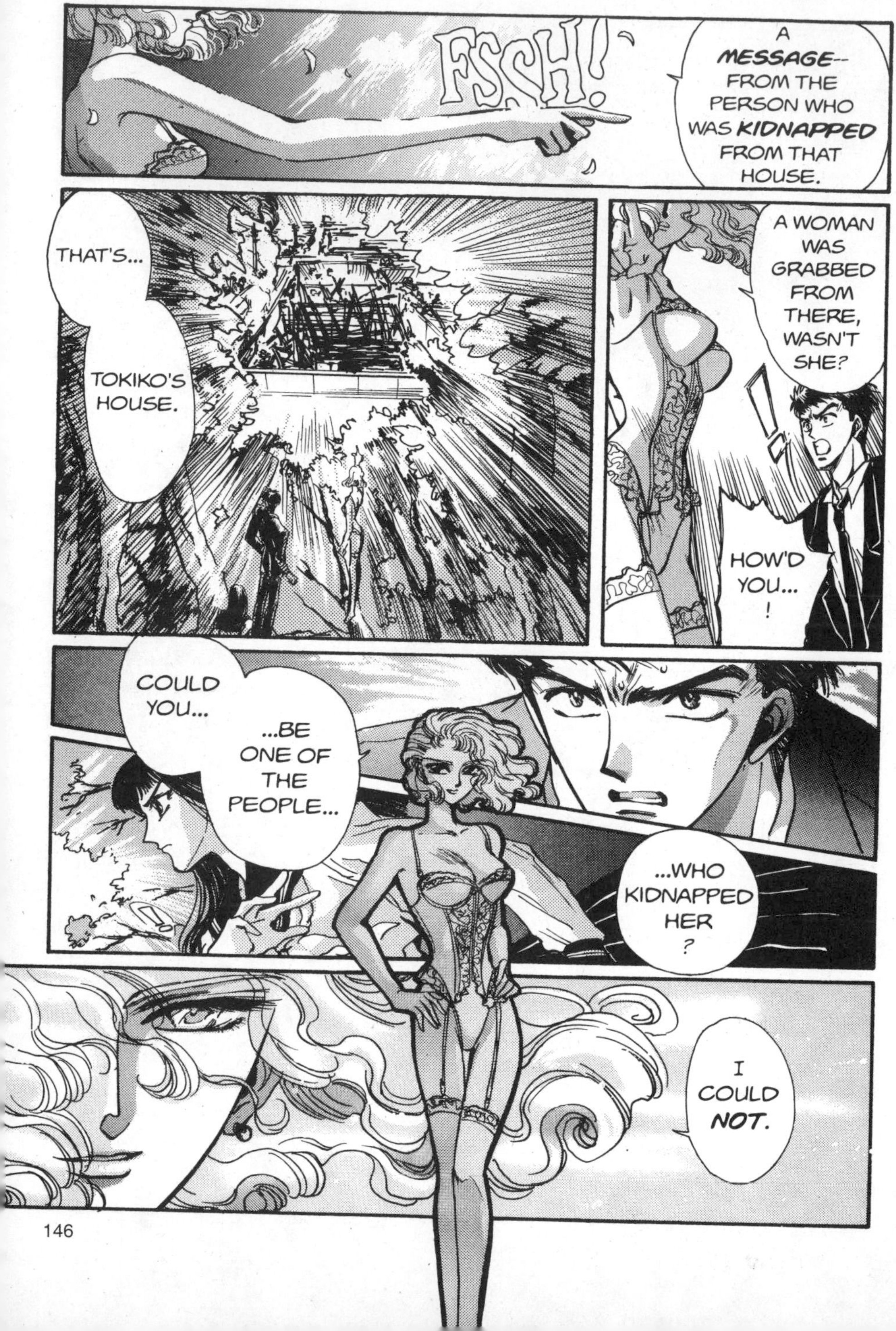
FSCH!
A MESSAGE-- FROM THE PERSON WHO WAS KIDNAPPED FROM THAT HOUSE.
THAT'S...
TOKIKO'S HOUSE.
A WOMAN WAS GRABBED FROM THERE, WASN'T SHE?
!
HOW'D YOU... !
COULD YOU...
...BE ONE OF THE PEOPLE...
...WHO KIDNAPPED HER ?
I COULD NOT.

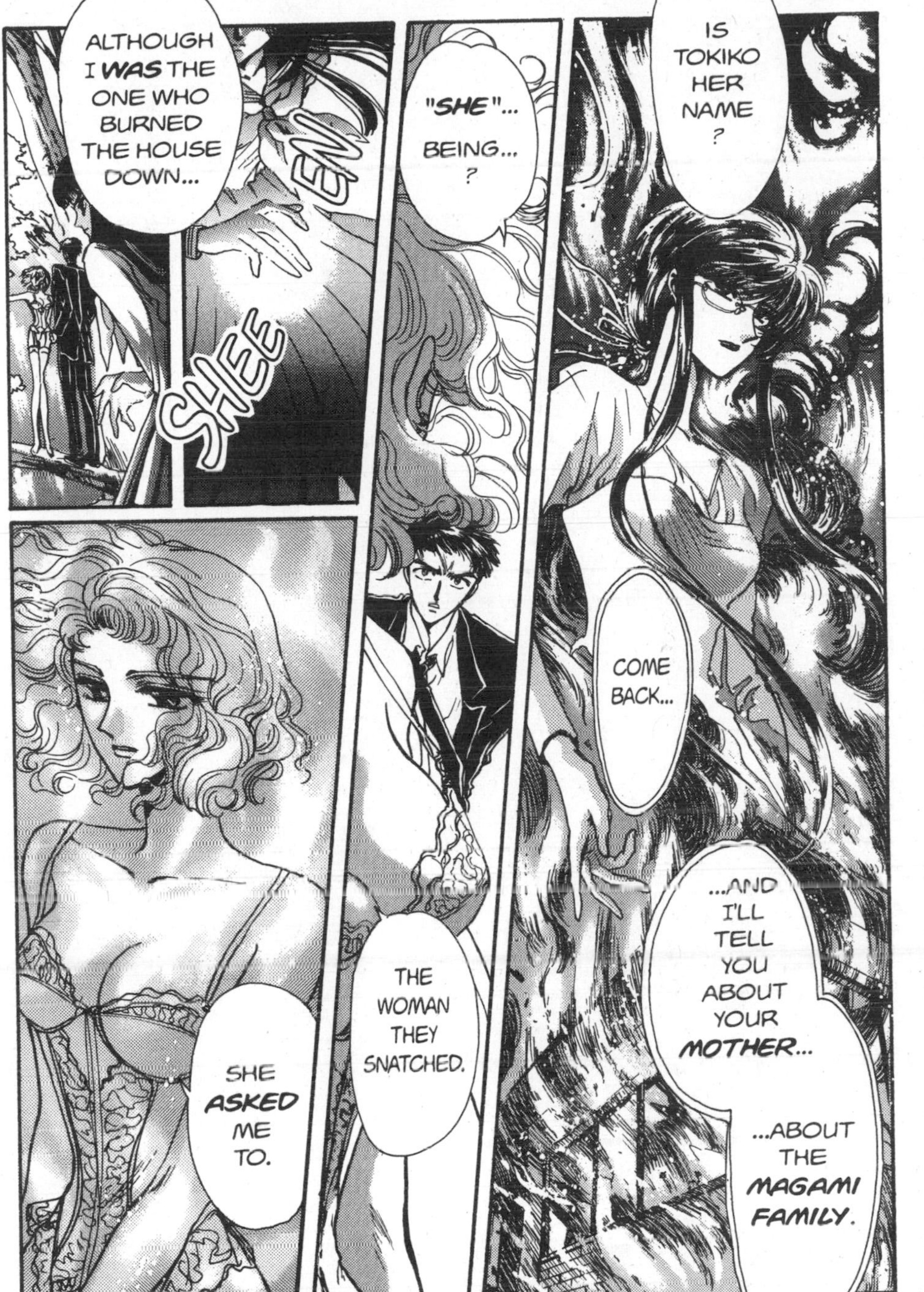

ALTHOUGH I WAS THE ONE WHO BURNED THE HOUSE DOWN...
EN
SHEE
SHE ASKED ME TO.
"SHE"... BEING...?
THE WOMAN THEY SNATCHED.
IS TOKIKO HER NAME?
COME BACK...
...AND I'LL TELL YOU ABOUT YOUR MOTHER...
...ABOUT THE MAGAMI FAMILY.

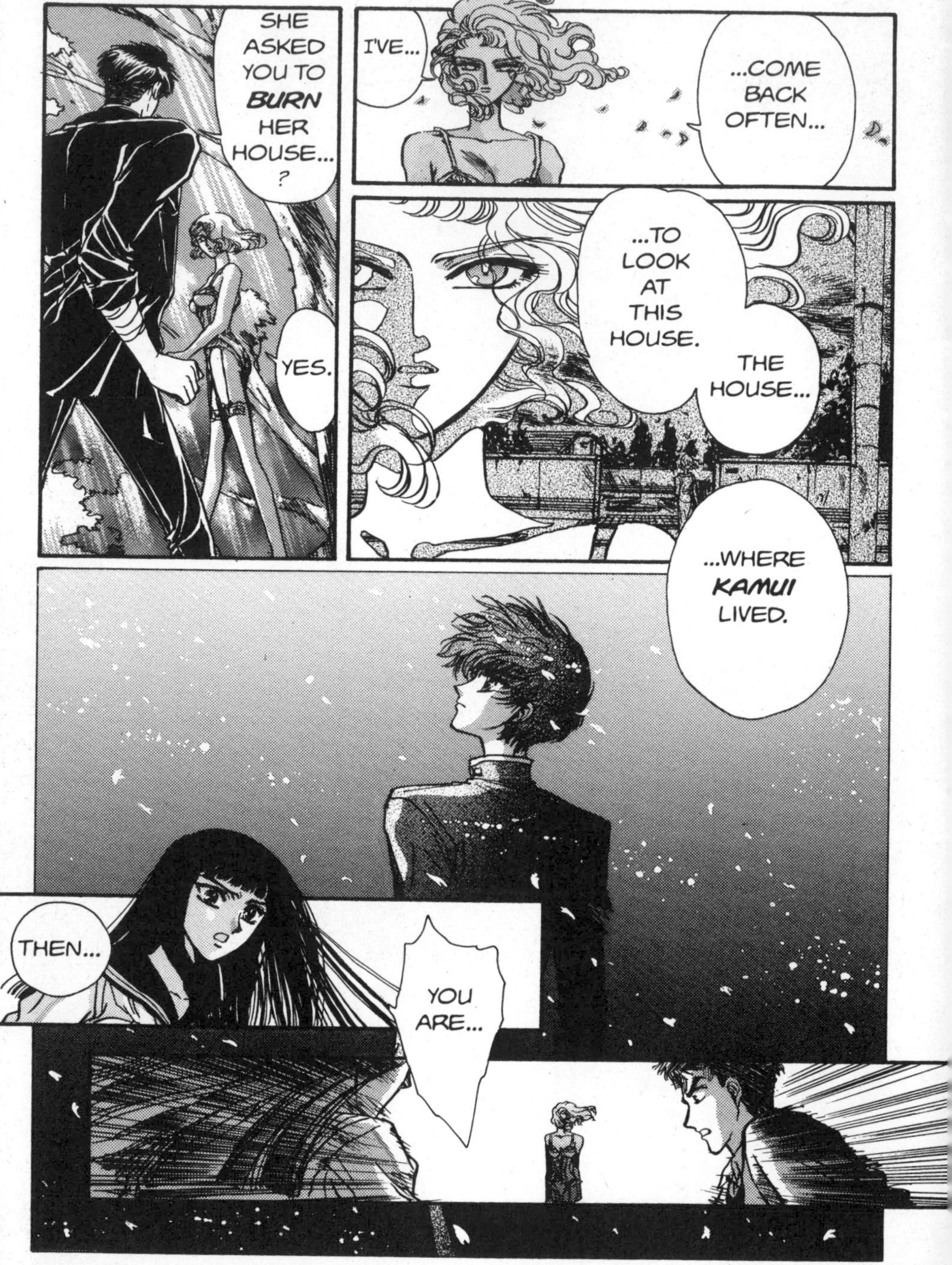
SHE ASKED YOU TO BURN HER HOUSE...?
YES.
I'VE...
...COME BACK OFTEN...
...TO LOOK AT THIS HOUSE.
THE HOUSE...
...WHERE KAMUI LIVED.
THEN...
YOU ARE...

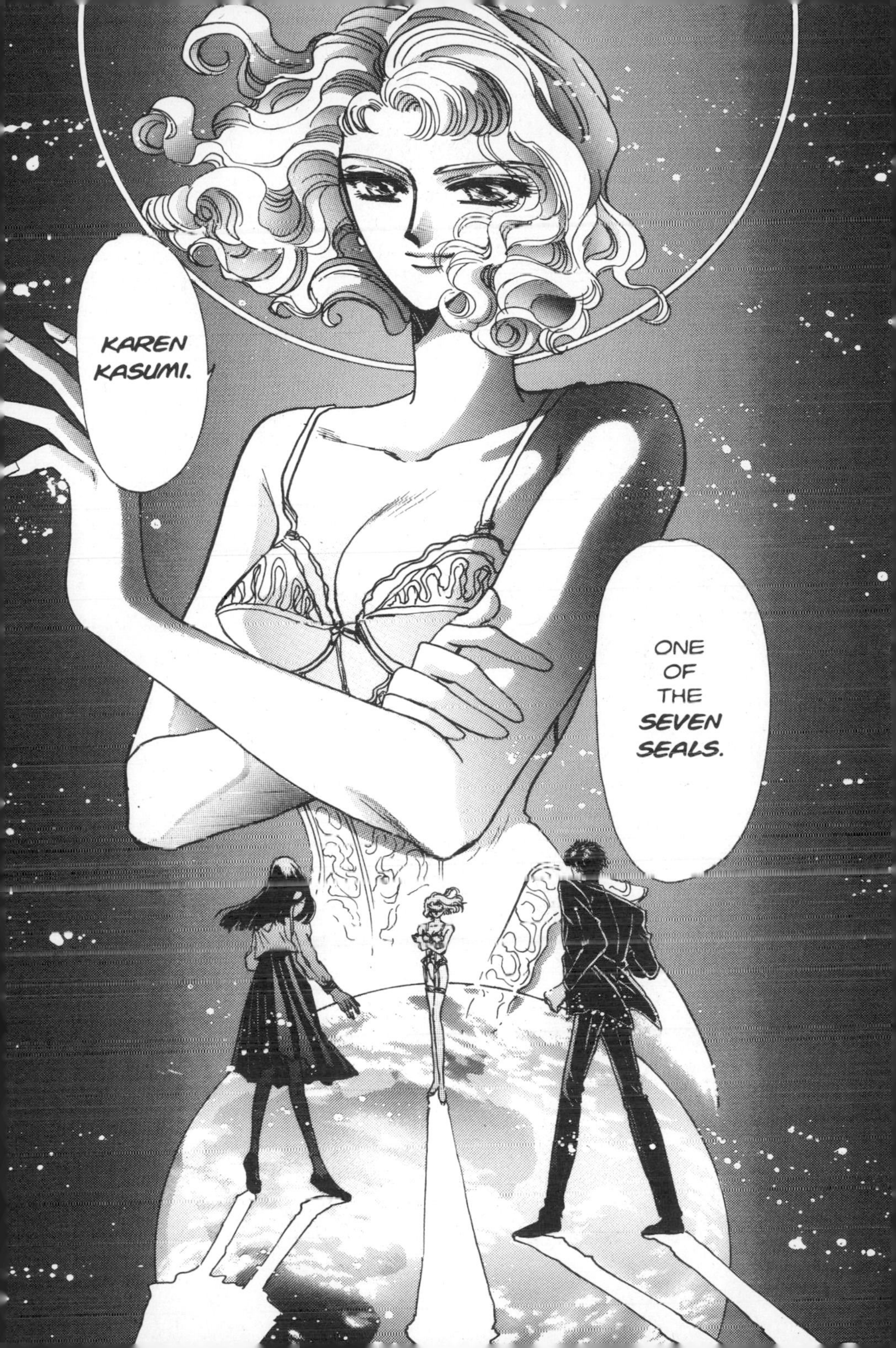
KAREN KASUMI.
ONE OF THE SEVEN SEALS.

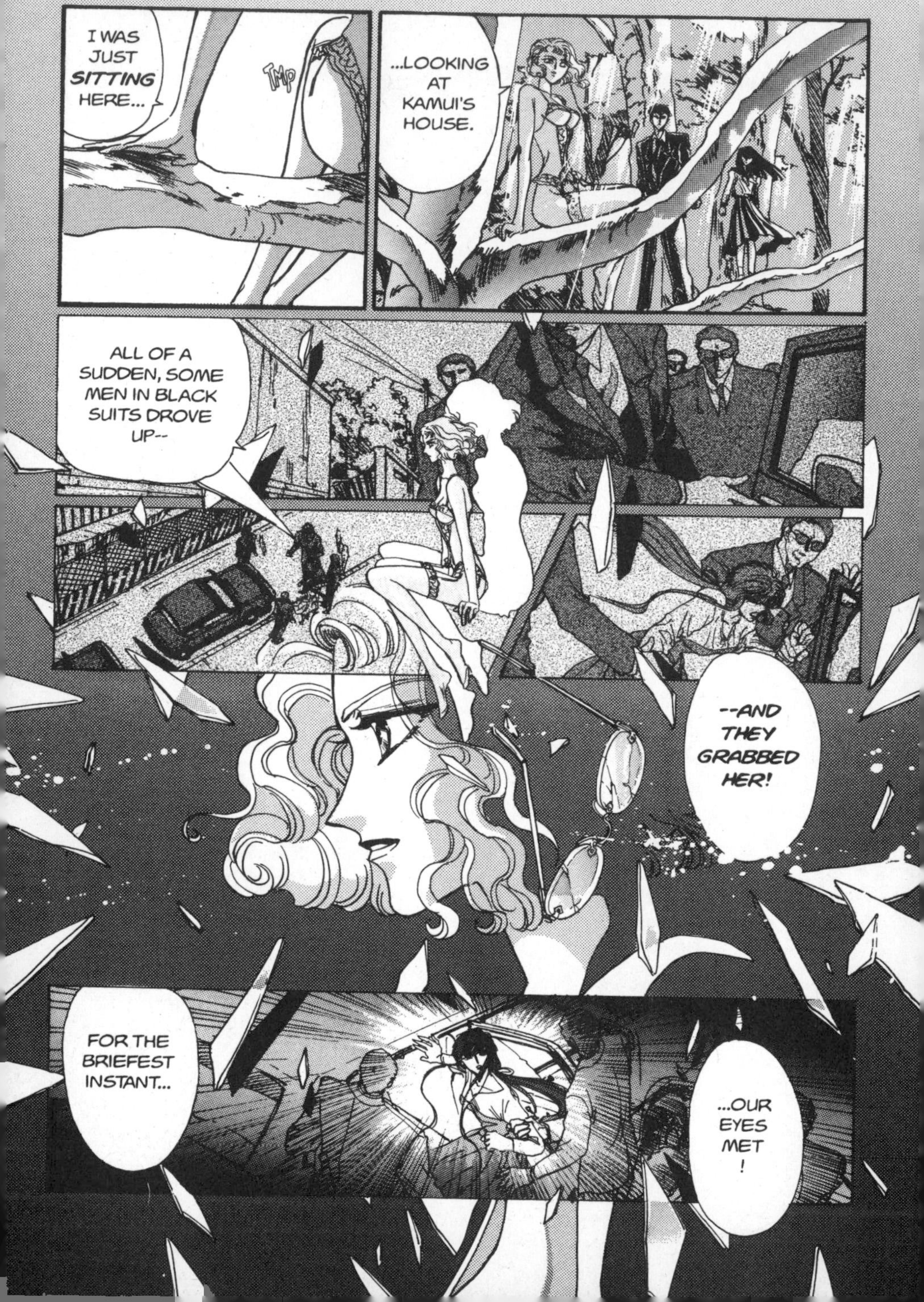
I WAS JUST SITTING HERE...
TMP
...LOOKING AT KAMUI'S HOUSE.
ALL OF A SUDDEN, SOME MEN IN BLACK SUITS DROVE UP--
--AND THEY GRABBED HER!
FOR THE BRIEFEST INSTANT...
...OUR EYES MET!

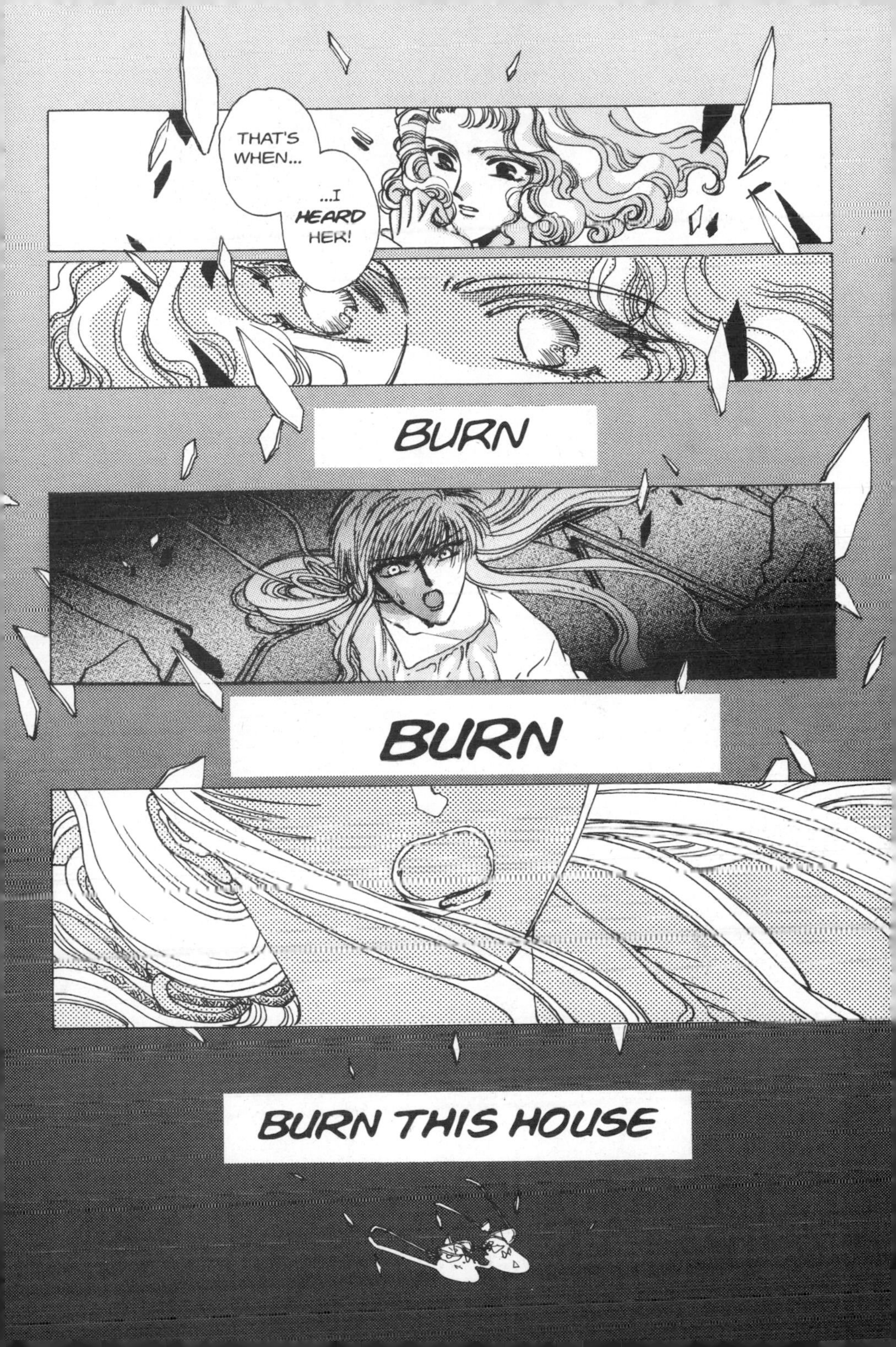
THAT'S WHEN...
...I HEARD HER!
BURN
BURN
BURN THIS HOUSE

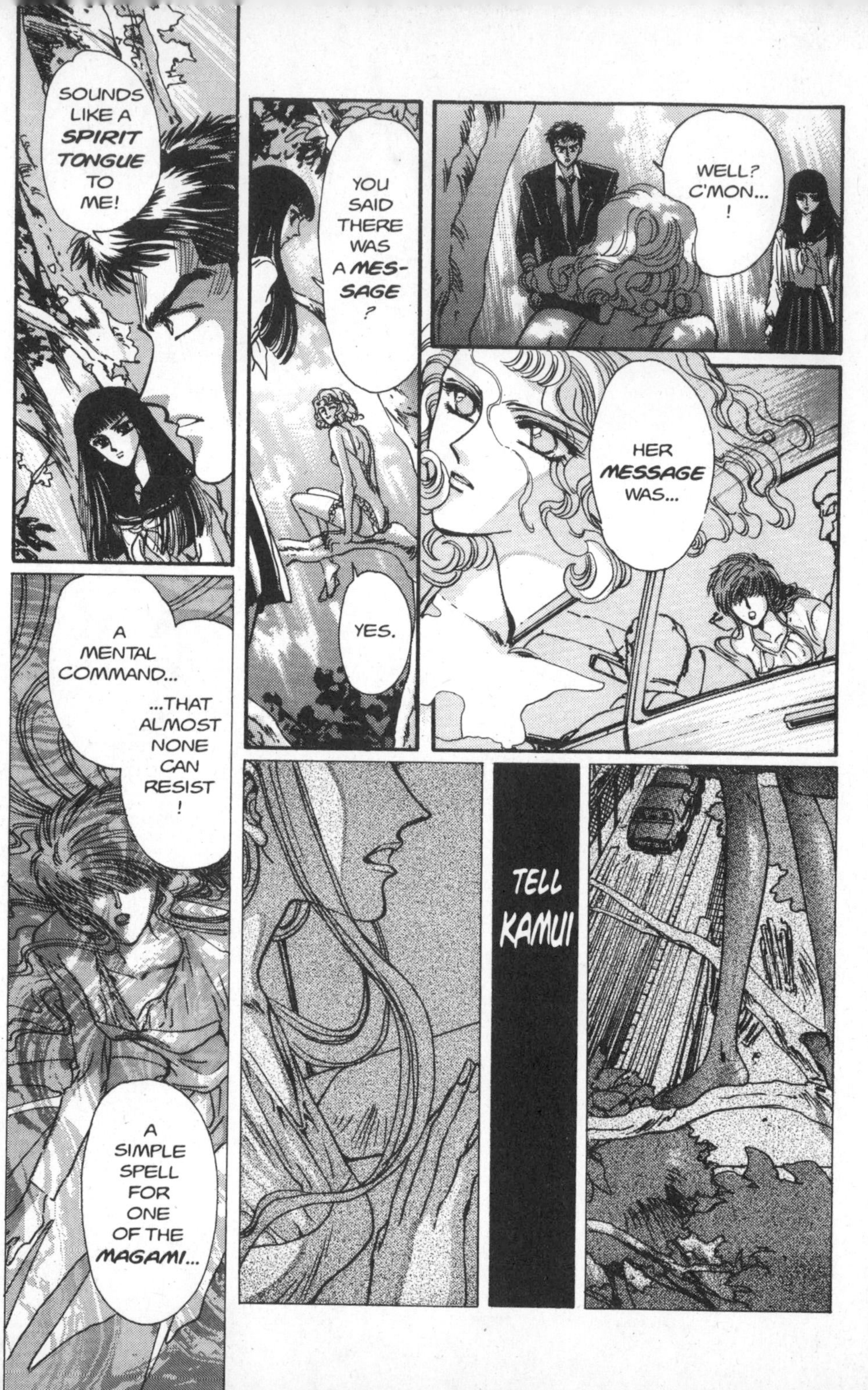
SOUNDS LIKE A **SPIRIT TONGUE** TO ME!
YOU SAID THERE WAS A **MES-SAGE**?
YES.
WELL? C'MON...!
HER **MESSAGE** WAS...
A MENTAL COMMAND...
...THAT ALMOST NONE CAN RESIST!
A SIMPLE SPELL FOR ONE OF THE **MAGAMI**...
TELL KAMUI

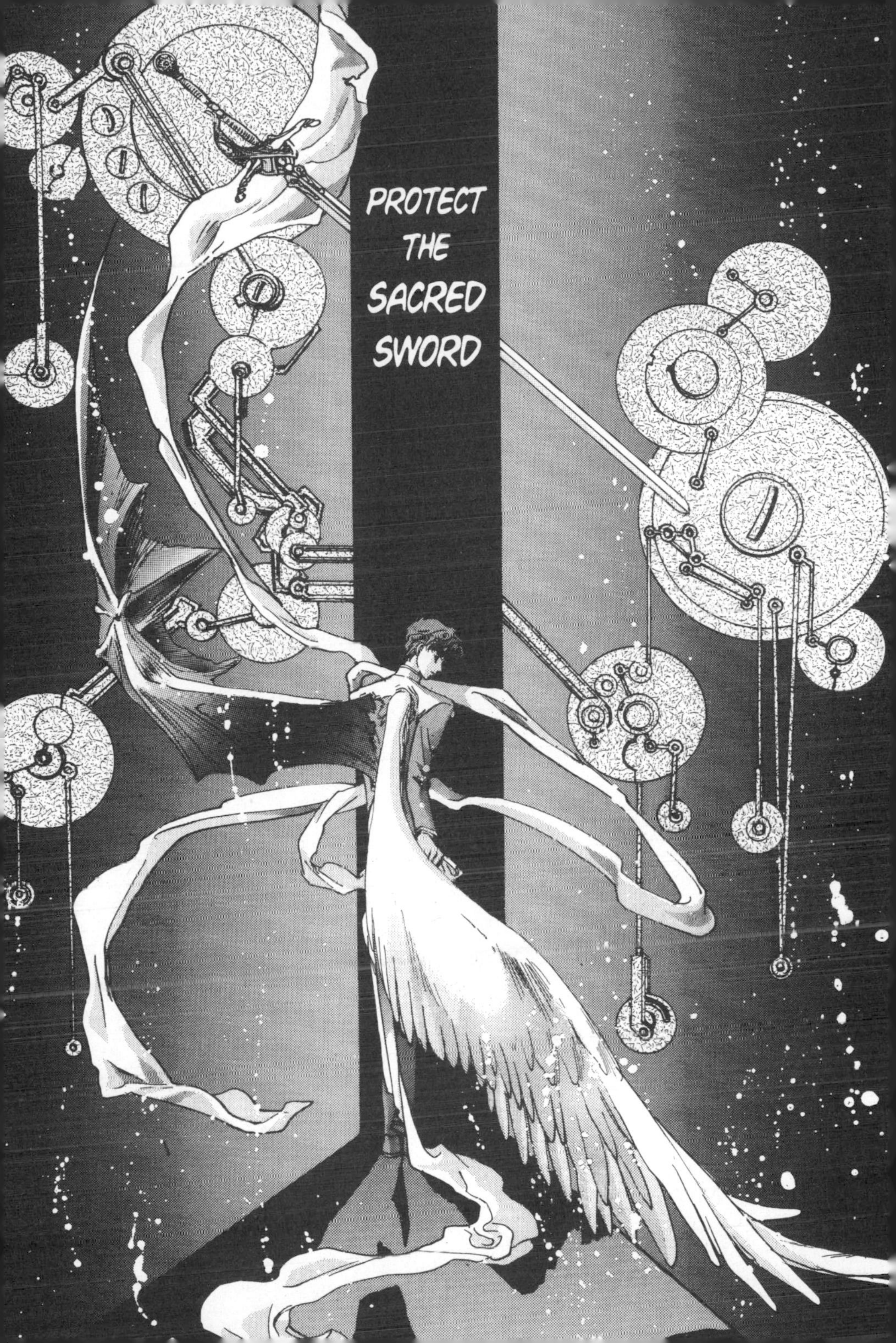
PROTECT THE SACRED SWORD

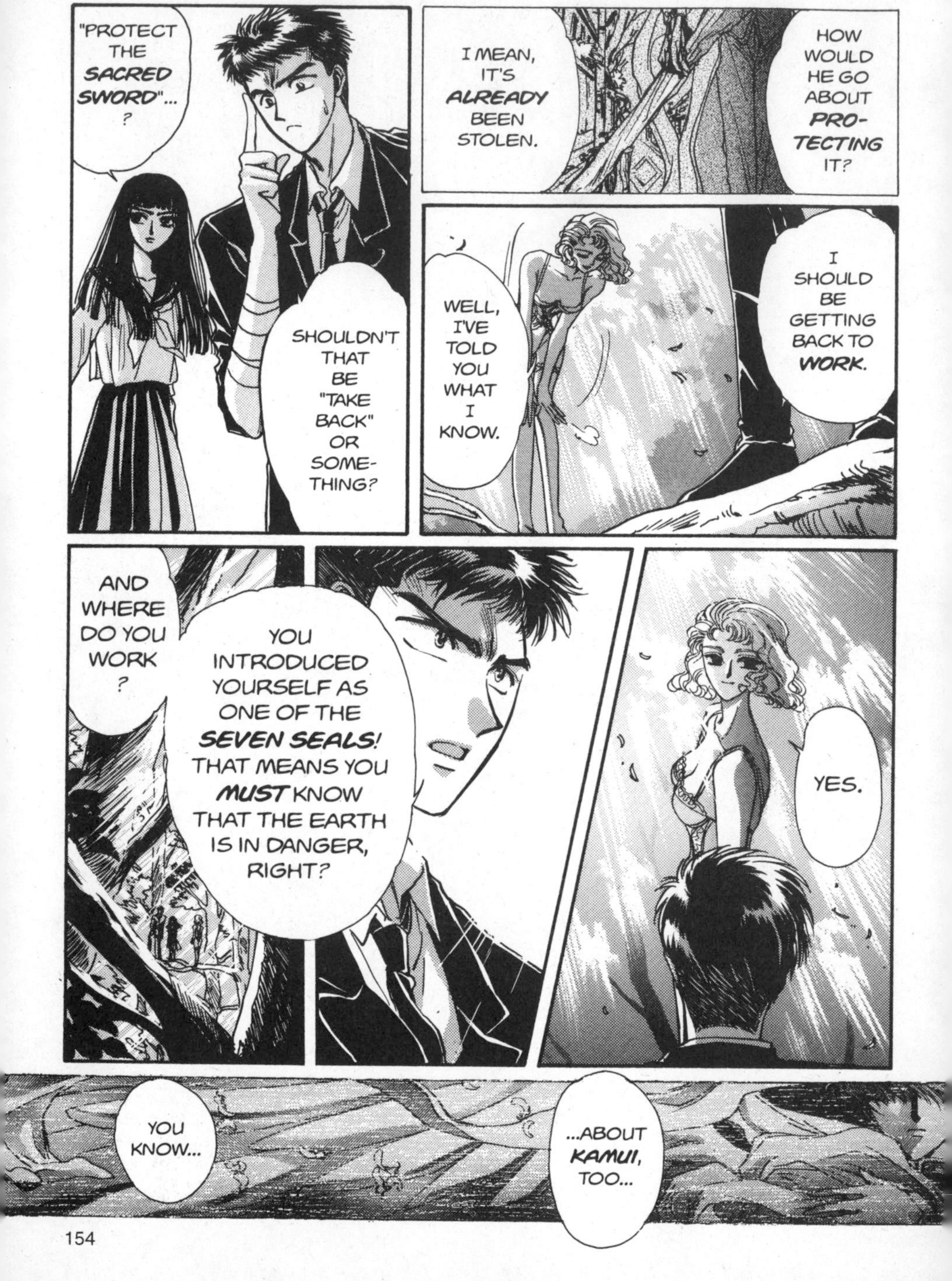
"PROTECT THE SACRED SWORD"...?
I MEAN, IT'S ALREADY BEEN STOLEN.
HOW WOULD HE GO ABOUT PROTECTING IT?
SHOULDN'T THAT BE "TAKE BACK" OR SOMETHING?
WELL, I'VE TOLD YOU WHAT I KNOW.
I SHOULD BE GETTING BACK TO WORK.
AND WHERE DO YOU WORK?
YOU INTRODUCED YOURSELF AS ONE OF THE SEVEN SEALS! THAT MEANS YOU MUST KNOW THAT THE EARTH IS IN DANGER, RIGHT?
YES.
YOU KNOW...
...ABOUT KAMUI, TOO...

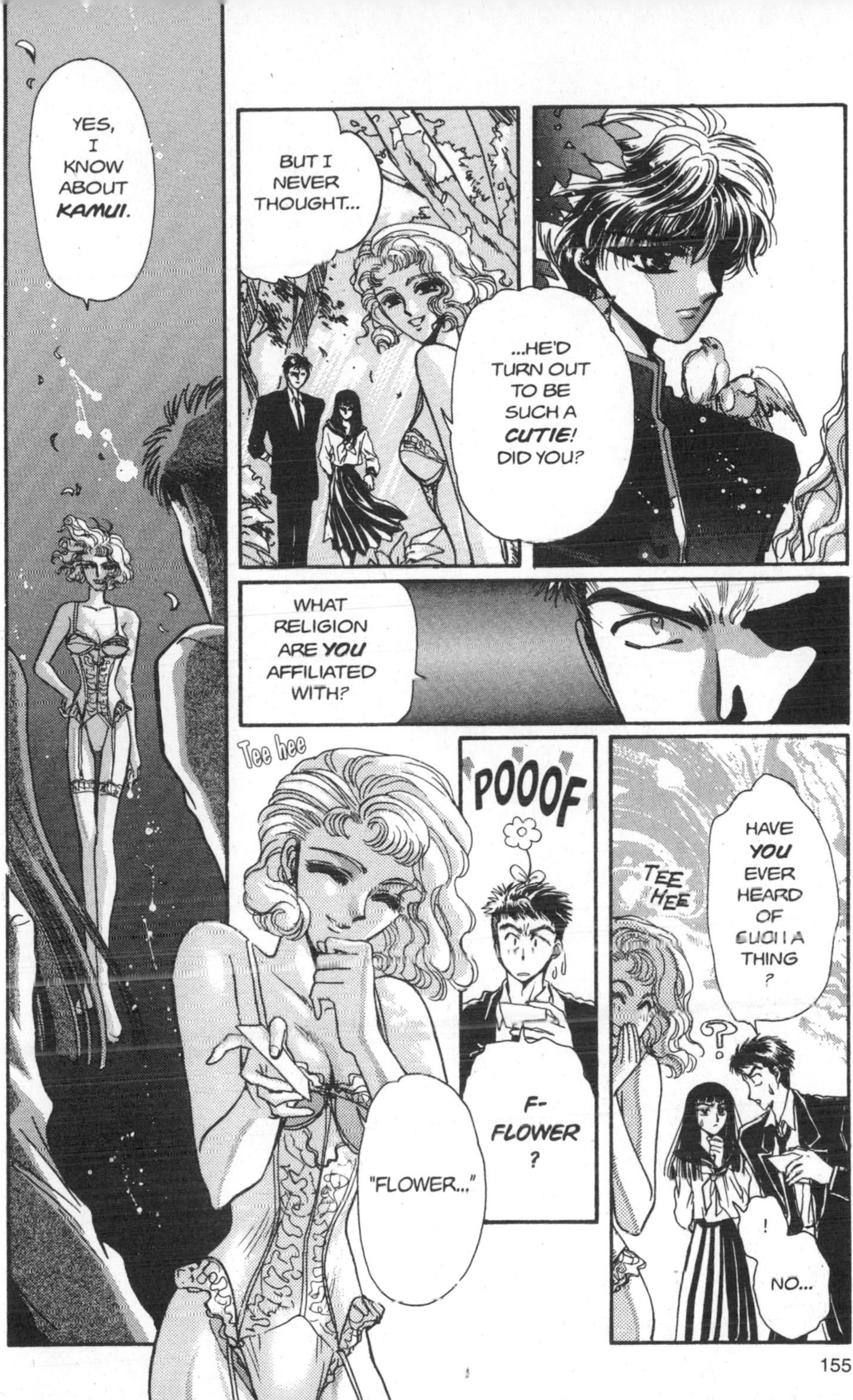

YES, I KNOW ABOUT KAMUI.
BUT I NEVER THOUGHT...
...HE'D TURN OUT TO BE SUCH A CUTIE! DID YOU?
WHAT RELIGION ARE YOU AFFILIATED WITH?
Tee hee
"FLOWER..."
POOOF
F-FLOWER?
TEE HEE
HAVE YOU EVER HEARD OF SUCH A THING?
!
NO...

BA-WHOOOSH

PLEASE-- VISIT ME SOME- TIME!

SMOOCH!

FWSSSSHT

FIRE !

SO *HER* ABILITY IS COM- BUSTION.

BUT WHERE DOES SHE...

THE ADDRESS IS ON THE BACK OF THE CARD.

TA DA!

Soapland
FLOWER

HOSTESS
Karen Kasumi

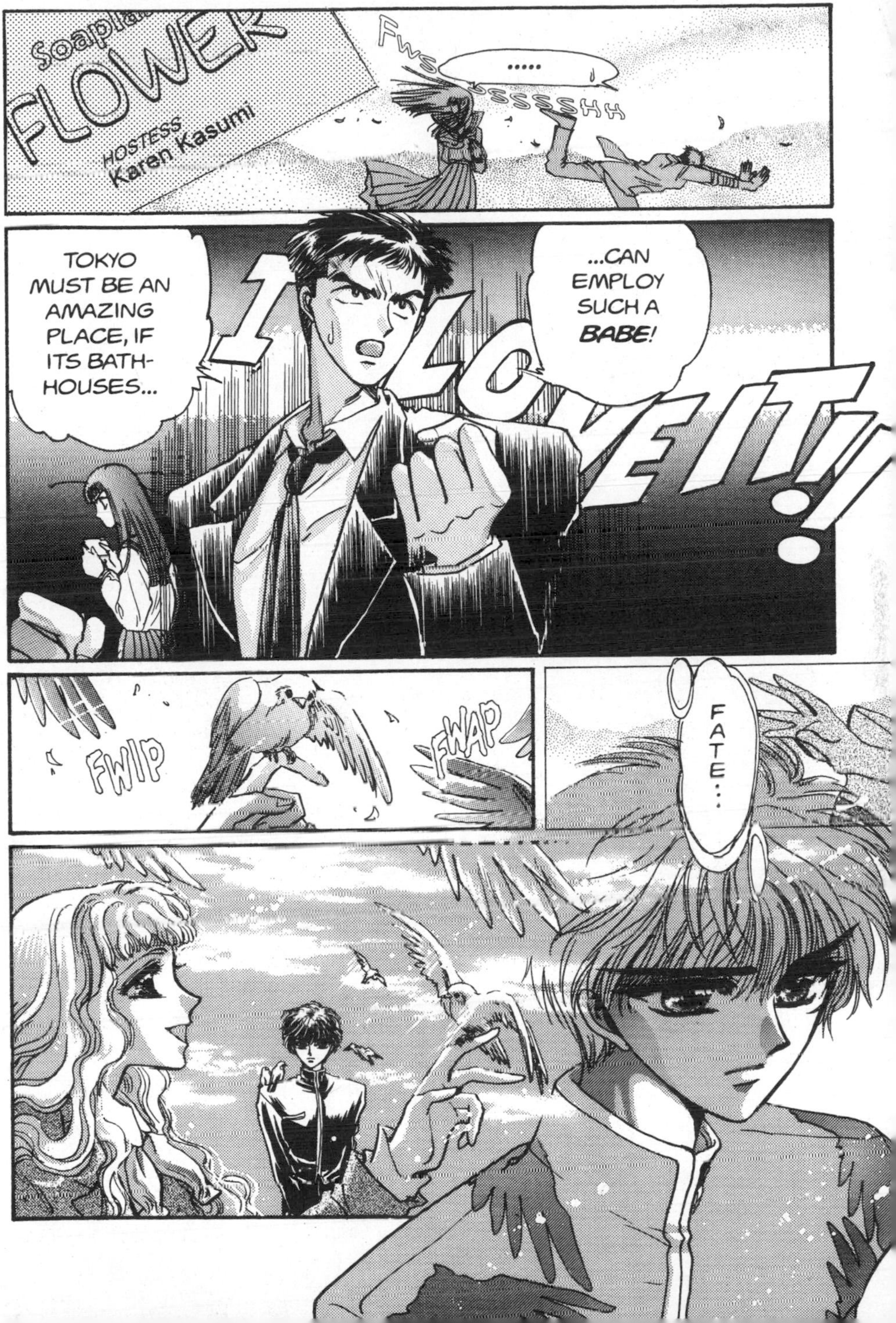
Soapla
FLOWER
HOSTESS
Karen Kasumi
FWSSSSSSSSHH
......
TOKYO MUST BE AN AMAZING PLACE, IF ITS BATH-HOUSES...
I LOVE IT!!
...CAN EMPLOY SUCH A BABE!
FWIP
FWAP
FATE...

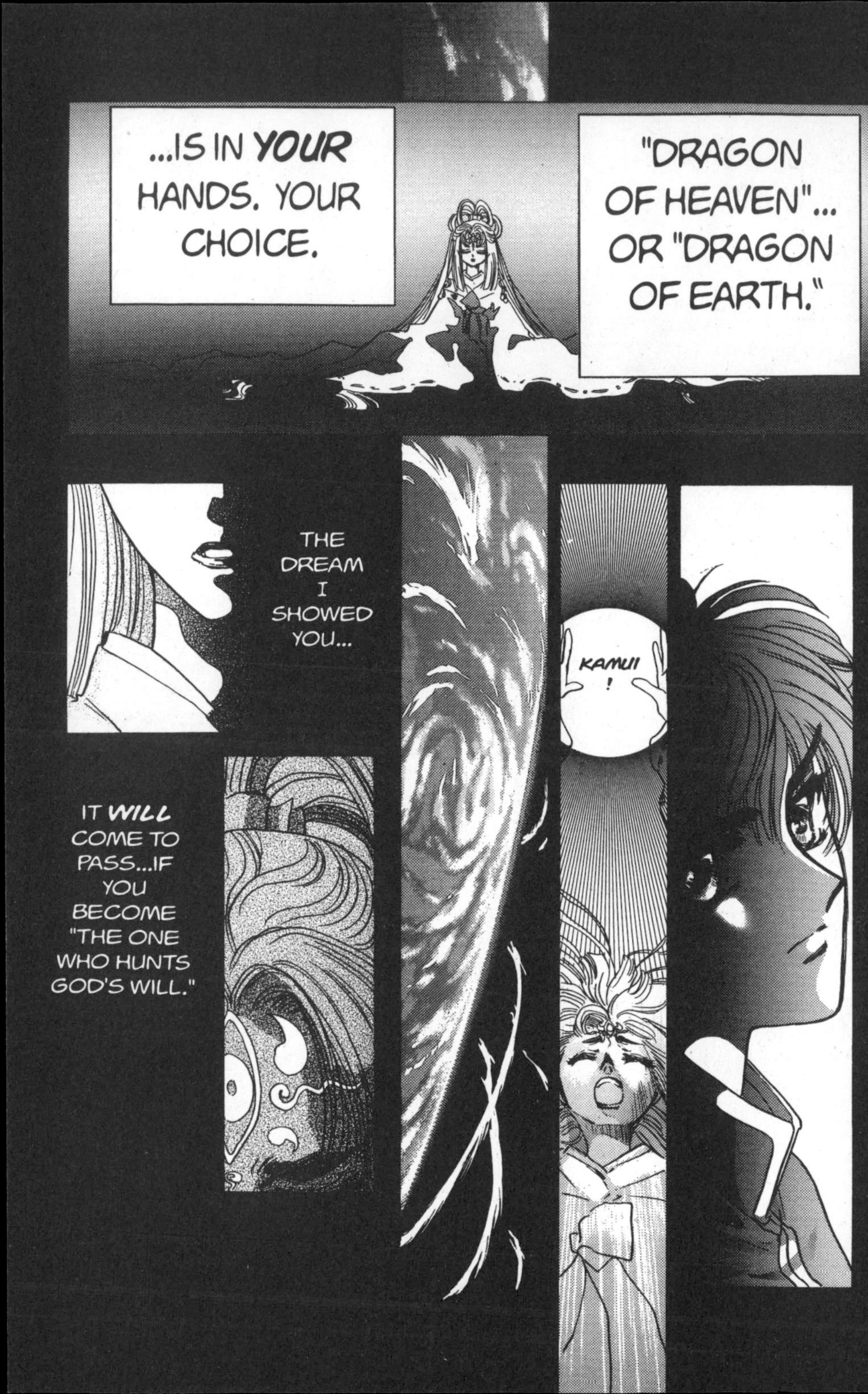
...IS IN YOUR HANDS. YOUR CHOICE.
"DRAGON OF HEAVEN"... OR "DRAGON OF EARTH."
THE DREAM I SHOWED YOU...
IT WILL COME TO PASS...IF YOU BECOME "THE ONE WHO HUNTS GOD'S WILL."
KAMUI!

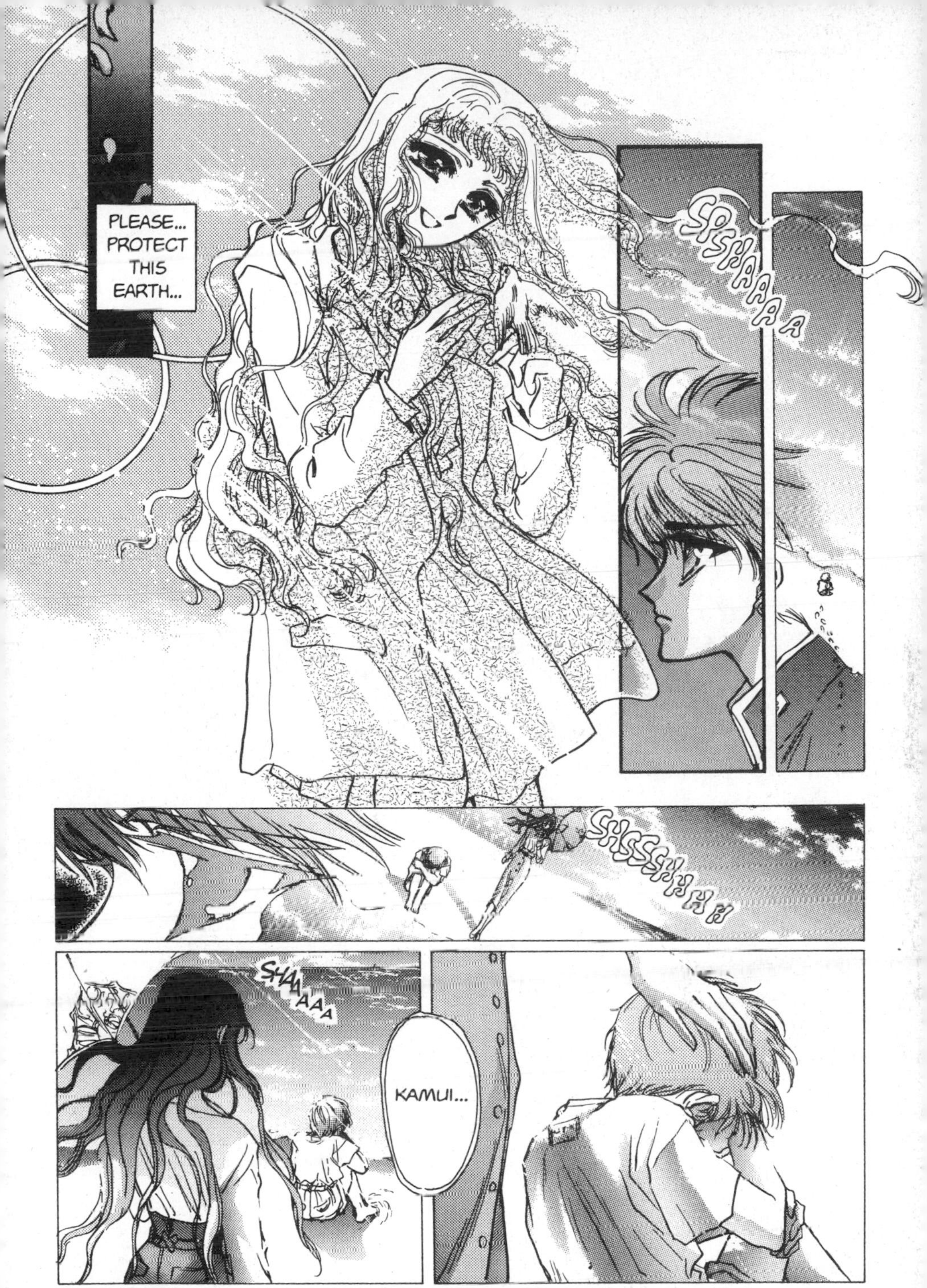
PLEASE... PROTECT THIS EARTH...
SPSHAAAA
SHSSSHHHH
SHAAAAA
KAMUI...

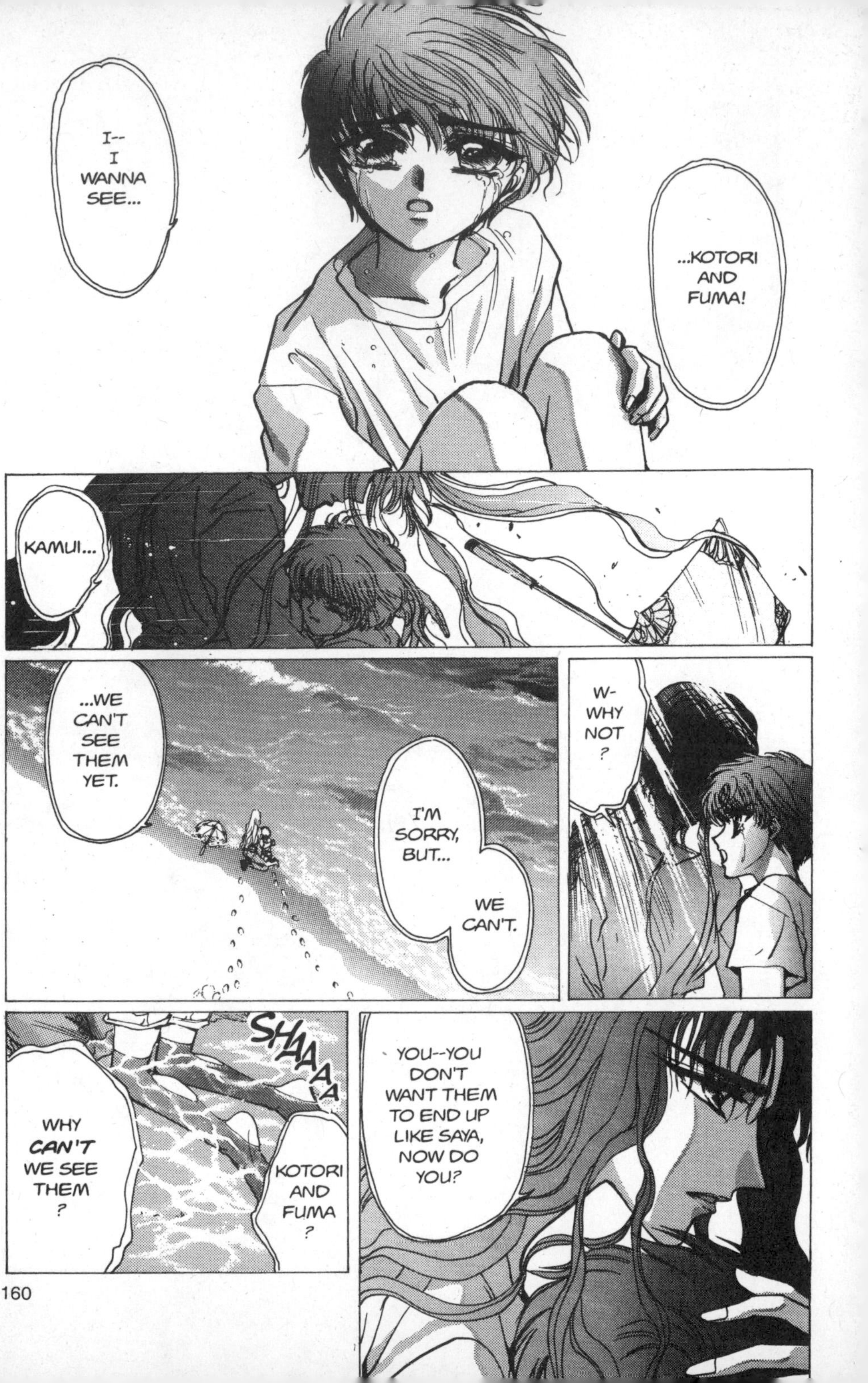
I-- I WANNA SEE...
...KOTORI AND FUMA!
KAMUI...
...WE CAN'T SEE THEM YET.
I'M SORRY, BUT...
WE CAN'T.
W-WHY NOT?
SHAAAA
WHY CAN'T WE SEE THEM?
KOTORI AND FUMA?
YOU--YOU DON'T WANT THEM TO END UP LIKE SAYA, NOW DO YOU?

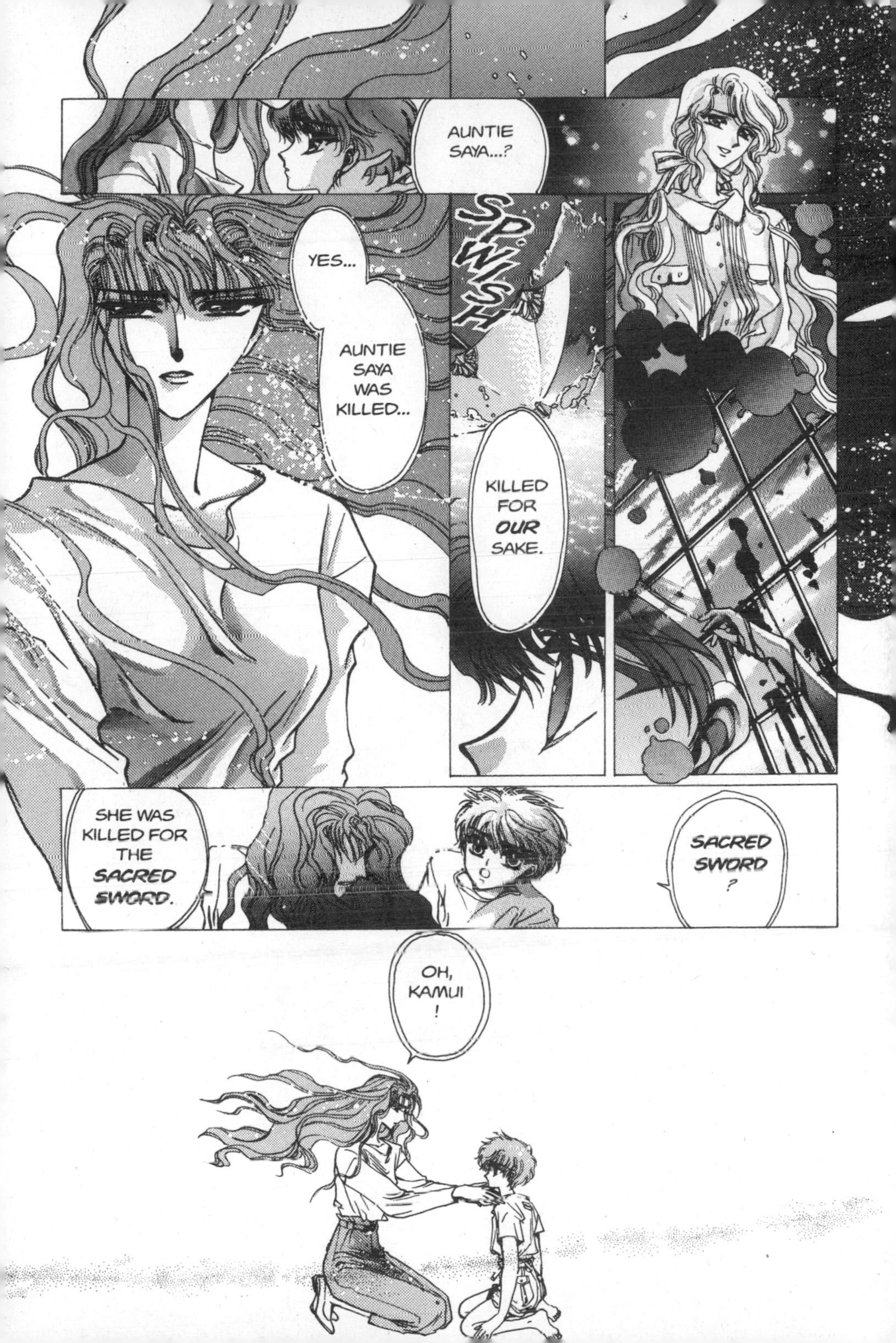
AUNTIE SAYA...?
YES...
AUNTIE SAYA WAS KILLED...
SPWISH
KILLED FOR OUR SAKE.
SHE WAS KILLED FOR THE SACRED SWORD.
SACRED SWORD ?
OH, KAMUI !

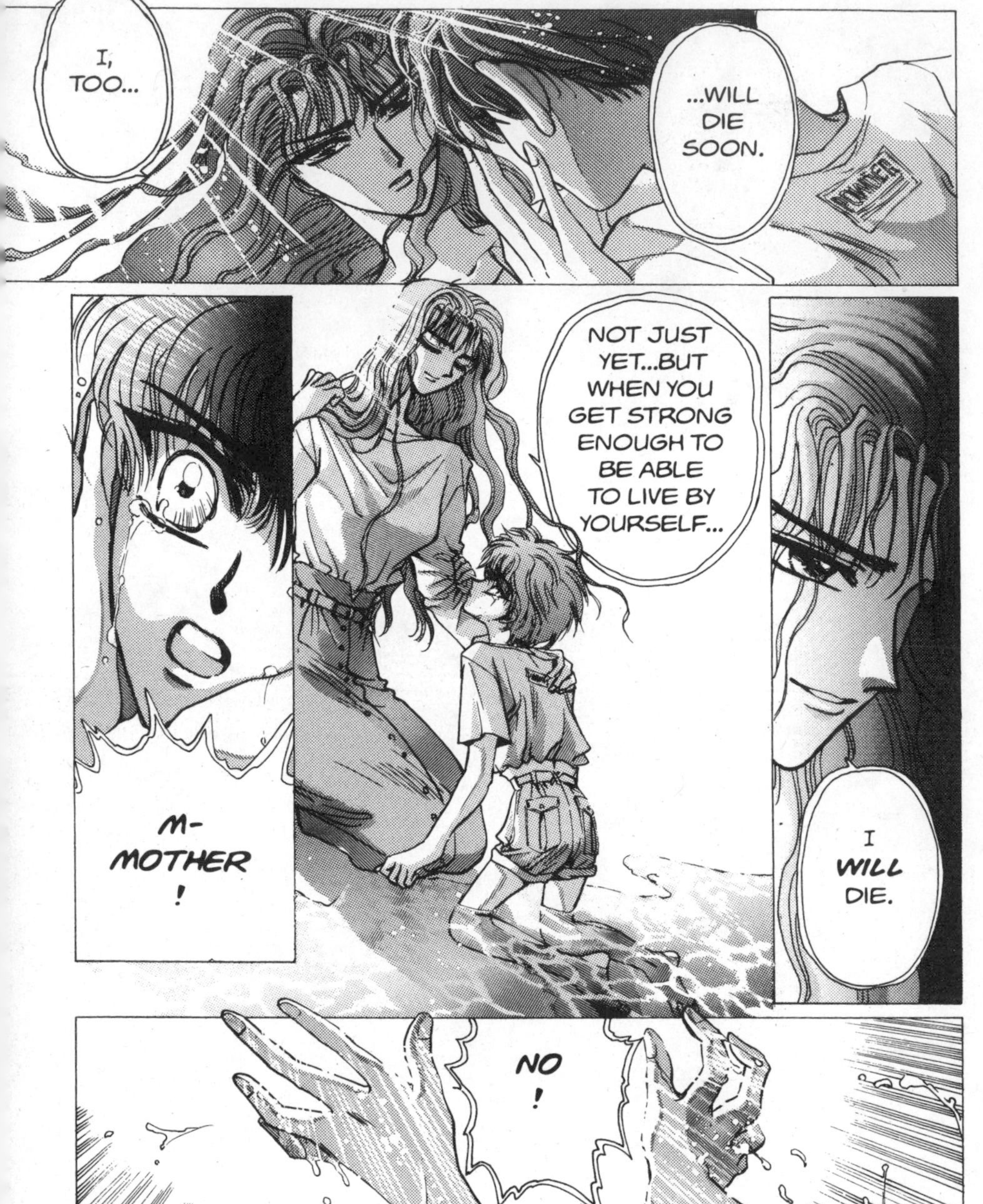
I, TOO...
...WILL DIE SOON.
M-MOTHER!
NOT JUST YET...BUT WHEN YOU GET STRONG ENOUGH TO BE ABLE TO LIVE BY YOURSELF...
I WILL DIE.
NO!

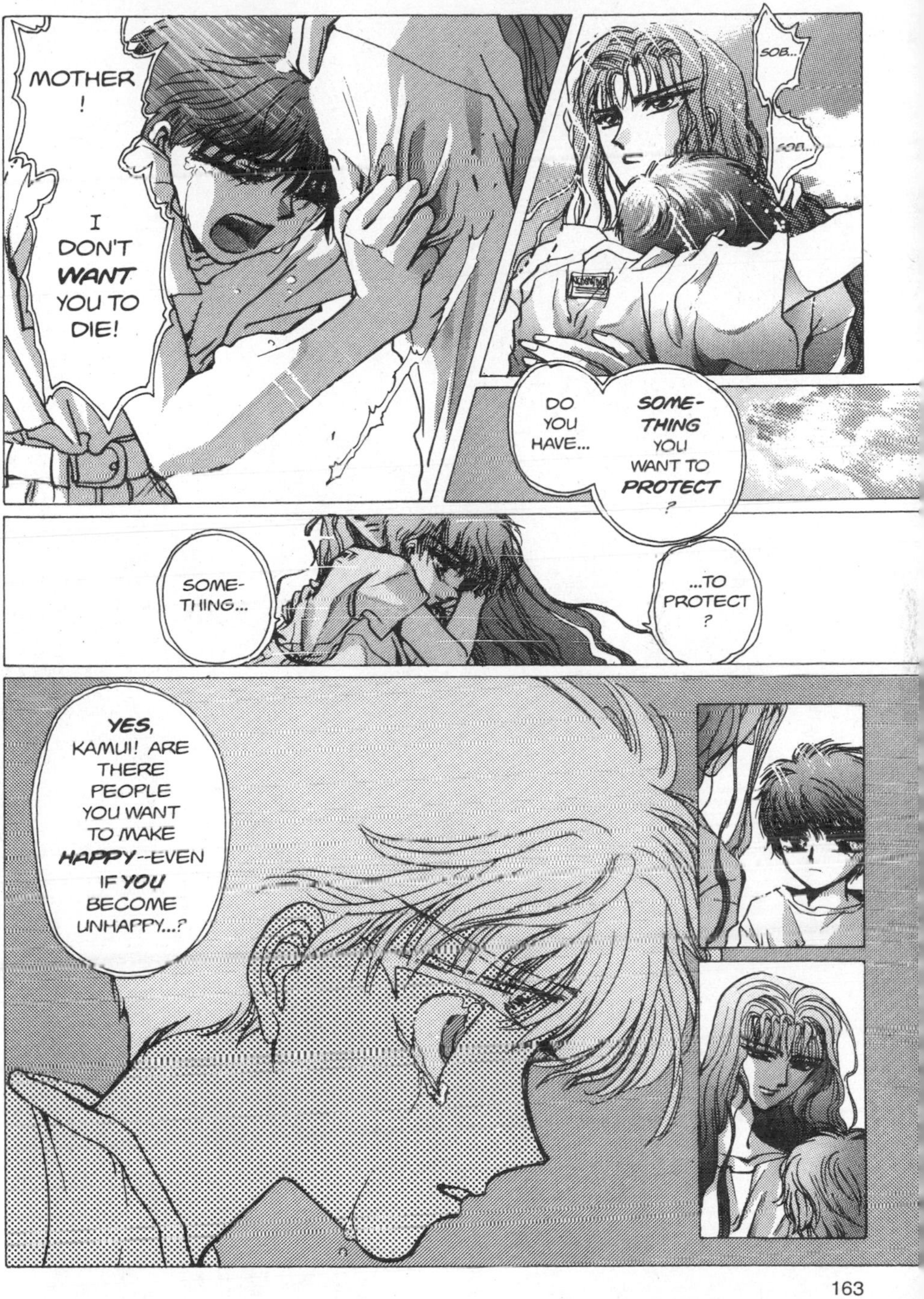
MOTHER!
I DON'T WANT YOU TO DIE!
SOB...
SOB...
DO YOU HAVE... SOMETHING YOU WANT TO PROTECT?
SOMETHING...
...TO PROTECT?
YES, KAMUI! ARE THERE PEOPLE YOU WANT TO MAKE HAPPY--EVEN IF YOU BECOME UNHAPPY...?

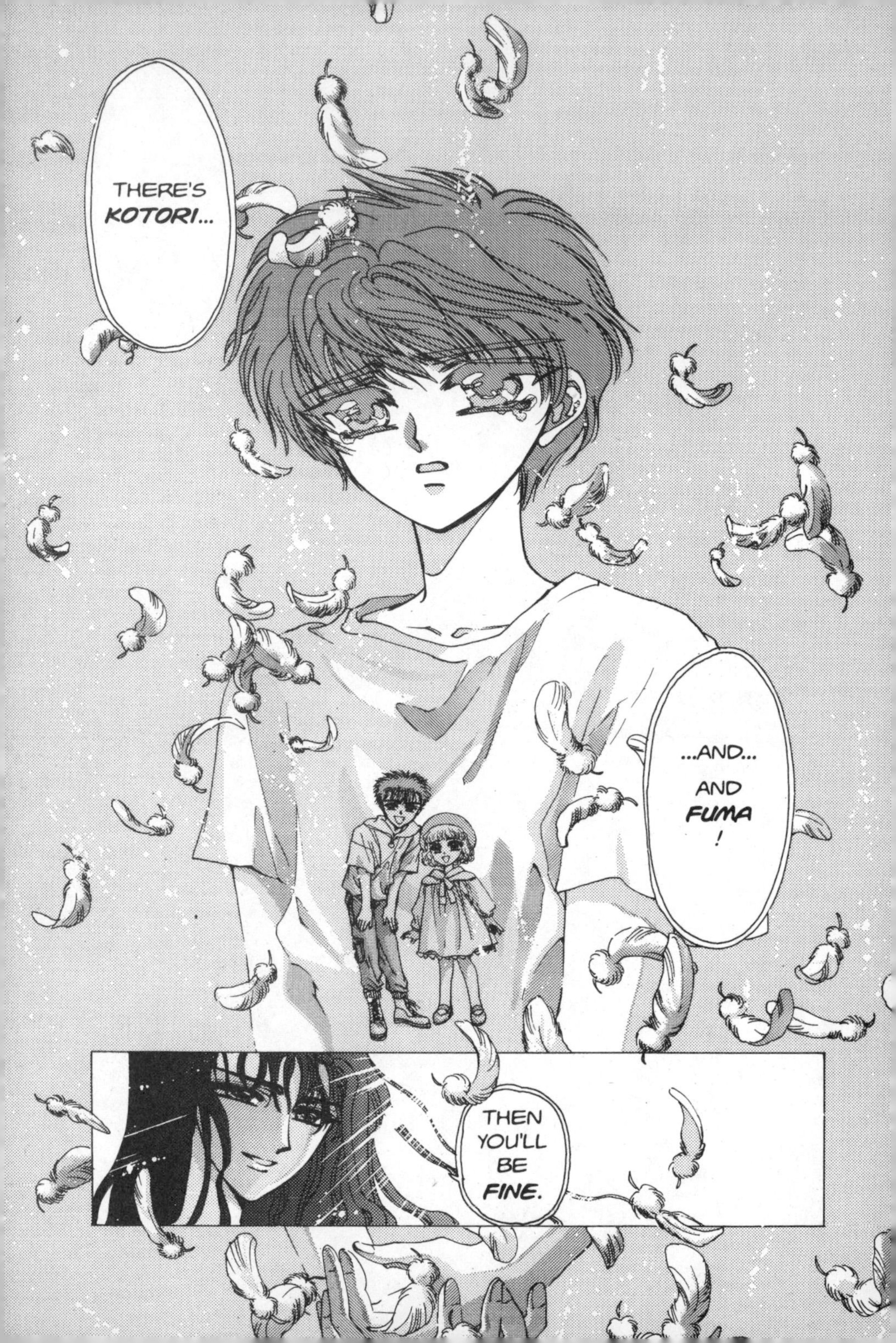

THERE'S KOTORI...
...AND... AND FUMA!
THEN YOU'LL BE FINE.

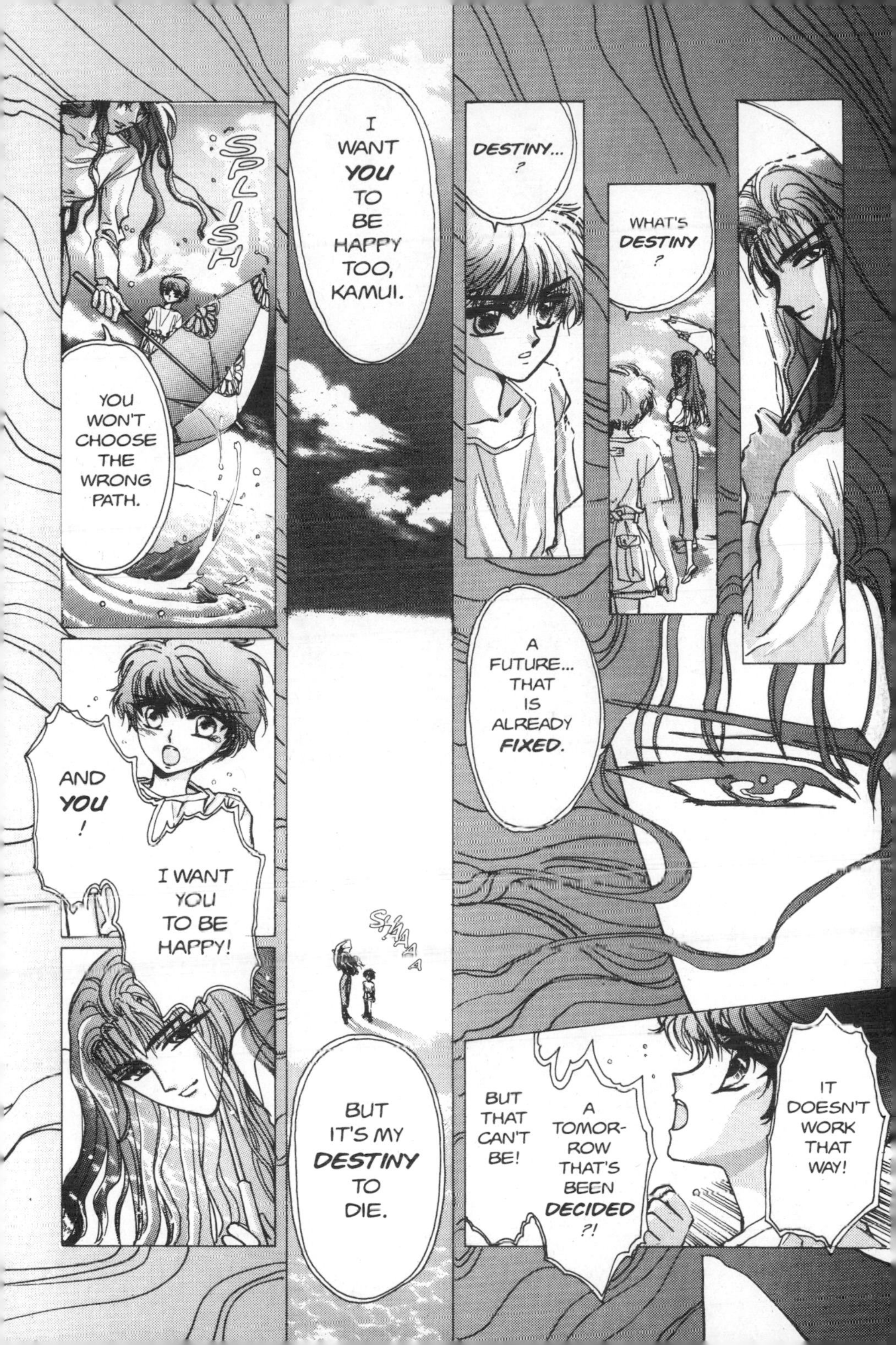
SPLISH
YOU WON'T CHOOSE THE WRONG PATH.
AND YOU!
I WANT YOU TO BE HAPPY!
I WANT YOU TO BE HAPPY TOO, KAMUI.
SHAAAA
BUT IT'S MY DESTINY TO DIE.
DESTINY...?
WHAT'S DESTINY?
A FUTURE... THAT IS ALREADY FIXED.
BUT THAT CAN'T BE!
A TOMOR-ROW THAT'S BEEN DECIDED?!
IT DOESN'T WORK THAT WAY!

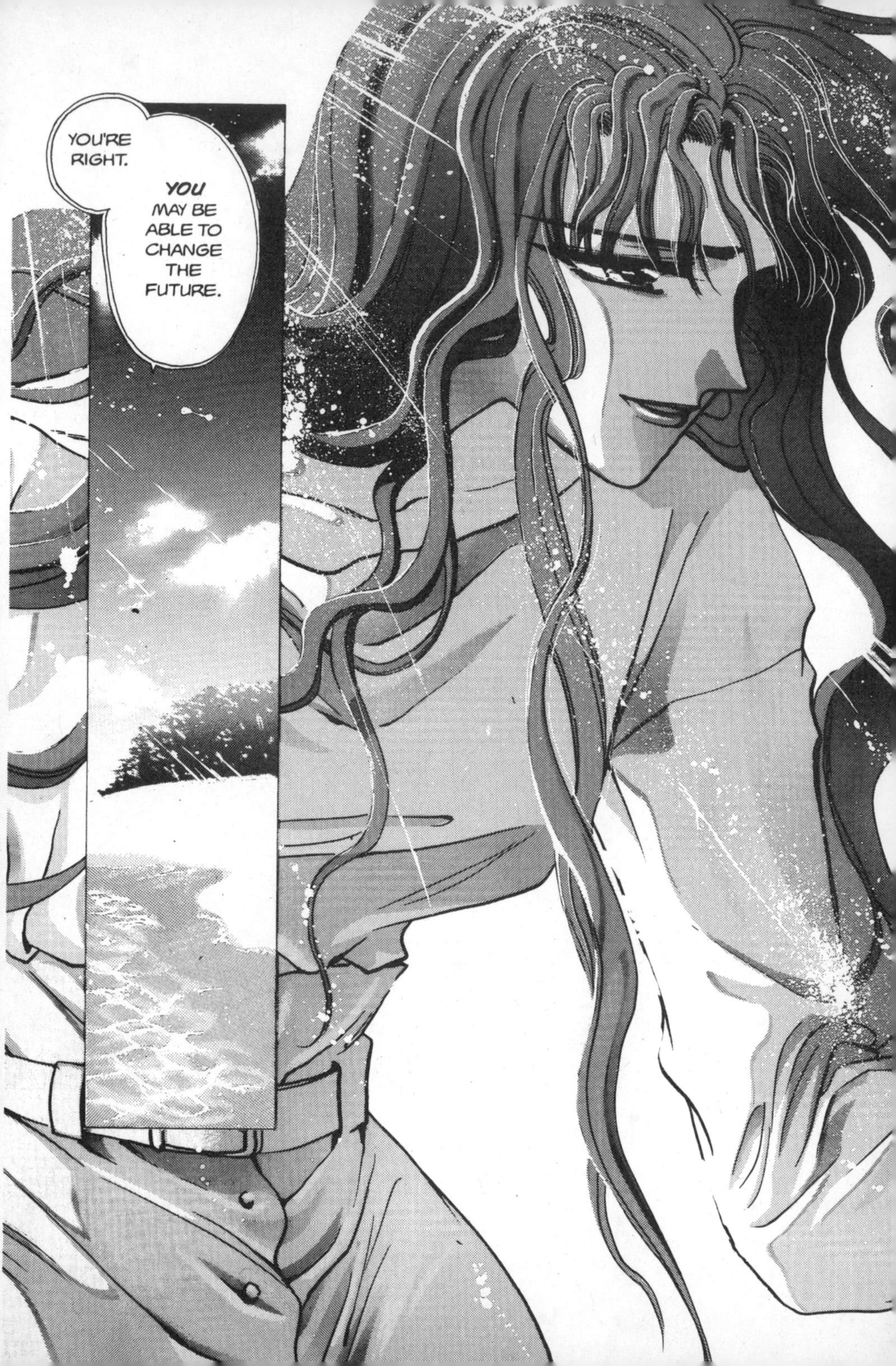
YOU'RE RIGHT.
YOU MAY BE ABLE TO CHANGE THE FUTURE.

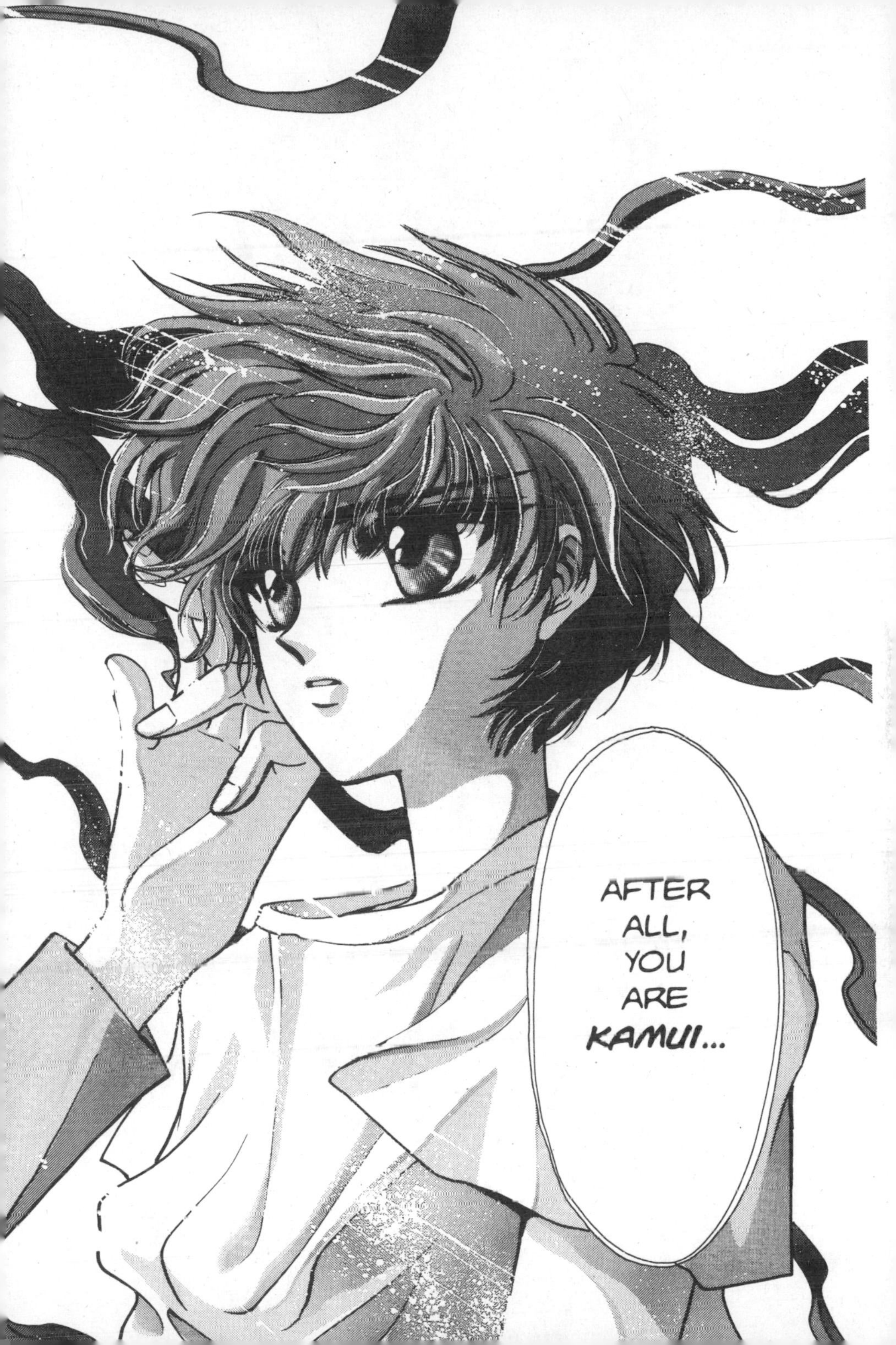
AFTER ALL, YOU ARE KAMUI...

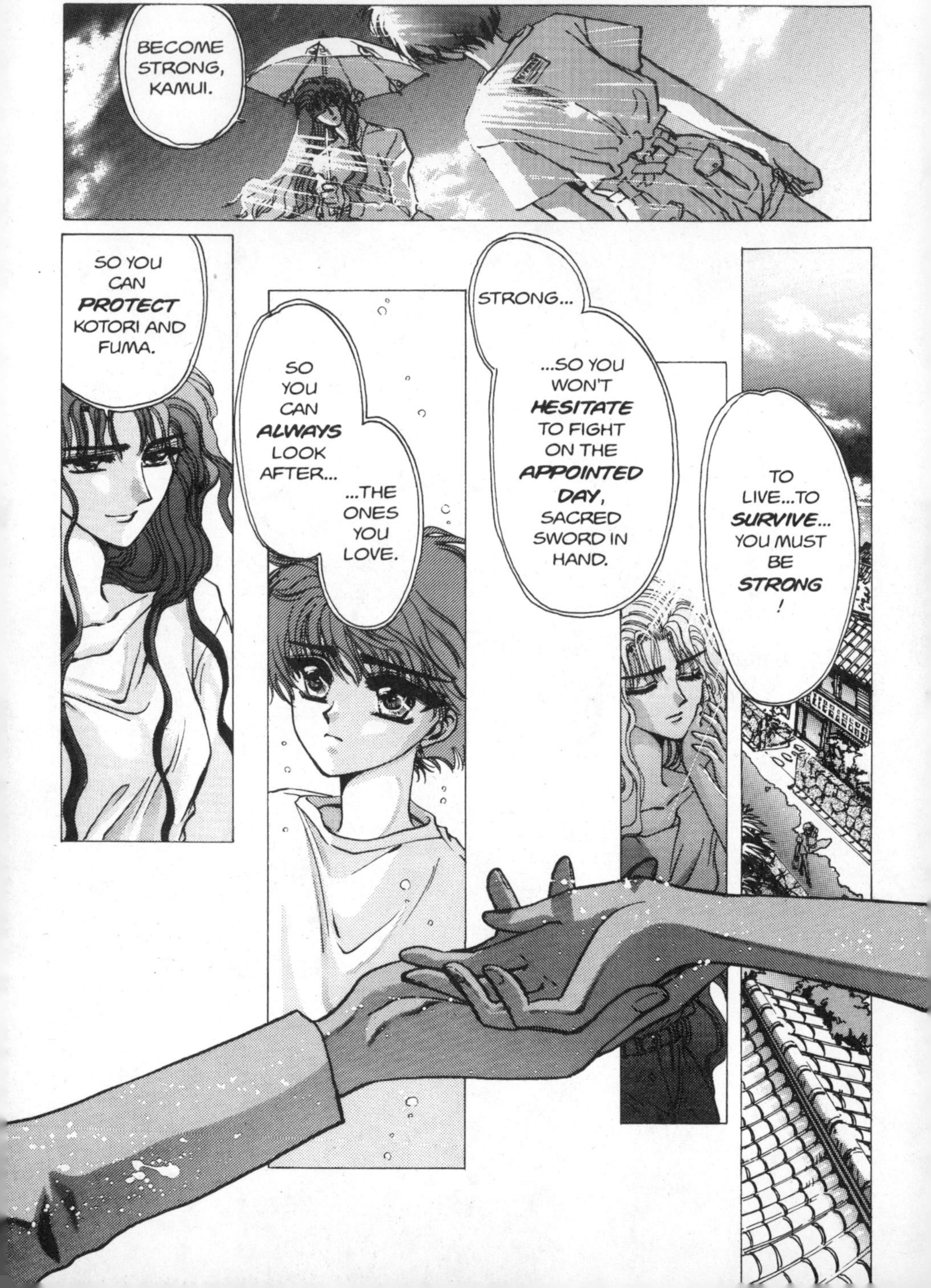
BECOME STRONG, KAMUI.
SO YOU CAN PROTECT KOTORI AND FUMA.
SO YOU CAN ALWAYS LOOK AFTER...
...THE ONES YOU LOVE.
STRONG...
...SO YOU WON'T HESITATE TO FIGHT ON THE APPOINTED DAY, SACRED SWORD IN HAND.
TO LIVE...TO SURVIVE... YOU MUST BE STRONG!

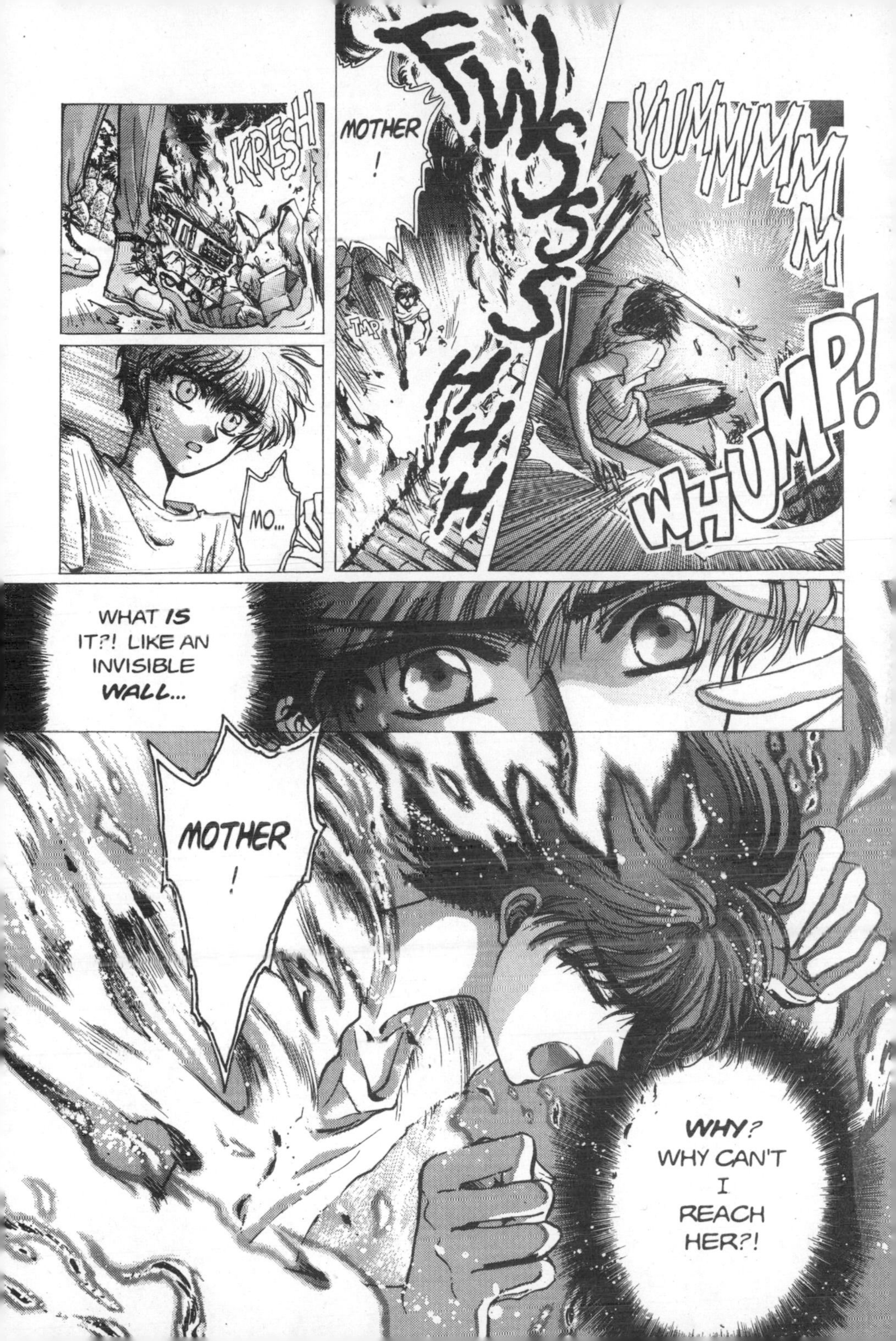
KRESH
MO...
MOTHER !
TMP
FWSSSHHHH
VUMMMMMM
WHUMP!
WHAT *IS* IT?! LIKE AN INVISIBLE *WALL*...
MOTHER !
WHY? WHY CAN'T I REACH HER?!

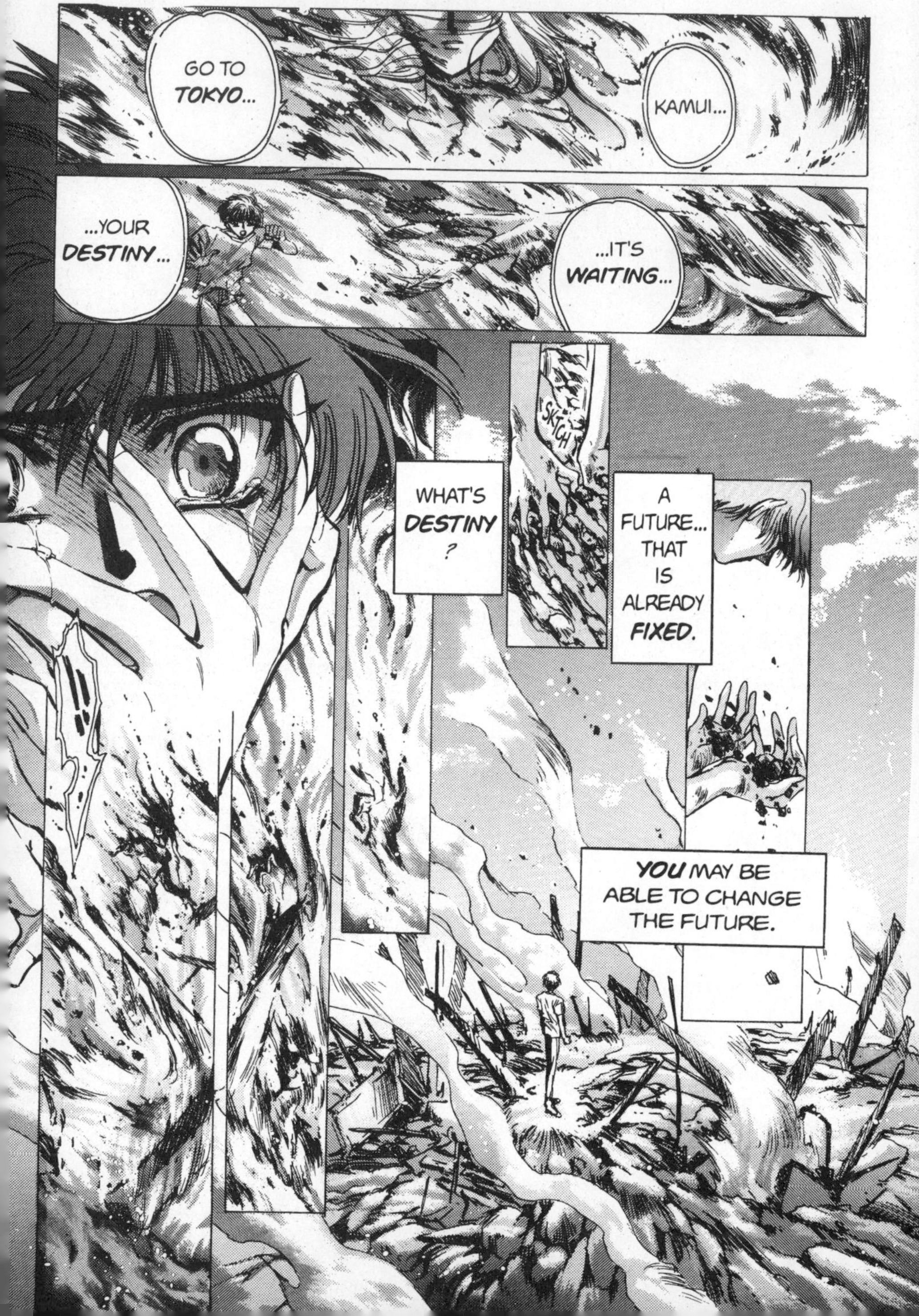
GO TO **TOKYO...**
KAMUI...
...YOUR **DESTINY...**
...IT'S **WAITING...**
WHAT'S **DESTINY** ?
SKTCH
A FUTURE... THAT IS ALREADY **FIXED.**
YOU MAY BE ABLE TO CHANGE THE FUTURE.

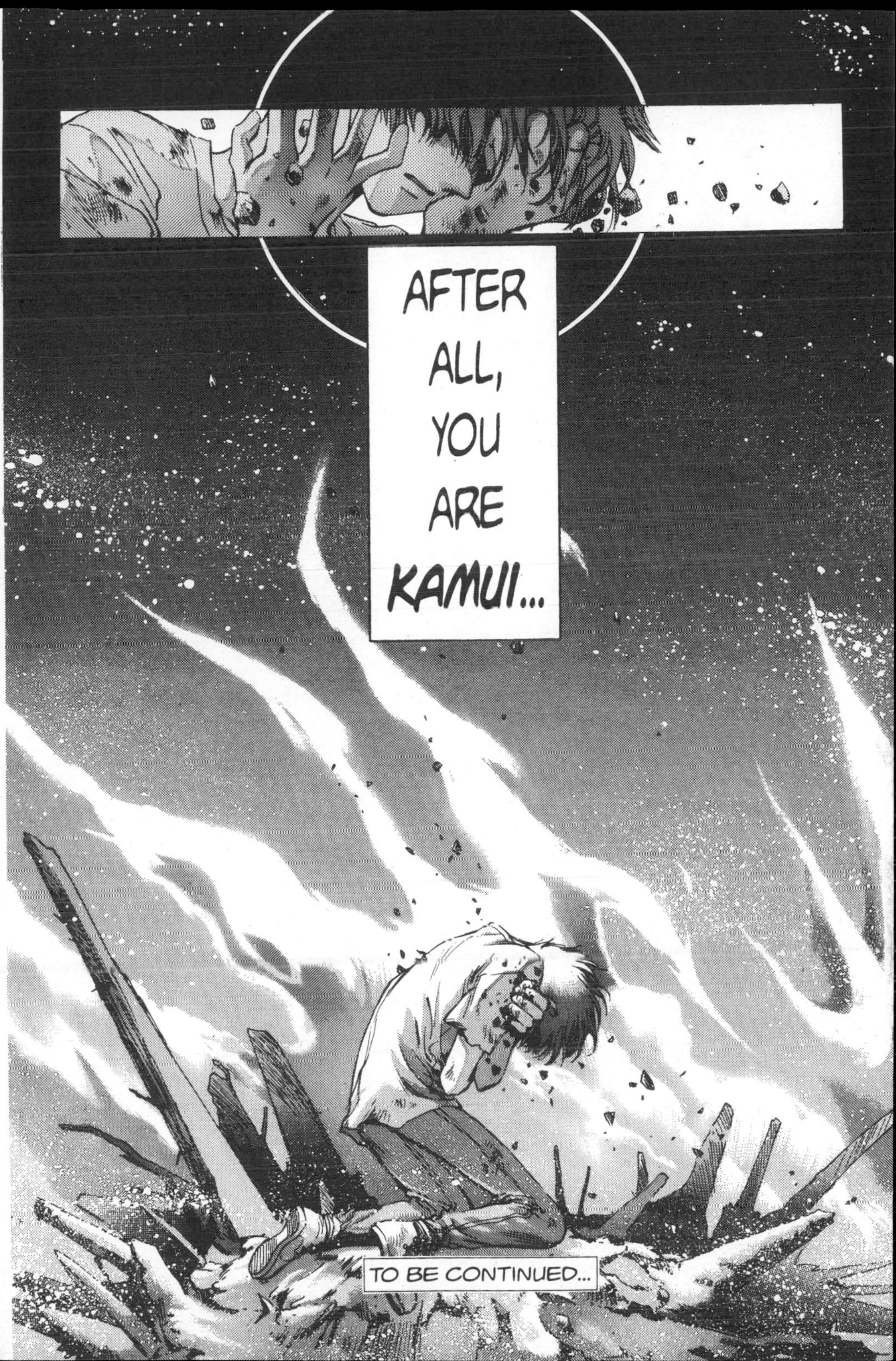
AFTER ALL, YOU ARE KAMUI...
TO BE CONTINUED...

X

SORATA ARISUGAWA

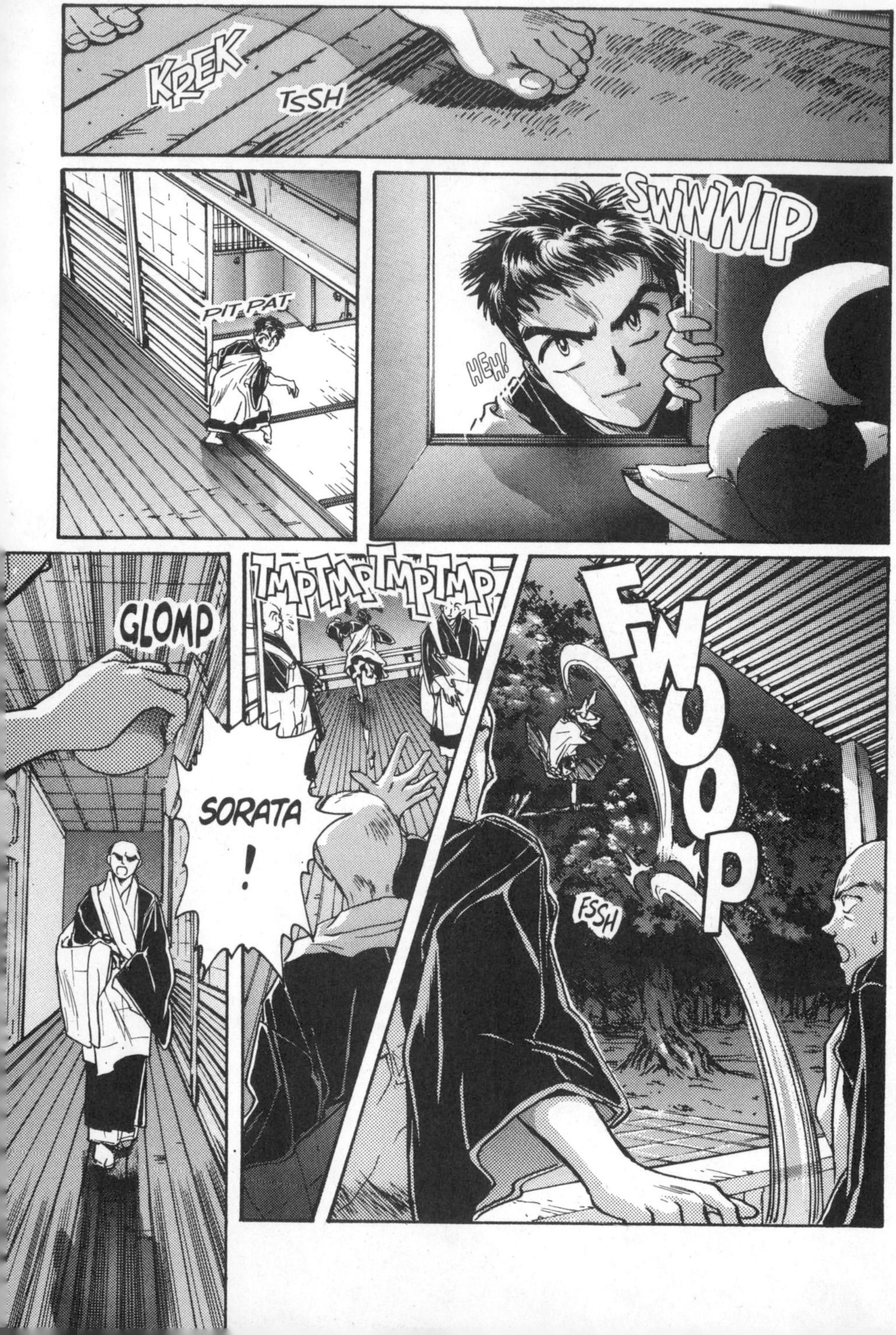
KREK
TSSH
PIT PAT
SWWWIP
HEH!
GLOMP
TMPTMPTMPTMP
SORATA
!
FWOOP
FSSH

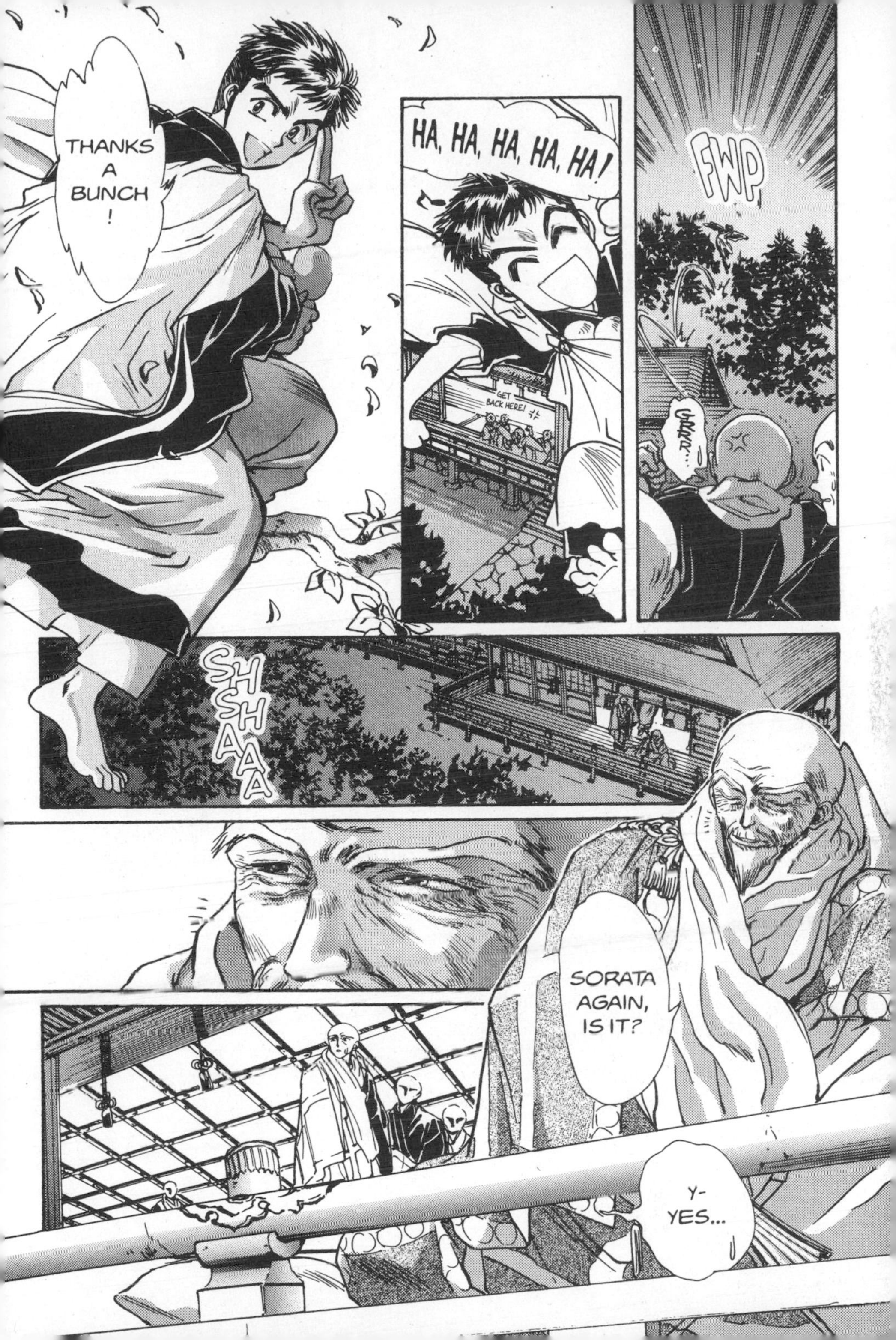
THANKS A BUNCH!
HA, HA, HA, HA, HA!
GET BACK HERE!
FWP
GRRR...
SHSHAAA
SORATA AGAIN, IS IT?
Y-YES...

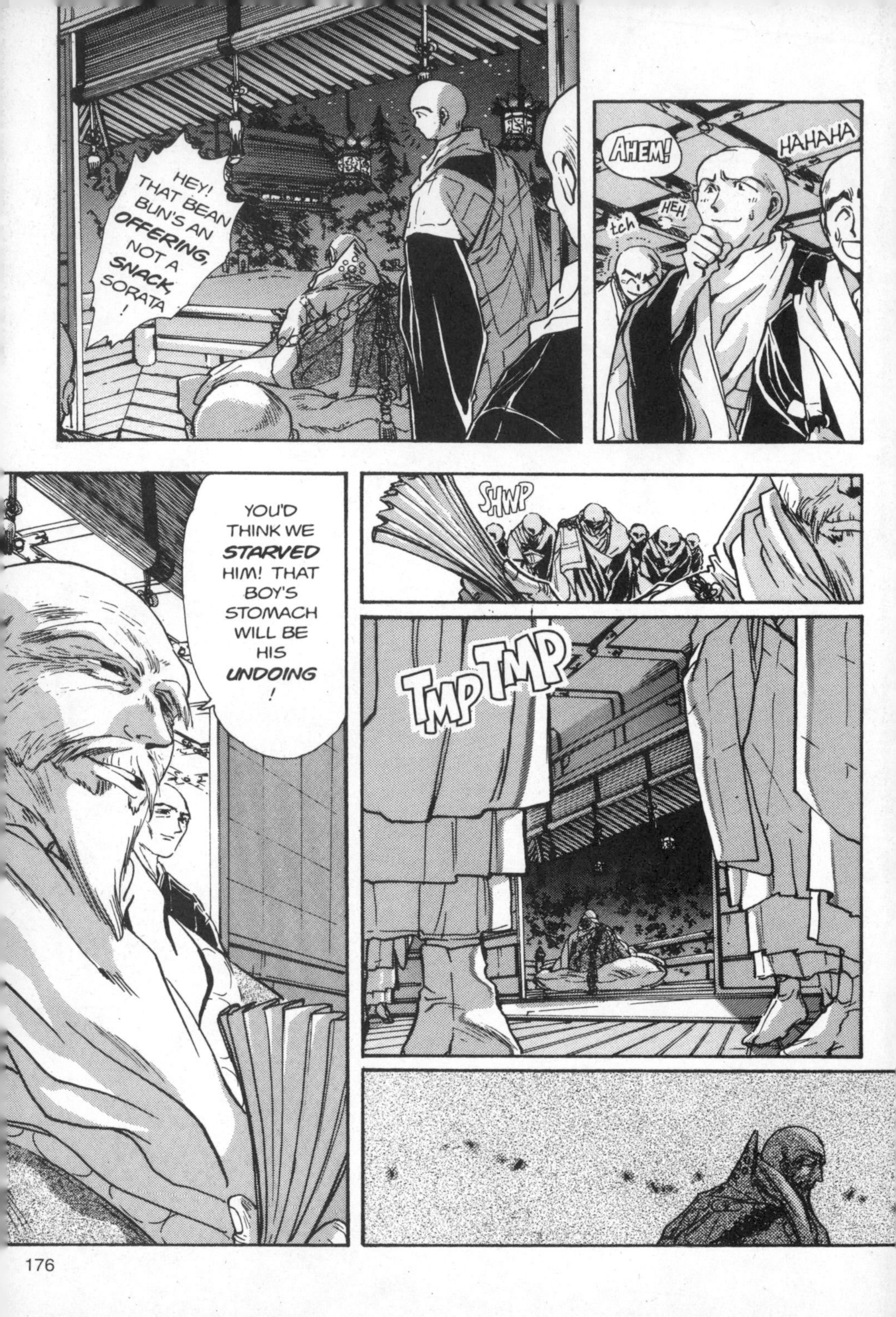
HEY! THAT BEAN BUN'S AN OFFERING, NOT A SNACK, SORATA!
AHEM!
HAHAHA
HEH
tch
YOU'D THINK WE STARVED HIM! THAT BOY'S STOMACH WILL BE HIS UNDOING!
SHWP
TMP TMP

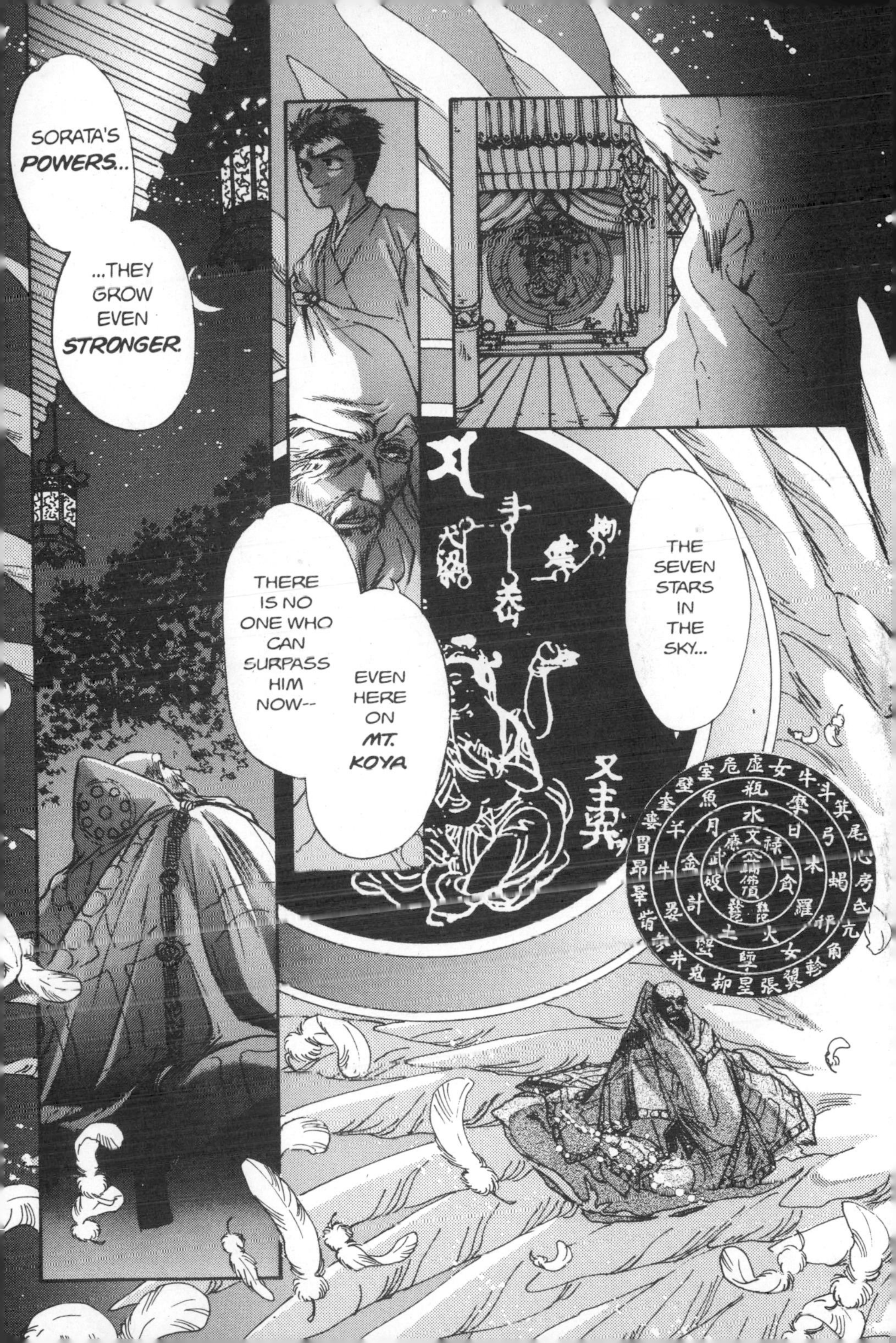
SORATA'S POWERS...
...THEY GROW EVEN STRONGER.
THERE IS NO ONE WHO CAN SURPASS HIM NOW--
EVEN HERE ON MT. KOYA
THE SEVEN STARS IN THE SKY...

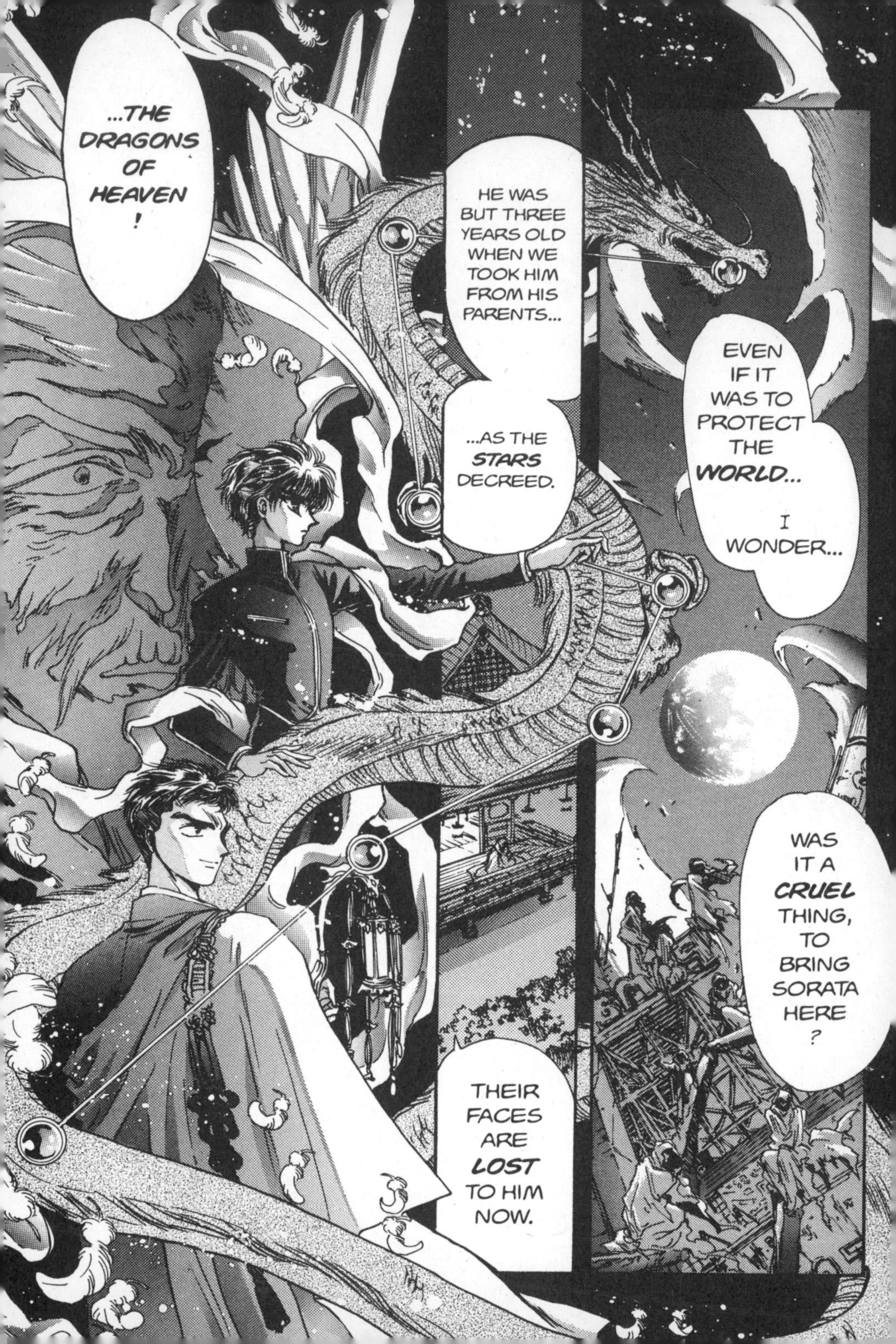
...THE DRAGONS OF HEAVEN!
HE WAS BUT THREE YEARS OLD WHEN WE TOOK HIM FROM HIS PARENTS...
...AS THE STARS DECREED.
THEIR FACES ARE LOST TO HIM NOW.
EVEN IF IT WAS TO PROTECT THE WORLD...
I WONDER...
WAS IT A CRUEL THING, TO BRING SORATA HERE?

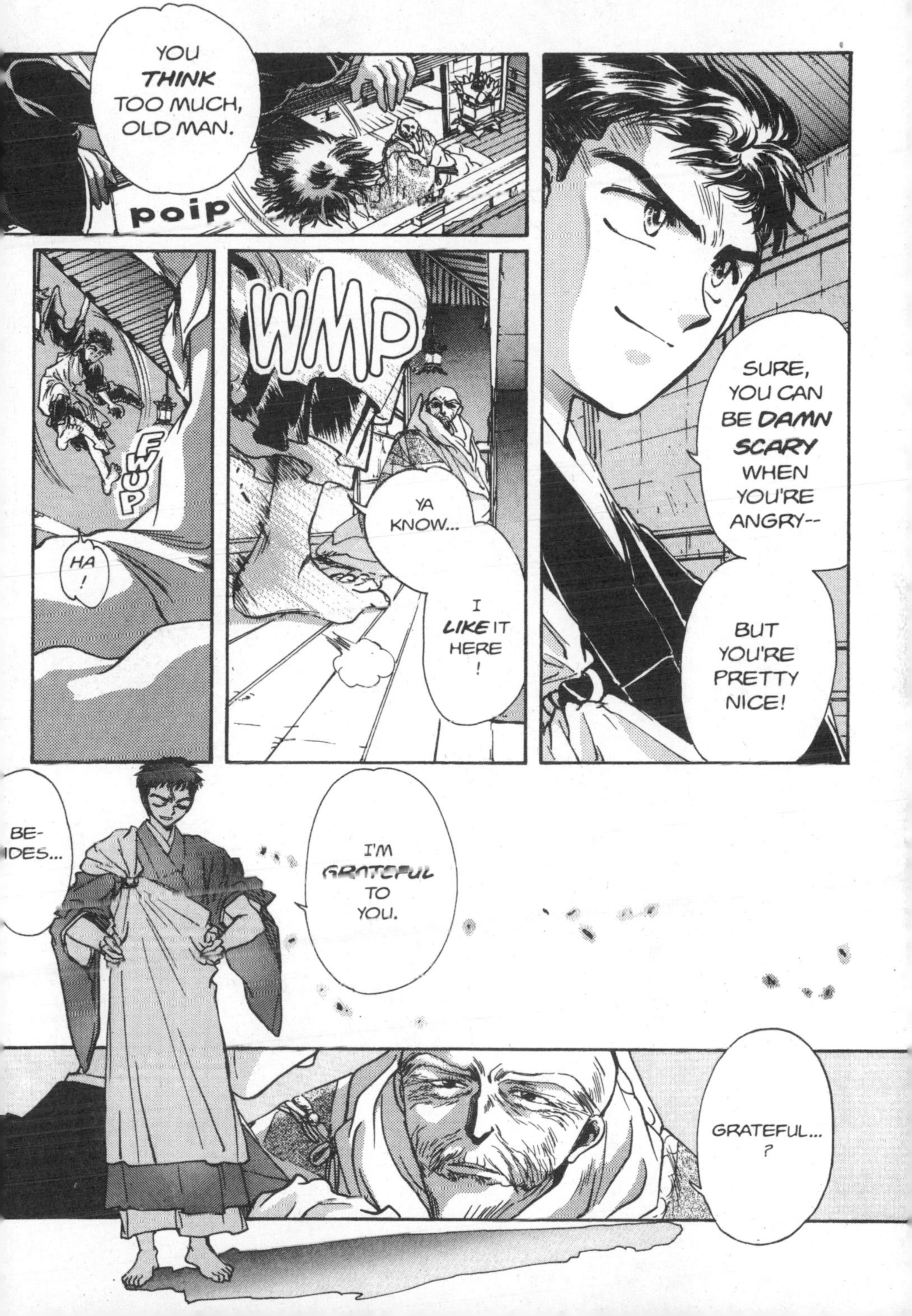
YOU THINK TOO MUCH, OLD MAN.
poip
SURE, YOU CAN BE DAMN SCARY WHEN YOU'RE ANGRY--
BUT YOU'RE PRETTY NICE!
FWUP
HA!
WMP
YA KNOW...
I LIKE IT HERE!
BE-IDES...
I'M GRATEFUL TO YOU.
GRATEFUL...?

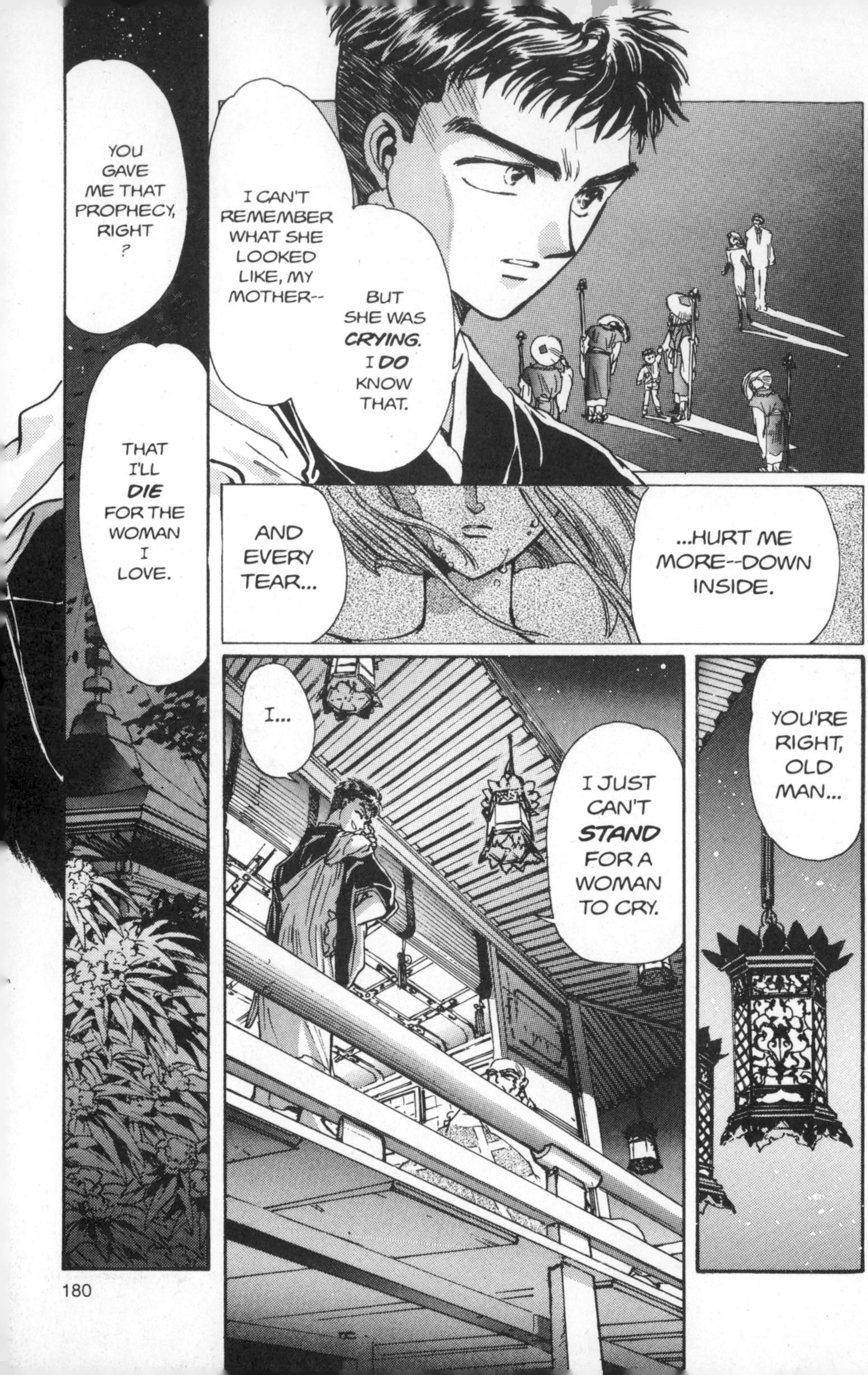
YOU GAVE ME THAT PROPHECY, RIGHT?
THAT I'LL DIE FOR THE WOMAN I LOVE.
I CAN'T REMEMBER WHAT SHE LOOKED LIKE, MY MOTHER--
BUT SHE WAS CRYING. I DO KNOW THAT.
AND EVERY TEAR...
...HURT ME MORE--DOWN INSIDE.
I...
I JUST CAN'T STAND FOR A WOMAN TO CRY.
YOU'RE RIGHT, OLD MAN...

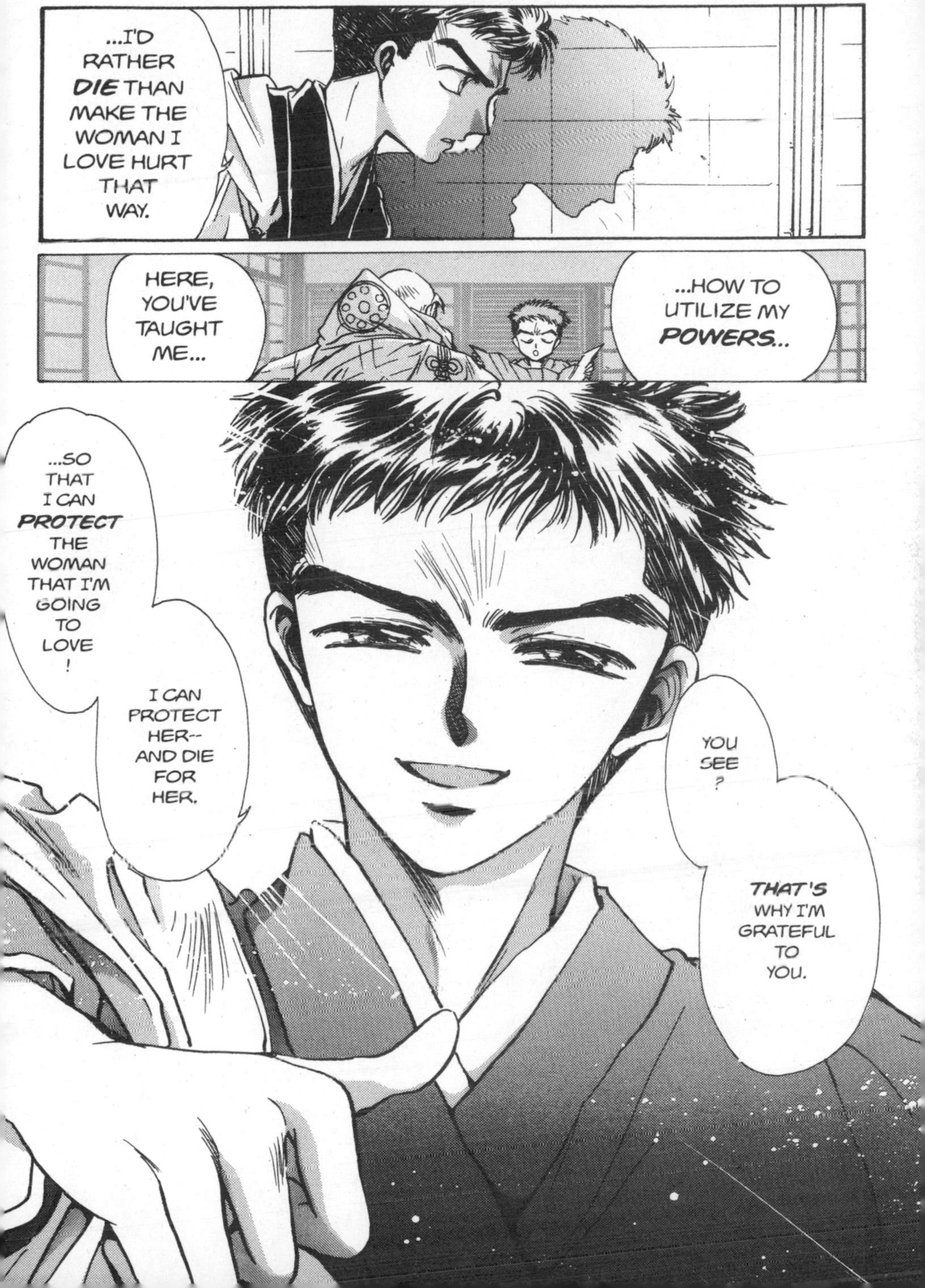
...I'D RATHER DIE THAN MAKE THE WOMAN I LOVE HURT THAT WAY.
HERE, YOU'VE TAUGHT ME...
...HOW TO UTILIZE MY POWERS...
...SO THAT I CAN PROTECT THE WOMAN THAT I'M GOING TO LOVE!
I CAN PROTECT HER-- AND DIE FOR HER.
YOU SEE?
THAT'S WHY I'M GRATEFUL TO YOU.

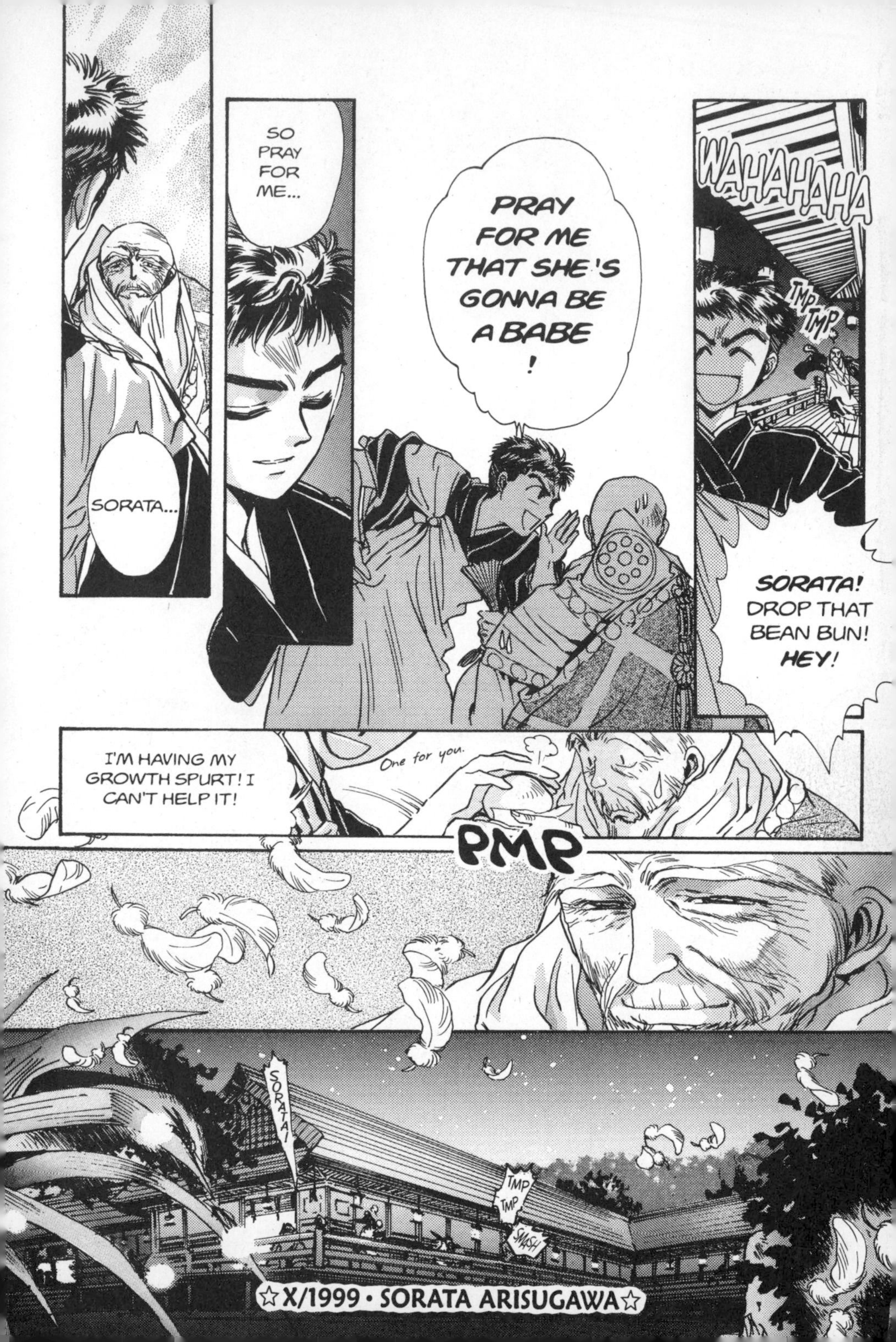
SORATA...
SO PRAY FOR ME...
PRAY FOR ME THAT SHE'S GONNA BE A BABE!
WAHAHAHA
TMP TMP
SORATA! DROP THAT BEAN BUN! HEY!
I'M HAVING MY GROWTH SPURT! I CAN'T HELP IT!
One for you.
PMP
SORATA!
TMP TMP
SMASH
☆X/1999 • SORATA ARISUGAWA☆